EXPERIMENTS IN DEMOCRACY

J. BENJAMIN HURLBUT

EXPERIMENTS IN DEMOCRACY

Human Embryo Research
and the Politics
of Bioethics

COLUMBIA UNIVERSITY PRESS
NEW YORK

Columbia University Press
Publishers Since 1893
New York   Chichester, West Sussex
cup.columbia.edu

Library of Congress Cataloging-in-Publication Data
Names: Hurlbut, J. Benjamin, author.
Title: Experiments in democracy : human embryo research and the politics
of bioethics / J. Benjamin Hurlbut.
Description: New York : Columbia University Press, [2017] |
Includes bibliographical references and index.
Identifiers: LCCN 2016011447 (print) | LCCN 2016030062 (ebook) |
ISBN 9780231179546 (cloth : alk. paper) | ISBN 9780231542913 (electronic)
Subjects: LCSH: Human embryo—Research—Government policy—United States. |
Stem cells—Research—Moral and ethical aspects—United States.
Classification: LCC QM608 .H87 2017 (print) | LCC QM608 (ebook) |
DDC 612.6/4—dc23
LC record available at https://lccn.loc.gov/2016011447

Columbia University Press books are printed on permanent
and durable acid-free paper.
Printed in the United States of America

Cover design: Bryce Schimanski
Cover image: Zernicka-Goetz Lab, University of Cambridge

For Molly

CONTENTS

Acknowledgments ix

INTRODUCTION: THE POLITICS
OF EXPERIMENT 1

1. NEW BEGINNINGS 39

2. PRODUCING LIFE, CONCEIVING REASON 79

3. REPRESENTING REASON 107

4. CLONING, KNOWLEDGE, AND THE POLITICS
OF CONSENSUS 133

5. CONFUSING DELIBERATION 179

6. IN THE LABORATORIES OF DEMOCRACY 209

7. RELIGION, REASON, AND THE POLITICS
OF PROGRESS 233

8. THE LEGACY OF EXPERIMENT 263

Notes 291
Index 343

ACKNOWLEDGMENTS

I am indebted and grateful to the many people who have engaged with me, encouraged me, challenged me, supported me, tolerated me, and loved me as this book took shape.

I am grateful for the support of my colleagues at Arizona State University. There are few institutions that would offer a home to a disciplinary misfit like me, yet at ASU one is invited to think and teach beyond the limits of the traditional disciplines. I am particularly grateful to Jane Maienschein for her guidance, encouragement, and support, and to the wonderful faculty and staff associated with the Center for Biology and Society. It was a privilege (and a hell of a lot of fun) to co-teach for several years with Jason Robert. Some of the ideas in this book crystallized through the exchanges Jason and I had in and around those classes.

A collaborative project with Hava Tirosh-Samuelson that was (I thought) unrelated to this project unexpectedly informed in it in significant ways. In addition to being an exceptional collaborator and colleague, Hava provided mentoring and professional advice that were truly invaluable. The sustained line of conversation with Linell Cady and Gregg Zachary that grew out of that project with Hava also influenced this project. When Gaymon Bennett joined ASU and that conversation, it began a period of exceptional dialogue, collaboration, and friendship that shaped this book in profound ways.

This project was supported by fellowships at the ASU Institute for Humanities Research and the Brocher Foundation, and by a grant from the Faraday Institute's Uses and Abuses of Biology Grants Programme. The Institute for Global Law and Policy provided me with an unexpected but incredibly enriching environment for encountering ideas that informed this project. I am grateful to David Kennedy for creating that environment and for welcoming me into it.

The research for this book could not have been done without the many people who graciously agreed to tell me their stories. In numerous cases, people gave far more generously of their time than was necessary. Though he had agreed to only an hour, Paul Berg allowed our conversation to spill over to three and a half. Charles McCarthy spoke to me at great length, providing me with not only an exceptionally valuable account but also enthusiastic encouragement for my project. Leon Kass not only provided illuminating information but also offered insights about the importance—and challenges—of the project of bioethics that significantly affected my thinking. Exceptional even among this group was Richard Doerflinger, who gave me almost an entire day, as well as access to the extraordinary wealth of materials in the US Conference of Catholic Bishops archive.

This book bears the mark of ideas the took shape in long-ago, late-night conversations with Jeff Skopek and Paul Kalanithi. Not a day passes when I do not miss my dear friend Paul and the sensitivity, seriousness, and sense of humor with which he approached the world. Conversations with Akiba Lerner, Brian Sullivan, Ben Howard, and Nasser Zakariya also informed this project more deeply than they know. With friends like these, one is reminded that in this sort of work, the pleasure of dialectic is its own reward, and that, combined with friendship, there is little in life that is better.

The book benefited from numerous colleagues' comments and criticisms. A dialogue with John Evans that began when I was a graduate student has immeasurably deepened my thinking. I am also grateful to Steve Hilgartner, Pierre Benoit-Joly, Clark Miller, Dan Sarewitz, Giuseppe Testa, Kaushik Sunder Rajan, Margo Boenig-Liptsin, Emma Frow, David Winickoff, Sobita Parthasarathy, Dan Wikler, Laura Stark, Carter Snead, Charis Thompson, Chris Jones, Jenny Reardon, David Solomon, Phil Sloan, Sundhya Pahuja, Sang-Hyun Kim, Brice Laurent, Ingrid Metzler, Charlie Peevers, Stuart Newman, Marcy Darnovsky, Robin Lovell-Badge, Alex Wellerstein, Ruha Benjamin, Amy Hinterberger, and Rachel Douglass-Jones. My thinking was sharpened and enhanced through conversations with each of these people. For their insights and their friendship, I am most grateful.

I received formative feedback when I presented my research at the Yale Interdisciplinary Center for Bioethics, at the STS Circle at Harvard, and in the Workshop on the Ethical, Philosophical, Legal and Theological Dimensions of Adult and Alternative Stem Cell Research at Notre Dame and at various meetings of the Science and Democracy Network. I am grateful to the hosts and the engaged and responsive audiences. Portions of chapters 3 and 4 were worked out in the *Notre Dame Journal of Law, Ethics and Public Policy*, and were presented at the journal's annual symposium in March 2015.

I am grateful to the editorial team at Columbia University Press, who have made the process of publishing this book a genuine pleasure. Thanks in particular to Kathryn Schell for finding me, and to Patrick Fitzgerald and Ryan Groendyk, whose capable hands (and patience) have made this process easy.

Thanks to Jake Early for his input on the cover design.

The STS program at Harvard was my intellectual home throughout graduate school, and still remains a home away from home. The intensity, energy, diversity, richness, and exceptional caliber of this scholarly community is unmatched by anything I have ever encountered. It was a privilege to come up as a scholar within the STS program, and it remains a great pleasure to engage with its ever-expanding community. One of my most important intellectual partnerships and friendships that grew out of the STS program has been with Krishanu Saha. Kris combines a creative, insightful, and easygoing intellectual style with a genuine and serious commitment to making sure that the scientific enterprise of which he is part is undertaken in the service of the good. It has been and remains a great pleasure and privilege to work with him. The Science and Democracy Network has also been a formative environment for me. For the last decade I have each year looked forward to the days of intensive exchange at the SDN meeting, and to seeing the numerous faces that have over the years become close friends.

Neither Harvard STS nor SDN would exist but for Sheila Jasanoff's extraordinary dedication of both spirit and labor, nor indeed would the field to which this book and its author aspire to be part. Sheila's brilliance as a scholar, her commitment to understanding and to building the ideas, opportunities, and resources necessary to achieve it, and her fierce loyalty to those who would join her in these endeavors are nothing short of extraordinary. Sheila is a person, rare in our world, who believes with conviction that ideas matter. She also believes that ideas are the province of people and institutions, and that to live well we must both understand what ways of knowing give shape to our world and work toward building worlds for which genuine understanding is a primary aspiration and humility is a foundational ethos. This book is, more than anything, a result of being part of the world she has built. In that respect it is, through and through, a reflection of the many virtues of that world, even if only a pale one. It is itself, therefore, too an expression of its author's profound gratitude to the person who built it, and an attempt to repay a little bit of the immense debt that he owes her.

My family deserves enormous thanks—for nurturing, supporting, enduring, and loving me as this book took form. Although I did not know it at the time, research for this book began decades ago when my father convinced his twelve-year-old son to tag along to his classes. One of the seeds that grew into this project was planted by a conversation that he and I had when I was a young teenager after we witnessed a heated exchange between the geneticist David Cox, who would later serve on the National Bioethics Advisory Committee, and bioethicist Leon Kass, who would later chair the President's Council on Bioethics. It was the opportunity to encounter such moments first hand, and the intense father-son conversations that often followed, that set me on the trajectory of which this book is a product. For my father's inexhaustible commitment to nurturing his son's nascent mind and spirit—then and now—I am profoundly grateful.

My three beautiful daughters, Tamsin, Hazel, and Tess, came into being in the decade during which this book was conceived, researched, and written. The joy, unpredictability, meaning, and love they bring into my life on a daily basis constantly remind me to be at once humble about and committed to my vocation. This book is about the making of a future that will belong to them. They remind me each day why I care about that future, that seeking to understand the world is not an end in itself but must be in the service of living well within it, and that there is more to living well than thinking well.

My wife, Molly, deserves more thanks than I can ever convey. She has believed in me, encouraged me, suffered me, understood me, and loved me in ways that no man could rightly ask or expect. In a world that is becoming less inclined to reward the slow labor of scholarship or to venerate a commitment to serious thought where what one achieves inevitably falls short of what one aspires to, she remains convinced of the virtues of my work, even in moments when I do not. For her faithful love, notwithstanding the gap between my aspirations and achievements in all walks of life, I am endlessly grateful. It is because of her dedication to me that this book is dedicated to her.

EXPERIMENTS IN
DEMOCRACY

INTRODUCTION

▄▄▄▄▄▄▄▄

The Politics of Experiment

On July 25, 1978, the birth of a little girl, ordinary enough on most days, made international headlines. Born to an English couple of modest means in a country hospital, this child was conceived differently from the billions of human beings who had preceded her. This tiny, newborn baby was evidence that a revolution in human reproduction was underway. She was born to parents whose bodies, for all of their efforts and prayers, had failed to cooperate with the natural laws of procreation. Louise Brown, daughter of Lesley and John Brown, was the first child in the history of the human race to be conceived outside her mother's body. She was a product of the laboratory, of disembodied sex that removed the enshrouded secrets of human genesis to the transparent glass dishes of the laboratory bench.

The uncertain futures that accompanied that moment were rooted in a very present certainty. Louise Brown's infant form made concrete the existence of a new biological entity, radically novel, though formed from ancient precedents, a being whose nature and future were rendered uncertain only by the circumstances of its generation: the in vitro human embryo.

Following the first successful attempts at artificial fertilization in the late 1960s and Louise Brown's birth in 1978, the in vitro embryo emerged into the public sphere as a locus of imagination and controversy. It was an object of scientific ambition, technological possibility, moral anxiety, and ethical ambiguity. No longer hidden in the dark interior of the womb, no longer an undetectable presence in its first weeks of being, the human embryo, in its in vitro environment, could be seen, described, and governed as if it were an autonomous entity. Displaced from the embodied process of procreation, it emerged as an isolated entity of uncertain moral status. In time, it became a material input in biological research and a site of production from which were ushered other biological entities of ambiguous moral significance. Located in a liminal zone between reproduction and research, it became a central figure in American democracy's efforts to devise new ways to evaluate and govern its technological future.

The in vitro human embryo heralded a period of profound perturbation not only in the earliest stages of human life, but in democracy's modes of reasoning about it. Separated from the normal biological rhythms of reproduction, developing human life became subject to new forms of control and intervention. And, as the human embryo became implicated in novel technological systems, the script of human conception could be separated from the story of procreation and made to figure in other human dramas.

This book explores the decades-long American debates about research on the human embryo. From the birth of Louise Brown to the derivation of human embryonic stem cells at the turn of the millennium, human embryo research figured centrally in a series of profound transformations in the landscapes of both bioscience and democracy in America. Norms, practices, and novel institutions of deliberation and governance developed to address advances in the biosciences. At stake in the human embryo research debates were imaginations of the right relationship between science and democracy. These imaginations shaped, and were shaped by, new approaches to bioethical deliberation and governance. Thus, at the heart of the debates was a question of great consequence that transcended the technoscientific possibilities of the moment: How should a democratic polity reason together about morally and technically complex problems that touch upon the most fundamental dimensions of human life—through what institutional mechanisms, guided by what forms of authority, in what language, and subject to what political norms and limitations? The central project of this book is to examine how those questions were answered in practice, and with what consequences for the politics of governing life in the era of biotechnology.

GOVERNING SCIENCE

Louise Brown was born during a period of soul searching about the proper relationship among science, state, and society. In the decade that preceded her birth, the power of emerging technologies to fundamentally reshape human life had become a focus of public debate. Prominent scientists had begun to comment upon the emerging powers to understand—and to remake—human life, and upon the roles and responsibilities of science in shaping the future.[1] Novel technologies had engendered new ambiguities at the edges of life. Life-support technologies rendered the boundary between life and death biologically, juridically, and morally uncertain.[2] Early successes in organ transplantation gave a new life-saving potency to bodies in transition from person to corpse, even as those bodies were taking on a utilitarian function that came with the potential for abuse.[3]

The rapid expansion of American biomedical research after the Second World War created an ever-increasing need for experimental bodies in biomedical research.[4] A series of scandals involving research on human beings that culminated with the public revelation of the Tuskegee syphilis study in 1972 convinced the American public of the need for external assessment and oversight of the ethical dimensions of research.[5] Responsibilities of care to patients and the aspiration to advance biomedical knowledge, long understood to be harmonious elements in the vocation of medicine, were recognized as being potentially in conflict.[6] A bright line was drawn between matters of scientific and ethical judgment, and new forms of oversight and ethical review were integrated into the growing bureaucracies of big bioscience.[7]

The dramatic postwar advances in molecular biology culminated in powerful new tools for genetic engineering. Techniques of recombinant DNA (rDNA) that were developed in the early 1970s offered the means to make fundamental interventions in the stuff of life, eliciting first-order questions about what sorts of interventions were worthy, safe, and appropriate, and also, more fundamentally, about who should make such judgments and on the basis of what authority.[8] As this new chapter opened in human dominion over life, so too questions arose about which secular institution, science or law, would authorize and delimit the corollary responsibilities of stewardship. The emergence of recombinant DNA techniques marked a moment of conceptual transition from ideas of life as subject to natural evolution to visions of life as potentially reworkable according to the purposes and desires of technician-designers—a conceptual transition that continues to unfold in domains such as synthetic biology.[9] Life itself could increasingly be seen as a platform for producing novel compositions of biological matter and, with them, novel industrial or military applications, new forms of property, and risks of unknown nature.

Where the natural order of things had previously supplied relative clarity, these developments produced ambiguities. In each case, perturbed boundaries—between living and dead, begotten and made, cared for and exploited—also created novel responsibilities of judgment and action. Choices had to be made, reasons given, responsibilities allocated, and action taken in order to re-establish the clear normative lines that these developments had disrupted.[10] Questions arose as to who was to imagine—and govern—humanity's unfolding biological future and using what modes of ethical reasoning.

Thus, the 1970s saw not only a series of remarkable technological developments affecting the biosciences, and not only a variety of attendant challenges of governance, but also new questions about the place of science in American democracy: as a generator of futures, as a source of uncertainty and risk, as a reservoir of expertise, and as an object of governance. From these moments of emergence and controversy began a decades-long period of experimentation with a repertoire of discourses, institutions, and modes of public reasoning to contend with problems in the biosciences whose moral and scientific complexity strained existing institutions.

This study examines this period of discursive and institutional experimentation within the context of a uniquely challenging and still unresolved problem: how American society should relate to developing human life in the laboratory. For nearly five decades, this question has been a fixture of public bioethical debate and controversy in the United States. This history of the experiments—both scientific and democratic—that unfolded around this question illuminates the imaginations of the right relationship between knowledge and norms, science and politics, that emerged within, and whose legacy continues to shape, American approaches to governing life.

GOVERNING LIFE IN THE LABORATORY

Human embryo research offers a powerful case for examining the politics of public bioethical debate in American democracy from the mid-1970s onward.[11] Other controversial issues in biology and medicine that arose in the 1970s gave way to codified rules and routinized practices of governance within a decade or less. By the 1980s, death had been redefined to accommodate life-prolonging technologies, a regime of ethical oversight had been integrated into human subjects research, and federal guidelines had cleared the way for rDNA research and the rapid rise of a biotechnology industry. Controversy died down as regimes of oversight were constructed to calm a worried public, if not to wholly resolve ethical and political uncertainties. However, in the United States at least, human embryo research remained both ethically and politically unsettled, even as uses of in vitro fertilization (IVF), and thus the laboratory production of in vitro human embryos, expanded rapidly. In the decades since, advances in molecular and cell biology have led researchers to imagine an ever-widening range of experimental uses of human embryos. These new scientific and technological possibilities have repeatedly reawakened public controversy. From assisted reproduction to stem cell research to gene editing,[12] the promises of biomedical innovation have continued to face off against widely held reservations about surrendering the stuff of early human life to the status of raw material for research. Decades after the advent of IVF, the question of what norms should govern human embryo research remains as uncertain as ever.

Uses of human embryos in research changed significantly over the course of the period this book covers.[13] From the late 1970s through the end of the 1980s, human IVF and embryo research were closely connected with assisted reproduction. This was largely because the laboratories that had access to human embryos tended to be those that were in the business of creating them for would-be parents. After the birth of Louise Brown, public discussions of IVF and embryo research also remained focused primarily on reproductive technologies. The IVF embryo was generally seen as a technologically displaced element of human procreation. Its presence in the laboratory tended to be of short duration, the brief period between retrieval of ova and the transfer of cleaving zygotes to the recipient womb. Potential research uses were mostly (but by no means universally) imagined to be related to reproduction, whether in perfecting IVF techniques, understanding the biology of human fertilization and early development, or developing better contraceptive technologies.

During the 1980s, IVF-assisted reproduction became an increasingly common practice in the United States, with the total number of children conceived in vitro rising from dozens in the early 1980s to hundreds of thousands by the 1990s.[14] Assisted reproductive technology (ART) became a lucrative and largely unregulated private sector enterprise, and IVF became a consumer good available to the would-be parents who could afford its high price tag. In a competitive marketplace, the success rates of clinics mattered greatly. Given the inefficiency of the process and the low odds of a successful pregnancy, clinics tended to fertilize most or all of the available eggs, transferring only a small subset to the would-be mother's womb. Beginning in the mid-1980s with the development of cryopreservation techniques, the remaining embryos were generally frozen for subsequent implantations. One consequence of these practices was to produce a surplus of embryos whose creators no longer wanted them for reproductive purposes and could therefore potentially be repurposed for use in research. By the early 2000s, there were an estimated four hundred thousand frozen embryos in the United States.[15] A decade later, there were more than a million.[16] As this vast population of embryos grew, scientists imagined an increasing range of experimental contexts in which they could be put to use.

From the late 1980s until the derivation of human embryonic stem cells in late 1998,[17] the projects of human embryo research became progressively more distant from human reproduction. The creation of Dolly, the cloned sheep, in 1997, suggested that somatic cell nuclear transfer, the technology used to produce her, might also be applied to human cells, offering a means for generating human embryos genetically identical to existing adult humans.[18] The derivation of human embryonic stem cells from human embryos in 1998 heralded powerful new therapeutic possibilities. With these developments came optimistic declarations of the biomedical benefits that would flow from them. By the early 2000s, human embryonic stem cell research was at the center not only of a rapidly emerging scientific field, but of American politics as well. The tiny embryonic stem cell loomed large in news headlines even in a period dominated by the war on terror and ground wars in Afghanistan and Iraq. Widely heralded as an endless frontier of medical and economic benefit, and edging out genomics as the soon-to-be revolutionary life science of the twenty-first century, the IVF embryo also became a lightning rod for sustained political disagreement.

As research involving human embryos figured in an ever-widening range of scientific domains beyond reproduction, the in vitro embryo too came to be conceptually displaced from its procreative origins, not least through the frameworks of analysis that sought to clarify its ontological and moral status. That status—biological and normative—engendered profound uncertainty in society about what human life is, when it becomes worthy of protection, and what instrumental uses it can be put to in the service of advancing scientific knowledge and technology.

MAKING MORAL STATUS

The vast majority of bioethical debate about human embryo research in the United States has focused on determining the moral status of embryos and on evaluating whether particular arguments—scientific, philosophical, or theological—about that status ought to inform public policy. For the most part, this body of work wades into well-worn debates about the moral status of the human embryo without questioning the ethical frame defined by the term itself. Yet, that frame was not given in advance. Initially, debates about how to govern the new capacities for control over early human life were broader. At issue were questions about harms and benefits, distributive impacts, and the social and technological trajectories that new technologies might portend. Actors in these debates questioned what uses of emerging technologies were appropriate, what departures from biological precedents might mean for social and moral norms, and what images of human nature, dignity, and purpose ought to guide new capacities to control life.[19] Curiously, as the range of imagined uses widened, the embryo came to be seen as a potential research object, and ethical deliberation became progressively more narrowly focused on the embryo's "moral status." Eschewing attention to the broader context and purpose that brought IVF embryos into being, the frame of moral status instead sought to establish the standing of the embryo as a thing in itself, so that answers about what instrumental uses of it were permissible would logically follow.[20] Put simply, the desire to use the embryo as an experimental object informed and delimited how it was approached in moral terms. The abstract notion of "moral status" was in this sense a direct reflection of scientists' desire to repurpose the spare IVF embryo from a potential child to an experimental object.

Importantly, from the very beginning of these discussions, questions of moral status were seen as turning in important ways on the embryo's biological status.[21] Thus, discussions about how the embryo should be treated were transmuted into questions of how it should be known and described and of which biological features of the embryo could clarify, or even settle, the crucial moral questions. The question of the embryo's "status" opened a site of "ontological politics" in which the questions of what the embryo *is*—and how its nature should be known—and the normative question of how it should be treated came to be simultaneously at stake.[22]

Approached in this way, the frame of moral status elevated the role of ontological (and, therefore, scientific) accounts of the embryo in ethical deliberation. This proved to be enormously consequential. It reconstituted the basic fault line between proponents and opponents of human embryo research as a disagreement between competing ontological accounts—accounts of what the embryo *is*. The normatively open-ended task of articulating what norms should govern society's relationship to the human embryo gave way to a narrower assessment of which features of its biological status could and should inform collective moral judgment. Debates about moral status, therefore, were translated into debates over how scientific knowledge should figure in public bioethical deliberation and thus over the right relationship between science's epistemic authority and democracy's modes of collective moral sense-making. The question of the embryo's status also became simultaneously a problem of constructing and evaluating arenas of public reasoning: of segregating reasonable disagreement—the lifeblood of democracy—from unacceptable ontological (and thus moral) confusion. Most surprisingly, the status question became the basis for a long-running debate about what language should be used to describe the embryo in order to align public discourse with scientific knowledge in the name of rendering public debate reasonable.

Generally speaking, bioethics tends to treat epistemic and normative judgments as occupying distinct institutional spheres: science and ethics, respectively. Science deals with facts and ethics with values. Science stands outside politics, whereas ethics deals with the political in its most fundamental sense, as collective judgments about the good. Indeed, the notion that science and politics, knowledge and norms, belong to wholly distinct spheres of social life is a cultural commonplace. This commonplace has been reproduced and institutionalized in the very structure of the science–bioethics relationship. Science is thought to have jurisdiction over matters of scientific practice and knowledge, whereas bioethics is considered to have jurisdiction over the value-laden dimensions of research and over the evaluation of the normative significance of technologies' social effects.

Yet, this neat and clean construction is belied by actual practice. In practice, the parameters of ethical reasoning are coproduced with parallel scientific judgments: Ontological and moral accounts are developed together and mutually constituted.[23] This is not merely a matter of cross-traffic between institutions; for instance, ethics bodies consulting scientists for information deemed relevant to ethical judgment. Rather, ontological accounts profoundly shape the practical, conceptual, and even discursive configuration of ethical deliberation. This relationship is particularly evident in the ethical debates that emerged around the embryo. These debates reflected underlying imaginations of the right relationship between science and politics and of the forms of public reasoning appropriate to this relationship. As we shall see, bioethicists drew upon the authority of science not just to construct accounts of the technical objects of ethical assessment, but of the forms of *ethical* reasoning appropriate to public deliberation in a democracy.

Thus, the narrow focus on the moral status of the embryo was consequential for how bioethics bodies constructed the range of relevant reasoning. By displacing other questions, for instance, about the implications of new technologies for human dignity or the meaning of human nature, the frame of moral status made the embryo itself the primary object of deliberation. Insofar as the status of the embryo became the single most important ethical determination, judgments about what should be done shifted into the hands of those who could claim authority to declare what the embryo *is* and how knowledge about its biological status should inform public moral reasoning.

THE POLITICS OF PUBLIC BIOETHICS

Public bioethics bodies played an important role in the human embryo research debates. This was not because they exerted a particularly strong influence on policy. Indeed, for the most part they did not. But they did shape wider public and policy debates in lasting and consequential ways. They are also an important new element in the repertoire of democratic governance. Though it has come to be a quintessential bioethical problem, defining the parameters of ethically acceptable research is first and foremost a problem of politics—the politics of collectively envisioning the good and of assuming responsibilities of democratic governance.

In the case of human embryo research, the question of whether the federal government should fund such research was the primary focus of public debate. This in turn raised the second-order question of how citizens' moral views about developing human life should inform public policy. The same question has persisted around abortion, and it has been widely noted that the political contours of embryo research were profoundly informed by the politics of abortion. Yet, the former was by no means merely an expression of the latter. The constitutional issues surrounding abortion focused on individual liberty and the limits of state authority. With human embryo research, by contrast, public institutions would directly support with taxpayer money activities in which human embryos would be destroyed. In this respect, human embryo research transformed the question of what protections are owed to incipient human life, long a focus of abortion politics, into a collective problem that could no longer be left to the domain of individual liberty. It became necessary for American democracy to contend directly with the question of how society should relate to human life at its earliest stages of development.[24] So too, it became necessary to develop deliberative techniques and institutional structures for doing this. Public bioethics bodies were an important element in that emerging repertoire. Indeed, the first task of the first federal bioethics body in the United States was to address precisely this question.[25]

Bioethics became an important fixture in the democratic governance of emerging biotechnologies starting in the 1970s.[26] Public concerns about "social and ethical issues" in the biosciences catalyzed the development of a scholarly field, professional expertise, novel institutional structures, and an administrative regime to oversee research, all of which are today grouped under the heading of "bioethics." All of these moves respond to a felt democratic imperative to come to terms with the "impacts" and "consequences" of emerging biotechnologies. Put simply, bioethics denotes the organized response to considerations that are ordinarily seen as belonging to the society side of the science–society nexus. In this sense, public bioethics, the focus of this book, can most fruitfully be analyzed as part of the repertoire of democratic governance that has emerged in U.S. politics in the last fifty years in conjunction with the increasing role of science and technology in public life.

"Ethical issues" have come to operate as a kind of shorthand for the class of problems in the biosciences for which society wishes to hold science responsible. "Ethics" delineates a boundary even as it names a problem. It assimilates questions about the future and meaning of technology with a particular repertoire of theoretical languages, administrative practices, and institutional forms. I argue that ethics, understood in this narrowly technocratic way, fails to capture the actual work of bioethics in contemporary American politics. We see how broader ideas of democracy are at stake and are given articulation by focusing on key moments of transition when "ethical issues" shift from an ambiguous territory of democratic responsibility to formalized reasoning within authorized institutions and idioms. I demonstrate that in framing ethical issues, bioethicists simultaneously construct accounts of the forms of public reasoning that are appropriate to democracy but not achieved in practice. Ethical "experts" then position themselves as competent to reason on society's behalf, even as they narrow the range of reasons and forms of discourse that need to be included in deliberation. At the same time, they occlude the constructions of democracy that underpin these moves because the objects of deliberation are formalized as "ethical issues"—in the territory of expert bioethics—rather than marked as matters of democratic governance. Thus, defining the "ethical issues" becomes a means for circumscribing the range of concerns that are deemed reasonable, in effect delimiting what democracy demands by first defining the forms of disagreement that a (putatively) well-informed understanding of the issues will tolerate. At the same time, such moves assert underlying constructions of reasonableness and democratic legitimacy, even though these concepts are essentially contested features of democracy.

Bioethics, because it is concerned with science and medicine, depends in important respects upon scientific expertise. At the same time, bioethics claims expertise in matters of moral judgment, matters that in secular, liberal, public life tend to be seen as belonging to the sphere of private belief and personal judgment—that is, as the sorts of things about which there can be no superior expertise. As sociologist John Evans has observed, bioethics navigates between these positions partly by claiming to have expertise about (and, therefore, jurisdiction over) a particular category of problems—namely, ethical questions that arise in the technically complex domains of biology and medicine.[27]

Bioethics also retains its position by functioning as a mechanism of governance to which society can delegate responsibility for addressing certain problems. This applies to bioethics as a mechanism of ethical assessment and oversight, whether in committees evaluating research in a university or public bioethics bodies supplying advice to governments. It likewise applies to bioethics as a domain of scholarly practice; for example, the huge body of ethical, legal, and social implications (ELSI) research supported by the Human Genome Project to address (and, some would argue, defuse) public concerns about the social effects of genetic technologies.[28] Evans compellingly demonstrates that professional bioethics carved out its jurisdictional space by narrowing the parameters of public debate to exclude other discursive and intellectual approaches such as theology. I build upon these insights by examining the ways bioethics bodies recruited the political authority of science to underwrite their own claims of competence to reason on behalf of the wider public. I argue that a fuller account of the position that bioethics has come to occupy in governance, and of the forms of authority and credibility that it draws upon to do so, requires symmetrical analysis of the interplay between scientific authority and culturally powerful conceptions of public benefit, right reason, and democratic order.

Put in theoretical terms, this is a study in coproduction.[29] I approach relationships between knowledge and norms as a consequence, rather than a cause, of social arrangements. On a methodological level, a coproductionist lens treats notions of the right relationship between facts and values, knowledge and norms, and science and politics, not as given in advance, but as historically situated cultural, political, and moral commitments. Coproduction requires a "symmetrical" approach to investigating both knowledge and norms (and associated institutions of social authority). That is, this framework requires setting aside a priori constructions of what distinguishes knowledge from norms, facts from values, and science from politics, instead examining the moves made by social actors to assert, reinforce, challenge, or adopt these distinctions. The boundaries that a coproductionist approach takes as analytic objects may reflect commitments that are so widely shared and so deeply held that they are invisible to social actors. They literally go without saying. Yet, at the same time, those actors are constantly engaged in boundary work that maintains or reconfigures these commitments.[30]

In extending the reach of David Bloor's principle of symmetry from knowledge to normativity, I am following the theoretical lead of Sheila Jasanoff and others.[31] These scholars have interrogated the coproduction of knowledge and norms in law, regulation, and the politics thereof, showing how ways of knowing—"civic epistemologies"—are embedded in, configured by, and constitutive of political cultures.[32] My analysis is deeply indebted to this pioneering work. My innovation is to take democratic theory itself as an object of analysis by examining how it is deployed within—and made to regulate practices of—deliberative democracy. I focus in particular on sites such as bioethics bodies whose legitimacy requires a different sort of apologetics than more established apparatuses of governance.

My study approaches public bioethics as a site of coproduction in which ideas of science, democracy, and the right relationship between them were constructed. The public bioethics bodies that contended with embryo research in America differed significantly in their practices and approaches, but they struggled with the same basic problem: How could they claim to stand in for the wider public whose ethical concerns they claimed to represent? This problem of "standing in" points to a fundamental tension in the project of bioethics as a form of expertise. The mandate of public bioethics bodies is to reason on behalf of the wider public. Bioethics walks a fine line between representing plural, publicly held views ("all sides of the issue") and constructing accounts of "reasonable" views— in effect, those views that *would* be publicly held were the public competent in moral reasoning. I show how each of these bodies contended with what political theorist John Rawls called "the fact of reasonable pluralism"—the inevitable diversity of reasonable moral positions held by a political community—by constructing accounts of the forms of reasoning appropriate to collective moral sense-making.[33] By reasoning on behalf of the public, they positioned themselves as able to perform a deliberative role that wider society has neither the capacity nor the will to do for itself. In effect, they constructed an account of an ideally reasonable public, and positioned themselves as reasoning as such a public would reason.

These bodies used a variety of different strategies to position themselves as legitimately standing in for the public. Regardless of the particular approach, however, these bodies all claimed to represent the public by representing good public reason. Most remarkably, in claiming to stand in for public values, bioethics bodies tended to rely upon a notion of science as an extra-political authority that can be drawn upon to delimit, discipline, and secure the range of reasonable pluralism appropriate for collective moral sense-making. Deference to scientific judgment was not just a matter of incorporating authorized knowledge into ethical deliberation. Rather, bioethical authorities drew upon the authority of science in constructing accounts of what forms of public reasoning were appropriate to making judgments about morally and technically complex matters.

Jasanoff has described the ways courts construct the boundary between science and law so as to lean on the exogenous authority of science in shoring up forms of legal argument.[34] My analysis of public bioethics reveals similar dynamics, yet in a different institutional context. Like courts, bioethics bodies depend on reason, rather than representation of political interests, to underwrite their authority. However, as constitutionally authorized interpreters of law, the courts are also an arena of widely acknowledged expertise. Legal expertise is usually a prerequisite of juridical authority. In contrast, bioethics is not linked to a codified and politically legitimated body of technical knowledge such as law. It claims authority over matters of moral belief—matters that in a liberal society belong in principle to each and every citizen. As such, public bioethics bodies find it necessary to justify their authority and political role by constructing themselves as "expert" in delivering the forms of moral reasoning and judgment appropriate to democratic governance. To enhance their legitimacy, I argue, they lean, much as courts do, on the cultural authority of science; but, unlike courts, bioethics bodies at the same time construct explicit normative accounts of how science *ought* to figure in public reasoning that treat deference to science as obligatory for democratically legitimate judgment.

Public bioethics bodies function in these respects as "experiments in democracy." These bodies, though different from the sorts of abstract processes or scripted experiments imagined by scholars of deliberative democracy,[35] are a productive site for uncovering the subtle ingredients that inform ideas of public reason in contemporary American politics. They are, in other words, "natural experiments." Indeed, the results of these experiments reveal much about the ideas of public reason that have taken shape in relation to technically complex problems and thus about corollary notions of what forms of democratic representation (that is, of "standing in") are appropriate to governing scientific and technological societies— what views must be considered, what voices heard, and what kinds of judgments rendered. Each of the bodies that I examine constructed a different account of how it could claim to stand in for the polity, but each in some way relied upon the notion that scientific knowledge stands outside politics to do this. The differences among these bodies cannot be accounted for in the extant vernaculars of moral or political theory. Rather, they reflect tacit cultural imaginations of democracy and right public reason, which this study excavates. Underpinning the work of these bodies were background notions of how the state and its citizens should relate to knowledge: to what is known and how it should be known, including the language in which knowledge should be described and deliberated.

Science and technology figure centrally in late modern democratic politics and are increasingly a focus of calls for new forms of deliberative democracy. This includes, for instance, mechanisms of public engagement to elicit policy-relevant public values.[36] While I do not engage directly with those projects, my analysis is relevant to them. These projects of democratizing science, too, are situated within—and configured by—particular political cultures. This is evident in recent calls for more inclusive deliberation in public bioethical debate.[37] Those calls affirm the importance of free and equal participation in democratic deliberation, but they leave intact assumptions about the conditions of possibility for deliberative democracy—in particular, notions of what must be known and how it must be known in order for people to participate in reasoned public debate. Such assumptions are highly consequential for who gets to speak, and in what terms, not only because they shape the epistemic framing of particular ethical questions, but because they reflect tacit assumptions about right modes of public reasoning. For instance, the Presidential Commission for the Study of Bioethical Issues, the public bioethics body created by President Barack Obama, has identified democratic deliberation as a key pillar of public bioethics.[38] At the same time, the commission suggests that this pillar must in turn be grounded in an educational campaign for public "ethics literacy" so that citizens acquire the capacity to participate in *reasoned* deliberation.[39] Democratic deliberation in this vision is not a construct defined by the will of the people. Rather, it is configured by underlying, ostensibly neutral, expert presumptions about what competencies are required and what the rules of engagement should be. These presumptions are seen as non-normative because they simply have to do with being "knowledgeable" or "informed." But this, I intend to demonstrate, is a faulty assumption: The baseline criteria for determining reasonableness are inescapably normative.

These presumptions of public bioethics are at once powerful and hidden. They have important consequences for how normative questions are asked and addressed, how the stakes of deliberation are constructed, and what perspectives are represented at the table. Yet, the ways they configure and constrain deliberation are systematically overlooked, even in the work of the Presidential Commission for the Study of Bioethical Issues, which is chaired by Amy Gutmann, a leading theorist of deliberative democracy.[40] Thus, my analysis speaks to issues that lie at the very center of contemporary democratic theory. I argue that science occupies a "constitutional" position in contemporary democracy and that this position is simultaneously underwritten and occluded by the notion that science stands outside politics.

THE CONSTITUTIONAL POSITION OF SCIENCE

One of the fundamental elements of a constitutionalist conception of democracy is the notion that a *demos* requires a shared normative repertoire and common language to reason together. Indeed, a constitution functions as a normative touchstone and a shared vocabulary for elaborating duties, rights, and entitlements. An enormous body of political theory has attended to the role of such vocabularies in constituting and regulating political modernity. Yet, processes and institutions of knowledge making, though critical to political life in contemporary scientific and technological societies, are essentially neglected in this body of scholarship. This applies in particular to the role of authorized knowledge in shaping the shared normative vocabularies and modes of public reasoning that constitute and regulate political life.

Sheila Jasanoff has observed that, as science and technology have reshaped fundamental aspects of social life, they have engendered transformations in identity, sovereignty, and citizenship that are properly described as *constitutional*. These forms of constitutional reordering reside not in the black letter of law, but in the "norms of constitutional relevance [that] are tacitly constructed in the daily hum of technological societies: norms that are embodied in technological standards and practices, hardened into material instruments and artifacts, entrenched within professional discourses, and legitimated through public policy."[41] They also reside in the political role that scientific authority plays as a reserve power, one that is deferred to in resolving questions of constitutional significance without itself being subjected to constitutional norms. With the concept of "civic epistemologies," Jasanoff has elaborated the ways scientific expertise is drawn upon in processes of political judgment. She has shown that different societies employ different forms of trust and reason in subjecting knowledge claims to tests of credibility and relevance for making collective choices.[42] Civic epistemologies are modes of constitutional ordering but sit below the surface of codified law. She has shown how, in U.S. political culture in particular, scientific authority is constructed as an exogenous resource, called into arenas of legal and political judgment to clarify matters of duty and justice.[43]

My analysis builds upon these insights to examine the ways *normative* accounts of public reasoning are underwritten by the ostensibly exogenous authority of science. In my case studies, the constitutional remit of science reached into domains of collective moral sense-making that were seen as utterly distinct from the sphere of scientific knowledge. Actors in the embryo debates constructed accounts of how citizens in a democracy should reason together that positioned science as the right authority to determine the terms of debate. This shaped not only how epistemic claims entered the political arena, but also the criteria of reasonableness that regulated debate—that is, criteria for the forms of discourse that were deemed appropriate (and inappropriate) to public moral deliberation. Thus, the political position of science was constitutional insofar as science became an arbiter of authorized speech in the democratic arena.

With the term *public reason*, I am referring to normative ideas of the forms of reasoning appropriate to public life in a liberal democracy. In an extensive body of work, Jasanoff has developed an innovative, constructivist approach to studying modes of public reasoning. I cannot here elaborate the many dimensions of this work that are relevant to my study except to note that I follow her lead in interrogating how culturally situated imaginaries of "rightness" inform practices and institutions of public reasoning.[44] Her work has illustrated the productivity of a framework that draws more of the matter of the world into its accounting of practices of reasoning, attending in particular to why modes of reason take the forms they do and win acceptance in the ways they do. I follow Jasanoff and others in science and technology studies (STS) in showing that political and ethical theory are not independent of social life. Rather, they are constituted through the very discursive and institutional processes that treat them as exogenous resources to justify themselves.

Here, I examine explicitly normative constructions of public reason in political theory, specifically in the tradition of John Rawls. In this conception, *public reason* refers to the normative ideal of the forms of reasoning appropriate to public life in a liberal democracy. Rawls's idea of "public reason" and his associated account of the deliberative foundations of democracy have been extremely influential in contemporary political theory. It is normative conceptions of "public reason" of this sort that I take as my object of analysis. In this respect, my usage of the term *public reason* differs slightly from Jasanoff's. For my purposes, "public reason" is also an actor's category—that is, it is a concept that was explicitly used and elaborated in the social processes I examine. I am interested in how actors imagined ideal public reasoning within these processes and the ways they called for norms and rules of debate that would realize that ideal. For these actors, public reason is a normative concept. It refers to an image of right reason to which the public ought to aspire. I do not advance my own normative account, but instead examine how actors in the embryo debates advanced their own accounts of how the public ought to reason together, drawing on what cultural and political resources, and grounded in what underlying imaginations of rightness.

One primary and explicit focus of the debates around human embryo research was whether and under what circumstances democracy should intervene in the workings of science. Less explicit but equally consequential was the question of what role science should play in shaping the terms of public debate and ensuring the quality of public reasoning. As we shall see, the question of how to treat the embryo was transmuted into questions of power: Who has the authority to declare matters of fact and to render moral judgments? Who determines the right language in which to reason together about the embryo's status? And, most remarkably, what is the role of scientific authority as a foundation for, and as an arbiter of, public reason?

Instead of ethics acting as a brake on science, we will see that bioethics bodies, along with a host of other actors, drew on the authority of science to define the parameters of right public reason, even down to the very words employed in public debate. In doing so, they relied upon a culturally entrenched imaginary of science as an extra-political source of authority.[45] This imaginary positioned scientific experts as occupying a privileged role in the debate, supplying the common language for public deliberation and defining the factual baselines to which moral judgments had to conform—in effect, defining the range of claims that could be made about what *ought* to be done by declaring what *is* the case. This power to shape the terms of debate is what I refer to as "the constitutional position of science"—constitutional because science is seen not merely as a source of relevant factual knowledge about the world, but as a foundational source of authority in taming the tumult of politics into the orderliness of right public reasoning. I show how scientific authority was repeatedly drawn upon as a resource to construct accounts of right public reason and democratic legitimacy. This played out in practice; for instance, as public debates about how a biological entity *ought* to be treated came to focus instead on what it *is* and how it should be named.

Bioethics bodies sometimes drew explicitly on democratic theory in constructing accounts of how the public ought to reason about the embryo. I attend in particular to the ways they drew on deliberative democratic theory. Questions about the forms of reasoning and practices of delibera-tion that are appropriate to democracy are a central focus of deliberative democratic theory, particularly in the tradition of John Rawls.[46] Rawls's work, and the lines of thinking that have developed from it, have come to dominate American political philosophy. I engage with Rawlsian delib-erative democratic theory for two reasons. First, it reflects the same tacit assumptions about science that I see at work throughout much of the embryo research debates (arguably because both Rawlsian political theory and American public bioethical debate are products of the same political culture). Second, Rawls's ideas of public reason, overlapping consensus, and reflective equilibrium were used by some of the ethics bodies I exam-ine to justify their approaches to standing in.

Two observations are pertinent here. First, deliberative democratic the-ory overlooks the tacit "constitutional" position of science in American democracy. Second, and more importantly for my analysis, this under-theorization of the role of science has profound consequences for the ways that democracy is imagined and enacted. Thus, my intent is not to engage with Rawlsian theory on its own normatively oriented turf, but rather to examine how Rawlsian ideas function "in the wild,"[47] as features of politi-cal culture come into play that are overlooked in (and, I would argue, rein-scribed through) dominant accounts of democracy.[48] Rawlsian ideas of how a polity should reason together were used to discipline public debate, and scientific authority was recruited to legitimate this disciplinary move. This is remarkable because Rawlsian approaches presume that science is not a form of political authority, even, I argue, as they create a normative opening for science to occupy a position of political authority—indeed, a constitutional one. To illustrate this, I briefly sketch below how this double move figures in Rawlsian theory itself.

THE IDEA OF PUBLIC REASON

The notion that the fact–value boundary is clear and unproblematic is a foundational assumption in Rawlsian deliberative democratic theory. It reflects a commitment to the idea that facts are extra-political, neutral, and common by definition, whereas values are plural, political, and essentially contested. I do not intend to critique these philosophical claims directly, but rather to explore how they function "in the wild"—in effect, to take them as objects of social analysis as they circulate through domains of political practice. Normative democratic theory meets social life when it is used to justify or evaluate particular democratic practices. Furthermore, one can read democratic theory itself as embedded in, and an expression of, political culture. Seen in this way, theories of democracy are themselves culturally situated artifacts. As such, they draw upon and codify an already existing cultural common sense about the right ordering of things.

Rawls's idea of public reason is a solution to the "fact of reasonable pluralism," the social fact that members of a political community inevitably hold a variety of irreconcilable "comprehensive doctrines." Pluralism poses a challenge for collective political judgment, particularly where a community aspires to modes of political judgment that neither merely aggregate individual preferences nor are simply majoritarian. Deliberative democrats in the Rawlsian tradition see aggregative processes (like voting) as far inferior to procedures of political judgment that are grounded in sustained, collective deliberation—simply put, democracy done well requires talking things over before deciding:

> According to the deliberative conception, a decision is collective just in case it emerges from arrangements of binding collective choice that establish conditions of *free public reasoning among equals who are governed by the decisions.*[49]

Thus, the central idea behind deliberative democracy is "to tie the exercise of power to conditions of public reasoning."[50]

The function of public reason is to ground political legitimacy in deliberation without suppressing reasonable pluralism. Rawls's idea of public reason requires citizens to provide justifications that all other citizens will find reasonable "by appealing to beliefs, grounds, and political values it is reasonable for others also to acknowledge," even if they disagree with those reasons.[51] Ideally, everyone would be convinced by the best reasons. But in the real world, people will disagree, so everyone must use reasons that seem at least reasonable, if not convincing, to everyone else. This is the principle of reciprocity. It requires that, "when citizens make moral claims in a deliberative democracy, they appeal to reasons or principles that can be shared by fellow citizens."[52] Nonpublic reasons are inappropriate to public reasoning in this scheme of things because they do not comport with shared conceptions of reasonableness:

> Shared guidelines for inquiry and methods of reasoning make that reason public, while freedom of speech and thought in a constitutional regime make that reason free. By contrast, nonpublic reason is the reason appropriate to individuals and associations within society: it guides how they quite properly deliberate in making their personal and associational decisions.[53]

Rawls positions public reason as a constitutional essential. A stable constitutional regime "should specify not only a shared, but if possible, a clear basis of public reason, and one that can publicly be seen to be sufficiently reliable on its own terms."[54] Political values must conform to the requirements of public reason, which "bar theological and other comprehensive doctrines from deciding the case."[55]

Thus, for Rawls, public reason is a *regulative* concept. In his theory, a commitment to the rules of public reason is a normative prerequisite for enacting deliberative democracy. It is a duty of citizenship that participants in a political community offer public reasons when engaged in political deliberation. In effect, the norms of public reason define the terms of participation by excluding reasons that are not held in common. In practice, however, the idea of public reason plays a disciplinary function in delimiting the kinds of reasons that can be offered by participants in a political community. This is the intended goal of Rawlsian democracy. Put into practice, the idea of public reason is meant to shape the practices of a political culture such that that political culture eventually incorporates those practices as norms. Indeed, the rules of public reason are meant to play a kind of pedagogical role in shaping members of the political community. As political theorist Joshua Cohen puts it, in limiting the kinds of reasons that can be given in political deliberation, "public reasoning itself can help to reduce the diversity of politically relevant preferences because such preferences are shaped and even formed in the process of public reasoning itself."[56]

SCIENCE AND PUBLIC REASON

Rawls imagines the questions confronted in political deliberation to be values questions by definition. Issues of knowledge are distinct because they are apolitical. Yet, in drawing this line, he in effect carves out a special space for the place of scientific authority in democratic deliberation:

> Faced with the fact of reasonable pluralism, and granted that, on matters of constitutional essentials, basic institutions and public policies should be justifiable to all citizens (as the liberal principle of legitimacy requires), we allow the parties the general beliefs and forms of reasoning found in common sense, and the methods and conclusions of science, when not controversial. . . . So we say the parties have that kind of general knowledge and they use those ways of reasoning. This excludes comprehensive religious and philosophical doctrines (the whole truth as it were) from being specified as public reasons.[57]

Thus, the "methods and conclusions of science" (when not controversial) occupy a special category of reasons: reasons that citizens cannot evaluate for themselves but must accept a priori as reasonable. In Rawls's thinking, scientific knowledge is reasonable not because others find it to be so, but because it is grounded in fact. However, in practice, the "methods and conclusions of science" are claims advanced under the mantle of scientific authority. From a constructivist perspective, scientific accounts are not given in advance, but are put forward by particular people in particular social and historical contexts and are subject to the credibility conditions specific to that social context. Reframed in terms that acknowledge science's social grounding, knowledge is the product of a community of reason.[58] And yet, veiled behind the label of (uncontroversial) science, this community's reasons are not (according to Rawls) answerable to the demands of public reason. The idea of public reason as an obligation of citizens, but not of scientists, to offer reasons in terms of "beliefs, grounds, and political values [that] it is reasonable for others also to acknowledge"[59] places science and the public in an asymmetrical and unequal relationship. Claims that are advanced by scientific authorities as uncontroverted knowledge are treated as de facto reasonable, whereas those views that are marked as depending upon moral pictures of the world that are not accessible to others are de facto excluded as nonpublic reasons. Thus, scientific voices are privileged in public reasoning because they are seen as offering incontestable reasons. At the same time, any other kind of claim that is incontestable is excluded precisely because public reasons must be contestable in order to be public.

Approached symmetrically, however, the boundary between scientific and nonscientific claims is not given in advance. The distinction is drawn by social actors through social processes. While, from an epistemological perspective, one can give accounts about what distinguishes facts from values, in social life, those distinctions are regulated by actors who are seen as able to authoritatively draw this line. My interest here is not whether the categories of "fact" and "value" are epistemologically meaningful independent of the contingencies of social life. On the contrary, my interest is what these categories mean—and how they are used—in social life. In this respect, I am working in a well-established tradition in sociology of knowledge. My primary object of analysis, however, is not knowledge as such, but its place in normative accounts of right public reason and the configurations of political authority and power that come into being as those accounts are put into practice.

Note that in Rawls's account, scientific authority is elevated to a privileged position not by displacing democracy as the locus of political authority, but precisely because science is seen as exemplary of the kind of reasoning that is the legitimate basis of political authority: universal reasons. Put differently, science is simultaneously figured as outside politics and as achieving the forms of pure reason to which politics ought to aspire. Thus, science is privileged both as an epistemic source of facts that inform (and constrain) public reasoning about values and as a self-governing deliberative community. As an epistemic authority, science supplies the foundational account of things as they are upon which values deliberation is built and to which it must therefore defer. Second, as a deliberative institution, science is seen as exemplary of the form of reasoning to which public reasoning ought to aspire. Indeed, the "republic of science" is a well-established cultural construct wherein the social practices of scientists are seen as producing a form of life—science—that "does" reason better than any other social community. Science is, in this construct, autonomous and authoritative. To be science, science is—and must be—sovereign. In the words of Michael Polanyi, "The soil of academic science must be extraterritorial in order to secure its rule by scientific opinion."[60]

Rawls's idea of public reason respects science's territorial sovereignty, while also giving it an unrestricted passport to enter into the arena of public reason. Needless to say, there is no reciprocity in this immigration arrangement: Science is instantly naturalized to the territory of public reason, whereas the lay public is unwelcome in the republic of science. Some scholars have suggested that this asymmetry is unjustified and can be remedied by expanding the circle of science to include a wider range of actors in processes of knowledge making.[61] I argue, by contrast, that what keeps that asymmetry intact is not merely an account of how to produce robust knowledge. What keeps it intact is an imaginary of liberal politics wherein the relationship between knowledge and norms, between science and politics, is in effect constitutional: For the integrity of its own processes, democracy depends upon the integrity, indeed the sovereignty, of science.[62]

In social practice, this means scientific authorities enjoy a privileged position of political authority. They are invited to offer reasons that cannot be contested and must be deferred to, not merely on the basis of epistemic warrants—that is, because they are considered to be correct—but because their reasons meet and exceed the *normative* requirements of public reason and thus demand deference. As a result, science is politically privileged (because scientific reasons are seen as public reasons by definition) at the same time that its position of social authority is occluded (because its reasonableness is seen as deriving from its truth status, not from a priori political authority). In this sense, science occupies a constitutional position—because the image of right reason codifies the *political* asymmetry between science and public as foundational, necessary, and appropriate.

This construction of the political authority of science is different from the kind of intrusion of technocratic authority into democratic space about which thinkers such as Jürgen Habermas have worried. It is not the "colonization" of the life-world of value-focused politics by instrumental reason. Rather, it is precisely the commitment to robust values deliberation that confers a political privilege upon scientific reasons. It is not technocratic displacement, but democratic deference. Scientific authority steps into a space *created* by a theory of public reason—a theory that sees itself as not needing to engage with science because it lies entirely on the fact side of a posited fact–value distinction. By treating knowledge and values as distinct, and locating democracy entirely in the latter domain, this theory has the perverse effect of according scientific authority a privileged position of political authority in practice.

As noted above, Joshua Cohen has suggested that public reason is pedagogical as well as normative. In this vein, he observes that the idea of public reason offers a model for designing institutionalized power, first to shape wider public culture, and second to achieve the aims of deliberative democracy, even in the absence of extensive public participation in deliberation: "We can work out the content of the deliberative democratic ideal and its conception of public reasoning by considering features of such reasoning in the idealized case and then aiming to build those features into institutions." In other words, by building the (disciplinary) functions of public reason into the design of political institutions, those institutions can *stand in* for a deliberative public by reasoning as the public ought to reason.[63]

As we shall see, a variety of actors in the human embryo research debates positioned themselves as doing precisely this. They addressed the "fact of reasonable pluralism" by bridging the chasm that separates the ideal of deliberative democracy from what they saw as the fact of an unreasonable public, and they relied upon the authority of science to do it. In practice, this entailed partitioning the field of possible participants into the reasonable and the unreasonable, using deference to science as a key criterion of reasonableness. In some cases, bioethics bodies reached directly into the repertoire of Rawlsian political theory to justify such moves. In other cases, however, actors made very similar moves without having recourse to (or indeed having knowledge of) the theoretical apparatus described above. Yet, even where there are no such direct links between political theory and political practice, the case studies offered in this book illuminate unexamined cultural assumptions that are also embedded in Rawlsian ideas. This is because both the Rawlsian idea of public reason and the tacit notions of reasonableness advanced in public debate spring from the same political culture. That political culture's (formal, big "C") Constitutional commitment to liberal pluralism has simultaneously conferred upon science a (informal, small "c") constitutional position as a universal, secular authority, capable of supplying a common foundation for politics.

Deliberative democratic theory emerged in part as a solution to the specter of technocracy.[64] Yet, in the tacit constitutional regime this study describes, public claims paradoxically get silenced by an explicit, normative commitment to robust deliberation. The admonition that citizens are to speak freely is structured in the background by a notion that such speech must first be emancipated from the constraints of unreason by being disciplined into scientifically authorized discourse. This dispensation invites one to systematically overlook the dynamics of the coproduction of knowledge and norms: those moments at which knowledge is called upon as a resource to order democratic practices and when democratic imperatives configure notions of what must be known, and to what end. Thinkers such as Habermas who celebrate the discursive foundations of democracy have treated technocratic authority as at odds with robust deliberative democracy. Habermas's solution is to maintain a normatively grounded separation between technocracy and democracy.[65] Yet, technocratic colonization of democracy comes, I argue, not only through the intrusion of an exogenous "instrumental reason" into political life, but also—and more consequentially—through the political elevation of epistemic authority in the name of democracy's own norms, particularly where science promises to bring order to the welter of value-laden public views, and thereby becomes an arbiter of right reasoning.

THE FIGURE OF SCIENCE

Throughout this book, I refer to "science" and "scientific authority." This language risks reifying the conception of science as a singular and well-defined entity and may appear to run roughshod over the distinction between science as such and particular scientific claims or actors who may or may not authentically speak for science.

Indeed, decades of STS scholarship have examined the processes by which disparate modes of inquiry are gathered together under the heading of "science" and come to bear that label.[66] This includes, for instance, constant boundary work whereby "science" is defined by reference to what it is not;[67] processes of negotiation and configurations of credibility whereby the mantle of facticity is conferred upon epistemic claims;[68] the constellation of social, material, and semiotic relations drawn together in the "actor networks" that constitute scientific knowledge;[69] and the ways in which knowledge and norms are coproduced in practice, even as these relations are rendered invisible by institutionalized distinctions between science and politics.[70]

My analysis proceeds in the same constructivist tradition. However, my aim is not to contribute to the already substantial body of work that examines the construction of scientific facts and technological artifacts. With the exception of the coproductionist scholarship noted above, this literature has tended on the whole to focus on the construction of facts to the neglect of norms and institutions, leaving a significant lacuna in theoretical accounts of the place of science in modern life. Yet, the relationship between science and politics is not limited to the political "uses" of exogenously constructed and black-boxed facts. As such, it cannot be adequately understood by interrogating the social processes of fact construction alone. Through symmetrical analysis of the interplay of scientific authority with normative and political conceptions of social benefit, secular reason, and democratic order, I show that the lopsided attention to the construction of knowledge overlooks fundamental dimensions of the coproductionist relationship between two of modernity's most powerful institutions: science and democracy.

By examining debates about an ontologically unstable object of significant moral concern—the human embryo—I show that the crafting of
right norms is every bit as intricate as the crafting of right knowledge,
and that the one is implicated in the other. In this respect, my aim is to
contribute to the growing field of scholarship on the "coproduction" of
science and politics.

Approached in this way, decomposing the singular "science" into a
tangle of hybrid actor networks that sit beneath its surface gives one little
analytic purchase on the ordering moves that are made at the frontiers
of science and technology. I am interested less in how particular epistemic claims came to be credible than in how they came to be normatively significant. Their normative significance derives, I argue, not from
their epistemic status, but from a conception (or, better, an imaginary)
of secular public reason that confers political authority upon (those who
speak for) scientific knowledge. Thus, those who speak with authority
about scientific knowledge do so by standing in for "science" as figured
in this imaginary.

Thus, the "science" that is the focus of this book is a figure in the
normative political imagination. Yet, it is not merely a figment of that
imagination. It is, at the same time, a set of very real epistemic, material, social, institutional, and, I would argue, moral configurations. When
scientists are called upon, for instance, to testify before a bioethics committee, they represent and speak for "science." They do not merely stand
for the accumulated knowledge that scientists have produced or the
social–material–semiotic configurations that constitute that knowledge.
They represent a social institution, one that was foundational for the
project of modernity[71] and remains so for its present political form.[72]
Approached as a social institution that occupies, as described above, a
constitutional position within the secular political project of modernity,
science is (and always has been) quintessentially modern. This is so not
least because science figures as a citadel of secular reason in the normative political imagination. In this sense, "science" is not a sui generis
institution. It did not bootstrap itself into its privileged political position through the prowess of its powers of technique and demonstration. Rather, it acquired (and retains) its position because it occupies

an essential—indeed, a constitutional—place in an aspirational political imagination of the right ordering of secular public life. Put differently, to the extent that, as Bruno Latour has famously claimed, "in our modern societies most of the really fresh power comes from sciences—no matter which," this is so not because "it is in laboratories that most new sources of power are generated."[73] It is so because the institution of science is woven into the fabric of imaginaries of modern political order—imaginaries that regulate—and are therefore realized by and reinscribed through—social practices.[74] Science is authorized to be seen as the maker of facts that *should* move through the world, and it is in this way that the normative figure of "science" is constituted.

Thus, when I refer to "science" or "scientific authority," I am referring to that figure of science at work in these imaginaries in practice. From the perspective of social analysis, there is no given-in-advance "true" science upon which social actors can draw, even if the notion that there is such a science plays a regulative function in politics. To be sure, I draw no principled distinction between "science" and the individual scientists or scientific claims that figure in my empirical cases. "Science" is implicated in the claims of particular social actors, and vice versa. I treat all forms of science symmetrically, because my project is to understand the social dynamics of these debates, not to evaluate who was "right"—or, as actors in the embryo debates put it, who was "true" to science and who was "politicizing" it.[75] The latter approach would entail an asymmetrical "sociology of error"; that is, it would examine how the bad wrongs arose, rather than examining how notions of rightness (and, correlatively, wrongness) are formed in the first place. Such a sociology of error would stray into the normative territory of defining the right relationship between science and politics and identifying instances of failure. I, by contrast, want to take precisely such drawing of definitions and declarations of failure as my objects of analysis. Rather than weigh in on which account of scientific authority was the right one, I take the very making of such claims as an object of social inquiry. Put in terms familiar to STS, in my analysis, "science" is an actor's category, not an analyst's category—it is a term employed by the actors in this story and is meaningful to them. My analytic project is to understand how it was employed, with what meanings, and to what ends.

FROM EXPLANATION TO UNDERSTANDING

Relatedly, there are a number of explanatory moves that have become commonplace in accounts of the human embryo research debates—moves that I intentionally refuse. One is to treat the social interests of actors as sufficient to account for what those actors did. Although in any particular case, one can argue that a given scientist did not really speak for science, but instead for his or her own particular interests, this explanatory move obscures the fact that actors who claim to speak for science are slotting themselves into an already recognized position of political authority. In the absence of that position, social interest would not translate into the same social effects. Indeed, it is the pre-existing and collectively acknowledged political authority of science that gives political force to the declaration that someone is "playing politics with science." The ideal is reinforced even as the particular individual is accused of violating it. Thus, "genuine" scientific expertise is constantly affirmed as an essential ingredient in democratic judgment, including by impugning a particular actor's claim to expertise as disingenuous. Therefore, an approach that focuses narrowly on social interests neglects the political dynamics that produce the conditions of possibility for scientific authority in the first place. It also, therefore, occludes the collective political commitments that push problems of democratic judgment onto the terrain of the politics of knowledge.

As noted above, another frequent move is to explain political conflicts over human embryo research as purely the extension of political ideologies associated with abortion politics. It is a commonplace to see the debates over human embryo research as abortion politics by other means. There is no question that the deep political division around abortion in the United States exerted tremendous influence in the controversies over uses of the in vitro human embryo. With that assessment I have no argument. My argument is with the claim that the politics of abortion are sufficient to account for the phenomena examined here. Reducing the embryo research controversy to a footnote in the history of abortion politics ignores some of its most salient—and consequential—features. The embryo debates extend the political fault lines around abortion into complex new territories.

While abortion politics play a critically important part in this story, the aim of my analysis is to look beneath these well-worn political conflicts to the ideas of knowledge, reason, and legitimate authority that were often shared by *both* "sides," and which therefore shaped the contours of the political debate. The notion that all explanatory roads lead to abortion politics, and thus to the unbridgeable ideological gap that separates Right from Left, hides the features of political culture and the collectively held imaginaries of right reason that shaped the contours of politics—including the parameters of disagreement themselves. The technical features of IVF and the technological possibilities associated with stem cell research fundamentally altered how science figured in the public debates over society's obligations to the human conceptus, exposing important differences between debates over abortion and human embryo research. Most importantly, mapping the ideological interests of particular actors—for instance, counting up the balance of pro-life versus pro-choice members of public bioethics bodies—reveals little about how they constructed their own modes of reasoning or judged them as adequate to stand in for public debate. At stake in those moves were notions of the proper relationship between scientific and democratic authority in producing right public reason.

This study, therefore, does not seek to evaluate the successes or failures of science or democracy; nor does it describe the political effects of already well-known social interests. My aim is to bring to the surface underappreciated dimensions of the relationship between science and democracy in U.S. politics. Insofar as I have a normative project, it is oriented not to the question, "What should we do?" but to the prior, more basic question, "How should we understand?"[76] It is only once we fully recognize the forms of power and authority that shape our thought-world that we can confront the question of "What we should do?" with enlightenment. It is this project of understanding that this book seeks to advance.

METHODS AND STRUCTURE

This book incorporates a number of disciplinary domains and approaches. My approach, to begin with, is most straightforwardly a historical project. It traces the development of a controversy together with the social and material practices, discourses, institutions, and imaginaries that shaped and were shaped by it. It is a genealogical project in the Foucaultian sense.[77] My theoretical analysis of the embryo debates, however, draws upon the theoretical tools of science and technology studies, and in particular the attentiveness of coproductionist STS to the complex interweaving of knowledge and norms in making social order.[78]

Bioethics figures centrally in my story, not as a set of principles for normative decision making, but as an emergent domain of thought, a reservoir of expertise and authority, and a new apparatus of governance. Bioethics is, in this respect, an object of study, but, I hope, it is also an interlocutor. One of my aims is to relocate some of the foundational, if abstract, commitments of bioethics within a wider political culture, with the hope of exposing dimensions of lines of reasoning that are unacknowledged even (perhaps especially) to those who initiate them.

My research relies more heavily on the raw discourse of deliberation than on the simplified and purified products of it found, for instance, in reports by elite commissions. The thousands of pages of transcripts from a public bioethics body reveal far more about its processes of reasoning—and the imaginaries that underwrite them—than its published conclusions. This book draws heavily on transcripts of the deliberations of public bioethics bodies, congressional hearings, advisory committee meetings, legal cases, and other primary sources. I also conducted several dozen interviews with key figures, including scientists, ethicists, policymakers, lobbyists and activists. I attended hearings, conferences, workshops, lectures, and other public events. In addition, I rely on reports, policy documents, and a wide range of other published materials.

My analysis proceeds chronologically, using key moments and controversies as empirical cases. Chapter 1 examines the period from the mid-1960s to 1980. During this period, scientific advances were made in human in vitro fertilization and embryo culture, leading to the birth of Louise Brown, the first child conceived through IVF, in 1978. During the same period, congressional concerns with the ethics of biomedical research led to the formation of the first national bioethics bodies in the United States. The chapter shows, in particular, how the Ethics Advisory Board (EAB), constituted in 1978 to provide a case-by-case review of ethically complex research proposals, struggled to find an acceptable framework of ethical analysis for IVF, particularly given the EAB's desire to mark its conclusions as but one possible approach amid a legitimate plurality of public views. The EAB's reasoning drew an analogy between artificial and natural reproduction as a strategy of limiting the range of ethical questions and avoiding the problem of the moral status of the embryo. Nevertheless, it confronted moral status in a limited way. Two of its least principled determinations—on the embryo's moral status and on a fourteen-day limit to in vitro embryo culture—proved to be its most consequential contributions. The EAB was dissolved in 1980, beginning a de facto moratorium on human embryo research that lasted until 1993.

Chapter 2 examines the 1980s, when the in vitro embryo went from a rare laboratory object to an element of widespread clinical practice. By the late 1980s, there were hundreds of IVF clinics in the United States treating thousands of patients annually. In response to the rapid growth of this largely unregulated industry, the American Fertility Society (AFS) established an ethics committee in 1985. Treating biological facts as extra-political and morally neutral, the AFS Ethics Committee adopted a technocratic approach to the deliberation of the moral status of the embryo, introducing a new scientific term—*preembryo*—in an effort to discipline public discourse into taking only relevant facts into account.

Chapter 3 examines events of the early 1990s, focusing in particular on the deliberations of the National Institutes of Health (NIH) Human Embryo Research Panel (HERP). In 1994, Congress passed legislation that ended the de facto moratorium on human embryo research. The NIH established the HERP to provide an ethical assessment of public funding in this area. The HERP was created at a moment of increasing scientific interest in human embryo research from domains well beyond reproductive biology. The panel drew on John Rawls's theory of public reason to imagine an ideal polity bound together by a commitment to reasoned engagement and organized around rationally secure, scientific knowledge. However, Congress and the president reacted strongly against the HERP's recommendations. In 1995, Congress enacted a ban on the use of Department of Health and Human Services appropriations for human embryo research.

Chapter 4 explores the period from the mid-1990s until the end of the Clinton administration in 2001. During this period, two scientific

developments, mammalian cloning and human embryonic stem cell culture, transformed both scientific research and ethical deliberation. The
scientific breakthroughs also initiated a period of heated political debate
at both the state and federal levels, prompting a vigorous reassessment
of the obligations of the state to science and to its citizens. The National
Bioethics Advisory Commission (NBAC), formed in 1996 by President
Bill Clinton, advanced a new theory of public reason, soliciting explicitly
theological moral accounts and translating them into an ostensibly common currency of secular reason. Characterizing electoral and legislative
politics as failed deliberation, the NBAC positioned itself as the authoritative organ of public reason, translating the fraught politics of the public
square into what the commission viewed as reasoned, and neutral, common premises.

Chapter 5 examines the politics that surrounded George W. Bush's
embryonic stem cell policy. The President's Council on Bioethics (PCB),
formed by President Bush in late 2001, took a radically different approach
to ethical reasoning from the bodies that had preceded it. In its discussions on cloning, the council attempted to ground its deliberations in
a shared language that would open up space for ethical disagreement,
rather that limit it in the name of producing consensus as preceding ethics bodies had done. The council's project of finding a common language
was appropriated by a group of scientists who set about to discipline and
reform the language employed in public deliberation over human cloning.
Invoking science as an extra-political authority on matters of fact, they
sought to change the terms of debate by replacing politically provocative
terms, such as *human cloning*, with the ostensibly less confusing and more
accurate *nuclear transplantation to produce pluripotent stem cells*. Behind
their claims was a tacit idea of public reason formed on the notion that
reasoned deliberation depends upon having a common language, one that
is authorized by the extra-political authority of science.

Chapter 6 follows the politics of the embryo into the states. As popular frustration with federal research policy mounted, legislative efforts
emerged at the state level to encourage and, in some cases, fund human
embryonic stem cell research. The most radical of these was Proposition 71,
a referendum in California to dedicate $3 billion to human embryonic
stem cell research. Such state-level initiatives sought to make the public

the direct custodian of its own values debates. Proposition 71 was intended as a direct democratic rejoinder to what its supporters saw as an overly restrictive federal policy. Before the people could speak, however, they needed to be informed about the matter upon which they were voting. The chapter examines a pair of court cases associated with the California initiative in 2004 and a ballot initiative in Missouri in 2006. The litigation focused on the terminology used in the voters' guides in each state. Here, the scientists who had positioned themselves as custodians of public reason sought to intervene in a most fundamental exercise of democracy. The courts faced the question, framed by scientific experts, of whether the term *cloning* was a factual misrepresentation that would confuse the public and pervert the democratic process or the kind of value-laden political speech that is the essence of democratic politics and sits at the apex of constitutional protection.

Chapter 7 turns to the politics of the public square, focusing in particular on California's stem cell ballot initiative. Controversy shifted from the focus on moral status to a debate about the state's dependency upon science to secure the well-being of the lives in its care. The chapter explores how an imaginary of innovation emerged around the human embryonic stem cell, eliciting new accounts of citizenship and the public good. It examines how actors constructed science and public reason as secular institutions allied against the unwarranted intrusion of religion into processes of democratic judgment. I argue that the figure of science as generative of technological futures produced more than an instrumental relationship between science and the state. It also underwrote an emergent democratic solidarity and an imagination of citizenship. I argue that notions of democratic representation, the public good, and the moral economy of science were rearticulated around an imaginary of innovation, eliciting a parallel re-examination of the social contract between the state and its citizens.

Chapter 8 concludes by reflecting upon the scientific and political developments that ended the stem cell controversy of the 2000s. I observe that the most lasting consequences of this political moment may lie less in the scientific and technological trajectories that it engendered than in the imaginations—and institutions—of democracy that emerged out of it. The embryo debates gave rise to sensibilities and approaches that continue to shape public bioethical debate in the United States. The contours of the debates that this study examines are not limited to the controversy around human embryo research. They reflect the dynamics of public reasoning about the meaning of emerging biotechnologies for our visions of progress and the good. Thus, the experiments in democracy that this study examines have—and will continue to have—a consequential legacy for the governance of science and technology, and, therefore, so too for the human future.

1

NEW BEGINNINGS

When Louise Brown, the first child conceived in vitro, was born on July 25, 1978, the image of her tiny newborn body was overwhelming evidence that a revolution in human biology was underway. Between the anatomical blockages to the Browns' legacy and the image of a joyful and exhausted Lesley Brown with tiny Louise cradled in her arms, had come the interventions of a mysterious, yet clearly powerful, medical science. The compelling presentation of this remarkable technological achievement arrived not in a medical journal, but in the maternity ward. The demonstrative power of this moment left little room for doubt about the reality of these emerging powers, though ample room was left for mystery. The details of the act of procreation that had given rise to Louise Brown remained hidden from the world: the displacement of the oocyte from opaque body to transparent glass, conjugation and synthesis of gametes, the cleavages of cell from cell in the first steps of embryogenesis, the efficiency of the process, the presence (or nonexistence) of embryonic siblings sharing the same dish—all of these details remained shrouded in darkness. An unprecedented conjugal act had taken place, that much was self-evident, but the details of its circumstances and its meaning for the social order remained unclear. What was clear, however, was that the technology that had produced Louise Brown also offered unprecedented powers of control over embryonic human life.

This chapter explores the early moments in the development of debates around human embryo research in the United States. It examines the technical, moral, and political uncertainties that emerged alongside the in vitro human embryo as a material presence in American laboratories and clinics. It follows the lines of early bioethical debate that took shape around emerging human biotechnologies, examining the framings, discourses, and novel forms of authority that shaped them.

During this period, political cleavages, epistemic differentiations, and conceptual axes developed that would prove to have profound consequences for the future of both scientific practices and the forms of ethical scrutiny and governance to which they were subject. The early development of the technology of human in vitro fertilization (IVF) was deeply informed by the surrounding medical, legal, and political environments. Ambiguously positioned between biological matter and human being, between research and therapy, and between radically distinct moral outlooks and imagined futures, the developmental forces that shaped the question of human embryo research reflected broader imaginaries of the right ordering of science, technology, and democratic politics. As the in vitro embryo became a familiar presence in the laboratory and clinic, a corollary set of increasingly familiar concepts, logics, and normative understandings also emerged in ethical deliberation about the status—ontological and moral—of this entity.

THE BEGINNINGS OF BIOETHICAL DEBATE

Control over human reproduction represented a central focus of emerging public anxieties about advances in biotechnology in the 1960s and 1970s. It was partly within this context that the category of issues and corollary forms of expertise that would later acquire the label of "bioethics" took shape. Initial discussions tended to be grounded in anticipation of a fast-approaching future in which humanity would wield the technological power to direct its own evolution, promising new forms of flourishing in some visions and a dehumanized "fabricated man" in others.[1] Prominent scientists like Julian Huxley, Hermann Muller and J. B. S. Haldane envisioned radical technological transformations of human life, not least through the control of reproduction, asking the question, as Huxley put it, "What are human beings for?"[2] Emerging biotechnologies seen in this light raised broad but fundamental questions about human purpose and dignity that looked beyond specific emerging technologies to the visions of transformation and control in which they were implicated. These technologies also raised fundamental questions about the right relationship between science and democracy, particularly vis-à-vis the role of publicly articulated values in shaping agendas of technological development.[3] These broad topics captured public attention during the late 1960s and early 1970s.[4]

In the early 1970s, however, scandals related to human subjects research channeled public attention toward an apparent deficit in oversight in this self-evident ethically weighty domain. In 1974, U.S. Congress developed a new mechanism for dealing with such issues: the public ethics body. Created by the National Research Act, the National Commission for the Protection of Human Subjects of Biomedical and Behavioral Research set about to articulate the principles and practices that would guide ethical oversight in human research matters. Its work immediately preceded the birth of Louise Brown and heavily shaped ethical and policy deliberation on IVF.

The first U.S. public ethics body charged with assessing questions related to IVF was the Ethics Advisory Board (EAB) of the Department of Health, Education, and Welfare (HEW; now the Department of Health and Human Services [HHS]). The board's work, though largely forgotten, played an important role in shaping approaches to ethical deliberation over human embryo research. Some of the board's judgments had consequential ramifications in subsequent debates, though in ways the board itself could not have anticipated. This chapter examines these beginnings, from the utopian visions of reproductive control of the early twentieth century through the efforts of the EAB to grapple with the suddenly real technology of human IVF and the deep ethical uncertainties that accompanied it.

A TEST-TUBE BABY

Louise Brown's birth elicited a tremendous response in the United States and around the world. Though it was a surprise to most, revealed only a few weeks before Louise's birth, the technical feat of reproduction through IVF had long been anticipated. A number of researchers had been actively engaged in experimental work on human in vitro fertilization for some time. In vitro fertilization and embryo transfer (ET) efforts had been undertaken concurrently in the U.S, the U.K., Australia, and India. The researchers who "produced" Louise Brown, Robert G. Edwards and Patrick C. Steptoe, had been working closely in this area for years. They had announced what was perhaps the first clearly successful human in vitro fertilization and embryo culture nearly a decade before the birth of Louise Brown. On the basis of their success in fertilizing human ova in vitro in the late 1960s, Edwards predicted in 1971 that human IVF with successful embryo transfer to the womb and pregnancy was "close at hand."[5]

Edwards and Steptoe's efforts were themselves not unprecedented. Others had made similar attempts, though claims to success were generally met with skepticism. In 1944, John Rock, a renowned Harvard University obstetrician, announced he had successfully fertilized and briefly cultured a human oocyte in vitro.[6] In the mid-1950s, Columbia University gynecologist Landrum Shettles claimed to have achieved in vitro fertilization, though not with any reliability. He later recalled that in these experiments, "fertilization was as rare as hen's teeth."[7] In 1961, Italian researcher Daniele Pettrucci claimed to have cultured a human embryo in vitro for 29 days. He destroyed the embryo, he claimed, because it had developed into a "monstrous" form.[8] (He never published his work, and his claims were never verified.)

Related work in animal species had been ongoing for some time. In 1934, Gregory Pincus at Harvard Medical School fertilized rabbit oocytes in vitro and achieved pregnancies in recipient rabbits. Though Pincus claimed the pregnancies resulted in live young, the experiment could not be repeated successfully until 1959 when M. C. Chang produced live-born rabbits through IVF and transfer.[9] Pincus's and Chang's work laid the foundation for extensive IVF research in nonhuman mammals and, ultimately, in humans.[10] Experimental work in laboratory animals went well beyond simple efforts to perfect IVF as a reproductive tool. For instance, in 1971, Johns Hopkins–based embryologist Yu-Chih Hsu cultured mouse embryos beyond the blastocyst to the early somite stage.[11] But it was the work of Robert Edwards from the mid-1960s onward that drew the most attention.

Edwards made clear from the outset that his efforts were therapeutic: he wished IVF to be a tool for treating infertility by producing pregnancies in bodies that could not accomplish it on their own.[12] He argued that, although it is reasonable for certain social concerns to attach to this research, IVF was in essence a therapeutic attempt to overcome a medical disorder and nothing more. Nature had failed the infertile, and the proper role of the physician—and of the technology of IVF— was merely to assist the body in circumventing its own failure. Thus, in Edwards's words, "Infertility is a defect to be remedied if possible by medical attention."[13]

There was, however, significant skepticism that the uses of this technique would remain so well circumscribed. Many saw this emergent domain as more closely associated with technologies of human transformation, including species transformation. IVF was one of several essential tools that would allow radical control of human biology: what one prominent religious commentator in the 1970s described as "ending reproductive roulette" and another saw as a step on the path to "species-suicide."[14] During the 1960s and 1970s, the most vocal critics of technologies of human genetic engineering—which included IVF—were theologians.[15] Figures like Paul Ramsey were concerned with the broad meaning of the project of human self-mastery that the new biotechnologies portended. For individuals such as Ramsey, these technologies signified an aspiration to transgress the natural order: an impulse to "play God" and bring about a "second genesis" that rejected the goodness of the first.[16]

Expressions of concern regarding human IVF came from scientific quarters as well. In 1971, Nobel Prize–winning geneticist James Watson raised concerns about in vitro fertilization as a potentially dehumanizing technology. He told the U.S. House Committee on Science and Aeronautics that the birth of a child through IVF might be seen within a year and that "techniques for the in vitro manipulation of human eggs are likely to be general medical practice within 10 to 20 years."[17] Watson argued that research in this area was distressing not so much for its potential application to overcoming human infertility as because these techniques were critical steps on the path to human clonal reproduction. He pointed to the recent research of Oxford embryologist John Gurdon on frog cloning as indicative of the trajectory of the science.

In 1962, Gurdon had successfully generated adult frogs by transferring the nucleus of an intestinal cell from a tadpole into an enucleated frog egg. The resulting adult frog was genetically identical to the donor of the intestinal cell.[18] These techniques, Watson argued, were, in principle, transferable to mammalian species. And, "if the matter proceeds in the current, nondirected fashion, a human being—born of clonal reproduction—most likely will appear on earth within the next 20 to 50 years."[19] Given this likelihood, he argued, it was urgent that democracy respond in advance to this technological future. It is "absolutely essential," he argued, that the government take action to track these scientific developments in order to "inform the public as a whole" and shape national science policies. Judgments of the regulation of such activities, from in vitro fertilization to clonal reproduction, are decisions "that the people as a whole must make." Watson argued that "if we do not think about the matter now, the possibility of having a free choice will one day suddenly be gone."[20]

A 1972 *Journal of the American Medical Association* editorial expressed similar concerns, noting that "Physicians, scientists, philosophers, theologians are astir with thoughts and pronouncements on genetic engineering, especially with growth of a fertilized ovum in vitro (already achieved) and with cloning." The editorial stated that though some of these technical possibilities seemed remote, in vitro fertilization and embryo transfer were on the immediate horizon. It urged a moratorium on further research on human IVF and ET until the associated ethical questions could be resolved.[21] That the editors of one of the most prestigious medical journals in the world took this stance is indicative of the widespread reservations about the emerging technologies of human reproduction in the early 1970s.

Yet neither these imagined futures nor the corollary anxieties about their moral meaning were new. A number of prominent biologists in the 1920s and 1930s had envisioned that IVF would become a critical tool in the eugenic management of the human species. In a lecture delivered in 1923, J. B. S. Haldane imagined a future in which human reproduction would be technologically managed. Not only would fertilization take place in vitro using oocytes from cadaveric ovaries, but fetuses would be grown outside the body in artificial wombs, a technology Haldane dubbed "ectogenesis."[22] It was these predictions that inspired Aldous Huxley's image of "Bokanovsky's process," the industrial reproductive organ of his dystopian *Brave New World*.[23] Haldane's vision of the future inspired other eugenicists, most notably Herbert Brewer and Nobel laureate geneticist Hermann Muller. Muller and Brewer, who began corresponding in 1935, described a eugenic future in which genetic enhancement of the species would be achieved though the careful technological management of reproduction. Both had been excited by the 1934 report that Harvard endocrinologist Gregory Pincus had fertilized rabbit ova in vitro and successfully transferred the rabbit embryos to a host uterus, producing live births.[24] Brewer called in vitro fertilization "penectogenesis," a preliminary step toward ectogenesis.[25]

Others anticipated this transformation of life with more equanimity. A 1935 article in the *Washington Post*, imagining life in 2035, noted that in addition to metal buildings and disposable clothes, we might expect "test-tube babies." But these radical transformations of life, the author suggested, were perhaps not different in kind from those already experienced. Remarking on Pincus's recent fertilization of rabbit oocytes in vitro, the author predicted that, "just as we became accustomed to automobiles and planes and tomato juice and cod liver oil, future generations may be entirely calm about even—horrors!—test-tube babies."[26] A 1937 editorial in the *New England Journal of Medicine* associated Pincus's research with the shifting sexual mores of early twentieth-century America, commenting, "If such an accomplishment with rabbits were to be duplicated in the human being, we should in the words of 'flaming youth' be 'going places.'"[27]

Thus, the idea of human IVF had for a long time been conceptually entangled with other kinds of radical interventions in human life, including eugenics, directed evolution, and genetic manipulation. Though these worries persisted beyond the birth of Louise Brown, by 1978, the rhetoric of IVF as a technique of genetic control had already begun to fade. Brown's birth significantly reinforced this change in perspective. The familiar and disarming scene of the newborn child with tired but proud parents was suggestive more of a medical miracle than a Frankensteinian experiment. NBC Nightly News anchor David Brinkley reported she was a "normal, beautiful baby."[28] As one headline noted, she entered the world "healthy, crying her head off."[29] The editors of the *Chicago Tribune* declared baby Louise's birth "a historic medical triumph" and a "time to rejoice with

Lesley and John Brown." Acknowledging a "flip side possibility for harm," they nonetheless expressed confidence that "human beings will be able to use this new power over reproduction for the benefit of childless couples like the Browns and not to tinker irresponsibly or malevolently with human biology."[30] The New York Times found an exemplar of this natural human prudence in Lesley Brown herself. In an editorial entitled "Conceiving the Inconceivable," the Times noted approvingly that Mrs. Brown had specifically requested not to be informed of the sex of her baby during pregnancy. "Given the power to bypass nature, she nonetheless aspired to preserve its mysterious ways."[31]

Ethical concerns over the experimental use of IVF began to shift away from the mechanization of human reproduction toward a focus on the embryo itself as a research object. This adjustment in attitude extended beyond the popular mind to the thinking of some critics of biotechnology such as Leon Kass. As a young physician and molecular biologist, Kass had become concerned about the implications of emerging biotechnology for human life. In the early 1970s, Kass expressed considerable reservations about the introduction of IVF into the practices of human procreation. In 1971, he wrote that the development of technological control over reproduction would result in the "transfer of procreation from the home to the laboratory and its coincident transformation into manufacture." Should this be carried to its logical end with technologies of ectogenesis, a "complete depersonalization of procreation" would result, a prospect he considered "seriously dehumanizing."[32] By late 1978, his concerns about strictly reproductive applications of IVF had softened, though he continued to worry about the possibility that they might disrupt traditional notions of lineage. Kass's strongest concerns about the technique had more to do with genetic manipulation of the embryo and experimental work in the laboratory than with strictly reproductive applications by married couples. He suggested that although under certain conditions, IVF-assisted reproduction would be a reasonable emulation of natural human reproduction, even a small divergence from this narrow path might initiate a slide down a slippery slope away from procreation and toward manufacture, resulting in radical abuses. He saw the temptation of purely experimental applications of IVF as among the most treacherous aspects of this narrow path.[33]

Though some prominent figures dismissed Kass's concerns as excessive, the effort to articulate reasonable boundaries to the application of IVF was a common feature of the ethical discourse surrounding this technology in the 1960s and early to mid-1970s.[34] Before the mid-1970s, IVF was generally seen as belonging to the same category as other anticipated technologies of genetic control. From 1975 to 1978, with few technical advances reported since the early 1970s, this conversation quieted down, and relatively little appeared in the emerging bioethics literature on IVF. With the birth of Louise Brown, however, IVF once again became a focus of widespread discussion, but with a shift in valence. By the late 1970s, experimental concerns over the use of IVF began to shift away from the manipulation of a future child toward a focus on the embryo itself. Although many did remain concerned about the potential uses of IVF for genetic manipulation and reproduction-as-manufacture, a new focus emerged and became prominent: the use of in vitro human embryos as laboratory research objects.[35] This shift in emphasis shunted the human embryo into another vein of ethical discussion in biomedical research: the deliberations on human subjects research of the 1970s and the work of the National Commission for the Protection of Human Subjects of Biomedical and Behavioral Research.

EXPERIMENTING WITH HUMAN LIFE

From the 1930s until the early 1970s, much of the consternation (and enthusiasm) surrounding human IVF focused on its power to transform the species. A second, largely distinct set of public conversations began in the late 1960s that dealt primarily with the human being as a research subject. Whereas imagined technological possibilities figured prominently in discussions of the good and evil of human genetic engineering, in discussions on human subjects research, the primary object of concern was uses of human subjects in generic research settings.[36] The former approach asked what technological projects were appropriate to human flourishing. The latter was concerned with the basic entitlements of persons that must be met in the context of research, regardless of its scientific or technological aims.

Formal attention to human subjects research grew out of responses to experiments performed by Nazi scientists on concentration camp inmates during World War II. Investigation of these experiments led to the articulation of ethical principles for research involving human subjects in what came to be known as the Nuremberg Code.[37] From the early 1950s onward, regulation of human subjects research became an increasingly prominent concern within HEW. Initially approached as an internal regulatory matter, it became a subject of increasing congressional scrutiny by the mid-1960s, particularly as the National Institutes of Health (NIH) budget grew.[38] The issue received renewed attention with Henry Beecher's 1966 editorial in the *New England Journal of Medicine* in which he drew attention to systemic abuses of human subjects in medical research.[39] In 1968, Dr. Christiaan Barnard created an international sensation with the first successful heart transplantation surgery. Radical new developments in biomedicine such as Barnard's surgical success, combined with a succession of research scandals, led to increased public interest in the ethics of human experimentation and a series of congressional interventions. In 1968, Senator Walter Mondale (D–MN) introduced a bill to establish a "Commission on Health, Science and Society," in effect, a public bioethics advisory body. In its original conception, this commission would have had a broad remit, ranging from human experimentation to technologies of mind control, from organ transplantation to reproductive technologies.[40] These efforts proved unsuccessful at first. But congressional interest in human experimentation was catalyzed by the revelation in 1972 of the now infamous Tuskegee syphilis study.[41] Senator Edward Kennedy held hearings that ultimately led to the passage of the National Research Act on July 12, 1974.[42] It was this act that led to the creation of the National Commission for the Protection of Human Subjects of Biomedical and Behavioral Research.

The charge of the national commission was "to conduct a comprehensive investigation and study to identify the basic ethical principles that should underlie the conduct of biomedical and behavioral research involving human subjects and to develop guidelines which should be followed to assure that such research is conducted in accordance with those principles."[43] Among the specific requirements detailed in the act was that the commission study research on live human fetuses.

Fetal research was the subject of an emerging public controversy in the early 1970s. This controversy was the result of a set of nontherapeutic experiments on previable human fetuses. For instance, several research teams had attached fetuses to perfusion machines to oxygenate their blood in an effort to develop an artificial placenta.[44] In one experiment, human fetuses were kept alive for up to twelve hours, during which time the fetuses performed "vigorous" movements of the head, body, and limbs.[45] Another group studying the "isolated perfused human fetal brain" removed the heads of human fetuses and circulated oxygenated blood through the carotid artery to study metabolism in the fetal brain.[46] After the U.S. Supreme Court handed down *Roe v. Wade* in 1973,[47] opening the door to unrestricted elective abortion of previable fetuses, there was mounting concern about the use of human abortuses in biomedical research.[48]

The National Research Act was in part a response to these concerns. It prohibited federal support of research on fetuses from induced abortion until the national commission had issued its findings.[49] The act imposed a deadline of four months for the committee to complete its study of fetal research and issue recommendations to the HEW secretary.

Research on the fetus was among the most contentious of the issues faced by the national commission. In its ethical analysis, the commission was careful not to engage in an assessment of the status of the fetus as such. Instead, it framed the issue as a complex problem of proxy consent. Fetal research was differentiated from other forms of human subjects research not by a difference in the ontological status and corollary moral obligations to the research subject, but by the unique difficulties of obtaining consent. The national commission's report, *Research on the Fetus* made this very clear:

> Throughout the deliberations of the commission, the belief has been affirmed that the fetus as a human subject is deserving of care and respect. Although the commission has not addressed directly the issues of the personhood and the civil status of the fetus, the members of the commission are convinced that moral concern should extend to all who share human genetic heritage, and that the fetus, regardless of life prospects, should be treated respectfully and with dignity.[50]

Thus, the commission drew no in-principle distinction between the fetus and other human subjects. The same obligations applied to all human subjects, including other groups from whom obtaining informed consent was difficult, including children, prisoners, and the mentally infirm. The commission's deliberations were organized around typologies of consent rather than ontological distinctions between types of research subject. In other words, what differentiated these categories of subject one from another were differences in their respective abilities to consent to research risks, not differences in the intrinsic moral worth of the subjects themselves.

On their surface, the conclusions of the national commission on fetal research bear this out. The committee emphasized that in research involving human subjects, the "integrity of the individual is preeminent," and therefore there are "certain boundaries that respect for the fetus must impose upon freedom of scientific inquiry."[51] At the same time, it emphasized that research on the fetus, like all research on human subjects, was in certain cases the only means to bring about "significant advances in health care."[52] The report noted, "While the exigencies of research and the moral imperatives of fair and respectful treatment may appear to be mutually limiting, they are not incompatible."[53] The commission concluded that research on the fetus was not substantially different in kind from other forms of research on human subjects and, therefore, that existing review procedures required by statute (Public Law [P.L.] 93-348) and HEW regulations (45 Code of Federal Regulations [C.F.R.] 46) for human subjects research were sufficient for fetal research, so long as the research did not expose the fetus to more than minimal risk.[54]

However, in adopting the minimal-risk standard, the commission introduced an ambiguity into the application of its findings in cases of induced abortion. Although the report concluded that "the woman's decision for the abortion does not, in itself, change the status of the fetus for purposes of protection" (the report referred to this as "the equality principle"), it acknowledged that the meaning of "minimal risk" was potentially different for the "fetus-to-be-aborted" and the "fetus-to-go-to-term."[55] Certain activities that might cause substantial risk to a fetus-to-go-to-term would not be treated as risky for a fetus-to-be-aborted, either because the risks would not manifest until a point in development at which the fetus would presumably already be dead, or because they would not amount to a greater risk of harm than the fetus would already have faced as a consequence of elective abortion.

Elective abortion was treated as an extrinsic circumstance—a private matter that was segregated from public ethical judgment. Therefore, it was circumstantially, but not morally, relevant to determinations of appropriate public action. Indeed, the commission was insistent that any research intervention would not unduly interact with or alter these circumstances. It stipulated that the research protocol should not affect the physician's recommendations on the advisability, timing, or method of abortion and that there should be no inducements offered to procure an abortion for research purposes.[56]

Here the commission was incorporating a demarcation between public and private ethical domains that had recently been supplied by the Supreme Court. With *Griswold v. Connecticut* in 1965 and *Roe v. Wade* in 1973, the U.S. Supreme Court articulated a clear distinction between the public domain of state intervention and the private domain of individual decisional autonomy.[57] Griswold had declared the use of contraceptives by married women to be outside the purview of the state. *Roe v. Wade* extended this logic to elective abortion, though in a less coherent and substantially more controversial form. In both decisions, reproduction-related practices were found to be protected under a right to privacy that the court discerned primarily in the due process clause of the fourteenth amendment.

In *Roe v. Wade*, the court tried to make clear that the recognition of a constitutional right to abortion entailed neither a moral sanction of abortion by the state nor a denigration of the moral significance of the developing fetus (though on this latter point the opinion was not altogether clear). Rather, the court treated public interference with elective abortion as an undue intrusion of the state into the domain of individual privacy. The court found viability—the in-principle possibility of survival independent of the mother—as the relevant boundary that separated individual rights from public interest in the well-being of the fetus. Thus, the decision sought to differentiate public and private spheres of moral action rather than the moral status of the fetus at different stages of development (though it is questionable whether the court successfully avoided the latter).

The national commission directly adopted the court's logic, treating viability as an important boundary in nontherapeutic research on the fetus-to-be-aborted, though the commission located that boundary at twenty weeks' gestation rather than the Supreme Court's twenty-eight. Prior to twenty weeks, the proxy consent of the mother was acceptable because the fetus could not have a future life independent of its mother, even in principle. No decision to act (or not act) by the researcher could, the commission reasoned, in any way provide an opportunity for the aborted fetus to survive.

The commission explicitly recognized that the previability–viability distinction was technologically contingent and would therefore require periodic reevaluation. The report's discussion of viability consisted of a review of the state-of-the-art in neonatal medicine with little reference to the moral relevance of the previability–viability distinction. The distinction was treated neither as a moral differentiation of types of fetus nor as an ontological marker of personhood. Rather, it was a boundary that guaranteed the complete (moral) containment of abortion within the private space of the decisional autonomy of the mother.[58]

Notwithstanding the commission's explicit affirmation of the "equality principle," and designation of the fetus as a human subject, the report had the effect of constructing two distinct categories of research subjects to which different ethical duties attached: the fetus-to-be-aborted and the fetus-to-go-to-term. These categories were the product of a strong separation between public and private spheres of decision-making and moral responsibility. The fetus-to-be-aborted was a product of the mother's constitutionally protected liberty, and as such, the national commission treated the future abortion as an amoral background fact for the purposes of public ethical assessment and regulation, a fact to be taken into account like any other in the assessment of research risk.

The commission's work, and the regulations that resulted from it, had four main effects on the human embryo research debates. First, the commission's approach to research on the fetus, in particular the way it treated private choices as circumstantial background facts in assessing public ethical obligations to the human subject, was reproduced in approaches to embryo research. The availability of embryos that were created (and would potentially be destroyed) as a result of private, reproductive choices would later be treated as a morally neutral background fact, at least for the purposes of public ethical assessment. Such choices came to be seen as relevant to public science only insofar as they were the supply lines for research materials.[59] Second, the public–private boundary that the U.S. Supreme Court drew in *Roe v. Wade* was taken up as a constitutionally grounded fault line that separated public and private spheres of moral judgment. If the practice was a private matter, the thinking went, so too was the moral meaning of it. Third, the national commission's focus on assessing the research subject's ability to consent to risk rather than the technological context, purpose, or goal of research was adopted in the moral evaluation of the in vitro human embryo as well. Ironically, as we shall see, the commission's decontextualized, consent-focused approach, which prescinded from defining the ontological and moral criteria for "personhood," had the effect of making a moral-ontological assessment of the embryo unavoidable. Finally, the commission's recommendations, codified in federal regulations in 1975, laid the regulatory groundwork for a public ethical assessment of IVF.

In light of contentious "problems of interpretation" of how the minimal-risk standard should be applied in practice to the fetus-to-be-aborted, the commission recommended that some other body be made responsible. Specifically, it suggested an apparatus be established to allow "ethical review at a national level in which informed public disclosure and assessment of the problems, the type of proposed research and the scientific and public importance of the expected results can take place."[60] This recommendation paved the way for the first American public ethics body that would directly address the question of in vitro human embryo research.

REGULATION OF IVF

The national commission did not deal specifically with in vitro human embryo research. Although early drafts of the National Research Act included provisions directing the commission to examine IVF, this requirement was absent from the final legislation. In 1973, as Kennedy was holding hearings on human experimentation, a HEW departmental study group concluded its deliberations on the limitations of informed consent. Fetal research was among the areas specifically addressed. The conclusions of the study group were published in the *Federal Register* in November 1973.[61] Among the group's provisions was a requirement that "agency 'Ethical Review Boards' are to be established to provide rigorous review of the ethical issues in research, development and demonstration activities involving human subjects in order to make judgments regarding societal acceptability in relation to scientific value."[62] A "special categories" section included "the abortus," "the fetus in utero," and "products of in vitro fertilization."[63] Under "products of in vitro fertilization," the study group stated, "No research involving implantation of human ova which have been fertilized in vitro shall be approved until the safety of the technique has been demonstrated as far as possible in sub-human primates, and the responsibilities of the donor and recipient 'parents' and of research institutions and personnel have been established. Therefore, no such research may be conducted without review of the Ethical Review Board."

The National Research Act was passed before these proposals could be promulgated as regulations, and the national commission was given jurisdiction over these issues. HEW proceeded to collect public comments and published the results of its findings in 1974 for the use of the national commission in its deliberations.[64] In 1975, regulations were proposed in light of the commission's findings on fetal research.[65] The department noted that in recommending "ethical review at the national level," the commission had given an "implicit" recommendation for the establishment of an ethics advisory board. Therefore, the requirement that an EAB review IVF was preserved in the proposed regulations.

In December 1976, HEW secretary David Mathews signed the charter creating the first (and, as it turned out, only) ethics advisory board.

THE ETHICS ADVISORY BOARD

In December 1976, President-elect Jimmy Carter appointed Joseph Califano to be HEW secretary. Califano called upon San Francisco–based attorney James Gaither to assist with the HEW transition under the incoming Carter administration. Gaither and Califano were old friends from their service under President Lyndon B. Johnson.

During the transition, Califano discussed with Gaither the complex ethical questions emerging within HEW and requested that Gaither finish out his service to HEW by assembling an ethics advisory board and serving as its chair. Gaither was given a list of the twenty most distinguished ethicists in the country to choose from, but he rejected the list because he considered a panel of experts in "the science of ethics" unqualified to render judgments of ethical acceptability on behalf of the public. Following his intuition about the conditions under which such a body could claim to stand in for the public, he adopted a representational model rather than an expert advisory one, a move that would prove to be relatively unique in the history of public bioethics in the United States. Gaither recalls thinking that "the only way to get at [ethical questions] is to have a diversity of opinion so that you really are rendering a judgment of ethical acceptability across a broad range of beliefs. Yes, one or two ethicists would be helpful, but then you have to reach out more broadly."[66]

Gaither, with the assistance of vice-chairman David Hamburg, assembled a diverse group of members including two ethicists, one of whom was a Jesuit priest.[67] Gaither conceived of the work of the EAB as providing a focused review mechanism for complex ethical questions; he distinguished the board's case-specific focus from the national commission's more abstract project of articulating broad ethical principles. The "science of ethics," he reckoned, was different from concrete "decisions about what is ethical."[68] The EAB would focus on the latter, reviewing specific questions within the narrow confines of the particular case.

In his introductory remarks at the first EAB meeting on February 3, 1978, Gaither commented that the EAB's authority to "look at any issue in the health field with significant ethical implications" was "in many ways . . . just a different rubric for looking at serious policy issues."[69] The EAB remained true to this framing of its task, consciously limiting itself to grounded and narrow determinations of ethical acceptability while largely avoiding explicit recourse to ethical theory.

THE EMBRYO

When the EAB was formed in late 1977, IVF was not considered to be a pressing locus of ethical concern. NIH director Donald Fredrickson told Gaither that, although it might eventually come before the board, the reproductive use of IVF was likely at least five years away.[70] Among the board's first tasks, however, was the assessment of a grant application that proposed to study human fertilization in vitro with no intention of transferring the resulting embryos to a recipient uterus. The research proposal was submitted to NIH by Vanderbilt University professor of obstetrics and gynecology Pierre Soupart. In the spring of 1978, the Soupart proposal was placed on the agenda for the November EAB meeting. In July, Louise Brown was born.

With the EAB already in place, the federal government was well positioned to respond rapidly. At a congressional hearing in the summer of 1978, Gaither reassured the House Subcommittee on Health and Environment that HEW had already set in motion an ethical assessment of IVF by the EAB.[71] In August, Secretary Califano instructed the board to expand its assessment of the Soupart proposal into a comprehensive report on the research and reproductive use of human IVF. The board began its deliberations on IVF on September 15, 1978, less than two months after Louise Brown's birth and long before any comparable body in any other country.

The board faced significant unknowns, not least of which were the scientific details of Louise Brown's conception and the numerous attempts that had failed. The EAB initiated a systematic consultation of scientists, ethicists, theologians, legal experts, and social scientists. The board also undertook a significant public consultation, holding eleven hearings in cities across the nation. Deliberations on IVF would last until May 1979, when the board issued a unanimous report. The report found IVF to be "ethically defensible but legitimately controverted" and left it to others to determine the relative priority of IVF research within federally supported biomedical research.[72]

Gaither considered it of utmost importance that the report be unanimous. To this end, he worked hard to keep deliberations focused and narrow. He encouraged the group to identify logics for its arguments that were more grounded in the precedents of existing practices and attitudes than in nuanced ethical theories or in broad principles. With these strategies, Gaither was reflecting his professional background as a lawyer and, in particular, his appreciation for the approach of U.S. Supreme Court Justice Earl Warren to school desegregation in *Brown v. Board of Education*. Gaither had served as Warren's clerk in the 1964–1965 session. He took special interest in the history of the *Brown v. Board of Education* case, learning from Warren how he had held back the decision until what was originally a split on the court could evolve into unanimity. Gaither saw Warren's efforts as exemplary of a statesmanship that had contributed to social cohesion in a moment of divisiveness. He saw the divided court in *Roe v. Wade* as exemplary of precisely the opposite dynamic; he counted the latter case as a deep disservice to the country.[73]

Gaither felt that the EAB could make a major contribution to public debate over IVF by building a consensus position among board members whose views on abortion differed. Most of the board's deliberations were devoted to finding an ethical framework that could deliver consensus. In early 1979, an informal poll of board members revealed a narrow majority of 7 to 6 in favor of federal support of IVF research. Staff members Barbara Mishkin, Charles McCarthy, and LeRoy Walters, all of whom favored federal support, urged Gaither to call a vote. Gaither refused, insisting that an ethical finding by narrow majority was not an ethical finding at all. According to Gaither, what is "ethical" is by necessity acceptable to a "broad range of thinking." The board kept at it for some months more, and slowly a consensus position began to emerge.[74]

Part of the basis for consensus was to offer only provisional conclusions. Despite an extensive and prescient discussion of the practical, legal, and ethical issues that might arise around IVF, the EAB's conclusions were narrow, tentative, and qualified as but one reasonable position among many.[75] The "ethical acceptability" of IVF was, the board explained, intended to mean only "ethically defensible, though legitimately controverted."[76] This tentativeness left a certain ambiguity in the board's conclusions: more than a decade later, the EAB report would be cited as supporting the positions of both proponents and opponents of embryo research. This tentativeness was partly intentional, however, since the EAB viewed itself as a standing body—somewhat like a common law court—that would likely be called upon to clarify and extend its prior conclusions as new situations arose.

Under Gaither's guidance, the board sought as universal and uncontroversial a framework for assessing IVF as possible, such that the broadest plurality of positions could be accommodated within it.

During the EAB deliberations, two somewhat divergent frameworks took shape. The first, and in some respects the dominant, approach was to assess the novelty of the technology by comparing it to natural human reproduction. The second approach ignored the uses and purposes of the technology and instead attended to ethical obligations to particular morally significant entities, be they the would-be parents or the embryo itself. This latter framework drew on the approach to human subjects research that had been developed by the national commission.

The EAB deliberations are worth examining in some detail, but not because they directly shaped policy or law. Indeed, the recommendations exerted their most significant effects by engendering regulatory inaction. Yet the EAB report provided a set of concepts and ethical demarcations that were extensively employed in subsequent deliberation. By tracing their genealogies to the EAB deliberations, I demonstrate how they were appropriated and transformed by later ethics bodies employing radically different notions of pluralism and reasonable consensus.

CONSENSUS BY ANALOGY

The Board was initially concerned that IVF with embryo transfer would expose the resulting child to unknown and potentially significant risk. At the time of the first meeting on IVF, very few specifics were known about Edwards and Steptoe's technique.[77] They had published only a letter in the *Lancet* in early August 1978, which gave few scientific details.[78] By the time the board concluded its deliberations, some more details were known, though many questions remained. Primary among them were questions of safety, particularly given that the memory of the thalidomide disaster was still relatively fresh. Gaither recalls, "What we were really worried about was not the right-to-life issue but the thalidomide issue. Were we getting into something here where we were going to be fostering the production of deformed human beings? Scared the living hell out of us."[79] The board solicited input from a range of embryologists, few of whom had any experience working with human in vitro fertilization. Despite requests from the EAB, Edwards and Steptoe refused to testify, instead promising a more detailed scientific publication in the near future.[80] The experts who testified before the EAB disagreed about whether IVF should be subjected to laboratory examination before being put to clinical use in humans. There was general agreement that the limited experience with mammalian IVF suggested that, although it might be difficult to culture viable embryos, any resulting babies were unlikely to suffer from gross birth defects of the sort that had resulted from thalidomide.[81]

After extensive testimony from experts, the board's concerns about the intrinsic safety of the technique began to wane. The early emphasis on embryology, however, had important consequences for the board's subsequent deliberations. The board took particular interest in several facts about Louise Brown. First, by all accounts she seemed perfectly healthy and normal. Second, she had been conceived through the retrieval and fertilization of a single oocyte without superovulation.[82] Third, the process was very inefficient. Of a large number of attempted in vitro fertilizations, more than thirty embryo transfers, and three pregnancies, Louise Brown was the only baby successfully brought to term.

The inefficiency of the procedure was initially a source of concern for some board members as well as for many citizens who testified at the public hearings.[83] To some members of the public, IVF seemed like a wasteful procedure. It responded exclusively to the parents' desire to procreate without regard to the nascent human lives that would be lost along the way. The primary objection to clinical IVF made in the public hearings was that the procedure required the creation of multiple embryos in order to achieve a pregnancy, with excess embryos being destroyed.[84] Yet, this very fact of inefficiency proved to be the critical element in the board's conclusion that IVF was ethically acceptable.

During the first meeting on IVF, the board heard from Dr. John D. Biggers of Harvard Medical School. Biggers, together with U.K. embryologist Anne McLaren, had achieved the first successful births of live mice after in vitro culture and embryo transfer.[85] He was a leading mammalian embryologist and as well positioned as anyone to comment on the work of Edwards and Steptoe. He presented an overview of the state of the science in human and animal embryology and IVF.[86] Among the scientific developments he reviewed were studies analyzing which subset of fertilizations led to live births in humans. These studies suggested a high rate of "embryo loss" in normal human reproduction. A significant percentage of human embryos conceived in vivo ceased to develop and spontaneously aborted very early in pregnancy. These data implied that a large percentage of human embryos fertilized in vitro would inevitably fail to go to term, even if transferred to a womb. Nature, it seemed, had produced an inefficient process in which discarding embryos was a matter of course.[87]

Board members who initially saw the inefficiency of IVF as an ethical problem were moved by Biggers's presentation. They now came to see the inefficiency of IVF as analogous to the inefficiency of natural reproduction. This had two significant effects. First, it helped establish embryo loss in IVF as a feature of nature rather than an artifact of the laboratory, thus shifting responsibility away from the technology (and those using it) onto the underlying biological system. Second, it allowed board members to argue that IVF was actually highly analogous to in vivo fertilization; it was roughly the same biological process, simply displaced to the laboratory. Given this analogy to natural reproduction, the board began to see IVF as merely a therapeutic rectification of failed biology rather than an artificial transformation of human reproduction. It was a technological effort to set right a biological dysfunction and in this respect was no different than any other technology of healing.

Jesuit theologian Richard McCormick in particular was affected by this scientific information. McCormick was a forceful member of the board; he spoke up often, and his interventions had a significant effect on the direction of deliberation and on the board's conclusions. Of all the members, McCormick harbored the greatest initial reservations about IVF. When NBC News reported on the birth of Louise Brown in July 1978, McCormick supplied the critical voice. Speaking of the likelihood that multiple eggs would be fertilized in the process of initiating a pregnancy, he noted that some embryos would be left over. He characterized this as the primary ethical question associated with IVF. "Now what do you do with these discards, what are they at the stage of cell division at which we find them? Are they human beings? Can they be destroyed?"[88]

The NBC report included footage of an in-production made-for-TV movie based on Aldous Huxley's *Brave New World*. "Of course this is fiction," declared the news correspondent as human fetuses in cellophane bubbles bobbed along on the conveyer belt, "but the birth of the world's first so-called test-tube baby has raised fears among some people that this fiction could one day become a reality."[89] As board deliberations proceeded, such dystopian images of IVF lost traction. Worries that IVF transformed human reproduction into laboratory manufacture receded. McCormick argued that if the risk of embryo loss in IVF could be brought into parity with natural reproduction, IVF could be thought of as analogous to nature and thus as a simple therapeutic intervention.

The analogy was not perfect, however. The board recognized that, though Louise Brown's mother Lesley had had only a single ovum fertilized, in future attempts, multiple ova might be used. This approach would likely entail transferring only a subset of the resulting embryos and discarding the remainder. The board argued that discarding embryos was not inconsistent with the natural process. It would be natural for some embryos to perish, even if they do so in vitro rather than in vivo. So long as the purpose of the operation was procreative and the outcome was indistinguishable from natural reproduction, IVF could be considered a restoration rather than a transformation of human reproduction. McCormick argued that the ethical acceptability of IVF depended on achieving as close an approximation to natural reproduction as possible. The analogy to nature, however, was measured not by similarity in material process but by purpose and end product. As McCormick stated during the board's deliberations,

It mimics the natural process if the death is there. It is something which is not intended, though it is foreseen. I just think that the ethical objection is against doing it artificially. It is unnatural. That is meaningless. As to zygote loss, I think that can be taken care of. Risks can be minimized to the point where they are about the same as they are in the natural process.[90]

The argument by analogy transformed the ethical questions around IVF in two ways. First, by characterizing the technique as a restoration, rather than a transformation, of human biology, the board was able to treat IVF as a technology of healing. On this basis, the board found it much easier to characterize IVF with embryo transfer as an "innovative therapy," thereby locating decision making in the private sphere of clinical medicine and leaving physician and patient to make judgments about the propriety of harms and benefits.

Second, the analogy to nature shifted the focus away from the IVF embryo as an entity and research subject toward the application of IVF as a reproductive technology. The fact of embryo loss allowed the board to partially avoid the question of whether the IVF embryo should be seen, let alone protected, as a human subject. In a review of the ethical literature, LeRoy Walters proposed that if IVF were seen as an "innovative therapy," many of the public bioethical questions—especially those related to the oversight of experimental research on human beings that the national commission had recently described—would give way to traditional forms of (private) clinical decision making. This idea, as well as the language of (innovative) therapy, was carried throughout the board's deliberations.[91]

In the public hearings, many critics had argued that IVF allowed an inappropriate degree of choice over who lives and who dies. Board member Robert Murray, a geneticist at the Howard University College of Medicine, summarized these objections as follows: "Man is doing the discarding versus Nature or God or the creator . . . doing the discarding, and they didn't trust man to do the discarding . . ."[92] The board used the analogy to nature to address this objection by recasting the choice to discard as an ethically neutral imitation of nature, thus minimizing the role of human choice and ethical responsibility. So long as the technology reflected nature, the death of the embryos did not require moral evaluation: one might just as well ask whether natural human reproduction was morally suspect. In McCormick's words,

If we distinguish between—you know, not everything that nature does may we do, because people die, and we cannot kill [un]necessarily, et cetera, but I think if we're talking about replicating, artificially, nature's achievements rather than her disasters it is a different type of issue and what we're doing here is replicating nature's achievements, even with some associated loss; we're replicating what happens in the natural process.[93]

The analogy to natural reproduction relied on technical scientific information about embryo loss, the main source for which was a single scientific paper.[94] In responding to public concern about discarding embryos, the board leaned heavily on this technical information. The first chapter of the report provided scientific background about "the normal human reproductive process." The majority of this section was a detailed discussion of the inefficiency of natural reproduction. It included detailed numbers reporting, for instance, that "only thirty-seven percent of human zygotes survive to be delivered subsequently as live infants." Other basic scientific information, such as the timing of fertilization, its location within the body, the processes of early embryogenesis in vivo, and the initiation of implantation, was conspicuously absent. That this information about embryo loss was the only background scientific information provided about the normal reproductive process demonstrates its centrality to the board's conclusions. The board used the biological fact of embryo loss to tether the technology of in vitro fertilization to the morally neutral precedent of natural reproduction using the bond of analogy.[95] In short, by constructing these processes as analogous, the board naturalized the technology of IVF.

The analogy to nature had important consequences not only for the board's conclusions but for the very way IVF was conceptualized in its deliberations. The argument by analogy placed the emphasis on the technology of IVF rather than on the embryos that it produced. It treated the IVF embryo less as an entity in itself and more as an element of a procreative process. As a result, the application of the technology (process) rather than the embryo (product) tended to be the primary object of moral evaluation. The board used the analogy to natural reproduction as a means of sidestepping the direct assessment of the "moral status" of the human embryo whenever possible. Other questions, such as that regarding the moral status of the IVF embryo, were thereby made secondary to the ethical assessment of the larger purpose of IVF. If nature were responsible for embryo loss, it was not necessary to address the question of the moral status of the embryo in the abstract. So long as IVF remained analogous to natural reproduction, the board reasoned, that question need not be addressed.

The analogy to nature, and thus to the remedial purpose of all medical interventions, also helped shift responsibility for ethical questions away from the polity at large. Insofar as responsibility for embryo death could be attributed to biological processes rather than human choices, one very common criticism of IVF could be dismissed on the basis of a more nuanced understanding of nature: an understanding that was inaccessible in normal human experience but was supplied by science. In this respect, a scientific picture of the underlying reality of nature supplied the foundation for a moral consensus. This consensus was built not on a convergence of value judgments but on an authorized account of nature that deflated the ethical questions themselves.

MORAL STATUS

Although the analogy to nature-dominated board deliberations, the problem of the moral status of the embryo was nevertheless present, if primarily in the background. The concept was introduced at the first meeting on IVF by staff member and bioethicist LeRoy Walters. Walters characterized two possible positions on moral status: first, that the embryo is a genetically unique human organism from conception onward and thus has the moral status of a human person; second, that the morally relevant features of the human organism, such as sentience, develop over time, and thus the conceptus acquires the moral status of a human person at a later developmental stage. Walters framed the difference between these viewpoints as turning on the question of how to move from *is* to *ought*: from a set of known facts to an ethical conclusion. However, the *is* questions that were at stake—and the technical knowledge that was seen as relevant—were different than in the argument by analogy. The question of moral status approached "the embryo" in the abstract, thereby separating it from the context of a procreative process—whether natural or technologically assisted. Instead, it took the embryo as a generic object of moral assessment. Walters's account, which mirrored a substantial subset of the existing bioethical literature, treated moral status as intrinsic to the conceptus itself, and independent of surrounding circumstances. Were the question of moral status to be adequately answered, he suggested, it would settle most other ethical questions about embryo research.[96]

This decontextualist approach mirrored the national commission's approach to human subjects research. The national commission made an important mark on the EAB, though primarily through its staffing. Executive Director Charles McCarthy had served on the national commission, as had Staff Director Barbara Mishkin. Mishkin and McCarthy, together with Georgetown ethicist LeRoy Walters, were largely responsible for drafting the EAB report on IVF.[97]

The national commission had articulated a set of principles that applied to all human subjects under all circumstances. This principlist approach, ultimately codified in the Belmont Report, sought to articulate the obligations of the researcher to the human research subject irrespective of the context or purpose of the research.[98] Central among the Belmont principles was the ethical commitment to "respect for persons." The ontological category of the person was assumed and treated as a constant. Respect, then, applied equally to all persons.

The principle of respect for persons is rooted in a notion of the sovereignty of the individual subject, both as a decisional agent and as a vulnerable body.[99] According to the national commission, the principle of respect applied to the individual research subject and was the foundation for autonomy and the requirement that consent be given prior to involvement in any research activity. In the event that a subject is unable to make considered judgments and give consent, respect requires that the subject be protected from risk of harm.[100]

As discussed above, the national commission distinguished between categories of human subjects in terms of vulnerability to harm and the ability to consent, not in terms of essential, ontological differences between categories of subjects. For instance, the differences between an adult and a fetus were defined vis-à-vis the ability of the subject to assume responsibility for research risks, not according to ontological differences between types of humans. The boundary between the human subject and other research objects (such as tissues or animals) was considered to be marked by a bright line, though one that was taken as given in nature, self-evident, and hence essentially untheorized in the commission's work. The national commission simply extended human subject protection to "all who share human genetic heritage."[101]

The in vitro embryo was approached differently. The board's discussions of moral status were informed by the decontextualist and principlist framework of the national commission. Building on the Belmont principle of "respect for persons," the board asked what ethical obligations the researcher has toward the IVF embryo by asking what sort of respect was due to it. But unlike the commission, which took the category of the person as a given and devoted ethical attention only to the appropriate way to show respect, the problem of the moral status of the embryo first required a corollary ontological account of personhood to address the issue of respect.

Adopting this framework required that the embryo be taken as an abstract, generic entity, independent of where, how, and for what purpose it had come into being. If the embryo were considered to be a person, it would be afforded the same respect as any other human subject. If it were not, the obligations detailed in the Belmont report did not (and could not) apply. The bright line of Belmont principlism could not accommodate the ends-focused ethical evaluation of the argument by analogy. In order to draw the embryo into the existing framework of federal research ethics, it had to be located on one side or the other of a morally unequivocal, ontological bright line.[102]

Thus, insofar as the board felt the need to be consistent with the norms and approach that the national commission had endorsed, it had to confront precisely the complex question that the commission had sidestepped in order to make its principlist approach tenable. The national commission's strategy to avoid asking morally "thick" ontological questions forced the board to face exactly those questions.

John Evans has described the transition from the "thick," ends-focused discourse of 1960s bioethics to the "thin," means-focused discourse of principlist bioethics. My observations square with his analysis but offer a further insight. When the board adopted the "thin" frame of principlism, it also needed to address the "thick" questions of what kind of being the embryo is and what its moral significance is. The first step was dependent upon the second. Put simply, to "thin" debate, "thick" questions were merely displaced from formal ethical debate, so they had to be asked in some other way. I argue that they were asked in ontological terms and thus in the putatively morally neutral idiom of scientific knowledge.[103]

This principlist approach to moral status, which ignored context and purpose, and the argument by analogy to nature, which was grounded directly in context and purpose, produced deep tensions. To the extent possible, the board tried to avoid a decontextualist evaluation of the embryo's moral status. McCormick, in particular, assiduously attempted to draw questions back into the ends-focused frame of the analogy to nature.

McCormick's approach encountered the most difficulty when the board confronted the question of whether the IVF embryo could be used as an object of laboratory research. The Soupart proposal set precisely this question before the board. Pierre Soupart was one of many scientists eager to use IVF in basic studies of human embryology. His proposed protocol entailed creating in vitro embryos with donor gametes specifically for research, with no intent to produce a pregnancy.[104] A number of scientific experts told the board that experimental work on the human embryo in vitro would be a powerful tool for understanding the process of fertilization, the emergence of genetic problems in the human conceptus, and other difficult-to-access features of human reproduction and embryogenesis. Similar claims were made by scientists and physicians at the public hearings.[105] Advocates were quick to point out that such research would be clinically valuable. One scientist told the board that such research was essential for reproductive applications of IVF, both for assessing its risks and for improving the efficiency of the procedure.[106] Another proposed that the in vitro embryo would be useful for developing other therapeutic tools and technologies, including new contraceptives.[107]

Though McCormick was adamantly opposed to IVF without embryo transfer through the first several months of deliberations, by the spring of 1979, he was prepared to allow it. With his conversion, any lingering hesitation harbored by other board members dissipated. McCormick's change in position resulted from a shift away from the argument by analogy to nature toward a moral-ontological assessment of the embryo itself. This change in focus came primarily from a discussion with another prominent Catholic theologian, Charles Curran, who testified at the fifth meeting of the EAB.[108] Curran began his presentation with a statement of the primary methodological principle of Catholic moral theology: "Catholic theology [has] always asserted that faith and reason can never contradict one another." In practice, he explained, this has meant that "the Catholic tradition has tended to use human reason as a way of understanding and arriving at ethical conclusions. In fact, its famous teaching of natural law was basically human reason directing us to our end in accord with our nature."[109] Curran explained two philosophical implications of this approach. First, although the conclusions of Catholic moral theology must conform with established dogma, they are not specifically derived from it. Therefore, they are not theological as such and can be advanced in purely secular terms. Second, an a priori assumption in this approach is that there is no distinction between natural law and moral law. Faith and reason never contradict each other, so rational accounts of nature have a direct bearing on moral discernments. Adopting a binary approach to personhood, Curran argued that the moral category of the person cannot accommodate ambiguity or intermediacy: "You either are or you aren't."[110]

Curran proposed a biological criterion that he considered determinative of the moral status of the embryo: individuality. He argued that "truly human life begins somewhere about the second or third week after conception" because "at this time we have present the individual."[111] He argued that because in some cases the human embryo prior to implantation will spontaneously separate into two, resulting in monozygotic twins, it is not until implantation is complete and twinning is no longer possible that the embryo becomes an individual.

Curran's argument exerted an important influence over the outcome of the board's deliberations. Curran and McCormick were old friends and both residents of the Washington, D.C. area. Following Curran's testimony at an EAB meeting in Seattle, it happened that Curran, McCormick, and staff director Charles McCarthy were on the same flight back to Washington, D.C. The flight was virtually empty, and the captain declared free cocktails for all. The three men sat together, enjoying their drinks and discussing the embryo. Their discussion was lively and open, less constrained than the more formal dialogue that had taken place in front of the media lights earlier that day.[112] All three men had a substantial background in Catholic moral theology (McCarthy had been an ordained priest and had been a professor of political philosophy at the Catholic University of America until 1970).

McCarthy recalls that Curran, over the course of the flight, seemed to convince McCormick that the moral status of the embryo was the only important question. He argued that, from the Catholic perspective, the analogy to nature was morally largely irrelevant. If the embryo were a human person, discarding embryos would be unethical no matter what the circumstance. If the embryo were not a "truly human life," then it could be used instrumentally, so long as other prudential concerns were taken into account.[113] By the next EAB meeting, McCormick had altered his position to match Curran's, and he affirmed that IVF without embryo transfer could be acceptable under certain circumstances.

This change in McCormick's thinking represented a strange convergence of the underdetermined category of the human subject in Belmont principlism and the highly developed natural law framework of Catholic moral theology. For the latter, the demarcation of the human from the nonhuman was a critical boundary. The human was the *imago dei* and inviolable. The 1869 instruction of Pope Pius IX that the conceptus should be protected from the moment of fertilization onward was predicated on the categorical obligation to protect the human being from wanton violation. The Vatican had not (and still has not) developed a specific dogma defining when in human development "hominization"— classically thought of as the moment of ensoulment— takes place. Before 1869, the Church's teaching on abortion was based on the Thomist (and Aristotelian) teaching that the human being was not present until well into development. But given advances in understanding of mammalian embryology in the nineteenth century,[114] Pius IX expanded the prohibition on interference with pregnancy to the moment of conception. He made this change on prudential grounds; though the precise moment of hominization was theologically uncertain, prudence required that the conceptus be protected from the moment of fertilization forward.[115] Theological teaching, however, was very clear that the emergence of the human being was sudden and definitive, not gradual. For all the uncertainty about where precisely the line was located, Catholic teaching held that it was a bright line.[116] Curran's views were in keeping with the Catholic bright line, but he disagreed with the prudential privileging of conception. In developing his position, he drew on embryological knowledge that had not been commented on directly by the Holy See and would not be until 1987.[117]

McCormick found Curran's argument convincing. However, in changing his position, McCormick did not abandon the analogy to nature. Rather, he shifted the level at which the analogy was drawn from the single instance of clinical IVF to the technology as a whole. He argued that IVF without embryo transfer was acceptable only insofar as the purpose and long-term effect of the research was to enhance IVF assisted reproduction. Nevertheless, once the possibility of research on the human embryo had been opened up, the question of moral status became far more present in board deliberations and figured prominently in the report. The result was that concepts developed in human subjects research ethics, most notably the concept of respect, were applied to the human embryo.

The board's ultimate conclusions about moral status suggested that there was a relationship between the ontology of the embryo and the norms that should govern its use, but it was silent on the nature of that relationship. The concept of "moral status" served as a kind of placeholder for uncertainty—both about the biological features of the embryo that had moral implications and about the kind of moral theory that would allow one to move from these observations to a moral position while preserving the tentativeness of recommendations in light of pluralistic public disagreement. The concept of moral status allowed board members to agree on the ethical acceptability of certain uses of the embryo without explicitly agreeing on an underlying ethical rationale. What precisely the moral status of the embryo *was* remained ambiguous, even as its moral status was invoked to justify treating it as less than a human subject. But it was the *concept* of moral status, and the recommendations that grew from it, that proved to be among the most influential features of the EAB report. Therefore, it is worth dwelling briefly on a moment of the board's deliberations that illustrates how the relationship of *is* and *ought* in the assessment of moral status was left undertheorized and ambiguous.

An initial draft of the report, written by the EAB staff, linked embryo loss with the notion that the embryo does not have the same moral status as a human subject:

> After much analysis and discussion regarding both scientific data and the moral status of the embryo, the Board is in agreement that the human embryo is entitled to profound respect; but this respect does not necessarily encompass the full legal and moral rights attributed to persons. *In reaching this conclusion, the Board noted the high rate of embryo loss that occurs in the natural process of reproduction* and concluded that some embryo loss associated with attempts to assist otherwise infertile couples to have children of their own through *in vitro* fertilization is not ethically distinguishable.[118]

Some board members objected to this language. Ethicist Sissela Bok argued that the issue of whether the process of embryo loss is natural or not is irrelevant to what sort of "respect" the embryo is due: "If we are not too worried about the embryo loss, it's not because it happens in nature. That's not it. It's because of the lower moral and legal status that we accord the embryo. Now, that may be a little more uncomfortable to say, but I think that's what this has to be based on."[119]

Harvard Medical School professor Mitchell Spellman, seeking to preserve the fragile consensus of the board, responded by shifting the focus away from the embryo by invoking the argument by analogy:

> I think it might clarify it if we added something which said in effect, it's a reasonable goal to expect that *in vitro* fertilization and embryo transfer could achieve success within . . . limits of embryo loss already observed in nature. . . . There's an inefficient process in nature relatively speaking, and it's reasonable that there is now technology which could replicate that.[120]

Nothing was resolved in deliberations; the arguments continued to persist in parallel. The staff resolved the disagreement simply by delinking moral status from embryo loss. The phrase "in addition" neatly replaced the previous formulation, "in reaching this conclusion," which had logically linked the two concepts:

> After much analysis and discussion regarding both scientific data and the moral status of the embryo, the Board is in agreement that the human embryo is entitled to profound respect; but this respect does not necessarily encompass the full legal and moral rights attributed to persons. *In addition, the Board noted the high rate of embryo loss that occurs in the natural process of reproduction.* It concluded that some embryo loss associated with attempts to assist otherwise infertile couples to bear children of their own through *in vitro* fertilization may be regarded as acceptable from an ethical standpoint.[121]

THE OBSCURE ORIGINS OF A BRIGHT LINE

The longest-lasting conceptual contribution of the board to the embryo research debates was also its least principled. The board unanimously recognized that for pragmatic reasons a time limit must be set on how long embryos could be cultured in vitro. Concerns had been raised about ectogenesis—the laboratory culture of human fetuses—in public comments and by some experts, most forcefully by Leon Kass. For the board, setting a time limit was a convenient policy response to these ethical concerns. A limit would preclude negative scenarios without requiring the board to comment on their likelihood or ethical significance. A boundary, the members agreed, must be established.

Yet the board never developed nor advanced any strong arguments for locating a boundary at a specific developmental stage. In the end, the report recommended that "no embryos will be sustained in vitro beyond the stage normally associated with the completion of implantation (14 days after fertilization)," but it gave no principled explanation or discussion of the rationale behind this limit.[122] Gaither, who in an interview with me readily recalled many details of the board's deliberations and conclusions, and who worked closely with the staff on many of the elements of the report, had no recollection whatsoever of the fourteen-day recommendation.[123] Judging from the recollections of Gaither and the staff and the transcripts of deliberations, the fourteen-day limit was a pragmatic, unprincipled, and essentially undiscussed addition to the EAB report. This is significant since, as we shall see in subsequent chapters, a fourteen-day limit on in vitro culture has since become a kind of unquestioned grundnorm and one of the most widely replicated policies on human embryo research around the world. It is a limit that has been—and continues to be—repeated over and over as the generally accepted ethical boundary between when an embryo can be used in research and when it transitions to a more morally significant stage that precludes instrumental use. Thus, the relatively arbitrary origin of the fourteen-day limit invites us to attend to both the contingent genealogy of this norm and the ways in which it was subsequently overlaid with justifications, both normative and ontological.

Fourteen days was ready-to-hand for a variety of reasons. Some had argued for a change in moral status at implantation, most notably Charles Curran, though the board had shied away from coming to definitive conclusions about these arguments. In part, this was because the board was primarily focused on the reproductive use of IVF, and embryos cultured beyond the initiation of uterine implantation at five or six days of development would not be viable for transfer. Furthermore, culture beyond the first several days of development seemed at that point to be technically infeasible, although Robert Edwards would later report that he had cultured an embryo to nine days some years earlier.[124]

But, most importantly, a boundary set at more or less than fourteen days would have required a reason. LeRoy Walters, who was responsible for drafting much of the report, raised this issue on several occasions during the EAB deliberations.[125] The federal fetal research regulations afforded the full protections of a human subject to the embryo, but only from the time of implantation. However, this was not for principled moral reasons. In the regulations, "the fetus" was defined as the human conceptus post-implantation (approximately fourteen days after fertilization) simply because it was not possible to detect the presence of the conceptus in vivo prior to that stage. The boundary was a function of the available technology at the time the regulations were drafted. This was explicitly acknowledged by HEW.[126]

When the proposed regulations were published for public comment, some commentators objected to the definition of pregnancy, suggesting that it ought to be defined "conceptually to begin at the time of fertilization." HEW responded,

> While the department has no argument with [this] conceptual definition . . . it sees no way of basing regulations on the concept. Rather, in order to provide an administrable policy, the definition must be based on existing medical technology which permits confirmation of pregnancy (46.303[c]).[127]

By drawing a bright line at fourteen days, the EAB was merely keeping its policy recommendations coherent with existing federal regulations. For the board, it was it was simply a convenient, if arbitrary, solution.

The fourteen-day limit was reaffirmed by virtually every subsequent ethics body that examined human embryo research, nationally and internationally. It became an article of regulatory faith seeking understanding.

THE COLLECTIVE PROBLEM OF INDIVIDUAL CHOICE

In the end, the board affirmed respect for liberal pluralism over all its specific ethical and policy recommendations. Even though the argument from analogy had allowed the board to circumvent certain ethical questions and construct a kind of consensus, the board nevertheless recognized that its recommendations contradicted the moral positions of many American citizens. It took great care to highlight the tentativeness of its conclusions. In designating certain forms of research "acceptable from an ethical standpoint," it was not claiming that they were "clearly ethically right," but rather that they were "ethically defensible, but still legitimately controverted."[128]

By treating IVF as analogous to natural procreation and describing it as an "innovative medical procedure," the board was also able to draw upon a notion of liberty and privacy associated with matters of reproduction. In an extensive discussion of constitutional issues related to IVF, the EAB report opined that the Supreme Court would likely find persuasive the claim that "restriction of access to in vitro fertilization is interference with the fundamental right of marital privacy and with their right to choose whether and in what manner to achieve procreation." But the report qualified this with the suggestion that the persuasiveness of the claim would likely depend on "how closely analogous" the IVF procedure was to other protected activities. A single woman seeking the assistance of a surrogate was much less likely to prevail than a married couple seeking IVF who had no alternative means of having a child of their own. The stronger the analogy to natural reproduction, the more compelling the claim.[129] Thus, the board positioned its own reasoning as analogous to the court's and drew upon the analogy to nature to discern continuity between a constitutional construction of privacy and its own approach to circumscribing public moral authority over the "legitimately controverted" ethical questions surrounding IVF.

Invocations of privacy bookended the board's deliberations. At the first board meeting in February 1978, Joseph Schulman, head of the Section on Human Biochemical and Developmental Genetics at the National Institute of Child and Health Development, told the EAB that the possibility of increased risk to the child derived from IVF was not sufficient to justify public interference in the private domain of reproductive choice.[130] In the last few minutes of the board's final meeting on IVF, chairman Jim Gaither commented on fears that the technology would be misused. He suggested that it was appropriate to entrust ethical responsibility for the use of such technologies to individual citizens and their privately held moral reasons:

> This is an area . . . so closely tied to fundamental decisions which humans have always been allowed in our society to make. And we do not want to be in the business of telling people that they cannot avail themselves of this.[131]

Yet many of the board's recommendations emerged out of concerns that, should IVF be left entirely to the private choice of individuals in a consumer-driven market, problems would inevitably emerge. The board became increasingly concerned about leaving IVF to the private sector after its public hearings.

During the hearings, a number of clinicians expressed their intent to experiment with human IVF whether or not federal dollars became available. Perhaps most notable among them were Drs. Randolph and Richard

Seed of the Reproductive and Fertility Clinic of Elgin, Illinois. The aptly named Seed brothers detailed plans to undertake a program of "artificial embryonation" in which a woman would serve as an egg donor for an infertile couple. She would be artificially inseminated with the sperm of the husband, the embryo would be flushed from her body (a technique the Seed brothers claimed to have mastered in cattle), cultured in vitro, and transferred to the uterus of the infertile woman.[132]

The Seed brothers' ambitious, if ill-conceived, experimental plans came to signify for the board what practices might emerge in the private sector if the government failed to regulate IVF.[133] Gaither recalled,

> All of as sudden you understood what would happen if we didn't say it was ethically acceptable. Like the backroom abortion practice, it was really scary, when you knew that people were going to do this whether it was legal or not. It really scared the hell out of you.[134]

The board believed that federal involvement in IVF research would provide both a measure of transparency and the leverage to require that institutions receiving federal funds adhere to federally mandated guidelines, here following the model of human subjects research oversight.[135] Thus, while privatizing the ethical questions around IVF by associating them with other reproduction-related practices, the board simultaneously articulated a responsibility of government to ensure that the technology was safe and would be safely used. The board advocated limited federal funding for research because such a limit would allow the federal government to regulate research practices by attaching ethical constraints to federal funds.

THE REGULATORY RESPONSE

The EAB report was delivered to HEW secretary Joseph Califano in May 1979. Though Califano had taken great interest in the work of the board and expressed his intention to see that work through, he was replaced as HEW secretary by Patricia Harris in 1979. After Harris became secretary, the EAB's IVF recommendations fell by the wayside. According to EAB staff director and then-director of the Office for Human Subject Regulation (OHSR),

Charles McCarthy, Harris neglected details of HEW-related biomedical research operations. He recalls the tremendous difficulty he had as director of the OHSR in reaching Harris for any purpose. In the final months of 1979, as the Carter administration wound down, all energies in the OHSR focused on the highest-priority tasks. With Reagan defeating Carter and entering office on an anti-regulation platform, McCarthy thought that years might pass before new federal regulations of any sort might be put in place. The OHSR's highest priority was promulgating the national commission's Belmont principles as federal regulations. Since the EAB recommendations on IVF were a lower priority, they were temporarily set aside. McCarthy recalls going to the farewell party for the HEW secretary the night before the change in administration and interrupting the festivities briefly to have Harris sign the changes to the human subjects research regulations (45 CFR 46) that had come out of the Belmont report.[136]

In 1978, Congress authorized the creation of a President's Commission for the Study of Ethical Problems in Medicine and Biomedical and Behavioral Research.[137] The president's commission was meant to replace the national commission, whose charter expired in 1978. The authorizing legislation allocated $20 million to support the president's commission, but by mid-1979, no appropriation had been made. In late 1979, the first task of newly appointed commission chairman Morris Abram was to find funds for the commission within the 1980 HEW appropriation. As the appropriation problem was being addressed, a HEW representative who did not fully understand the EAB's regulatory responsibilities was sent up to the Hill to discuss the issue. The conclusion Congress drew from the meeting was that two public bioethics bodies housed within HEW would be one too many.[138] The remaining funds appropriated for the EAB in fiscal year (FY) 1980 were reallocated to the commission with the understanding that the role of ethics advising would also be transferred. This result did not comport with the expectations of the executive directors of the two bodies. EAB director Barbara Mishkin and president's commission director Alexander Capron had discussed how the bodies would coexist, the EAB dealing with specific research proposals and the commission dwelling on larger bioethical problems, such as the definition of death.[139] But for the HEW secretary and Congress, that division of labor seemed redundant, particularly with a constrained federal budget in an era of aggressive deregulation. The EAB closed its office permanently in May 1980.

The work of the Ethics Advisory Board has been largely forgotten. But in important respects, its was highly influential. Certain boundaries and categories that were fashioned and formulated within EAB deliberations would come to circulate extensively in subsequent debates over human embryo research, most notably the fourteen-day limit to in vitro culture, the notion that the embryo is due "profound respect," and the concept of "intermediate" moral status—a moral status somewhere between human tissue and a human being. Despite the board's efforts to root its arguments in analogies to the embodied familiar rather than in analysis of the uncannily abstract, the embryo's "moral status" nevertheless became the primary object of ethical interrogation in the years that followed.

The national commission's principlism and its use of the public–private boundary as a means for segregating moral responsibility and containing ethical risk also persisted through the deliberations of the next three decades. The question, "What is the embryo?" came to be wrapped up with the normative question, "What are our obligations to it?" Knowing what "is" means and identifying the "we" came to be deeply entangled—in part because these issues addressed a question that was posed in a language that specifically avoided ontological questions and treated the relevant moral community as a given.

It is perhaps unsurprising that the argument by analogy and the efforts McCormick led to preserve the conceptual and practical nexus between IVF and procreation gained little traction. For those who wished to make the embryo circulate into novel spaces and applications, it was expedient to find a mode of moral evaluation that could be made to circulate with it. The seemingly immutable mobility of moral status and the fourteen-day rule met this requirement. In subsequent decades, they circulated with the in vitro embryo through novel research contexts, expanded clinical uses, and new approaches to resolving public bioethical problems.

During the next fifteen years, in vitro fertilization and human embryo research proceeded simultaneously, though primarily in the private sector and in a clinical context. The practices employed in this work would radically alter the circumstances, both moral and scientific, under which ethical deliberation would proceed.

2

PRODUCING LIFE, CONCEIVING REASON

n 1980, as the Ethics Advisory Board (EAB) was dissolved, no child had yet been born through in vitro fertilization (IVF) in the United States. By the early 1990s, however, clinical IVF was a widespread practice. Thousands of Americans had been conceived in the laboratory, tens of thousands of human embryos were in frozen storage, and hundreds of thousands of human ova had been fertilized in vitro in the United States. IVF had shifted from a radical, experimental technology to a consumer good, available at hundreds of clinics nationwide.

During the 1980s and early 1990s, controversy surrounding research on the in vitro human embryo opened a new chapter in American debates on developing life. During this same period, IVF became a common clinical practice, and an IVF industry grew into an essentially unregulated market driven by significant consumer demand. In 1981, the first American conceived in vitro was born.[1] Over the course of the next two decades, human embryos became an increasingly common presence in American laboratories. By 1987, approximately 5,000 IVF babies had been born worldwide, 1,000 of them in the United States. There were 220 IVF clinics around the world, conducting a total of 30,000 treatment cycles annually and producing more than 150,000 human embryos per year.[2] Approximately one-third of these were in the United States. One year later, the U.S. number had increased by fifty percent.[3] This dramatic rate of increase persisted well into the 1990s. By 2000, slightly less than one percent of all American children born that year had been conceived in vitro.[4] This dramatic change in American reproductive practices also transformed the circumstances that had to be taken into account in debates over human embryo research. Whereas the EAB had been faced with a new technology that had yet to be used on American soil, less than a decade later, clinical IVF had become widespread and entrenched in American society.

As IVF became a widespread clinical practice, the morally divisive issue of human embryo research was repeatedly raised. Over the course of the 1980s, the issue was altered by the shifting position of the embryo as a material presence in the clinic, by the political economy of IVF, and by the increasing interest in the use of the embryo as a laboratory research object independent of procreative intent. This chapter examines the consequences of the emergence of a market in IVF for ethical debates and governance of the new reproductive technologies. I argue that the material practices of clinical IVF, and the boundary between public and private spheres of judgment produced by federal inaction, shaped ethical and political approaches to human embryo research. In particular, I trace shifting approaches to the "moral status" of the embryo. As assessments of the embryo—biological and moral—were elevated in importance over questions of the appropriateness and meaning of the technology of IVF itself, a heightened significance was attributed to the very terms employed in public debate. One ethics body coined a new term, *preembryo*, in an attempt to encourage reasoned public debate and to reform public discourse to take into account (what it judged to be) relevant scientific knowledge.

THE CONSTITUTION OF HUMAN LIFE

In 1981, a piece of legislation titled the *Human Life Bill* was introduced in the U.S. Senate.[5] It purpose was to define the "person" of the fourteenth amendment as a human being from the moment of conception until death, thereby extending constitutionally guaranteed equal protection, life, liberty, and due process to human embryos.[6]

The *Human Life Bill* was a legislative effort to wrest control over abortion from the judiciary. Since the Supreme Court decided *Roe v. Wade* in 1973, pro-life factions in Congress had been waiting for an opportunity to push through a "human life" constitutional amendment. Such an amendment would have extended full constitutional protection to the human conceptus from the moment of fertilization onward. With the 1980 election of Ronald Reagan, it appeared that the amendment would have sympathetic support from the White House. However, in early 1981, it became clear that this much anticipated support would not be forthcoming. The *Human Life Bill* was conceived as an alternative strategy that would not require getting over such a high political bar.

In hearings on the bill, its sponsors brought forth a series of distinguished scientist-witnesses who described in careful detail the biology of fertilization and the process of human embryogenesis. Through the technology of in vitro fertilization, these witnesses argued, the discerning eye of science could now witness firsthand an event that had been invisible to the founding fathers: the inception of human life at the moment of fertilization. To the witnesses' eyes, the evidence was unequivocal: the individual human life begins with fertilization. The witnesses insisted that their claims were utterly incontrovertible statements of scientific fact.[7]

A cell biologist from Harvard Medical School read a series of quotations from embryology textbooks that stated that fertilization initiates the life of a new individual organism. This fact, she argued, was so uncontroversial as to be unremarkable: "No study or experiment has ever refuted these scientific facts, and no competent scientist denies them. Thus, one is being scientifically accurate if one says that an individual human life begins at fertilization or conception."[8]

To the question, "When does a person begin?" geneticist Jérôme Lejeune supplied "the most precise answer . . . available to science."[9] "Life," he said, "has a very very long history, but each individual has a very neat beginning—the moment of its conception."[10] This longstanding supposition had been experimentally confirmed and made settled fact, he argued, with the birth of the first baby conceived in vitro. In light of this development, "to accept the fact that after fertilization has taken place a new human has come into being is no longer a matter of taste or of opinion. The human nature of the human being from conception to old age is not a metaphysical contention, it is plain experimental evidence."[11] Another witness agreed: "The work of Edwards and his associates in England with test-tube babies has repeatedly proved that human life begins when the ovum is fertilized and the new combined cell mass begins to divide."[12] Given this unambiguous experimental result,

"Now we can say, unequivocally, that the question of when life beings is no longer a question for theological or philosophical dispute. It is an established scientific fact."[13]

Subcommittee Chairman John P. East (R-NC) drove this point home, repeatedly asking the witnesses to clarify whether these statements were personal interpretations of the experimental data or could be read unambiguously from empirical observation of nature. The witnesses unwaveringly affirmed the latter.[14]

Scientific witnesses called by the opposition vigorously disagreed. Dr. Leon Rosenberg, a respected geneticist from the Yale School of Medicine countered that, "I know of no scientific evidence which bears on the question of when actual human life exists."[15] Rosenberg asserted that "the notion embodied in the phrase 'actual human life' is not a scientific one, but rather a philosophic and religious one."[16] Others expressed similar views, not least among them the National Academy of Sciences (NAS). In a declaration, the NAS asserted that the bill "purports to derive its conclusions from science, but it deals with a question to which science can provide no answer. . . . Defining the time at which the developing embryo becomes a person must remain a matter of moral or religious value."[17]

Harvard law professor Laurence Tribe asserted the same epistemological boundary, but in terms of the constitutional limits of the state. He argued that defining the moment at which life begins was a problem of law, not of scientific knowledge, and that it had already been addressed by the U.S. Supreme Court. The court was not faced with a "deep dark mystery" of "what a fertilized ovum is." "It is not," Tribe argued, "as though the court labored under the misapprehensions of an Aristotle, believing that until some point late in pregnancy the fetus was inert, not alive."[18] Rather, the very nature of the question made it inappropriate for the court to answer it. The court had sidestepped the question of when human life begins not for lack of knowledge, but because the state has no business intervening in matters of conscience. Although the moral issues were "mysterious and puzzling," the legal issue was "extraordinarily clear."[19]

The chief officer of the general assembly of the United Presbyterian Church argued that in rendering its decision, the court had opted not to "impose any position, any assumption, any conclusion, upon anyone." The court had left "the individual free to exercise his or her own religious convictions as to when human life begins, as to when personhood begins." The answers to such deeply personal questions "should not be imposed by legislative fiat."[20] To do so would enshrine a particular religious view as the law of the land, he argued, which would violate the establishment clause, whose purpose was to prevent precisely such transgressions of the boundary between private belief and public law.

This constitutional argument was repeated by all critics of the bill, who generally also saw an epistemological distinction between fact and value—the beginning of human life could not be scientifically known because it was not a scientific question.[21] The sole exception was embryologist Clifford Grobstein. Grobstein was Professor of Biological Sciences and Public Policy at the University of California, San Diego, and had been writing about the moral status of the human embryo since the late 1970s. In a 1979 *Scientific American* article, Grobstein described significant changes that take place at the completion of implantation and with the formation of the primitive streak at the gastrulation stage, changes that distinguish the "preimplantation embryo" from the "postimplantation embryo." First, Grobstein observed, the preimplantation embryo has a significantly lower likelihood of surviving to term than the gastrula (i.e., an embryo that has reached the gastrulation stage at approximately twelve to fourteen days of development). A higher percentage of embryos spontaneously abort before this stage than after. Second, he suggested, the preimplantation embryo has not undergone discernable differentiation beyond separation of the inner cell mass from trophoblast cells.[22] The inner cell mass, which gives rise to all tissues of the fetus, is homogeneous in the preimplantation stage. It is a collection of cells, not yet a multicellular organism. That assessment, he asserted, is confirmed by the fact that the preimplantation embryo is able to give rise to two distinct embryos through fission, or twinning.[23]

Twinning, Grobstein argued, demonstrates that, though genetic individuality is established at fertilization, "multicellular individuality" is not: "The preimplantation period can be regarded scientifically as one of preindividuality in a developmental sense." Since "persons, usually defined, are multicellular individuals . . . developmental individuality appears to be a prerequisite of personhood."[24] Grobstein allowed for legal and philosophical considerations in defining personhood, but for the preimplantation embryo, the prima facie biological evidence was, he argued, so compelling that philosophical questions could not be meaningfully raised. The scientific facts of the matter rendered normative questions moot. He acknowledged that a purely scientific account would not satisfy "individuals committed to a religious view of the matter" but felt that it was not the purpose of public policy to respond to private religious concerns.[25]

In the *Human Life Bill* hearings, Grobstein presented a rationale for privileging the role of scientific evidence:

> This matter cannot be settled by science, but it is also not a matter that can be settled without examining carefully what we know scientifically about the process of development. What we know scientifically is part of our objective knowledge, and objective knowledge has advantage because it is potentially accessible and common to all parties in a dispute.[26]

Note that Grobstein was advancing an account not only of specific, relevant scientific knowledge, but also of the right relationship between scientific knowledge (and authority) and democratic judgment, drawing upon the commonsense notion that value-laden collective deliberation must begin with, and be constrained by, what is "common to all parties in a dispute." Scientific knowledge, he asserted, is common by definition. I do not mean to suggest that Grobstein was constructing a democratic theory, let alone a wolf of a political argument in the sheep's clothing of science. Rather, he was uncritically invoking a commonsense notion of science as extra-political, universal, and value neutral, and of secular public reasoning as necessarily and rightly constrained by scientific authority. This commonsense commitment was no less evident in the disputes between, for instance, Lejeune and the NAS over whether the beginning of life is a matter of universal fact (and thus of utterly uncontroversial textbook science) or of individual moral judgment (and thus by nature irresolvable and subject to disagreement). Yet Grobstein's intervention was different. He invoked the separation of scientific and political spheres to open a space for articulating a scientifically authorized ontological account that would—and should, he argued—delimit the range of what can be reasonably debated in the political sphere. The ontological account would function as a conversation stopper by exposing certain moral perspectives as intrinsically unreasonable—that is, at odds with the norms of secular, public reason.

Grobstein argued that because the features generally associated with personhood develop gradually, science could not definitively point to a moment at which the human conceptus becomes a person; furthermore, such "definition depends on what the purposes are, and the purpose is not the business of science to decide but the business of the body politic."[27] Therefore, he argued, science could not supply a positive definition of when a morally significant person comes into being, but it could provide a negative one. It could rule out answers that do not comport with the objective, commonly held, scientific evidence and thereby play a critical gatekeeping function by defining when the biological criteria are met for asking philosophical and legal questions. Scientific accuracy was an obligatory passage point for entry into public moral deliberation[28] because scientific knowledge was the most basic source of epistemic and discursive common ground in public deliberation. Scientific knowledge, according to Grobstein, is independent of subjectivity—what one philosopher has called "the view from nowhere,"—and, as such, can define the reasonable limits of public deliberation.[29]

Grobstein's account created a space for science in deliberating a question that some had characterized as entirely outside the boundaries of science. The demarcation of the scientific from the moral presented by Leon Rosenberg, the NAS, and others spoke to the unacknowledged target of the *Human Life Bill*, the constitutional right to abortion. In *Roe v. Wade*, the Supreme Court had held that no definitive beginning of human personhood could be identified without drawing on private moral and religious belief. Accordingly, the question of when life begins in a meaningful constitutional sense was left to the conscience of the citizen.[30]

Grobstein's arguments, however, grew out of an entirely different object of concern: the human embryo in vitro. He wrote extensively on external human fertilization and the preimplantation embryo beginning in the late 1970s.[31] Grobstein had also followed the deliberations of the EAB. He had testified before the board and submitted a document that was included in background materials appended to the EAB report.[32] Grobstein believed that the human embryo in vitro was inevitably going to become an object of public regulation. As such, questions that, in the case of abortion, could be left to the citizen would, he thought, have to be publicly deliberated. His intervention in the *Human Life Bill* debate was motivated by this conviction. He concluded that the constitutional affirmation of individual autonomy would be inadequate to resolve the moral status of the human embryo in research contexts. A common ground would be required for reasoning together about the embryo, and he saw science as the appropriate authority to define what is—and therefore must be treated as—"common to all parties in a dispute." Through the mouthpiece of organized science, nature itself would supply the common ground for public reasoning.[33]

Grobstein's intervention mostly fell on deaf ears. Given that the problem of society's relationship to the in vitro human embryo had not yet acquired much public attention, his arguments seemed speculative and esoteric. The *Human Life Bill*, though extensively deliberated, did not garner the necessary support in the Senate to advance. By 1982, it was dead. The life of Grobstein's idea, on the other hand, had only just begun.

AMERICANS IN VITRO

As the hearings on the *Human Life Bill* began in late April 1981, another beginning was taking place. An embryo that had been generated in vitro was completing the process of implantation in her mother's uterine wall. Nine months later, in December 1981, she was born Elizabeth Carr, the first American baby that had been conceived in vitro. She added a North American presence to the small international community of test-tube babies, which at the time numbered less than twenty.[34] Elizabeth's birth came just weeks after an article in the *Lancet* predicted that IVF would become a routine outpatient procedure in years to come.[35] By late 1981, there were five clinical centers providing IVF services in the United States.[36] That number grew rapidly throughout the early 1980s. By the late 1980s, there were several hundred American IVF clinics, though fewer than half of them had successfully produced a baby.[37] This exponential growth, combined with a lack of regulation and professional standards, was cause for concern among the leading figures in the U.S. fertility industry.

Elizabeth Carr was conceived at the Jones Institute for Reproductive Medicine at Eastern Virginia Medical School. Founded in 1980 by Howard and Georgeanna Jones, the Jones Institute rapidly became the premier IVF clinic in the United States. Howard Jones had long been active in research on human IVF and had collaborated with Robert G. Edwards as far back as the mid-1960s.[38] In early 1983, Jones produced the first set of American twins born through IVF.[39] Jones pioneered the use of superovulation in reproductive IVF. He used pituitary gonadotropins to stimulate multiple ovarian follicles to release multiple ova. This technique allowed multiple eggs to be fertilized and multiple embryos to be produced in a single cycle. This allowed transfer of more than one embryo to the recipient mother, significantly increasing the chances of achieving pregnancy. Elizabeth Carr was the first birth that resulted from this superovulation technique. It rapidly became the norm in clinical IVF and remains so today.[40] Because this technique produced multiple ova, and thus multiple embryos, it often produced more embryos than would be transferred. These "left-over embryos" quickly came to be a primary object of moral concern.

As the use of IVF rapidly expanded in American reproductive medicine, and the federal government made no moves to regulate it, Howard Jones believed that it was time for the IVF industry to regulate itself.[41] Jones kept a close eye on international developments in IVF regulation. When the U.K. House of Lords commissioned an advisory body to examine IVF, Jones remained in conversation with his British colleagues, including members of the committee.[42] The Warnock Committee, named for its chair, Oxford moral philosopher Mary Warnock, produced its seminal report in 1984.[43] Jones met Mary Warnock at the House of Commons on the first day the regulation of IVF was being debated.[44]

By the mid-1980s, a number of countries had initiated public ethical and regulatory assessment of IVF, including the U.K., Canada, and Australia. Although the United States had been very early in its own public bioethical assessment of IVF, the momentum petered out with the dissolution of the EAB in 1980. In 1984, Jones persuaded the American Fertility Society (AFS; now the American Society for Reproductive Medicine) to step into the breech by establishing an ethics body to examine issues associated with the new reproductive technologies.[45]

ETHICS OF THE NEW REPRODUCTIVE TECHNOLOGIES

In November 1984, AFS president Dr. Charles B. Hammond defined the mandate for such an ethics committee. The committee would be responsible for the ethical assessment of the rapidly emerging variety of technologies and techniques of assisted reproduction. The committee would allow the AFS to "take a leadership position in addressing ethical issues in reproduction."[46] The AFS hoped the findings of the committee would be broadly disseminated and adopted, satisfying the concerns of the fertility industry and the wider public about the need for standards and regulation.

By February 1985, the AFS had assembled the committee. It included four senior IVF practitioners, one endocrinologist, two developmental biologists (one of whom was Clifford Grobstein), one lawyer, and two ethicists. The ethicists were LeRoy Walters and Richard McCormick. The committee held eight meetings between February 1985 and April 1986 at locations across the country.

The society went to some lengths to support the ethics committee. As one committee member recalled, the hotels were exceptional, the meals lavish, and the gatherings pleasant and light-hearted.[47] Meetings were closed to the press and the public. The committee relied primarily on internal expertise, bringing in outside experts only a handful of times. Report chapters were drafted by individual members. They were read aloud at meetings and revised collectively by the committee.[48] The committee examined a wide range of assisted reproductive technologies and practices, ranging from the routine to the hypothetical. These included cryopreservation, gamete donation, and gestational surrogacy, among others.

The core of the report was an assessment of the "biologic status" and moral and legal status of the human embryo. Indeed, Howard Jones originally envisioned an ethics body that would do just this by answering the question, "What is the moral status of the object we are dealing with?"[49] This, he believed, would address all subsidiary questions. Although the AFS ethics committee would ultimately address a wider range of issues, the centerpieces of its work were analyses of the "biologic" and "moral" status of the IVF embryo.

Biologic status was, according to the committee, grounded in scientific knowledge—in morally neutral, dispassionate scientific observations about the nature of the preimplantation embryo. *Moral status*, by contrast, reflected informed judgments about "our moral obligations" to the embryo and the "rights" it possesses.[50] The report explored whether the embryo's biological characteristics "are relevant for the treatment to be accorded to the developing human entity between fertilization and birth when it is undergoing rapid and progressive biologic change."[51] It argued that they were.

NATURE'S LIMITS

One of the primary findings of the committee was that human embryos should not be cultured beyond fourteen days of development. The fourteen-day limit was not a novel construction. The EAB had set a limit for in vitro culture of human embryos at fourteen days, and ethics bodies in Canada and the U.K. had also adopted fourteen days as a proposed regulatory limit on in vitro culture. For the EAB, however, this had not been a principled demarcation so much as a deferral to existing regulations on fetal research.[52] However, this demarcation of convenience was subsequently appropriated, treated as principled, and reproduced by other ethics bodies, including, in particular, the AFS committee.

The report's chapter on biologic status was authored by Clifford Grobstein.[53] It proceeded linearly through a list of biological features and made many of the same arguments that Grobstein had advanced in other writings and in the *Human Life Bill* hearings. These included the notion that the early embryo does not exhibit "developmental individuality in the sense of singleness" until the formation of the embryonic axis during gastrulation. The reasoning was as follows: this developmental change corresponds (in vivo) with several other markers, one positional, one temporal, and one diagnostic. First, the position of the embryo in the body of the mother is stabilized by the time of appearance of the primitive streak. The process of implantation (which begins at roughly seven days) is complete, and the embryo has become embedded in the uterine wall. Second, these events generally take place at gastrulation, which occurs at roughly fourteen days of development. Third, these events correspond with a set of physiologic changes in the mother that, with the technology available in the 1980s, were used as diagnostic indications of pregnancy.

Taking these facts together, the committee drew a bright line at fourteen days. According to the committee, this was a line given by nature. Indeed, the biological changes in the embryo that occurred at fourteen days were so significant, it argued, that the term *preimplantation embryo* was not sufficient to convey the magnitude of the transition. The committee thus coined a new term for the pregastrulation conceptus: the *preembryo*.[54]

THE BRITISH PREEMBRYO

On their surface, the AFS committee's findings were very similar to those of the U.K. Warnock Committee. The parallels in ultimate recommendations are significant, yet the reasoning behind those recommendations differed significantly. The Warnock Committee in the U.K. also adopted a fourteen-day limit. The Warnock report noted that, although "biologically there is no one single identifiable stage in the development of the embryo beyond which the in vitro embryo should not be kept alive," a clear statutory boundary was required "in order to allay public anxiety."[55] The report explicitly set aside the issue of when life begins, noting that such problems are "complex amalgams of factual and moral judgments."[56] Instead, it moved directly to the ethical question of "what status ought to be accorded to the human embryo."[57] When the Warnock Committee looked for a developmental reference point that would lend itself to such a boundary, the formation of the primitive streak was ready to hand. The primitive streak "marks the beginning of the individual development of the embryo" and could, the commission reasoned, serve as a biologically sensible marker to which a legally necessary bright line could be attached.[58] Thus, the Warnock Committee reasoned backward from the practical necessity of regulation to a commonsense moral ontology of the embryo.[59]

Parliament resisted adopting the Warnock Committee's recommendations because there was significant opposition to research on human embryos. With legislation at a standstill, a consortium of IVF groups established a voluntary licensing authority (VLA) to implement the Warnock recommendations. In 1985, the prospects for human embryo research in the U.K. looked dire. The *Unborn Child Act*, which would have banned embryo research, looked like it might pass. In April 1985, Royal Society president Andrew Huxley lamented that the public debate over human embryo research was "taking place against a background of widespread ignorance" and confusion, confusion exacerbated by "an unfortunate ambiguity in the word 'embryo.'" According to Huxley, this confusion derived from the use of the word *embryo* to refer both to the preimplantation conceptus and gastrula, though before the appearance of the primitive streak, "it cannot be said that a definitive embryo exists."[60]

At a VLA meeting in late 1985, the term *preembryo* was proposed as an alternative to *embryo* for the first fourteen days of development.[61] The term was coined independently, but nearly simultaneously, at both a VLA meeting in the U.K. and during the AFS ethics committee deliberations in the United States.[62] Anne McLaren, a distinguished embryologist and a member of both the Warnock Committee and the VLA, quickly became a strong advocate for the term *preembryo*. In a letter to *Nature* in April 1986, McLaren wrote,

> . . . as the only embryologist on the Warnock Committee of Inquiry into human fertilization and embryology, I was wrong in not insisting on a logical and unambiguous terminology. I missed the first meeting, at which it was decided to apply the term "embryo" to all stages from fertilization onwards, but that is no excuse. . . . Traditionally, the embryo is the entity that is formed only at the primitive streak stage, the entity which then develops into the fetus and ultimately the baby. In recent years embryologists (including me) have adopted the sloppy practice of using the same term for the entire product of the fertilized egg, most of which differentiates before the formation of the primitive streak into the tissues that will protect and nourish the future embryo . . . *The embryologist knows what is meant; the uninitiated must be left gasping.*"[63]

Even though the committee was aware of the biological changes that occur during the first fourteen days following fertilization, according to McLaren, this misses the point. McLaren felt that it was not a matter of understanding the features of the embryo, but of being able to say unequivocally what it *is*, and "the embryo does not exist for the first two weeks after fertilization." Responding to the claim of a fellow commissioner that terms like *preembryo* were "cosmetic words," manipulated to "polarize an ethical discussion," McLaren invoked the British empiricist faith in common sight, uncomplicated by sophistical manipulation of meaning:[64] "Cosmetics hide, clarity illuminates. I strive for clarity, and regret that I have not done so more effectively in the past."[65]

The Warnock report was clear that the fourteen-day boundary was an effort to marry the necessity of regulatory boundary drawing to an empirically discernable transitional stage in embryogenesis. The primitive streak was not ethically prescriptive, but a convenient biological discontinuity upon which a practical, legal boundary could be overlaid. The committee therefore grounded the bright line in the unequivocal measure of time rather than the biological assessment of ontological status.

This decision was criticized in some corners of the British scientific establishment. The Royal College of Obstetricians and Gynaecologists suggested that because the conceptus might develop at an irregular rate in vitro, and may never develop to the point of gastrulation, the appearance of the primitive streak itself—that is, biological status, not age—ought to be the criterion for limiting in vitro culture.[66] Nobel laureate and Royal Society president Andrew Huxley made a similar argument, suggesting that if the primitive streak failed to appear, "culture could be permitted well beyond the fourteen-day limit without risk of formation of a definitive embryo."[67] The U.K.'s *Human Fertilisation and Embryology Act* of 1990 adopted a somewhat compromise position, limiting culture to either the appearance of the primitive streak, or fourteen days, whichever came earlier.[68]

As both Michael Mulkay and Sheila Jasanoff have shown, the concept of the preembryo played an important role in reorienting British debate, ultimately contributing to the passage in 1990 of the *Human Fertilisation and Embryology Act*.[69] The uptake of the preembryo–embryo distinction in British politics reflected what Jasanoff has described as a "confidence of an empiricist culture persuaded that observable distinctions exist in the real world, that they can be witnessed in common, and that they accordingly form a stable basis for public policy."[70] As Jasanoff observes, science is central to British witnessing in common because it is seen as coherent with, rather than distinct from, collective political sense. She notes that Mary Warnock's plea to Parliament invoked collective responsibility to see and judge rightly, rather than mere epistemic correctness: "It is our moral duty to make a distinction in this case between the pre-embryo and the embryo . . . and to act on this distinction."[71] As I demonstrate below, this stands in significant contrast to the distinction between scientific and political judgment that informed the AFS committee's construction of the preembryo.

THE AMERICAN PREEMBRYO

The American Fertility Society ethics committee drew similar ethical conclusions to the Warnock Committee but grounded them in a very different logic. Whereas the Warnock Committee, through elite consensus, had imposed a regulatory bright line, the AFS committee discerned a clear natural boundary that could in turn be made to delineate a boundary between good reasoning and bad in public debate.

Drawing on arguments previously developed by Grobstein, the committee report stated that the potential of the zygote to develop into a (rights-holding) adult human being is "theoretic and statistical."[72] As only one in three embryos "accomplishes" development to term, and development is in any case conditional upon implantation, the preembryo does not have the same potential as the (post-implantation) embryo. Because the prembryo has attenuated potential and is not yet "developmentally individual," the committee concluded that the biological changes initiated with gastrulation constitute a change in "status." The transition between these stages was of "sufficient magnitude" to treat it as a change in kind; the primitive streak was literally a line drawn by nature that distinguished two different sorts of beings.

The committee considered this line of reasoning to be prior to and in no way informed by moral evaluation. It drew what it saw as a fundamental *scientific* distinction between the conceptus before and after gastrulation. Such a refinement in understanding, the committee judged, required a refinement in language. The committee decided that the adjectival modification of *embryo* by *preimplantation* was not sufficiently precise to unequivocally convey the facts of the matter: "The zygote, cleavage and early blastocyst stages should be regarded as preembryonic rather than embryonic. Such terminology reserves the term 'embryo' for the rudiment of the whole being that first appears in the second week after fertilization."[73] Prior to this point in development, the committee suggested, the conceptus should be called a *preembryo*, not an *embryo*.

The committee made very clear that this new terminology was strictly scientific: it was warranted by recent developments in scientific understanding and the need for descriptive accuracy in discussions of the human conceptus. It was "not intended to imply a moral evaluation of the embryo."[74] Yet, this natural demarcation supplied a critical foundation for rearticulating the ethical questions associated with in vitro fertilization. The report suggested that "uncertainties and disputes about preembryo status result from the failure to distinguish carefully between the pre-embryos and more advanced embryos and fetuses." Once this "common tendency" is overcome by a more refined scientific view, the committee argued, it becomes clear that an "independent analysis" of the preembryo is required.[75]

The inception of the term *preembryo* was significant for two reasons. First, it was the first effort in the embryo research debates to structure public moral deliberation by modifying technical language. The term *pre-embryo* was intended to discipline public discourse into taking account of (what the committee judged to be) the relevant facts such that the public would then necessarily reformulate its moral positions. Second, the committee presented *preembryo* as a strictly *scientific* term, a product of a value-neutral "view from nowhere"—one that reflected the scientific facts that were essential for making reasonable ethical and policy judgments without being determinative of those judgments. The committee's rationale for coining the term reflected an underlying imagination of right public reasoning wherein public debate is grounded in a scientifically authorized epistemic common ground—in Grobstein's terms, that which "is common to all parties in a dispute." Thus, the term was intended to serve both a scientific and democratic function. According to Charles McCarthy, who joined the committee in 1989, the term was crafted to be both "scientifically accurate and meaningful to the public."[76]

The story of how the term itself was synthesized bears this out. As the committee discussed what term might be suitable to capture relevant features of the embryo's "biologic status," Jones proposed the term *proembryo*. Jones had been educated in Classical languages, and he was bothered by the etymological disharmony of the Latin prefix *pre-* being joined to the Greek root *embryo*. Other committee members expressed concern that in the American vulgate, the *pro-* prefix might be interpreted to mean "in favor of the embryo," whereas *pre-* would more unambiguously signify "prior to" and therefore "not yet." Jones was persuaded.[77]

The committee drew ethical conclusions directly from the scientific demarcation. The preembryo was due heightened ethical consideration only if it were to become a future embryo or fetus. Respect for the preembryo was, in this case, respect for a future child. However, if the preembryo was not intended for transfer, it warranted no greater respect than any other human tissue.[78] It should not be treated as a person because "it has not yet developed the features of personhood, is not yet established as developmentally individual and may never realize its biological potential."[79] Thus, the committee's construction of moral status followed directly from its account of the biologic status of the human preembryo; although questions of moral status were epistemologically segregated from biologic status, resolving the latter simultaneously resolved the former. Indeed, the term *status* frequently appeared in the report without an adjectival modifier. Biological status was sufficient to eliminate certain moral questions simply by rendering them unreasonable.

Thus, the fact–value distinction was fundamental to the committee's approach (in contrast to Mary Warnock's), even as the concept of the preembryo embodied an idea of the right relationship between knowledge and norms (and thus between science and politics). According to Howard Jones, there was unanimous agreement within the committee that it was "clearly necessary" to have a term to refer to the conceptus prior to gastrulation, and the rationale for this was strictly scientific. In an interview, he told me, "It was a matter of having a word to talk about this structure that wasn't an embryo and which could turn out to be things other than an embryo." At the same time, the term was intended specifically for ethical deliberation. The term "had to do entirely with trying to evaluate the moral status of the human preembryo."[80] The term was invented as a contribution to what the committee saw as an ill-informed public debate.

The term *preembryo* was rapidly taken up in scientific discourse. By 1986, it appeared in *Henderson's Dictionary of Biological Terms*,[81] and it was increasingly being employed as a term of art in scientific publications, especially among those who published in *Fertility and Sterility*. Proponents of the term encouraged scientific colleagues to use it in their publications; they also continued to argue that ethical and policy discussion of embryo research should incorporate the term (and with it a putatively more accurate scientific picture). By the late 1980s, the term was in wide use, in some cases side by side with and undistinguished from the term *embryo*. It appeared in texts as varied as American judicial opinions and scientific articles in journals such as *Science*.[82]

At the same time, it also encountered significant resistance. *Nature* declared the term a "cop-out."[83] John D. Biggers, a professor of cell biology at Harvard, declared it a disingenuous political ploy and an abuse of scientific authority.[84] Pro-life critics declared it a hoax and a bastardization of scientific truth.[85] It was litigated in court, with one famous decision (and its reversal) turning partly on the accuracy of the term.[86] Regardless, whether espousing or impugning the term, actors affirmed the tacit boundary between science and politics; *preembryo* was seen as either reflecting or violating the right relationship between scientific knowledge and political judgment. The notions that political judgment should be grounded in authorized scientific knowledge and that (genuinely) scientific terms should discipline public discourse went unacknowledged and unquestioned.

THE CASE OF THE MISSING EAB

As we saw in the previous chapter, beginning in 1975, federal regulations required specific approval of any research on in vitro human embryos by an ethics advisory board.[87] With the dissolution of the EAB in 1980, there was no longer a public mechanism for ethical review of embryo research proposals.

Throughout the early to mid-1980s, the Department of Health and Human Services (HHS; formerly the Department of Health, Education, and Welfare [HEW]) went through a series of secretaries, none of whom treated reconstitution of the EAB as a priority. During the same period, fetal research had become a locus of controversy, particularly focused on a fetoscopy research proposal approved by the EAB in 1979. The study had been approved on the grounds that it did not expose the fetus to new risks. Since the study subjects were to be aborted anyway, the risk of miscarriage was not judged to violate the minimal-risk standard of the federal regulations. The renewed attention to fetal research in Congress contributed to the passage in 1985 of the *Health Research Extension Act*. The act called for Congress to form a biomedical ethics advisory committee and put in place an "equality principle" stipulating that all human fetuses must be treated the same, whether in utero or not and whether to be aborted or not. It also prevented HHS from waiving review for any research for which the 1975 regulations had required EAB review until November 1988.[88]

During the 1980s, a number of requests were made to HHS to reconstitute the EAB, including requests from the American Fertility Society in 1983, the National Advisory Child Health and Human Development Council in 1984, and the American Association for the Advancement of Science (AAAS) in 1986.[89] In May 1986, the AAAS board adopted a resolution strongly urging the secretary of HHS to authorize the reestablishment of the EAB and offering to nominate qualified members. The board advised that the absence of the EAB had "created an obstacle to the advancement of science."[90] Several months later, HHS secretary Otis R. Bowen responded to the AAAS request, stating that although the EAB had not been in place since 1980, the department had "developed a number of mechanisms to address the ethical aspects of biomedical and behavioral research." He named two such mechanisms, including the Human Subjects Working Group of the Recombinant DNA Advisory Committee and a recently convened panel to address the ethics of epidemiological research on human immunodeficiency virus (HIV) in prostitutes. Thus, he suggested, although no EAB per se existed within HHS, "other mechanisms are used to achieve the same purpose, namely, to obtain the best available advice concerning the ethical conduct of research." Furthermore, given that the Biomedical Ethics Advisory Committee would, once constituted, review fetal research regulations, it would be premature to re-establish an EAB.[91]

The lack of an EAB and the consequences of this for IVF research remained largely below the congressional radar through the mid-1980s. When Congress did begin to take notice, it was in response to other developments. On May 12, 1987, the Select Committee on Children, Families, and Youth of the House of Representatives held a hearing on the "The Alternative Reproductive Technologies: Implications for Children and Families," organized in response to developments in clinical IVF, most notably surrogacy and the *In re Baby M* custody case.

"Baby M" was the pseudonym for Melissa Stern, a child born as a result of a surrogacy agreement between William and Elizabeth Stern and Mary Beth Whitehead of New Jersey. Elizabeth Stern, a professor of pediatrics, had multiple sclerosis and was reluctant to become pregnant. The Sterns contracted with Whitehead, a homemaker, mother of two, and wife of a sanitation engineer, to be inseminated with William Stern's semen and to gestate and deliver the resulting child. Whitehead was to be paid $1,000 upon initiation of the operation and $9,000 upon delivery (and handover) of the baby.

Within twenty-four hours of giving birth, Whitehead changed her mind about relinquishing the baby to the Sterns. Litigation followed, and on March 31, 1987, Judge Harvey R. Sorkow of the New Jersey Superior Court stripped Whitehead of parental rights and awarded custody of Baby M to the Stern couple. Immediately after he finished reading his 121-page decision, Sorkow summoned Elizabeth Stern to his chambers where she signed papers permitting her to adopt Baby M. Sorkow based his ruling in part on the state's *parens patriae* responsibility to look after the child. Since justice could not be had for all parents, the court would "seek to achieve justice for the child."[92] The stir caused by the case brought renewed attention to IVF and the practice of surrogacy. The cover of the June 1987 issue of *Life* magazine was an image of the first "host uterus baby," a baby gestated in a surrogate womb with no genetic relationship to the gestational mother.[93]

The May 1987 Select Committee on Children, Families, and Youth hearing addressed concerns over the ethical and legal implications of practices such as surrogacy and examined the role that the federal government might take in responding to these largely unregulated practices. Representative Bruce Morrison (D-CT), who presided over the hearing, described it as an effort to "close the gap" between new technologies of reproduction and their social and moral consequences. "No more fundamental issues could ever come before the Congress," he asserted.[94] Witnesses lamented the lack of federal guidance and regulation of IVF and related reproductive technologies. Gary D. Hodgen, scientific director of the Jones Institute, recommended that HHS implement the 1979 EAB recommendations, although with some adjustment to allow for changes in technology and practice. He further argued that the EAB should be reconstituted in order allow IVF-improving research to go forward. "The door is locked" on federally funded research, he asserted. Allowing ethics review and "meritorious scientific studies aimed toward imminent medical breakthroughs" would serve the infertility patient and the public alike. It was, Hodgen argued, critical that concerns be allayed and for research to progress because "the public's trust in the miracles of biomedical research during the twentieth century is the largest single reason for our successes in health care. As the stewards of this irreplaceable confidence, we must see that the public's trust in scientific research will be preserved for the families of the twenty-first century." Endocrinologist Dr. Robert J. Stillman agreed. The EAB was an advisory body, not a legislative body. As such, its role was to draw together "all divergent views" in an effort to formulate advice for the federal government.[95]

Others saw the EAB as an antidemocratic concentration of power. Richard Doerflinger, a representative of the United States Conference of Catholic Bishops, worried that the purpose of a reconstituted EAB would be to provide unilateral approval of IVF experimentation without any mechanism for democratic deliberation or oversight. The previous EAB, he argued, had done its work well: all the abuses they anticipated had proved true.[96] Representative Dennis Hastert (R-IL) expressed concerns about the delegation of ethical authority more forcefully. In an exchange with Stillman, he asked for clarification of the EAB's role:

HASTERT: Do they [the EAB] decide when that sperm and egg becomes an embryo or not?
STILLMAN: I don't believe so.
HASTERT: What is it [its purpose] then?
STILLMAN: It's to bring to bear the idea of divergent group opinions of

experts with different opinions to suggest to policy makers and legislators the results of a deliberative process.

HASTERT: But this Board becomes more or less of a turnstile in a gate
whether that type of experimentation takes place . . . [the EAB] would
actually be a national turnstile of what's right and what's wrong. . . .

STILLMAN: What they suggest may have major ethical consequences and
what might by the deliberation—

HASTERT: So actually we have a board of people who are quote unquote
"experts" . . . and they're actually making moral decisions from a wide
spectrum—even at this table we have quite a divergent view of what's
right and wrong—but somebody in the place of the legislator . . . would
be making those decisions on whether this in vitro fertilization . . .
for the purpose of experimentation should take place or should not
take place.[97]

This exchange captures the political tensions around the idea of bioethical "expertise" and its role in representing public reasoning. For people
like Hastert, *bioethical expertise* suggested an unauthorized appropriation
of democracy's authority over public norms. Proponents of re-establishing
the EAB stressed its representative function, translating pluralism into
informed policy recommendations. The EAB was, in the words of the
AAAS, a model of "public participation and openness." Without the EAB
(and the public funding it would regulate), decisions were being made in
private by "ad hoc groups of experts." As a consequence, "an important
basis of credibility is lost."[98] This disagreement over the democratic role
of the ethics body became even more pronounced as subsequent ethics
bodies were formed in the 1990s and 2000s.

A NEW CONSUMER CLASS

In May 1988, the Office of Technology Assessment (OTA) published a
report called *Infertility: Medical and Social Choices*.[99] The four hundred–
page document was the most thorough and detailed examination of
human IVF that had been produced to date. It was strongly critical of the
"failure of any HHS secretary" to reconstitute an EAB since 1980. IVF was

"a powerful means for unraveling the mysteries of the human reproductive process," with implications for both human reproduction and contraception. But researchers in this promising area had "faced since 1980 the stifling effects of a de facto moratorium on federal funding of research involving human IVF."[100] This language was uncharacteristically sharp for the nonpartisan OTA. Project director Gary B. Ellis told a congressional subcommittee that the report's discussion of the EAB used some of the harshest language not only in the report, but in any report produced by the OTA.[101]

Chairman Ron Wyden (D-OR), who presided over the hearing, agreed with the OTA's assessment. As a result of the lack of federal action on IVF, there was "no public accountability at all" in the private sector. Furthermore, he argued, the efficiency of the procedure, and thus the aspirations of thousands of infertile couples, had been severely compromised by the lack of systematic, basic research on human IVF.[102] Bioethicist Arthur Caplan, echoing these sentiments, told the committee that it was "scandalous" that an ethics advisory board had not been created.[103] The problem, according to all of these perspectives, was that no EAB meant no publicly funded research on IVF, which in turn meant no public ethical oversight of human embryo research. Therefore, they argued, it was imperative to fund embryo research so that it would be subject to oversight. Funding it was an ethical responsibility.

At a June 1988 hearing and at a follow-up hearing nine months later, witnesses recited statistics to illustrate how routine IVF had become: $66 million was spent on IVF per year, and in a two-year period, 191 clinics had conduced 26,332 IVF cycles on 18,273 patients.[104] Yet, the product was lacking. Upward of 90 percent of couples, each of whom spent between $4,000 and $7,000 per IVF cycle and often went through two or three cycles, remained childless. Ellis, Wyden, Caplan, and others bemoaned the low efficiency of IVF and the corollary risk of consumer exploitation. IVF was compromised by the lack of investment in research, they argued, and what research had been conducted had been financed largely at the expense of infertile couples desperate to have a baby.

At the same time, they repeatedly reiterated that IVF was a widely accepted practice that was no longer experimental and thus ought not be considered questionable or controversial.[105] Given the multiplicity of

IVF clinics and the large number of IVF treatments, it was, according to Wyden, "downright silly" to ask whether the technique was still experimental.[106] Caplan agreed: "When people have reunions of families who have had help to conceive, it is probably moot. The questions have ended about the innovative status of this procedure."[107] In a parallel hearing in July 1988, Chairman Ted Weiss (D-NY) commented that as Louise Brown approached her tenth birthday, the birth of an IVF baby "no longer lifts an eyebrow."[108] Thus, the legislative discussion was shifting from safeguarding the citizen as an experimental subject to protecting the consumer in an unregulated market.

The blame for failing to protect this emergent class of consumers was largely laid on the lack of an EAB. With no EAB, research was stalled and consumers were, according to Wyden, condemned to "using the technology of the late 1970s at time when demand is increasing and couples hope to get access to the best technology."[109] Gary Ellis of the OTA declared that "the nine-year absence of an Ethics Advisory Board has . . . robbed infertile couples seeking IVF of the ultimate consumer protection."[110]

This framing of human embryo research as a responsibility of the state to the citizen-consumer galvanized HHS into action. In the July 14, 1988, hearing, Representative Weiss demanded to know why HHS had "ignored year after year" requests that the EAB be reconstituted. Assistant Secretary of Health Robert E. Windom responded by pleading ignorance and taking action. He told the committee that he could not account for the inaction of the four other HHS secretaries who had held the post since 1980, but that the current secretary had decided to change course.

On July 12, two days before the hearing, Secretary Bowen directed HHS staff to draft a new charter for the EAB. Despite a request by National Institutes of Health (NIH) director James B. Wyngaarden that HHS simply adopt the 1979 recommendations of the EAB, Bowen concluded that enough change had taken place in the intervening years that a fresh assessment was required. The draft charter was to be published in the *Federal Register* and followed by a sixty-day public comment period. Weiss questioned why, after eight years of waiting, HHS would move so slowly. He accused HHS of opting for a course of inaction simply to avoid controversy and criticism from the pro-life community. This, Weiss argued, was "a nonscientific . . . political kind of opposition." Where, he asked, "do you see your responsibilities when you see controversy coming on political grounds but as a scientist and a public health professional you see that the science comes down on the other side. Don't you think it's your obligation, in fact, for you to go with the science?" Windom responded that HHS could proceed responsibly only if the public were properly consulted.[111]

An EAB draft charter was published in the *Federal Register* on September 12, 1988, with a sixty-day comment period.[112] Several hundred comments were received, but no further action was taken. With the change in administration following the election of President George H. W. Bush and with Louis W. Sullivan replacing Bowen as HHS secretary, the project of reconstituting the EAB was dropped.[113] The incoming administration was already facing a divisive issue in fetal tissue transplantation research that would push human embryo research to the political margins until 1993.

From the late 1980s onward, fetal tissue transplantation had been much discussed to treat disorders such as Parkinson's disease, diabetes, and Alzheimer's disease. In 1988, the NIH convened a fetal tissue transplantation research panel to examine the ethical issues surrounding this technology. Its report, delivered to the HHS secretary in January 1989, recommended allowing fetal tissue research on electively aborted fetuses without a requirement of case-by-case EAB review.[114] The outgoing Reagan administration opted not to act on this recommendation, leaving the thorny issue for the Bush administration to address. In 1989, HHS indefinitely extended an existing moratorium on federal funding for research on fetal tissue from elective abortions. In 1990, Henry Waxman (D-CA) introduced the *Research Freedom Act of 1990* to override the moratorium and eliminate impediments to fetal tissue research in federal regulations. The bill included a provision for an EAB review of research and made the findings of an EAB binding, prohibiting override by the HHS secretary.[115] This and two other similar bills introduced in 1991 failed. In 1992, a new bill, the *NIH Revitalization Act* (S.2507), made a variety of changes to HHS policy, including lifting the fetal research moratorium, mandating expanded funding in key research areas, and requiring that women be included as research subjects in NIH-funded clinical research.

The bill was passed in 1992 but was promptly vetoed by President Bush for "ethical, fiscal, administrative, philosophical, and legal" reasons. In his veto message, Bush foreground the issue of fetal tissue transplantation research, stating the moratorium was not on research, but on sourcing research materials from electively aborted fetuses. He told the House that the moratorium "is important in order to prevent taxpayer funds from being used for research that many Americans find morally repugnant and because of its potential for promoting and legitimatizing abortion."[116]

As human IVF became an increasingly common procedure in the United States, the question of how the state should relate to the human conceptus was raised anew. As we have seen, that question arose not only around the constitutional limits of individual liberty, but around the use of the embryo as an object in the laboratory. The human embryo presented a difficult and ambiguous case. Because it was easily dissociated from its progenitors, was useful for a wide range of projects beyond simple procreation, and was more easily displaced from the constitutionally defined space of individual privacy, it destabilized the boundary between public and private, so dogmatically invoked in abortion debates. At the same time, federal inaction, partly underwritten by the EAB's judgment that traditional reproductive applications of IVF were innovative therapy and as such belonged in the constitutionally protected space of individual privacy, resulted in the creation of a sharp line between public and private spheres of practice.

As IVF was rendered a matter of private moral judgment (and thus a commercial product), huge numbers of human embryos were produced with neither public support nor oversight. However, private arrangements gone wrong, particularly in the new practice of surrogacy, caught policymakers' attention. When Congress examined IVF in the late 1980s, it encountered an already established industry with entrenched consumer expectations. Keeping with the 1980s political norm of deferring to the market, Congress approached its regulatory responsibilities not as a matter of setting limits on the technology, since policymakers judged that that horse had already left the barn, but as a matter of consumer protection.

Yet, questions remained about what uses of human embryos in research were ethical, whether such research could be federally funded, and in what terms these questions should be addressed. As the embryo was increasingly imagined as a research object, and thus as an entity distinct from a procreative process, moral deliberation came to focus almost exclusively on the "moral status of the embryo." Ethical deliberation centering on "moral status" tended to interrogate the embryo to reveal generic rights (or a lack thereof) that would apply regardless of specific circumstances. As the efforts to make moral sense of this entity progressed, the nexus between the embryo in vitro and the reproductive process that the EAB had sought to preserve was progressively attenuated. The embryo became an abstract concept, severed from specific biological, technological, and moral contexts. As a result, the embryo became a heightened site of ontological politics, as the question of how the embryo should be treated became ever more deeply entwined with the question of what it was. The stakes in terms of how people talked about the embryo were thereby heightened as well. The term *preembryo* was the first attempt by scientific experts to shape the terms of debate and to discipline public discourse into taking into account (what particular experts deemed to be) relevant ontological considerations. The committee looked to the authority of science to ground pluralistic disagreement in a common language. With this technocratic approach, the preembryo was intended to discipline public discourse through the use of a common, reasonable language in which universal facts would precede contingent, private values.

This discursive abstraction of "the preembryo" was mirrored by a material one. The advent of cryopreservation techniques allowed the embryo to be frozen and thereby separated from the constrained temporal dynamics of the reproductive process. As such, it could be separated in time and place from its moment of conception. Cryopreserved embryos variously became objects of litigation, instruments of indefinitely deferred reproductive choices, and resources for research use. The social fact of a growing number of embryos held in suspended animation would have profound consequences for debates in the 1990s and beyond.

3

REPRESENTING REASON

The twelve years from 1980 to 1992 spanned by the Reagan and Bush administrations saw essentially no changes in federal policy related to human embryo research. Yet, during that period, enormous changes had taken place in American practices of in vitro fertilization (IVF) and associated forms of embryo research. Most importantly, IVF had become a common and normal practice to produce human embryos for reproduction, many of which would not ultimately be used for this purpose. The federal government took some quite modest steps to monitor and regulate the IVF industry, but insofar as the industry's practices were regulated, it was according to the voluntary standards established by the American Fertility Society (AFS; now the American Society for Reproductive Medicine). The ethical judgments that underwrote those standards were grounded in an assessment of the status of the embryo. That assessment found the embryo to be lacking in those biological features that would justify ethical protections from use in research.

By the early 1990s, widespread use of cryopreservation techniques (freezing embryos) had dramatically increased the number of embryos present in American IVF laboratories. It became general clinical practice to fertilize as many ova as could be harvested from a woman and freeze any embryos that were not transferred to her uterus. If the first cycle did not produce a successful pregnancy, some of these embryos could be thawed and transferred. During the late 1980s, more than ninety percent of couples who attempted to get pregnant through IVF were unsuccessful. Cryopreservation significantly reduced the financial and physical unpleasantness of a second and third attempt. But for many of the embryos saved for later attempts to get pregnant, later never came.[1] As a result, the embryo ceased to be merely a fleeting presence in the assisted reproductive process. Embryos could be frozen in time indefinitely, thereby also putting off decision making about what they would be used for. By the early 1990s, the number of embryos left unused and, in many cases, abandoned in frozen storage at U.S. fertility clinics was mounting rapidly. Held in suspended animation, these embryos became a frozen presence and, in the eyes of some, a potential resource for research.[2]

Researchers also began to envision a widening range of uses for IVF embryos, for instance in studies of cancer genetics and human embryogenesis and tissue culture and in the study of an elusive category of self-renewing cells called stem cells. By the early 1990s, a number of other countries had had extensive political debates about IVF and human embryo research and had passed legislation governing activities in these areas.[3] Whereas Germany, France, and Australia had established relatively heavily regulated and restrictive regimes, the U.K. had constructed an environment that, although thoroughly regulated, was highly permissive of human embryo research. Concerns among American scientists about the lack of access to federal funding and the risk of being left behind by the British led to increasing calls for some form of oversight that would at the same time open up the National Institutes of Health (NIH) coffers for human embryo research.

A change in presidents brought changes in policy. On January 22, 1993, his third day in office and the twentieth anniversary of *Roe v. Wade*, President Bill Clinton issued five administrative orders, all dealing with abortion and reproductive rights.[4] Among them was an order that lifted restrictions on federal funding of fetal tissue research. The order declared that the findings of the 1988 Fetal Tissue Research Panel should be treated as having fulfilled the requirements of an Ethics Advisory Board (EAB) review. The order effectively rendered moot the primary source of disagreement over the *NIH Revitalization Act*. The provisions on fetal tissue remained in the bill, and, on June 10, 1993, the bill was passed.

Slightly altered from the 1992 version, the bill nullified the requirement for EAB review of research on IVF.[5] This provision was interpreted by the NIH as opening the door to all forms of research on in vitro human embryos (the human embryo in vivo was still treated as a full human subject in the federal regulations at 45 C.F.R. 46.201).[6] Grant applications for research involving human embryos began to flow into the NIH almost immediately.

With the door opened to public funding, the NIH determined that human embryo research was a sufficiently sensitive issue that an advisory body should be constituted to address ethical questions. In late 1993, an advisory panel was assembled to study the issues surrounding human embryo research and provide a report to the NIH Advisory Committee to the Director (ACD).

This chapter examines the deliberations of the Human Embryo Research Panel (HERP) and the reception of its recommendations by the wider scientific and political community. The panel's work was consequential for the embryo debates for several reasons. First, it developed an explicit account of the forms of public reasoning appropriate to the democratic assessment of the embryo's moral status, an account that would shape how other ethics bodies approached this question. Second, it took up some of the arguments articulated by the AFS committee and grounded them in an account of the right relationship between scientific and democratic judgments. Finally, its approach and its recommendations elicited a legislative response that still remains in place more than two decades later. The panel recommended allowing research on embryos left over from IVF, as well as allowing the creation of embryos specifically for research under certain conditions. In 1995, Congress responded with legislation that prohibited federal funding for research involving more than minimal risk to the embryo, effectively placing human embryos in the same category as other protected human subjects.

THE HUMAN EMBRYO RESEARCH PANEL

The HERP was composed of nineteen members, drawn from a range of disciplines including embryology, reproductive medicine, law, bioethics, sociology, and patient advocacy. A number of the members were intimately familiar with the ethical complexities associated with human embryo research. Mark Hughes was a pioneering researcher on human preimplantation genetic diagnosis and held a position at the NIH;

Kenneth Ryan was chair of the AFS Ethics Committee. The panel's charge was to ethically evaluate research on the in vitro human embryo. Germline genetic modification of human embryos was specifically excluded from the panel's purview, as was any activity already regulated under the fetal research rules. The panel was charged with defining the classes of research activities that were acceptable for federal funding, those that warranted further review, and those that should not be funded. The panel held five meetings between February and June 1994.

The panel's work came at a moment of transition in cell biology. More than a decade of fundamental research had been conducted since the derivation of embryonic stem cells from mouse embryos in 1981.[7] New techniques in cell culture and genetics were opening new avenues for studying embryogenesis. The imagined research uses of the in vitro human embryo had expanded significantly. Human IVF, though utilized almost exclusively for assisted reproduction, had become significantly more efficient by the early 1990s. The technique of cryopreservation was developed in the early 1980s and, by the early 1990s, had become widespread. By 1994, tens of thousands of embryos were frozen in time, suspended in baths of liquid nitrogen. Neglected, abandoned, or simply unneeded, these embryos were seen by some scientists as a vast reservoir of potential research material.

Whereas the EAB and the AFS Ethics Committee had focused on IVF primarily as a therapeutic tool to treat infertility, the panel focused exclusively on the human embryo as a potential research object. While clinical IVF was an important part of the background context, the panel treated the practice of clinical IVF as a potential source of embryos and not as the sole or even primary context of research. It was felt that public science could make use of the large surplus of embryos that the private sector, market-driven practices of the IVF industry had produced without being implicated in the process of producing them. Although many of the imagined applications of embryo research were related to reproduction, the panel emphasized the potential value of the human embryo for research on unrelated matters, such as the biological mechanisms behind cancer, toxicology, and as a source of human embryonic stem cells.

In fact, such uses of IVF embryos had been imagined as much as a decade earlier, though they had not been widely discussed in the United

States. In 1984, even as the Warnock Committee was assembling its report, Robert Edwards predicted that human embryo research would generate extraordinary new biological knowledge, including "the genetics of organogenesis, the causes of hydatidyform degeneration and the effects of teratogens on embryonic growth." "The list," he wrote, "is almost endless." He predicted that therapeutic applications might come through the culture and isolation of various sorts of stem cells that would be used as grafts in adults. Anticipating uses of human embryos that would be widely debated two decades later, he envisioned that "the donation of embryonic stem cells into damaged tissue could encourage their natural repair, a concept opening new forms of treatment of some fundamental disorders in children and adults." He also noted that problems with immune rejection might be circumvented with techniques including "the induction of parthenogenesis, androgenesis and gynogenesis, and perhaps even cloning, which could be applied to human embryos to make them resemble and compatible with an existing adult."[8]

By 1994, these possibilities seemed within reach. Some members saw the panel as a critical vehicle for opening up a fundamental, potentially revolutionary domain of human biological research. Dr. Patricia Donahoe, a pediatric surgeon and developmental biologist from Harvard Medical School, saw the panel as a means to shift authority over embryo research to the hands of the scientific community—to "return this research to peer-review."[9] Donahoe was opposed to strict regulatory limits, arguing that there was a tremendous amount to be gained from culturing the human embryo in vitro to gastrulation and beyond. Remarking on the therapeutic potential of what "one could pick up just a little bit later in gestation," Donahoe said, "it would be a shame for those therapeutic potentials if we limited ourselves to fourteen days, because there's going to be a revolution of understanding that will come out of this."[10] A decade earlier, Robert Edwards had expressed similar sentiments, notwithstanding the law of the land in the U.K.: "Culturing human embryos through their postimplantation stages of development could yield much information of scientific and clinical value."[11]

The panel was keen to open these research domains but hesitant to depart from the by then well-established precedent of the fourteen-day rule. The panel concluded that the pregastrulation embryo was an acceptable research object, that under certain circumstances it was acceptable to create human embryos and parthenotes specifically for research, and that, in the future, it might be reasonable to permit research on the human embryo beyond the appearance of the primitive streak.[12] Because in 1994 there were only two reports of human embryos that had been cultured in vitro beyond six or seven days: one to eight days, and one to thirteen, the idea of in vitro postgastrulation culture was somewhat hypothetical (though it had been accomplished in a mouse embryo as early as 1971).[13] But the panel was not deterred from discussing future research possibilities. It saw the embryo as a potential resource in a wide variety of experimental domains and projects, including blastomere splitting,[14] somatic cell nuclear transfer, embryonic stem cell culture, in vitro maturation of human oocytes from fetal ovarian tissue, and other research areas that had little or nothing to do with assisted reproduction.

STRAIGHT TO MORAL STATUS

Despite its broad charge, the HERP almost immediately zeroed in on the frame of moral status. With moral status came the ontological (and terminological) problem of defining the "embryo." In the first hour of the first meeting, during what was supposed to be simply a perfunctory introduction of the panel's charge, chairman Steven Muller asked for a "working definition of an embryo."[15] Duane Alexander, director of the National Institute of Child Health and Human Development (NICHD), present at the meeting to welcome the members, directed Muller to the panel's briefing materials. The glossary defined the embryo as "the developing human from about two weeks after fertilization until the end of the eighth week." That definition was, according to Alexander, "pretty much a standard one."[16] Other panel members disagreed, maintaining that the term referred to the conceptus from the point of fertilization onward. Within minutes, the panel was engaged in a discussion of the significance of gastrulation, twinning, and the formation of a body axis for the definition of the embryo, as well as the biological, social, and legal significance of these developmental markers.

Law professor R. Alta Charo suggested that a definition constructed with reference to existing law, rather than to biology, would be the most neutral course of action, since, whereas the letter of the law was clear, life, by contrast, supplied no neat or clean boundaries. Because existing regulations defined an embryo (in vivo) as coming into being at the time of implantation, Charo stated that it was therefore best to set aside "biological terms, which are fuzzy sometimes, and focus simply on something objective, like pre-implantation, leaving the only real ambiguity the moment of fertilization, which is indeed something that is a biological process."[17] Embryologist Brigid Hogan suggested pregastrulation rather than preimplantation because it is a "very very precise time" in embryogenesis and "that is the stage when an embryo becomes an individual." Charo heard this as a philosophical argument rather than a biological description. Hogan's definition implied gastrulation was a "legally significant moment or a socially significant moment." She suggested that the group define "what we're going to work on without necessarily tying ourselves to technical terms that have been used in arguments about philosophical status."[18]

This exchange was typical of the problems that preoccupied the panel in the following months. Not only would the definition of the embryo remain uncertain, but also the epistemic basis of its definition. There was disagreement over whether *embryo* referred to a biological entity "out there," to an emergent ethico-legal problem, or to a moral philosophical construction. Nevertheless, there was almost unequivocal agreement from the outset that the fundamental question before the panel was the moral status of the human embryo, however defined.

WORKING BOUNDARIES

The HERP discussed the fourteen-day boundary extensively. Although it opted not to depart from such a well-established norm, the panel was keen to reinforce the rationale behind it. Most members saw fourteen days as a temporal proxy for underlying biological transformations associated with gastrulation. Indeed, the panel assumed that the fourteen-day limit had always been grounded in the notion that gastrulation represents a fundamental biological point of transition.[19] Patricia King explained, "I understand the fourteen-day rule to have come about only because of the need for a definite period that people could focus on that was related to gastrulation. In other words, fourteen days became a proxy for gastrulation."[20]

The panel spent considerable time discussing whether guidelines ought to rely on a temporal proxy or on the biological event itself. There was strong support for the latter option. Brigid Hogan, an accomplished mouse embryologist, was concerned that the rate of development of the human embryo in vitro might not track its development in vivo. Limiting research to fourteen days might unnecessarily constrain it to stages far earlier than gastrulation. Agreeing, ethicist Ronald Green proposed, "We should put fourteen days out of our discourse and replace that with gastrulation as the marker event."[21] King suggested that in some instances the primitive streak might not emerge at all, in which case the embryo could be cultured indefinitely, since it would never actually cross into the morally significant category of the gastrula. Insofar as a time limit was considered, it was simply because a temporal period was more enforceable and less subject to judgment than a developmental marker.[22] Thus, the panel adopted the reasoning of the AFS Ethics Committee in many respects: Gastrulation was biologically significant, and, therefore, morally significant. The primitive streak was a line drawn by nature that provided a firm foundation for a limit codified in law.

There were, however, important differences in the panel's reasoning. Whereas the AFS committee had moved linearly from biological status to moral status, for the panel, this step was more complex. It was mediated by an explicit democratic theory and an account of right public reason. The panel concluded that gastrulation was a morally significant marker, not because the biological facts gave clear moral answers, but because the preponderance of reasonable moral arguments favored protecting the embryo only once it had reached this stage. The proponent of this approach and arguably the figure who most influenced the panel's recommendations was ethicist Ronald Green.

A professor of religion, values, and ethics at Dartmouth College, Green had been writing on the moral status of the human conceptus for two decades, though primarily in relation to abortion. Green was responsible for a subtle but consequential difference in the ways the panel and the AFS committee approached the primitive streak. Whereas the AFS committee had treated the transition from preembryo to embryo as a transition between natural kinds, the panel approached embryogenesis as a continuum and the scientific demarcation of stages more as a matter of human judgment than natural fact. In this respect, the panel, under Green's guidance, saw scientific descriptions of natural phenomena as analogous to moral reasoning; both were intended to lend order to complex phenomena.[23] The question, then, was whether a given account ordered things in a reasonable way. Because the panel's judgments about moral status would inform public policy, Green argued, no single argument could be decisive as long as there was public disagreement. Choosing the primitive streak as a decisive marker event represented, according to the panel, "a compromise among competing viewpoints."[24]

In making this judgment, the panel described itself as adopting a "pluralistic" approach. This pluralistic approach required that the panel avoid adopting any one criterion, such as genetic diploidy, sentience, or self-awareness, as the defining characteristic of human beings' morally significant status. It instead emphasized "a variety of distinct, intersecting, and mutually supporting considerations. According to this view, the commencement of protectability is not an all-or-nothing matter but results from a being's increasing possession of qualities that make respecting it (and hence limiting others' liberty in relation to it) more compelling."[25]

Green argued that the role of the public ethicist was not to identify the single best argument, but to pragmatically balance the various arguments: "Matters of determining the status of any kind of an entity or being really follow from a very complex, pluralistic, and essentially pragmatic process of thought and decision on all of our parts as members of society, in which a variety of criteria interact and work together to lead to a mounting sense of concern and ultimately to judgments of protectability about entities."[26]

The panel's report affirmed this construction of the role of public bioethics bodies in facilitating this process:

> Americans hold widely different views on the question of the moral value of prenatal life at its various stages. These views are often based on deeply held religious and ethical beliefs. It is not the role of those who help form

public policy to decide which of these views is correct. Instead, public policy represents an effort to arrive at a reasonable accommodation to diverse interests.[27]

The key concept here was the notion of the "reasonable."[28] The panel's reasoning leaned directly on the idea of public reason developed by American political theorist and moral philosopher John Rawls. Green had been a student of Rawls and had adopted and developed many of his teacher's ideas. It was through Green's influence that Rawlsian ideas figured so centrally in the panel's reasoning.[29] Although the panel's report explicitly cites Rawls only once, its "pluralistic" approach and the construction of right public reason in which it was grounded were deeply informed by the Rawlsian approach. Citing Rawls, the report stated,

> Public policy employs reasoning that is understandable in terms that are independent of a particular religious, theological, or philosophical perspective, and it requires a weighing of arguments in the light of the best available information and scientific knowledge.[30]

As noted above, Rawls developed the idea of public reason as an amendment to his theory of justice to accommodate what he called "reasonable pluralism"—reasonable disagreement between citizens on moral questions. He distinguished "reasonable pluralism" from "simple pluralism," the latter being closer to the raw politics of the public square.[31]

Rawls's idea of public reason requires that citizens provide justifications that all other citizens will find reasonable.[32] Public reasons must be purified of arguments that make recourse to private moral beliefs (or "comprehensive doctrines"), and, under ideal conditions, public reasons will be convincing to every reasonable person. In an ideal sense, public reason is the "view from everywhere"—a view Rawls constructed in his concept of the original position.[33] But under less than ideal conditions, the norm of public reason justifies excluding nonpublic reasons from deliberative politics; for instance, reasons that are grounded in religious views. Thus, for Rawls, public reason is a framework of rational engagement, but also a duty of citizenship, a kind of social contract that undergirds the legitimacy of democratic politics.[34]

Green argued that the panel's task was to sort public from nonpublic reasons and, in so doing, stand in for an ideally democratic and ideally rational community of judgment. Put in practical terms, the panel's pragmatic, "pluralistic" approach positioned it as an instrument for disciplining "simple pluralism" into "reasonable pluralism"—for designating and imposing criteria for the kind of reasons that must be taken into account in public discourse. Guided by Rawls's notion of public reason, the panel set about to determine what (and whose) arguments should be included in its pluralistic approach. The panel positioned itself as an arbiter of public reason, judging moral arguments not on their merits but on their reasonableness.[35] Arguments were given greater weight if the panel imagined a reasonable public would find them convincing. The more arguments drew on shared premises, the more weight they were given.

In his earlier scholarship on abortion, Green had argued that the moral questions surrounding abortion were misguided because of the way they approached the question of when in development personhood begins. Given that the criteria for personhood were essentially contested, "either we have once again entered a realm of irresolvable value conflict or something is wrong with the way the question is being approached."[36] He maintained that it was the latter, describing his insight as a "Copernican revolution" in thinking about life's beginning.[37] He suggested that in arguments over who we regard as a person, insufficient attention was being given to the "we." Drawing heavily on Rawls's concept of the original position, Green argued that the "we" must be regarded as a "community of judgment" in which only the qualified can participate: "The 'we' here does not include all who are human but only reasonably mature individuals with roughly 'normal' intellectual and reasoning powers, the kinds of persons we allow to serve on juries or to make social decisions generally."[38]

Under Green's direction, the panel positioned itself as a judge of reasons and arbiter of the community of judgment. By limiting its balancing decisions to "good reasons," the rational integrity and political legitimacy of the community of judgment were simultaneously safeguarded. Thus, the panel assumed the role of standing in for the community of judgment. As an appendage of the democratic state, it claimed authority over the question of moral status on behalf of society, constructing itself as representing the public by representing public reason. First sorting public from nonpublic reasons, it assembled those reasons it deemed reasonable until a preponderance tipped the scale.

In weighing arguments, the panel privileged those it thought could be challenged only through recourse to background beliefs, or, in Rawls's terminology, "comprehensive doctrines." Reasons that were incontestable except by violating norms of public reason were given the most weight. Conversely, the panel excluded arguments that seemed to make recourse (whether explicit or implicit) to comprehensive doctrines, particularly religious ones. For instance, the panel judged that "arguments for the embryo's status that rely on continuity, personal identity or the theological concept of ensoulment" are unreasonable because the individual is only definitively present at gastrulation—before that, the embryo can spit into two.[39] On the other hand, the panel felt that the belief that the embryo is not a person until after the formation of the primitive streak is reasonable because it is justified by reference to universal and incontestable scientific reasons, not controverted moral or theological ones.[40] The panel treated accounts that invoked scientific evidence as being closer to public reasons—closer to the "view from everywhere" with which all reasonable minds would necessarily agree.[41] By rejecting reasons that depended "for [their] force on a particular philosophical, religious, or ideological perspective" and "weigh[ing] arguments in the light of the best facts available and the best scientific information,"[42] the panel concluded that it is "*unreasonable* to put the claims of the preimplantation embryo before those of true persons."[43] In short, the panel drew the circle of reasonable pluralism and placed science at its center.

PRACTICING PUBLIC REASONS

The HERP also drew on Rawls's notion of reflective equilibrium. The panel treated the reproductive practices of citizens as equivalent to publicly given moral positions. The panel treated practices like the use of IVF and the intrauterine device (IUD) as a proxy for reasons; it treated them as a demonstration of the performance of individual moral judgments.

The panel justified this move by drawing on Rawls's notion of reflective equilibrium. Rawls had argued that rational moral actors by their very nature will not tolerate conflicting or rationally inconsistent positions. They will draw their moral beliefs and practices into what he called *reflective equilibrium*. He applied this concept to both the individual moral subject and to the political community as a whole, so that the practices and institutions of the state should reflect the moral positions of the reasonable polity and vice versa.[44]

During the panel deliberations, Green suggested that a task of the public ethicist should be to facilitate the process of arriving at reflective equilibrium by drawing together "theoretical approaches" with "hunches and judgments and practices." The ethicist must "bring these together in an amicable way, to arrive at what one philosopher has called 'reflective equilibrium' where our theory more or less matches some of our most deeply held intuitive judgments about a complex matter, as well as the practices that we commonly use that reflect certain judgments, and so on."[45] Following this line of thinking, the panel treated practices such as clinical IVF and the use of potentially abortifacient contraceptive devices, such as the IUD and the "morning-after" pill, as proxies for widespread moral intuitions about the moral status of the embryo.

Green argued that the notion of the genetic criterion of personhood

> runs up very badly . . . against the widespread acceptance of high rates of natural mortality at the preembryo level, something that few people seem to be exercised about. It runs up against certain widely practiced birth control methods, the IUD as an example, and morning-after pills and things of this sort, which are widely accepted in our society and which work essentially by preventing implantation in most cases. So a lot of judgments in reality—the absence of concern over the high mortality of pre-embryos in the natural course of things, these other practices—suggest that this view doesn't conform very well to the variety of our moral hunches and intuitions and practices.[46]

This "absence of concern" was translated in the report into a forceful source of reasons that outweighed arguments for protecting the embryo from the point of fertilization.[47] Thus, the concept of reflective equilibrium allowed the Panel to translate normal practices into normative positions by serving as the philosophical mouthpiece for the masses. By attributing reflective equilibrium to the individual citizen (between her moral beliefs and practices), private practices could be translated by the public bioethics body into public reasons. Then, the bioethics body could move on to achieving reflective equilibrium within political institutions by bringing science policy in line with the public's (unspoken) reasoning.

In treating practices as reasons, the panel dramatically expanded the community of reason-givers. Citizens became participants in moral deliberation, not through giving voice to public reasons, but through their private practices as patients and consumers. As such, the panel altered the conditions of participation so that the private reproductive practices of American women were transformed into participatory input into a deliberative process of policy making. A deliberative democratic public had been constituted out of a collection of consumers of particular technologies. By attributing to the citizen a commitment not only to ethical coherence among her own practices and beliefs, but also a desire that public policy reflect her (putative) positions, the panel transformed the use of technologies—and consumer participation in reproductive markets—into a medium of democratic expression. It made this move without asking any questions about what convictions, experiences, ambivalences, constraints, or social circumstances might inform individuals choices about these technologies. While the panel made much of the need to draw upon a plurality of appropriately public reasons, it discounted the capacity of the public to supply those reasons for itself. Indeed, the panel actively constructed the public as incapable of doing this, thus legitimating the notion that a public bioethics body can, should, and must stand in for the public.

REPRESENTING THE IGNORANT

The HERP did not emphasize public participation in its deliberations.[48] Instead, it treated public engagement primarily as task of public education. The most outspoken proponent of this view was democratic theorist and panel chairman Steven Muller. Muller dismissed the EAB's many public hearings as misguided: "I would much rather see some forums that would involve some of us or all of us in public discussion of our report after we have reached conclusions than to say that we really are so heavily dependent on public opinion that we should solicit the broadest range of even the most ignorant comment."[49] Muller was quick to dismiss unmediated public input, regardless of its form. He and other members of the panel tended to dismiss public expressions of deeply held moral sentiments as irrelevant to (and inhibiting) the panel's work.[50] For instance, he referred to the large volume of correspondence received by the panel, most of which was critical of human embryo research, as "the hate mail." Presenting the panel's findings to the NIH ACD, Muller noted that the panel had received over 25,000 pieces of mail, but that the vast majority reflected "not only massive public ignorance, but such ignorance manipulated into public hostility." This was, he argued, because the public does not know what the human embryo *is*. Members of the public "make no distinction between the embryo and the fetus. . . . As a result, the phrase 'human embryo research' conjures up a public image of vivisection, and even of ripping living flesh from the womb. Public statements about ex utero research or in vitro fertilization are, to most of our fellow citizens, incomprehensible gobbledygook in a foreign language."[51]

Muller was optimistic that the report itself might contribute significantly to public understanding. Until that pedagogical work had been accomplished, however, he thought that an ignorant public could contribute little: "The degree to which a public that has hitherto not focused on this topic can be helpful is questionable."[52] Muller saw the panel's task as separating tolerance for free speech from right reason. "Some speech is pure, absolute nonsense," and the role of "representative democracy" (an institutional category in which he included the panel) is to "immediately . . . point out that it is nonsense." This account of political authority fit neatly with Green's account of the ethicist as the arbiter of right public reason.[53]

By invoking public ignorance and the norms of public reason, the panel positioned itself as legitimately standing in for the public. Importantly, the panel explicitly rejected a stakeholder model of representation, instead grounding its claim to legitimacy in the notion that it *knew* best—knew the relevant science and knew how best to reason about its moral meaning. Muller observed that the criticism that the panel was biased toward allowing embryo research was probably accurate but suggested that this did not undermine its legitimacy. Rather, the panel was representative because it more closely approximated an ideally reasonable deliberative community than could ever be achieved in the public square.[54]

Muller's comments on representation aroused criticism. Daryl A. 'Sandy' Chamblee, acting deputy director for Science Policy and Technology Transfer and the NIH official responsible for HERP-related public correspondence, received numerous letters from members of the public expressing concern that their views were not adequately represented in the panel's work.[55] One made reference to Muller's remark about the panel's bias and inquired why "there are no representatives on [the panel] from the pro-life community."[56] In a four-page point by point response to the letter, Chamblee wrote,

> Panel members were selected for their knowledge, expertise, experience, perspectives, and for the thoughtful and careful approach they would take in fulfilling their important and sensitive assignment. They were not selected as representatives of particular interest groups . . . or proponents of specific viewpoints . . . members were not polled in advance for their views about the acceptability of this research.[57]

The letter also objected to the use of the term *preembryo* and to the links between panel members and the AFS, which had been "responsible for propagandizing" the concept. The concerned citizen wrote, "It is the 'pre-embryo' hoax that is the foundation for 'ethical' permissions for embryo and IVF research."[58] Chamblee responded that *preembryo* was simply shorthand for the preimplantation embryo and that, regardless of nomenclature, "the term will not be employed as a way of sidestepping the most challenging aspect of the panel's charge, i.e., addressing the competing views held about the moral status of the human embryo."[59]

Chamblee was quite concerned by the letter. She located the section in the transcript that she believed the letter was referring to, and hand-delivered a copy of the correspondence to NIH director Harold Varmus. In a cover memo she wrote, "I think this inquiry underscores the fact that the Panel members and staff have to be extremely careful in remarks made in a public forum on the issue of human embryo research. It is an extremely sensitive topic and every word that we say about it is likely to be scrutinized very carefully."[60]

Both panel and NIH leadership worried over their choice of words, and not only because they did not wish to appear to be "sidestepping" difficult problems. Panel members were generally favorable toward to term *preembryo*, and they unequivocally agreed with the ontological distinction it codified. Nevertheless, they opted early on not to use the term out of concern that the panel might be accused of obfuscating an important moral question. Yet, the panel remained concerned that the public was so ignorant of the subject of their deliberations that scientifically "accurate" language was "incomprehensible gobbledygook in a foreign language."

Political theorist, Duke University president, and member of both the panel and the ACD, Nannerl Keohane echoed these concerns: "I think some of the misperceptions and some of the controversy that this panel has clearly generated have to do with the way in which the name itself was framed—human embryo research. . . ."[61] Suggesting that the problem of public (mis)understanding could have been solved by giving the panel a different name, she noted that "most people who take the time to understand what we are talking about do not regard the single fertilized cell or the immediate cells which derive from it as an embryo." Noting that this would not change the minds of those dogmatically committed to the idea that "fertilization immediately creates a being which has the same moral status as a person," she suggested that for everyone else's sake, "it would be a good idea to use terminology which avoids the misperception that may get in the way of understanding what it is that we are trying to achieve."[62]

SELLING SCIENCE

NIH leadership echoed the HERP's worries about public ignorance and the problems it posed. These worries were the main focus of discussion at the December 1, 1994, meeting of the Advisory Committee to the Director (ACD) at which the panel presented its report. In presenting the HERP's policy recommendations, panel member and University of California at San Francisco professor of medicine and medical ethics Bernard Lo underscored how important the panel felt it was to bring human embryo research "under the aegis of NIH." Doing so, he suggested, would be an important "way to reassure the public that it was being carried out in a responsible and thoughtful way."[63] Other members of the group worried that oversight mechanisms would be ineffective as long as the public was opposed to the research itself. Numerous members of both the HERP and the ACD called for an "incremental" approach that would coordinate "public education" with opening up areas of research so that the public's reasoning could "catch up" with the panel's. This discussion suggested a necessary and inevitable evolution of public opinion toward being favorable to the research, even if public opinion lagged behind both the science and more enlightened attitudes about it. The ACD was confident that these changes in attitude would come, and that policy should therefore be made in anticipation of them, because they were confident that scientific advances and associated medical benefits would inevitably flow from human embryo research. In the words of ACD member and microbiologist Gail Cassell, "the benefits are unquestionable."[64]

Patricia King, who dissented on this point, worried that the panel's recommendations would be "too far out in front of public understanding and public consensus," a problem that "had only been heightened since the November elections" in which the Republicans had won a majority in Congress. However, she was confident that, "in time, the public will be where I think the members of the panel are already in understanding the importance of the research."[65] Other members of the group were similarly wary that Congress could "stop your money, your grants—that sort of thing—and make life generally uncomfortable."[66]It was imperative, then, "if *we* think this is the right thing to do . . . to bring the public along and to try to talk about how to inform the public."[67] It would be necessary to adjust the report to make it "as palatable as possible to the general public."[68] The group generally affirmed that the public would need to be educated in order to be able to see the reasonableness of the panel's recommendations. In a discussion of whether the NIH ought to defer to public concerns about specific forms of research, Green suggested that deferring to such perspectives would require "giving up . . . what was really our guiding concern, and that is facilitating research that is ethically permissible under reasoned judgment."[69] Muller affirmed the value of public deliberation in bringing public "unreason" into line with the panel's more enlightened "reasoned judgment." Suggesting that if the NIH organized a series of public engagement exercises—"a sort of series of public conferences where people could talk" about issues such as creating embryos for research—progress could be made, "not because they would resolve the issue, but because so many people would learn so much more."[70]

Numerous members of the ACD affirmed that, as the science progressed, the public would see its merits. The problem was, however, that only scientific experts (and those who had learned from them) could see the technological future that public ignorance was standing in the way of. Thus, the political challenge was getting the public to "see" like science so that citizens' unreasonable moral views would become reasonable ones. The NIH director invited the various institute directors around the table to speculate about what biomedical advances might arise in their respective domains as a result of human embryo research. Janice Zeller, a member of the National Advisory Council for Nursing Research, expressed skepticism that public opposition was purely an expression of ignorance of scientific facts and future biomedical benefits: "Letters that were submitted by apparently informed, educated individuals said that they still felt it was alarming and ethically wrong for us to favor and support this research."[71] Green disagreed with the premise that such individuals were informed:

One thing that is very, very important is that people have to understand what the issues here are and *what the facts are*. Many of the letters that we received mistook what we were dealing with.... I think *when people come to understand that we are dealing with the preimplantation embryo*, an embryo that is routinely discarded in the normal course of life—the figure that I mentioned of 60 percent and so on—when they fully begin to understand that, some of their *feeling and thinking will change* on this, when they see that some of the concerns they have, even with regard to the issues of abortion, are perhaps *irrelevant* here."[72]

The political imperative, according to the group, was to engender public deference to scientific judgment for now, since the public would inevitably come to see the error of its ways once the scientific potential of human embryo research paid off. The challenge was navigating this lag, moving forward in research without public support on the assumption that the public would retrospectively support it once it eventually saw the benefits of the research. Green continued, "Moving forward with research that proves truly beneficial or that shows its medical and practical benefits and that shows that we can practice research of this sort responsibly without undermining our humanity—as we do that, people's concerns about ends and means will moderate, I believe, but you can't do that unless you begin the research."[73]

The group spoke at length about the duty to educate the public specifically so that this presumably inevitable shift in thinking would take place. Edwin Rubel of the University of Washington suggested that "education of congressional representatives and congressional staffs" would "ward off the bombshells." Echoing the notion that the opposition derived from public misunderstanding of the nature of the research, he suggested that another strategy would be "to kind of rename this from human embryo research to fertilization research, which I think would defuse some of this."[74]

NIH adopted this strategy in preparing the press for the release of the report, educating reporters to see the embryo—and the ethical problems associated with its use in research—as smaller than they might imagine. A week before the release, the NIH held a briefing for science writers. At that briefing, every journalist was handed a sheet of white paper with a tiny dot in the middle and informed that the embryo that would be the object of research was no bigger than that nearly invisible dot.[75] This vivid (for being nearly invisible) representation of the embryo was repeated in many contexts, including in the report of the panel itself, which noted that the early-stage human embryo is "significantly smaller than the period at the end of this sentence."[76]

A slippage emerged between talk about educating the public and convincing it, what came to be referred to by numerous members of the discussion as "selling" the public on the importance of the research. Ralph Snyderman, dean of the Duke University School of Medicine, criticized the idea of opening up research incrementally. Drawing a distinction between "scientific incrementalism and political incrementalism," he suggested that, though the latter was certainty warranted, the former was not:[77] "We need to decide where the science is and then sell the report."[78]

Edwin Rubel of the University of Washington agreed. He suggested that "the best defense is a good offense." In a statement that captured the interchangeability of the notions of "educating" and "selling" the public in the discussion, he said, "It seems to me that to avoid the problems that Dr. Muller brought up in his opening statement [about the fact that scientifically enlightened discourse is "incomprehensible gobbledygook in a foreign language" to the ignorant public], that congressional staffs, the lay public, and Congress all *have to be sold it or educated* very, very thoroughly in terms of what are the benefits to mankind of this kind of research."[79]

Green affirmed this judgment about the need to engender public deference to science but elevated it from the level of political strategy to ethical imperative. Edward Stemmler, of the Association of American Medical Colleges, asked Green, "Is there an ethical question that comes from the knowledge that you are moving into an arena in which there is enormous ethical and moral controversy and in which a position taken without some due sensitivity to that is unethical?"[80] Green responded that attending to ethical disagreement was an ethical obligation because it had tactical implications for getting the right and reasonable position accepted in politics and policy. He said, "I believe the Roman Catholic tradition has a word for that. It is called prudence. Yes, I think the answer is very much that, that an ethics that ignores those realities and ends up defeating your purposes, in this case of facilitating research and improvements—that is a profound ethical question, that you have to consider your strategy and your tactics."[81]

SCIENTIFIC CERTAINTY OR SOCIAL IGNORANCE?

Throughout the extensive discussions at the December 1 and 2 ACD meetings, only one person commented that the confidence of the committee in the rightness of its judgments might be misplaced. On the second day, Ralph Snyderman stated,

In the discussions of education, which I'm totally in favor of, I think we ought to recognize that some of the individuals that need to be educated are ourselves as well. We need to understand that moving into this area is at least as big a step as was moving into recombinant DNA and gene therapy. In the mind of the public, I think it will be even bigger. As we go out and educate, I think we ought to be humble and understand that we also will be educated.

The modest suggestion that engaging the public should be considered a two-way street was the only one of its sort in the entirety of the panel's deliberations. I have argued that the panel's confidence in its judgments derived from the conviction that scientific reasons are exemplary of public reasons, and the public must therefore defer to ethical evaluations grounded in scientifically authoritative assessments. This was not a cynical position: It reflected a genuine and deep conviction about the fundamental unreasonableness of public concerns, and a thoroughgoing confidence in the panel's own construction of what forms of knowledge and modes of reasoning underwrote its own democratic legitimacy. This is evident in some of Chamblee's letters. Despite being particularly cautious not to dismiss public concerns out of hand (and worrying that panel members such as Steven Muller were doing this too overtly), Chamblee also readily dismissed certain public concerns as reflections of simple scientific ignorance. Numerous people wrote that they were concerned that the NIH might fund research on human parthenogenesis.[82] NICHD director Duane Alexander had specifically included parthenogenesis as an issue for the panel to address. Chamblee responded to all of these letters in the same way, dismissing moral concerns as irrelevant by virtue of being scientifically ignorant. She wrote, "I believe that these concerns arise from a misunderstanding of the biological potential of parthenotes . . . extracorporeal development of a human parthenote beyond . . . a few hundred cells is not possible biologically."[83] On June 16, 1994, a group of thirty-five senators wrote to Varmus expressing similar concerns about the HERP. Among these was the charge that the NIH was interpreting the *NIH Revitalization Act*'s language on IVF research too liberally. The HERP was discussing experiments that went well beyond the boundaries of IVF and posed "grave ethical problems of their own."[84] Research on parthenogenesis was offered as a specific example.

In a six-page letter, Varmus responded with virtually the same language that had been used in the many letters the NIH sent to private citizens. He suggested that parthenogenesis was an area of research about which there had been "much misapprehension in the public mind." Ethical concerns arose from a "misperception of the biological potential of parthenotes," which cannot progress "beyond a stage consisting of a few hundred cells."[85]

The congressmen were nonplussed. They replied with a detailed five-page letter that included several dozen citations of the HERP transcripts. "While you cite public misunderstanding of this area of research," they wrote, "your own letter seems somewhat confused about [parthenogenesis]." Noting that the panel had discussed the use of parthenotes for stem cell derivation, they wrote, "This creation of new life for the sole purpose of vivisection will be abhorrent to many Americans, and not because they *mis*understand what is going on. The fact that parthenotes may not be able to develop beyond an early stage of development is neither here nor there."[86]

On November 8, 1994, Varmus responded with a letter less than a page in length. This time, he invoked the pluralistic balancing of reasons rather than the superior knowledge of elites:

> I respect the fact that your personal beliefs about when personhood begins may preclude your agreement with the conclusions and recommendations of the Panel. . . . As the Panel acknowledges in its report, the development of public policy in a pluralistic society requires a consideration and balancing of diverse beliefs and interests.[87]

Even as Varmus put pen to page, a test of the panel's theory of democratic representation was in the making. November 8, 1994, was election day. By its end, the Republican party had won control of Congress, and the distribution of power in Washington was significantly altered. A week later, Varmus received a response. No longer in need of the rhetorical force of numbers, it bore the signature of a single congressman, Robert K. Dornan (R-CA). Less than five sentences in length, its message was crisp: "Given the new realities of Congress . . . let it be known that we plan to use every legislative means available to prevent federal funds from being spent on grotesque research of this nature. I hope you will keep this in mind as you consider the recommendations of the Human Embryo Research Panel."[88]

REGULATING REASON

President Clinton was more inclined to defer to public opinion than to the HERP's putatively public reasons. When the White House caught wind of the panel's tentative conclusions in the fall of 1994, Clinton's chief of staff, Leon Panetta, called Varmus, demanding that he denounce the panel for recommending that federal funds support the creation of human embryos specifically for research. Varmus refused.[89] On December 2, 1994, the ACD approved the HERP report and released it publicly. Within hours, Clinton issued an executive order prohibiting the creation of human embryos for research using federal funds. A year later, during congressional negotiations over the NIH budget, United States House Appropriations Subcommittee on Labor, Health and Human Services, Education, and Related Agencies members Jay Dickey (R-AR) and Roger Wicker (R-MS) wrote an amendment to the 1996 spending bill to prohibit the use of Department of Health and Human Services funds for any experiment that would create, harm, or destroy any embryo that was not already protected under the human subjects research regulations at 45 C.F.R. 46. From 1995 onward, the Dickey–Wicker amendment has been attached as a rider to every subsequent HHS appropriations bill. It remains in force.

The Human Embryo Research Panel offers a remarkable example of Rawls's idea of public reason put into practice. The HERP drew on the AFS committee's notion of the preembryo but skirted controversy over the term itself by assessing claims, not in terms of truth-to-nature, but by whether they comported with what it judged to be the norms of right public reason. It looked to the rational acuity of the ethicist to segregate public reasons from private beliefs, using the universality of the scientific "view from nowhere" as its touchstone. The panel's full-blown theory of public reason grounded the AFS committee's notion of the priority of (scientifically authorized) ontological judgments. Drawing on Rawls, the panel drew a circle of reasonable pluralism and placed science at its center. In so doing, the panel treated moral views that it saw as deriving either from religion-inflected perspectives or from scientific ignorance as nonpublic reasons and excluded them from its deliberations.

In this way, the panel claimed to be more capable of performing right public reasoning than the public itself. The panel reconstructed moral reasons out of the public's practices; for instance, by treating the use of contraceptive devices as an unequivocal affirmation of the embryo's insignificant moral status and, by logical extension, an endorsement of human embryo research. At the same time, the panel dismissed the public voices that spoke against its judgments, particularly those it could construct as unreasonable.

Yet, the panel's principled project of narrowing the range of debate ran up against the realities of political power. In constructing itself as standing in, it alienated those whose voices the panel deemed it unnecessary to give ear. The panel was chastised for excluding perspectives that were critical of human embryo research, particularly religious ones. Its approach elicited significant pushback from members of Congress, and ultimately led to a legislative ban on federal funding for human embryo research. As we shall see, the controversy touched off by the Human Embryo Research Panel grew significantly more intense with the remarkable scientific developments of the last few years of the twentieth century.

4

CLONING, KNOWLEDGE, AND THE POLITICS OF CONSENSUS

n February 1997, nearly two decades after Louise Brown was born, another birth announcement from the U.K. made international headlines. The *Observer* broke the story of a biological event unprecedented in the history of mammalian life: the asexual reproduction of an adult mammal. This time, there was no moving story of infertility conquered, no narrative of nature made whole. The birth announcement, made in the pages of *Nature*, informed the world of the first asexually produced mammal made from another adult mammal: a Scottish sheep named Dolly.[1] Two years later, researchers at the University of Wisconsin at Madison announced that they had cultured embryonic stem cells from human in vitro embryos.[2] This gave new significance to somatic cell nuclear transfer (SCNT), the technique that had produced Dolly, as a potential source of genetically tailored embryonic stem cells.

This chapter explores the debates that unfolded as a result of the creation of Dolly in 1996, and the derivation of human embryonic stem cells in 1998. During this period, human embryo research became an important area of federal policy as the hopes and fears surrounding human cloning and human embryonic stem cell (hESC) research pushed it to the forefront of American politics. Given the wide-ranging technological possibilities associated with cloning and hESCs, human embryo research drew greater attention from a broad political constituency. As the federal government reacted to the scientific developments of the late 1990s, debates transcended reproductive medicine and dwelt more generally on the public goods associated with the federal support of biomedical research.

As Congress and the White House debated what interventions were appropriate and what possibilities were already foreclosed by existing law, they encountered a strange set of problems: disagreements about what the controverted laboratory objects *were*. In the 1980s and early 1990s, the early embryo (or "preembryo") was generally treated as a fixed biological entity regardless of where and how it was produced. But after 1997, the discourse began to shift. Some characterized hESCs and cloned embryos produced though SCNT as products of human artifice, unprecedented in nature, and, therefore, materially (and morally) distant from the human embryo. They treated questions of moral status as subsidiary to questions of ontological status. Some claimed that because the SCNT-derived embryo was a product of engineering with no natural precedent, it was a technological artifact. Not easily classified as a natural kind, it could not be ontologically dissociated from the laboratory process that produced it. Others saw it as an expression of natural biological potencies, even when activated through technical means, and even if the resulting entity was less than fully functional. That it was the product of human manipulation was irrelevant; in form and potential, it was a product of its biological nature and should be approached as such for ethical purposes. In short, the question, "What *is* it?" became tied up with the laboratory origins and the larger social circumstances of these new biological entities. Moral disagreement often took the form of competing ontological interpretations, which elicited corollary questions about who is in a position to authoritatively answer questions about ontological status.

Importantly, these disagreements emerged most forcefully around discussions of what common premises undergird public reasoning, first in aligning biology and law in policymaking, and second in aligning scientific knowledge and plural moral perspectives in public deliberation. Questions of what the SCNT embryo *is* were simultaneously questions of who should speak for it and with what authority and whether such representations were value laden or value free. As a result, problems of epistemic and ontological representation of the entities in the Petri dish also became problems of representing elite scientific expertise and the pluralistic polity in public deliberation. Normative questions of who can and should speak in democratic deliberation were transmuted into questions of who could best describe what a complex laboratory materiality *is*, of what role such descriptions should play in ethical evaluation and public deliberation, and thus of the right relationship between epistemic and democratic authority.

I argue that these questions of "who knows" became seamlessly joined to questions of how to provide representation for a divided polity. Moral arguments were increasingly made in the authoritative language of facts, even as specific knowledge claims were challenged as value-laden politics masquerading as value-neutral fact. This was because, despite deep disagreements on matters both epistemic and moral, both sides of the debate were committed to the notion that moral evaluation depends on ontological (i.e., scientific) clarity and that assessing the facts of the matter and determining their meaning in moral terms are distinct processes, subject to different criteria of credibility and authority. At the same time, particular constructions of fact were endlessly contested, often by challenging the credibility and expertise of the person advancing them. Thus, even as particular fact claims were "politicized," the ideas of factual knowledge as a value-free space and ontological clarity as an essential foundation for public moral reasoning were consistently affirmed. This posture was at once epistemological and political: it reflected the notion that the foundations of public reasoning must rely on shared premises and shared language, grounded in (and disciplined by) an authoritative account of the material world. Thus, in this chapter, I continue to develop the larger argument of the book that American imaginations of the forms of public reason adequate to contend with morally complex problems in the biosciences have taken shape around a tacit democratic theory that privileges the role of scientific authority in supplying the terms—and thus the parameters—of public debate. As this chapter demonstrates, such an imagination is reinscribed even (and especially) where particular scientific claims are challenged as illegitimate politicizations of science.

NEW KINDS, NEW GENEALOGIES

Dolly was one of several million lambs born in 1996 in a country where sheep outnumber humans, but her birth was a singularity.[3] She was born on July 5 at the Roslin Institute, a veterinary research facility in the countryside outside Edinburgh. She was cloned from a mammary epithelial cell, an adult somatic cell from the mammary gland. This cell was drawn from a cell culture that had been in existence for some years. The donor sheep—the original to the clone—had died years before; the donor cell was taken from a laboratory cell line. In a moment of laboratory humor, the cloned sheep was given a name that referred to her mammary origins; her namesake, Dolly Parton, was apparently known to the Roslin team as much for her cleavage (which, as it happens, was artificial) as for her country music.

Dolly had been produced through a process called somatic cell nuclear transfer, in which an oocyte (egg) was harvested from a donor animal. The oocyte was then enucleated: a pipette was inserted into the oocyte, and the pronucleus (containing the maternal genetic material) was removed. The nucleus of a somatic cell was taken from another donor and transferred into the enucleated oocyte. The nucleus of the somatic cell provided the full complement of nuclear genetic material. The oocyte was then "activated" with a chemical and electrical stimulus, and it began to divide.

In an effort to demonstrate unequivocally that Dolly was the product of human artifice, her creators employed a variety of lineage-defying techniques. The sheep was generated from an oocyte taken from a Scottish Blackface ewe. The genetic material was removed from the oocyte and replaced with the nucleus of a cell from the udder of a Finn Dorset ewe. Since these varieties of sheep have very different appearances, one had only to look at Dolly to see that her genetic heritage came from the Finn Dorset cell, not the Blackface oocyte donor. After the newly constructed cell began to divide, the resulting embryo was transferred to the womb of a Scottish Blackface ewe so that there would be no question whether she was Dolly's genetic mother. One of 277 cloning attempts using mammary epithelium, and one of 29 embryos transferred to recipient ewes, Dolly was the sole live lamb produced.[4]

Shortly after Dolly was announced, the Oregon National Primate Research Center at Oregon Health Sciences University (now the Oregon Health & Science University) revealed that it had produced monkeys through nuclear transfer, though with blastomeres from early embryos rather than fully differentiated adult somatic cells. The announcement was seen as an indication that primate cloning, including human cloning, was in the offing.

The birth of Dolly made headlines around the world. SCNT was initially seen as paving the way to a radical new era of reproduction in the laboratory, but within a short time, it was the nonreproductive applications of SCNT that became a primary focus of debate. Scientists thought that if SCNT could be made to work with human cells, it could be used to generate custom-made immunocompatible tissues for cell therapy. The patient would donate a somatic cell, an embryo would be created through SCNT, and cells would be harvested. Because these cells would be virtually genetically identical to the patient who supplied the cell, they would likely be accepted by the patient's immune system as "self."[5]

Interest in this hypothetical application of SCNT was redoubled when, in late 1998, a group at the University of Wisconsin led by James Thomson announced that they had cultured human embryonic stem cell lines.[6] The cell lines were derived from the inner cell mass of blastocyst-stage human embryos (roughly five days postfertilization). The Wisconsin group used embryos left over from clinical IVF. At the blastocyst stage, the embryo has "compacted" into a hollow spherical structure. The sphere is composed of a one-cell-thick layer surrounding a fluid-filled cavity. In normal embryogenesis, this spherical structure, called the trophoblast, will give rise to the extra-fetal tissues, such as the placenta. A small mass of cells accumulates at one place on the inner surface of this spherical structure, and this mass of cells, called the inner cell mass (ICM), is thought to give rise to the cell lineages that form the body of the developing fetus. In hESC derivation, the trophectoderm is ruptured, and the ICM is dissected out, destroying the embryo. The ICM is then cultured through a series of transformations or "passages." The process, if successful, produces a line of cells that is immortal, self-renewing, and capable (in theory) of giving rise to every tissue type in the human body. hESCs appear to be an artifact of culture; they are not identical to the cells of the ICM, and equivalent cells have not been observed in nature.[7]

In a simultaneous announcement, another research group led by John Gearhart at Johns Hopkins University described similar cells cultured from the germ cells of electively aborted human fetuses. Gearhart's cells seemed to have roughly the same properties and were discussed alongside Thomson's cells, but given their different source, most considered them to raise a different set of ethical and regulatory issues.[8]

The derivation of hESCs was not unexpected. Similar cells from mouse embryos had been cultured in 1981. These cell lines had been an exceptionally productive resource in a variety of research areas, including genetics and cell and developmental biology, and had been used as a therapeutic tool to treat human disease models in mice with some success. ESC lines had also been derived from a number of other mammals, including nonhuman primates in 1995.[9] Robert Edwards had imagined culturing primordial stem cells from in vitro human embryos as far back as the early 1980s.[10] In 1994, hESC derivation from human blastocysts was a scientific possibility that the Human Embryo Research Panel (HERP) considered quite realistic and had addressed in its deliberations.

Precedents notwithstanding, the news of Thomson's and Gearhart's research was heralded as a profound achievement. Responding to scientific enthusiasm, the press offered unrestrained speculation about the meaning of this achievement for human health. A *San Francisco Chronicle* headline declared that the breakthrough "may yield a variety of cures within next ten years."[11] The Associated Press published a story titled "Steps Taken Toward Growing Organs."[12] The optimism of the press was due to the perceived promise of these cells as a therapeutic tool, an idea that had been primed by earlier discussions about SCNT as an individually tailored source of cells and tissues for cell therapy. Indeed, the Thomson paper concluded by drawing attention to the promise of hESCs as a bridge from bench to bedside: "Progress in basic developmental biology is now extremely rapid; human ES [embryonic stem] cells will link this progress even more closely to the prevention and treatment of human disease."[13]

SCNT and hESC derivation pushed the imagined experimental uses of the human embryo further from reproduction-related research toward tissue engineering for cell therapy. As reproductive medicine slipped off the research agenda, IVF and its associated practices, including in particular the production of excess embryos, became background social facts, naturalized to the imagined research projects as a source of biological materials. The potential beneficiaries of the research were, according to its proponents, innumerable: Myriad diseases and a multitude of American citizens stood to be cured through these new technologies.

ENGINEERING A REVOLUTION

Washington responded to Dolly with a sense of urgency. Although Dolly was a significant scientific development, the cloning technique had not yet been applied to primates, let alone humans. It posed no immediate public health threat or risk to human subjects. It had been successful only once in sheep, and significant scientific uncertainty remained about what in fact had been accomplished.[14] Yet, the achievement seemed to portend a technological future that demanded reaction.

On February 24, 1997, President Clinton requested the newly formed National Bioethics Advisory Commission (NBAC) to issue recommendations for a federal response. Reflecting the general sense of urgency, he set the commission a deadline of ninety days. A week later, he issued an executive order banning federal funding of research on human cloning and requested that the private sector adhere to a voluntary moratorium. The next day, Representative Vernon Ehlers (R-MI) introduced two bills, one banning federal funding for human cloning research and the other criminalizing it.[15] These were the first of a number of bills that would be introduced over subsequent years. The same day, the House Subcommittee on Technology of the Committee on Science held a hearing asking, "How far should we go?"[16]

Participants in the House hearing and a parallel Senate hearing characterized Dolly as marking a scientific revolution and so too revolutionizing human self-understanding. Many characterized cloning as novel, unprecedented, and profoundly destabilizing to the moral as well as scientific status quo. Chair of the Subcommittee on Technology Constance A. Morella (R-MD) declared that cloning had the potential to "immeasurably improve our human health condition with radical advances in medical research."[17] Comparisons were made to recombinant DNA, to IVF, to the splitting of the atom, and to the Copernican revolution.[18] For Senator Bill Frist (R-TN), cloning "challenged our imaginations over the centuries," as well as "our basic beliefs about what are the appropriate limits of human knowledge."[19] Ian Wilmut, leader of the research team that had created Dolly, had, in the words of Senator Edward Kennedy (D-MA), "broken the biological equivalent of the sound barrier."[20] Representative Lynn Rivers (D-MI) declared that cloning had brought about a "philosophical watershed."[21] Senator Tom Harkin (D-IA) predicted that cloning "held untold benefits for humankind."[22] To Senator Chris Dodd (D-CT), it was "a remarkable step forward."[23] Wilmut was similarly unrestrained. Responding to a question about the potential of cloning for treating disease, he speculated that in the future, there would be "no limits."[24]

Though few questioned that Dolly's creation marked a revolution, many expressed ambivalence and concern about the new order that such a technology could usher in. To Senator Frist, cloning held the potential for "both good and evil."[25] Senator Jim Jeffords (R-VT) declared, "This research at once completely fascinates me and scares me to death."[26] Senator Kit Bond (R-MO), sponsor of a Senate bill[27] that would ban cloning, was less equivocal: "Human cloning is something that we as a society cannot and should not tolerate."[28]

SCIENCE BEFORE THE LAW

Yet, lawmakers were uncertain about the role of law in shaping the future of this technology. "We are legislators," Jeffords told Wilmut and his co-witness, National Institutes of Health (NIH) director Harold Varmus, "and we have got decide what our role is. . . . Do you have any suggestions as to how far we should go . . . ?"[29] Policymakers approached the question of how to make this emerging domain of research accountable to public ethical norms as simultaneously a question of whether controlling the direction of technological change was within—or beyond—the powers of government. Though not often articulated directly, the latter question was constantly present in the cloning debates.

Although lawmakers had widely varying assessments of the implications of cloning, they tended to tacitly agree that government cannot guide, but only react to, technoscientific change. While some were convinced that urgent regulatory action was required to prevent cloning technology from running amok, others expressed doubt that research could be controlled even if policymakers took action. Senator Jack Reed (D-RI) observed that science "has a momentum of its own that is not easily constrained by what we or any other governmental body does." Echoing the U.S. Supreme Court's assertion in *Diamond v. Chakrabarty* that law cannot hold back science "any more than Canute could command the tides,"[30] Senator Harkin declared that "the march of science" could not be restrained by law: "What utter, utter nonsense to think that somehow we are going to hold up our hands and say 'Stop.'"[31] Furthermore, he insisted, any attempt to intervene in science would not only be futile, but contrary to human virtue. Characterizing science as a wellspring of progress that is natural, necessary, and good, and law as misguided where it contravenes this more righteous authority, he declared, "I think that to attempt to limit human knowledge is demeaning to human nature."[32] Wilmut agreed that "it is not possible or even desirable to regulate the way science progresses or the questions that it asks."

Despite disagreement about whether it was cloning or attempts to regulate cloning research that posed the greater risk to human life, participants in the hearings consistently characterized science as unpredictable, emergent, and governed by its own internal processes. Democratic institutions, therefore, inevitably lagged behind. Chair of the Committee on Science Senator Jim Sensenbrenner (D-WI) made the observation, repeatedly reiterated by others, that, "in the area of cloning embryos, it is obvious that science is ahead of . . . the law, morals and ethics." The notion that law lags behind science was used to assert both the autonomy of science and to delimit political responsibilities. The role of Congress, Sensenbrenner asserted, must be to reconnect them so that "science can carry forward."[33]

The law lag narrative is common in American discourse about science and technology. As an account of sociotechnical change, it runs afoul of the observations of a substantial body of science and technology studies scholarship on the interpenetrations of science and law and the coproduction of technoscientific and normative orders.[34] Here, however, I wish to question not the narrative itself, but the function that it serves in organizing imaginations of the dynamics of technoscientific change and corollary allocations of responsibility in governance.[35] Actors in the debates over cloning tended to interpret the significance of the (putative) law lag in one of two ways. First was the notion (first articulated in the 1930s by William Ogburn) that a disjunction between the creations of science and the institutional custodians of social order, such as law, was a potential source of social disorder. The task of the legislator was to react quickly when unanticipated changes came and adjust the law to accommodate the new. Democracy in this account is always and necessarily reactive, but reacting is considered a responsibility of governance. Society's institutions cannot produce technological revolutions but must respond to them by adjusting law to preserve social order.

Second was the notion that the lag between scientific change and law making is a natural and necessary consequence of science's generative potential, and, in order to preserve this potential, law must largely defer to science's own internal norms. Despite being "scared to death" by cloning, Jeffords was "comforted by the knowledge that throughout time scientific research has produced advances that outpace public discourse about the ethical, legal and social implications of scientific research and development." This was a common sentiment: Initial public response to a novel technology is bound to be unreasonable and counterproductive because the public can no more anticipate the implications of a technology than it can the technology itself. Therefore, in order for policymakers and the public to fulfill their democratic duties, they must rely on scientific experts to constrain the public imagination to focus narrowly on risks that are plausible and governable and avoid regulatory interventions that are likely (according to scientific experts) to inhibit progress. By drawing on scientific expertise, deliberative institutions would ensure that facts preceded values in the formulation of reasoned policy responses. On this view, the immediate governance challenge was not containing an out-of-control technology, but containing a premature legislative response driven by an unreasonable and reactive public. The blunt instrument of law, untempered by scientific knowledge, would inevitably produce a suboptimal sociotechnical order, regardless of its intent.

Both of these accounts constructed the democratic governance of science and technology as necessarily reactive. They differed primarily in their assessments of the extent to which science is self-governing and demands deference from law.

NIH Director Harold Varmus was a vocal proponent of the view that science was best positioned to govern itself because society was always a step behind. He told a Senate subcommittee that "legislation and science frequently do not mix very well"[36] and that Congress therefore often makes its greatest contribution in moments of technological revolution by doing nothing. He pointed to a number of precedents, such as recombinant DNA and gene therapy, where congressional action might have destroyed a nascent field but inaction had allowed the development of a large and productive biotechnology industry and myriad life-improving technologies: "Much deliberation was given to the question raised by the cloning of DNA. . . . The consequence of not having legislation to prevent such research is directly linked to the fact that we now have an extremely vibrant and benefit-generating biotechnology industry in this country."[37]

Representative George Brown (D-CA) also invoked the recombinant DNA controversy. He recalled hearings that the same committee had held exactly two decades before in March 1977, which contributed to a "broad educational process," one that helped Congress leave "the initial ignorance and anxiety behind, giving way to a process of education and rational discussion."[38] By moving slowly, the committee guaranteed that legislative action would lag behind innovation, following science's lead and allowing reasoned deliberation to emerge in the interim. This approach cast Congress as allied with science as an educator of public reason rather than as publicly authorized norm maker with jurisdiction over science.

The law lag was used to characterize the roles and responsibilities of bioethics and its relationship to both science and the public. Lawmakers and witnesses both pointed to public bioethics as being an important tool in the repertoire of government for managing the lag and engendering reasoned deliberation. Pointing to bioethics institutions such as the NBAC and the investments of the Human Genome Project in "ethical, legal, and social issues" research, Senator Jeffords suggested that such mechanisms could respond to impossible-to-anticipate circumstances like Dolly with measured reasoning, thereby mediating between scientific advance and willy-nilly public reaction.[39] Varmus saw the role of public bioethics in similar terms. He applauded President Clinton for asking the NBAC to deliberate for ninety days. In taking this time, the NBAC would enforce a legislative cooling-off period and thus allow time for more reasoned thinking, informed by scientific expertise, to emerge.[40] In these scenarios, technology comes first, and the social norms for governing it are developed in response.

For some, the mediating function of such institutions was especially critical for moments in which public anxiety would prove to be wholly unfounded. Senator Frist pointed to the initial fears around heart transplant surgery in the 1960s: "People were terrified. People did not know what to think. But after a reasoned discussion, after bioethicists helped us address that particular issue, and after it was taken through a balanced and reasoned public discourse, today I can come before you having performed hundreds of heart and lung transplants . . . and thirty years ago, no one knew what to think!"[41] Now, in the age of biotechnology, Frist argued, space for reasoned deliberation was more essential than ever. "The very velocity with which new discoveries of this type are taking place—and in the future they will occur even faster—makes it imperative that reasoned and balanced public discourse proceed alongside scientific discovery."[42]

R. Alta Charo, a lawyer and bioethicist who was also a member of the NBAC and a former member of the HERP, emphasized that the risks associated with cloning included the risks that public reactions posed to science itself. Echoing Varmus, she worried that public reaction would drive policy responses that would in turn frustrate technological futures, futures that the public was incapable of imagining and therefore ought not meddle with. Good governance requires, therefore, that the public, through its representatives, restrain its own undisciplined imagination, deferring to authoritative accounts of the future in order to act where, and only where, those accounts warrant. Charo told the Senate subcommittee, "These kinds of . . . discussions about the scientific advances that are at risk if we were to ban all such forms of research could be more important than any kind of legislation you ultimately come up with, because it will help us to understand what it is we are balancing and make a reasoned choice."[43]

The law lag narrative underwrote accounts of how scientific expertise, public education, and congressional action (or inaction) could together lay the foundation for reasoned deliberation and thus for the right kind of technological future. Both advocates and critics of legislative action saw themselves as adopting a necessarily reactive posture, responding to the unpredictable and sui generis products of technoscientific creativity. In seeing law as necessarily laggard, they treated ethical deliberation as secondary to scientific change. Emerging science and technology determined the bioethical agenda, not the reverse. In practice, this meant that public deliberation and policymaking were made to defer to scientific judgments about present and predicted technological developments. In short, science would declare what technological futures—and thus what public goods—hang in the balance. It would supply the facts (that is, authorized predictions about scientific and technological potentials) that would inform—and thus constrain—public moral deliberation.

The narrative of the law lag was constructed around the notion that technological change is inevitable, irrespective of society's actions. As a consequence, the technology of human cloning was talked about as though it were the most determinate piece of the puzzle, even though it was as yet only a figment of imagination. By contrast, law, policy, and the public sensibilities that might authorize it were seen as provisional and unstable in their convictions because they were being thrown off balance by a scientific revolution. The task of governance, then, was first a task of answering Charo's question: "What it is we are balancing?" In the law lag frame, that was seen as a matter for science to address: To render reasonable judgments about what ought to be done, policymakers and publics needed first to be informed by scientific experts about the nature of the technology and the possible futures it portended. Democracy must delegate to science the authority to define the focus of public debate, and must defer to scientific accounts of what risks and benefits are realistic, before asking whether such risks and benefits are bad or good.

Beneath these moves of delegation and deference were tensions between notions of scientific autonomy and public sovereignty. In what ways did democratic governance extend to science and with what source of legitimacy? In their attempts to construct warrants for public oversight of scientific research, policymakers simultaneously constructed accounts of science's sovereign territory and its constitutional role in defining the parameters of legitimate public reason. First was the notion that the remit (and responsibility) of law to regulate science applied primarily to those moments when scientists act outside of science's self-governing norms. Democratic oversight was for abuses, not quotidian uses, of scientific knowledge, since the former violate public morality, whereas the latter serve the public good by definition. Second was the notion that public intervention demanded epistemic (and, as I demonstrate below, ontological) clarity about what exactly law is seeking to govern. Ethically motivated interventions were justifiable only insofar as the facts were clear in public deliberation. I address these each in turn in the next two sections.

GOVERNING SCIENCE AND ITS OUTLAWS

The specter of public interference in science figured prominently in the debates about cloning, both within and beyond congressional deliberations. Responding to an invocation of Frankenstein's monster during a Senate hearing, Harold Varmus pointed to a different monster: "When I hear that research on cloning is something that ought to be taken away, I shiver."[44] Experts like Varmus argued that the integrity of science requires that it be autonomous and self-governing, particularly if society is to benefit from scientific progress. When policymakers proposed placing constraints on research, others worried that society would be denied important technological benefits as a consequence. While this view reflected a contradiction between the notion that the trajectory of scientific progress was inexorable and the notion that the technological future was fragile and endangered by democratic intervention, the contradiction was occluded by training the focus of public debate away from knowledge production itself and focusing policy instead on the applications (and abuses) of the resulting technologies. This came in two forms: the imagined social benefits that eventually would flow from research (assuming it was not unduly inhibited) and the prospects of the uses of scientific knowledge for purposes that were contradictory to these anticipated future benefits. (People referred to "misuses" of scientific knowledge, which implied that the knowledge itself was intrinsically virtuous, except in the hands of the vicious.)

Imaginations of abuses as exceptional and exogenous had the effect of legitimating "normal" science and its unexceptional uses.[45] The notion that normal science was self-governing and that its powerful tools must be subjected to regulation only when they were applied outside the arena of scientifically authorized practice was crystalized by the idea of "abnormal," apostate science, personified by the rogue scientist. Over the course of the cloning debates, a number of figures represented this rogue. By personifying scientific irresponsibility, these figures were a means for scientists to externalize moral violation, constructing it as an abuse by an individual outside the fold of mainstream science as opposed to a feature of cloning technology itself. What needed regulating, it was felt, was not science, but bad scientists, a distinction which attributed "badness" to individual (criminal) intent and cast normal science as intrinsically virtuous.

A parade of rogue figures emerged throughout the cloning controversy, each of whom had his or her fifteen minutes of fame. They included Panos Zavos, a Cypriot fertility specialist who claimed to have produced a cloned child, Severino Antinori, an Italian fertility specialist, and the Raëlians, a cult that celebrated free love, encounters with extraterrestrials (who travelled in flying saucers), and human cloning. Raël, the Raëlian movement's esteemed leader, testified in a U.S. congressional hearing in 2001. (He is perhaps the only person to have testified before Congress in a white robe, wearing a large medallion, and sporting a topknot.) But before the Raëlians, there was Dr. Seed.

In December 1997, at a conference on human reproductive technologies at the Illinois Institute of Technology's Chicago-Kent College of Law, a scientist named Richard Seed announced his intention to produce a child through cloning. The aptly named Dr. Seed held a Ph.D. in physics from Harvard and had long been involved in research on assisted reproductive technology, though on the margins of the field. He claimed to be assembling an expert team and the necessary financing to proceed with his endeavor. In 1998, a moratorium on federal funding for human SCNT research remained in force, but the private sector was largely unregulated, so there was nothing preventing Seed from proceeding. Seed's announcement prompted something of a media frenzy and earned him an interview with Ted Koppel on ABC's *Nightline*.[46] It also stoked the fires in Congress, eliciting a vigorous debate over the appropriate legislative response.

Seed was seen as the archetypal rogue scientist who, in violating the internal norms of scientific responsibility, reveals the necessity for (and role of) law. The role of law was to contain the threat of the outlaw, thereby preventing abuses of knowledge and technology while also preserving the

integrity of science. With Seed on the scene, views of the role of regulation that had previously appeared to be at odds were unified by the scandalous figure of the rogue scientist. With scientists and public officials'
univocal condemnation of Seed, Senator Dianne Feinstein (D-CA) discerned a politically unified "we": "I think what we're all responding to, as
policymakers, is this gauntlet that's been thrown down by one scientist."[47]
Senator Sherrod Brown (D-OH) declared that the American people were
unanimous on the issue, with the single exception of Richard Seed.[48] Representative Ehlers worried that a rogue like Seed would "simply go blithely
ahead" until he was successful, never mind the parade of "horribles" that
was likely to mark the way.[49]

In fact, this was history repeating itself. Almost exactly nineteen
years earlier, Richard Seed had testified before the EAB together with
his brother Randolph.[50] It was their testimony that had convinced the
board that IVF could not be left unregulated in the private sector.[51] But
like the EAB in 1978, Congress was concerned with not overstepping the
boundaries of scientific autonomy. Law had to be both precise and limited in its proscriptions, lest it inhibit science. Sherrod Brown argued,
"If Congress enacts legislation that goes beyond a strict ban on human
cloning . . . important biomedical breakthroughs may never be available
to the patients who so desperately need them."[52] This statement figured
SCNT research itself as quotidian and the abuse (and abuser) as the
exception. Representative Henry Waxman (D-CA) argued that in light of
a figure like Seed, legislation should be limited to the object of public concern: misapplications of the scientific technique, not the technique itself.
"Somatic cell nuclear transfer is just the latest tool of genetic research. It
is not the same thing as cloning human beings. That should be very clear
to my colleagues."[53]

This emphasis on abuse foregrounded the scientist's intent as the defining moral element. Waxman and others used this emphasis on intent to
draw what came to be an ontological distinction between SCNT used to
benefit human health and SCNT used to commit an act that science and
society alike found abhorrent, namely creating a "cloned human being."
Two kinds of cloning were discussed, each defined by its aims. In Waxman's words, "There is a big difference between cloning a human and
using cloning techniques to produce specialized tissues," and, he argued,

these uses must be kept strictly separate in public deliberation and policymaking. Therefore, it was "important that Congress not hastily ban this technique in an effort to do good which would have bad effects."[54]

This issue, according to Waxman, was not a problem of politics but a matter of scientific precision: A failure to grasp science's own norms would put law in the position of unwittingly violating science's own internal lawfulness: "There is no Democrat or Republican way to approach science. There is no Democrat or Republican way to ban cloning."[55] This was a common framing: To regulate human cloning, Congress first had to get the facts right and ensure that the language of the law followed from the scientific facts of the matter. This almost universally affirmed maxim had two important effects on the relationship between science and democracy in imaginations of right governance. First, scientific certainty (and thus expert knowledge) was seen as a foundation for democratic deliberation. It offered a shared, value-neutral common ground upon which to build public reasoning and policy. For society to react reasonably to an emerging technology, it first had to understand it. Second, it was only in light of a clear understanding of what impacts and consequences the technology would bring, including in generating beneficent technological futures, that society would be able to see where democratic intervention in science was warranted. To prevent the technology from running amok, society must first understand what the technology could do. In practice, the notion that value deliberation is dependent upon having prior epistemic clarity functioned as a means of rendering ethical judgments subsidiary to scientific ones. On the level of allocations of authority, it elevated ontological disagreements over moral ones and positioned custodians of knowledge—that is, scientific experts—in a politically privileged position.

DEMOCRATIC CONSENSUS, BUT ON WHAT?

In a 1998 hearing, Sherrod Brown asserted that "the American people are unanimous in their belief that Congress should prohibit the practice of human cloning."[56] This assertion was made repeatedly by policymakers from both sides of the aisle, as well as by the long parade of witnesses who testified in congressional hearings. Numerous cloning bills were introduced in Congress that reflected this unanimous belief. But at the same time, they reflected disagreement over what exactly this belief was about, namely over what human cloning is and what the term "human cloning" means. The question of what human cloning is was constructed as an ontological question that should be settled by reference to nature. The process of SCNT produced something, but what? The question of what *human cloning* means was constructed as a democratic problem: It was a matter of translating the crude expressions of the general will into precise and necessarily restrictive public policy. Both questions were construed as problems of representation, the former as a matter of accurately (and neutrally) representing in language the technical object of concern, the latter as a matter of giving adequate political representation to public moral concerns when the democratic public did not itself understand the technical details. The fundamental question that policymakers and experts raised again and again was this: When the public opposed human cloning, what precisely was the public opposing?

Thus, lawmakers confronted two problems of representation that were linked in important respects. First was the problem of political representation: of how elected officials should interpret and act upon public opinion. As the custodians of public values, and as representatives answerable to the democratic public, it was incumbent upon them to respond to widespread public concerns. This problem is familiar enough in representative democracy. Yet, in the cloning debates, there was much disagreement over what precisely these public concerns were about. This was the second problem, the problem of representing public reasoning: of matching public concerns about *human cloning* with an epistemically authoritative representation of what human cloning *is*, and thus determining which technical objects and practices the public was concerned about, and which they were not. While it was clear that there was widespread public concern about human cloning, these concerns were variously characterized as applying to the application of SCNT to human biomaterials, the production of a child through the technique, or cloning as represented in Hollywood movies. Members of Congress invoked political representation to justify legislative action—in a democracy the power to act for any reason lies with the people and their representatives. But, in the end, it was representations of public reasoning that most powerfully structured the debates. The notion that Congress needed to bridge the gap between what cloning is and what *cloning* means to the public in order to make law created an opening for scientific experts to define the parameters of right *political* representation. These experts claimed the authority to reconcile public opinion with an accurate account of what was happening in the laboratory, in effect to define what cloning is, to diagnose what the public was misunderstanding, and thus to declare what legislative action in the name of democratic representation was warranted by a now clarified picture of the public's reasoning.

Policymakers and scientific expert both invoked public ignorance to underwrite their respective claims to authority. Echoing the sentiments of Steven Muller, Nannerl Koehane, and other members of the NIH Advisory Committee to the Director (ACD) in the discussion of the HERP's recommendations, they asserted that, in the context of rapid technological change, the public was necessarily ignorant and, therefore, incompetent to make reasonable judgments about policy. Representative Morella, echoing the law lag narrative, characterized public misunderstanding as an inevitable effect of the radically new technology: "No other science issue is as dramatically misunderstood and feared since cloning comes saddled with lingering and troubling concerns about the very dimension of our human existence." The fact of public ignorance meant that in order to make policy, someone had to separate the chaff of public misunderstanding from the wheat of legitimate democratic concerns. While policymakers were charged with acting on behalf of the public will, scientific experts positioned themselves as best able to declare where public concerns aligned (or failed to align) with what was happening in the Petri dish.

Numerous experts asserted that there was a mismatch between what the word *cloning* meant to the public and what it meant to scientists. Even as policymakers characterized their bills as attempts to forestall the damaging effects that a hasty, ignorance-driven public "backlash" would have on science and technology, scientific experts characterized policymakers as subject to the same deficiencies and impulses as the wider public. In the rush to regulate, they warned, lawmakers and the public would impose unwitting and unwarranted constraints on self-evidently ethical science—self-evident at least to those who knew anything about it.

Gillian Woollett of the Pharmaceutical Research and Manufacturers of America expressed concern that public (and congressional) ignorance would lead to a ban on a wide range of uncontroversial activities. She pleaded with the House Committee on Science to make any legislation "as narrow as possible . . . to protect biomedical research and therapy that may involve the cloning of individual cells, genes and tissues."[57] Representative Ehlers affirmed this concern, asserting that it was the policymaker's role to ensure that advancing science and laggard society were brought into alignment. He proposed legislation as a preemptive measure: Policy action would demonstrate that things were being taken care of, thereby both allaying public anxiety and protecting science from the threat that public ignorance would lead to excessive regulation. Describing himself as a scientist working strictly in the interest of science (Ehlers holds a Ph.D. in nuclear physics from the University of California, Berkeley), he said, "I think if we don't ban immediately research on cloning of humans, we are likely to see a strong movement to ban research on cloning in general." His bill would kill two birds with one stone: It would protect science and provide "a golden opportunity to educate the public."[58] His legislation, limited to human cloning by SCNT, would satisfy the public before irreparable damage was done to science by hasty, politics-driven legislation.[59]

However, numerous scientists rejected the notion that policymakers could adequately play this mediational role. They asserted that policymakers such as Ehlers were wielding concepts (and words) in lawmaking whose scientific meanings those policymakers themselves did not fully understand. Some argued that the term *human cloning* was bound to cause confusion, not merely for the masses, but for everyone except the expert elite. In the summer of 1997, a few days after the NBAC issued its report on cloning, a representative of the Biotechnology Industry Organization (BIO, now the Biotechnology Innovation Organization) told a congressional subcommittee that between the NBAC report and various pieces of pending legislation, there were fourteen different definitions of *human cloning*.

Codifying public values in law therefore required terminological precision. Scientists positioned themselves as the relevant authorities to declare when the terms being used in political deliberation were correct and when they aligned (or misaligned) with what the public seemed to have in mind. Michael West, a cell biologist and chief scientist at Advanced Cell Technology, rejected Ehlers's bill as overly broad and technically imprecise because it focused on a technique and not on its (intended) uses. He stated that it "would ban the use of somatic cell nuclear transfer . . . even if the technology is used for purposes completely unrelated to the cloning of a human being." West agreed that "we ought to prevent the cloning of a human being" but worried that Congress was very likely to "overstep the bounds" because policymakers did not understand what "cloning a human being" entailed.[60] SCNT was likely to have important therapeutic applications in engineering "primordial stem cells" for transplantation. Used for this purpose, the technology was laudable, even if under other circumstances it could be abused:

> The problem with some of the pending human cloning bills is that they outlaw or make it a crime to conduct research if it *could possibly* be related to the cloning of a human being even if it is *not*, in fact, conducted for that purpose. They confuse what "might possibly be" with what "is," the "potential" with what is the "actual." This is why they are over broad and threaten biomedical research.[61]

West argued strongly for focusing regulation on prohibiting one potential product of SCNT—a child—without regulating the technique itself.

Proponents of a ban on human SCNT saw things differently. SCNT with human tissue would produce a human embryo regardless of whether that embryo was transferred to a womb for gestation or cultured to generate stem cells. Since the sole purpose of the technique was to produce an embryo of a predictable genotype, and because the instrumental uses of that embryo relied on technologies that were already applied to IVF embryos, *human cloning* meant the SCNT technique itself, not the more familiar processes of transferring an embryo to a womb and the human development that might follow after it.

Proposed legislation reflected this distinction. Ehlers's bill banned human SCNT outright. Senator Feinstein introduced alternative legislation that permitted human SCNT as a laboratory technique but criminalized the transfer of an SCNT-derived embryo into a human uterus. It also limited in vitro culture of an SCNT-derived embryo to the by then standard fourteen days by requiring that the embryo be destroyed before then.[62] Proponents of the Feinstein bill insisted that it banned human cloning while preserving a valuable laboratory research tool in SCNT.[63]

Opponents of the bill argued that it did not ban human cloning at all; rather, it simply limited the lifespan and uses of the resulting embryo. They nicknamed it the "clone-and-kill" bill, pointing out that it was unprecedented for the federal government to require by law that a developing human organism be destroyed.[64]

TERMS OF DEBATE

Political struggles emerged over who would control the definition of *human cloning*. According to Senator Bill Frist, "the challenge before the U.S. Congress today" was "the difficulty we have with definitions," particularly in an area with "tensions between ethics and science."[65] He explained that his carefully crafted bill excluded all human cellular cloning from "our proposed ban, with the single exception of the mass-production of live cloned human embryos," thus "protect[ing] this promising research in spite of the misinformation that has been put forward."[66] Implying that good law was grounded in solid facts, he insisted that it was necessary to be scientifically precise about what human cloning was and what the process of SCNT produced: "I do want to take a moment to clarify that the product of somatic cell nuclear transfer into an egg which is then charged to become a human embryo is indeed a human embryo."[67] Frist argued that a ban merely on transfer to a uterus, and not on the technique of human SCNT itself, would lead to the laboratory production of "an unlimited number of these human-cloned embryos," a prospect Ehlers described as "repulsive to the entire American public," and the reason "ninety percent of them want to ban human cloning."[68]

Indeed, the notion that SCNT produced an embryo was the sole reason for some groups to oppose it. For them, it was the destruction of embryos, not cloning per se, that was of concern. The National Right to Life Committee (NRLC), for example, was initially silent on the issue of human cloning. In contrast to the United States Conference of Catholic Bishops, the NRLC did not come out against cloning as a reproductive technology.

When the organization did take a position against SCNT, it was because it was concerned about the bills that mandated SCNT embryo destruction. It was not until it looked as though some form of cloning legislation would pass that the NRLC expressed support for a total ban.[69]

The NRLC challenged the claim that the use of SCNT to derive hESC cell lines did not produce an embryo. It looked to the discursive conventions of the pro-research scientific community to justify this claim, demonstrating that scientists frequently referred to both the products of IVF and SCNT as embryos. The NRLC and the United States Conference of Catholic Bishops each supplied Congress with a lengthy list of quotations from scientists, ethicists, the NIH, the NBAC, and others in which the product of SCNT was described as an *embryo*.[70]

Terminology became a major locus of disagreement by 2001, but from early 1997 onward, anti-research critics were already wary of technical terminology that implied ontological distinctions between the biological entities produced through IVF and SCNT. In March 1997, biologist and Jesuit priest Reverend Kevin FitzGerald told the House Subcommittee on Health and Environment that attempts to call SCNT embryos by another name were just a way of hiding a moral judgment in an (incorrect) ontological characterization: "[It] comes down to what sort of status we're going to give to the human embryos—I mean, we can call them primordial stem cells, totipotent stem cells, you know, a rose is a rose is a rose."[71]

In these disagreements over terminology, each side accused the other of obscuring important facts. Proponents of a complete ban on human SCNT accused opponents of an Orwellian attempt to hide the fact that cloning produced an embryo and that the ostensibly promising research applications of SCNT necessarily involved creating and destroying embryos. Proponents of limiting restrictions to a ban on creating a child through SCNT argued that public opposition to cloning was concerned with "creating a human being," not with an esoteric technical procedure for producing engineered stem cells.

On the surface, the debate over definitions appears merely nominal: a ploy to load an already loaded term with a politically expedient meaning to manipulate a public that was not paying close enough attention to notice. It is certainly the case that competing factions realized that controlling the terms of debate would give them a political upper hand.

But it is incorrect to say that the disagreement was merely nominal. It was also ontological and therefore epistemic. Waxman, reaffirming his opposition to human cloning, suggested that the notion that public opposition to cloning extended to using the technique to produce stem cells was false, even if a majority of Americans were opposed to the creation and destruction of embryos for research. This was because SCNT did not produce an "embryo":

> We're talking now about a new technology that allows the taking of a cell—just a cell, like a skin cell—and putting it inside an egg; and then you have now something different than we've ever had before. It's called a totipotent cell, created through somatic cell nuclear transfer. . . . [These kinds of cell] can be potentially a child, or potentially for skin to be transplanted. . . . I don't think it's an embryo, in the way that we've understood embryos in the past. An embryo, as we always understood is the egg fertilized . . . by the sperm.[72]

Ontological disagreements also became opportunities for testing expert credibility and reaffirming the clear distinction between matters of scientific fact and value-laden judgment. For instance, in an exchange between Republican congressman Greg Ganske (R-IA) and biologist Diane Irving, Irving argued that biological human life begins with the inception of the embryo, regardless of whether it is the product of natural fertilization or SCNT: "When a human embryo or human being begins is strictly a scientific question and should be determined by scientists." This was neither "opinion" nor "a religious or theological position," but "fully referenced, objectively known scientific facts, scientific facts which anyone can ascertain, simply by going to their local library."[73]

Ganske probed Irving's claims to reveal personal moral views on abortion behind ostensibly scientific claims, despite her protests that "I did not come here . . . to speak as an ethicist, as a philosopher, or as a theologian, or as a pro-lifer":[74]

GANSKE: Let me phrase the question a little differently. You stated that those first cells are human life.
IRVING: Yes, sir.

GANSKE: And on the basis of that, then you would not be for allowing an abortion. Your conception of life is that from the moment those cells, that genetic material from the male and the female, get together, that's life? Is that correct?

IRVING: That is not my opinion, sir, that is the opinion of the consensus of the scientific community.

GANSKE: I'm just asking. Is that your personal opinion?

IRVING: It is what I think is true, based on the scientific consensus that is out there.

Remarking that "this is starting to get very fuzzy," Ganske turned to Michael West, the senior scientist at Advanced Cell Technology, asking, "Well, then, are we going to call that an embryo?" West answered that he was not sure about the answer but that the question was a scientific one and not one that just "anyone could ascertain." It was a question for scientific experts that would have to be asked by taking the contested entity as an experimental object: "That's a very, very complex question . . . we need to take time and do more science and make judgments down the road."[75]

ALIGNING LIFE AND LAW

The derivation of hESCs in 1998 raised new questions about the limits on federal funding.[76] It also generated new problems of terminological clarity, even as it underscored how consequential terms could be once codified in federal law. Funding for research involving the creation or destruction of a human embryo had been banned by the Dickey–Wicker amendment (hereafter "Dickey") since 1995.[77] It was unclear, however, whether the statutory limitations on human embryo research applied also to hESCs. Dickey banned federal funding for research in which a human embryo was created, destroyed, or subjected to risks in excess of those allowed for research on fetuses under existing federal regulations. *Human embryo* was defined as "any organism not protected as a human subject under 45 C.F.R. 46 as of the date of the enactment of this Act, that is derived by fertilization, parthenogenesis, cloning, or any other means from one or more human gametes or human diploid cells."[78] (The "human diploid cells" language was added in 1997 in response to the cloning of Dolly, thus extending the category of *embryo* to include the product of SCNT). Before hESC lines were derived in 1998, any research conducted on human embryonic cells necessarily entailed research on the embryo from which those cells were derived. The fetal research regulations stipulated that non-therapeutic research involving anything beyond minimal risk could not be performed on a fetus. Dickey applied the same standard to the in vitro embryo. Therefore no invasive research could be conducted that was not directly therapeutic for the embryo.

Given the state of scientific practice in 1995, by outlawing the destruction of embryos, the law also banned all federal support for research on in vitro–derived human embryological materials because these could only be derived by destroying the embryo. It permitted research involving in vivo–derived embryological materials as long as there was a complete separation between the (private) choice to abort and the (public) funds used for research. But because hESC lines are immortal, derivation of the line from an embryo could be separated in time and place from research on the cells themselves. To some, this suggested a way to conduct research on early human embryological materials without violating Dickey. As long as the cells were derived without federal support, federal support for research on the hESCs themselves did not seem to violate the letter of the law.

In a memo dated January 15, 1999, to NIH director Harold Varmus, Department of Health and Human Services (HHS) counsel Harriet Rabb assessed the eligibility of human pluripotent stem cells for federal funding. She determined that, as long as federal funds were not used to support the derivation of the cells (and hence the destruction of embryos), research on hESCs was eligible for federal support. Because Dickey applied only to human embryos, if hESCs were not embryos, Dickey did not apply.[79]

Dickey defined a human embryo as "an organism." Rabb's memo noted that the law provided no definition of an organism, and that this was, in any case, not primarily a task for the law: "The question of what is an organism calls for a science-based answer."[80] Rabb turned to the *McGraw-Hill Dictionary of Scientific and Technical Terms*, which described an organism as an "individual constituted to carry out all life functions." Furthermore, an embryo, "as that term is virtually universally understood, has the potential in the normal course of events to develop into a living human being." Because pluripotent stem cells if transferred to a uterus would "not have the capacity to develop into a human being," they did not meet the scientific or legal criteria to be considered embryos.[81]

Rabb's interpretation complicated the boundary that Dickey had drawn between public and private. Recall that Dickey had over-ruled the Clinton administration's decision that embryos from private IVF procedures that would otherwise be discarded could be used in publicly funded research. Supporters of Dickey rejected the Clinton administration's judgment that public science could use left-over embryos without being responsible for their creation and destruction, since the decisions to create them and let them be destroyed were made by private parties exercising their freedom of choice. Clinton's policy embraced the view that since left-over IVF-produced embryos were slated to be destroyed anyway, using them in research amounted to salvaging what would otherwise go to waste.[82] Dickey instead required that in vitro embryos be afforded the same protections that human research subjects (including in vivo embryos) enjoyed under the federal regulations of federally funded research, thereby preventing federal research from making use of this byproduct of clinical IVF. But the hESC was a biological loophole that the drafters of Dickey had not anticipated. It could slip across the boundary that Dickey had sought to enforce because it did not fit the ontological category (and biological definition) upon which the Dickey prohibition was constructed.

Critics argued that Rabb's interpretation violated the spirit of the law and the norms it was intended to reflect.[83] In a congressional hearing, Richard Doerflinger, a representative of the United States Conference of Catholic Bishops, objected that the Rabb memo ran afoul of a well-established norm governing research uses of fetal tissues from elective abortions. The federal rules had constructed a firewall between private responsibility for a morally controversial act and the public benefit from it. Fetal tissue could not be used for research if the "timing, method or procedures" for the elective abortion were in any way influenced by the research use of tissue from the aborted embryo or fetus. Because hESC derivation would be undertaken specifically for research use, federal funds would necessarily be implicated in the "abortion" of the embryo. Thus,

Doerflinger argued, regardless of the embryo's biological status, the Rabb interpretation would encourage research uses of human embryos, thus contradicting the intent of the law.[84] Members of Congress agreed. When the NIH issued draft guidelines for hESC research based on the Rabb memo that allowed hESC research on privately derived lines, a group of conservative senators wrote to the NIH stating that the proposed guidelines were "contrary to the law and congressional intent."

To NIH Director Harold Varmus, however, the separations of powers between law and science mirrored those between the executive and legislative branches: "The law, to our minds, reads quite clearly and it is not our job to try to discern intent." The question was ontological (and thus scientific), and there was a "very clear distinction" between cells and organisms.[85]

WORDS AND BEINGS

While everyone acknowledged the clear legal and moral significance of the distinction between cell and organism, in the case of SCNT, the ontological boundary was fuzzy. Since the Rabb memo left open the possibility for federal funding on human embryonic materials that were not "an organism," the moral and legal stakes of the ontological status of the product of SCNT were accordingly quite high. So, too, therefore, were the stakes for who would give the authoritative ontological assessment. As we have seen, Waxman disputed the notion that the product of SCNT was an "embryo" because it did not meet the dictionary definition of the product of fertilization. Nevertheless, the language of Dickey had rendered Waxman's account of an embryo moot by making provision for unconventional modes of embryo making. A chorus of scientific voices began to emerge that challenged the notion that the product of SCNT reached the ontological threshold of "organism" and, therefore, "embryo."

For instance, stem cell biologist Rudolf Jaenisch, of the Massachusetts Institute of Technology's Whitehead Institute for Biomedical Research, argued that for any given SCNT blastocyst, the likelihood of successful development to term if transferred to a uterus was so minuscule that, in the vast majority of cases, it could not properly be called an embryo.

Given this, it was more reasonable to classify the product of SCNT as an artifact, wholly disconnected from human reproduction.[86] A similar argument was later made in 2002 by President's Council on Bioethics member Paul McHugh. A pro-life Catholic physician and chair of psychiatry at Johns Hopkins University, McHugh argued that the product of SCNT and the IVF embryo should be classified separately. They were both members of the "genus" of totipotent cell, he argued, but very different species. Although he opposed research on IVF embryos, he favored the research use of SCNT embryos. Given their distinct positions in his taxonomy, he proposed that the product of SCNT should not be called a zygote or embryo but a "clonote."[87]

These moves positioned scientists as best able to interpret the law because they were best able to discern which biological entities fit within the law's ontological categories. To Michael West of Advanced Cell Technology, the law's reliance on crisp ontological distinctions presented an opportunity for an entrepreneurial bioengineer. Both hESCs and the SCNT-derived embryo were products of the laboratory that could not have been easily anticipated in Dickey. West observed that the same applied to any laboratory construct that had been made in awareness of existing prohibitions. He noted the parallel between the present dilemma and concerns in the 1970s with the mingling of DNA across species. He proposed that the solutions of the recombinant DNA (rDNA) debate provided a model for resolving the present controversy. By using an attenuated strain of bacteria that could not survive outside the laboratory, rDNA scientists had simultaneously contained laboratory risks and public concerns with the research. They had thereby "allowed recombinant technology to advance and . . . to improve the human condition." West suggested that a modified version of SCNT, perhaps using human somatic cells and nonhuman oocytes, could generate entities "engineered to be defective in producing a fetus even if used in an inappropriate effort to clone a human being by implantation in a uterus."[88] Such a technology might provide a similar technological fix, guaranteeing that the ethical risks associated with hESC research would be similarly contained.

By disabling the genes for placental development, for instance, one could construct entities that did "not have the capacity to develop into an organism that could perform all the functions of a human being" and therefore would not become embryos subject to the federal restrictions under Dickey, at least according to the Rabb interpretation.[89] But, for science to take advantage of the malleability of living systems, corollary legal and ethical rules had to be fixed and clear. Therefore, West argued, it was imperative that a body like the NBAC define once and for all the parameters of what was ethically acceptable so that science could come up with clever ways to work around the rules without violating them.[90]

West's suggestion was not merely hypothetical. On November 12, 1998, one week after James Thomson announced that he had cultured human embryonic stem cells, another scientific announcement made national headlines. Advanced Cell Technology (ACT), a small, Massachusetts-based biotechnology firm led by Michael West, revealed information regarding an experiment that its scientists had conducted three years earlier in which an ACT-supported researcher had transferred human somatic cell nuclei into bovine oocytes,[91] producing several cleavage-stage "embryos" from which cells were derived and cultured.

ACT revealed its experimental results to the world through a rather unconventional publication: the *New York Times*. The company explained that its sole intention had been to generate "undifferentiated stem cells." The technology was "not designed to be used for the cloning of a human being."[92] Nonetheless, many, including the president of the United States, responded with a combination of uncertainty and horror. Glenn McGee, then a professor of bioethics at the University of Pennsylvania, worried that ontological uncertainty would paralyze governance: "What this whole business shows is that we are in a regulatory nightmare. It's going to be impossible to state whether these things are really human, let alone how to protect them."[93] Nicholas Wade of the *New York Times* observed that the issue blurred morally significant biological boundaries: "A perplexing feature of the hybrid embryo would be that it would start mostly bovine, then become mostly yet not entirely human."[94]

Numerous experts expressed skepticism at ACT's claims, given that they had not been subjected to scientific peer review.[95] Yet, West's intention in making the research public was to elicit clear answers from society on the boundaries of morally permissible research. Finding that the results were insufficient to warrant publication in a scientific journal, the company decided that it "was in the public interest to release the preliminary results to promote an informed and reasoned public discussion of the issues." It was an experiment in the "public acceptability" of such research.[96]

FROM (DE)ONTOLOGY TO REACTIVE CONSEQUENTIALISM

For a number of prominent commentators, things were not so simple. The flexibility of the new laboratory techniques destabilized the very moral concepts that had previously been the foundation for clear ethical proscriptions. With the technique of SCNT, they argued, the potential of living matter had been so profoundly expanded that morally significant bright lines between natural kinds had collapsed into a grey zone. As one prominent scientist put it, with SCNT "any live cell has the potential for full human life."[97]

These declarations came most strongly from the bioethicists who had been in the business of drawing those bright lines. In a 2001 Senate hearing on stem sell research, bioethicist Ronald Green declared that "all of our terms, all of our ways of thinking, have been scrambled . . . by technological and scientific advances." SCNT made the argument from potential for the embryo's moral status moot: "If I were to ask you five years ago or two years ago, 'What is a human embryo?' you'd say, 'Well, it is the product of human fertilization and it has these other qualities and characteristics.' These cloned entities, these organisms, are not the product of fertilization. Their inception, their origin, is completely different. They are novel in nature in that regard." The boundaries of natural potential that had historically distinguished the (morally significant) embryo from mere (morally insignificant) cells had been dismantled by SCNT: "In an era of cloning technology, every single cell in our body has the potential to be equated with these clusters of cells."[98]

Some argued that the new technologies transformed the very parameters of public reasoning. SCNT had dismantled the natural boundaries that separated the nascent human organism from other, less morally significant kinds. With this technological advance, every somatic cell in principle now had the same sort of potential that had previously been unique to the embryo. According the embryo an elevated moral status would logically require similar treatment of all human tissue. One especially strong proponent of this argument was former HERP member and, in 1997, current NBAC member R. Alta Charo. She observed,

> Until now, even the most important forms of embryo research have run afoul of objections to the manipulation of fertilized eggs, as these cells are genetically complete and possess the potential, albeit with human assistance, of being nurtured in the laboratory and then transferred to a woman for gestation until development progresses to birth. But if nuclear transplantation cloning ultimately proves to be successful . . . then any cell in an adult body could then be regarded as equivalent to a fertilized egg. It would be genetically complete, and therefore any skin or mammary cell could, with human assistance, be developed into a baby. Whether this observation affects prevailing reasoning about the respect due to fertilized eggs, embryos and our bodies in general remains to be seen.[99]

For Charo, the implication was clear. SCNT represented an ontological potential that rendered the deontological judgment of high moral status untenable. Reasoned judgment would have to shift focus from the embryo's intrinsic status to the consequences of its use:[100] "The prospect of nuclear transplantation cloning presents a new approach to balancing respect for embryonic human life with medical and scientific advances made possible by embryo research."[101]

Charo later argued that SCNT should indeed change prevailing moral reasoning. In an essay subtitled "Logical Consequences of the Argument from Potential in the Age of Cloning," she asserted that SCNT forces one to better articulate the "real reasons for opposition to things such as research on human embryos. Better articulation, in turn, leads to some possible compromises in that debate, compromises that just might provide an avenue for permitting embryo research to go forward."[102]

SCNT, however, entailed human intervention. Because the SCNT-derived embryo and the hESC were artifacts of the laboratory, their natural histories implicated the activities of a technician in a way that the notion of the preembryo had not. This way of seeing the embryo—as a product of the lab and thus situated within social intentions and interventions—came to include IVF-derived embryos as well. Arthur Caplan, a prominent bioethicist, testified before the Senate that "it is wrong to say that all embryos are alike."[103] Caplan argued that the morally defining feature of an embryo was not its nature, but its intended use. Because embryonic potential depends upon human interventions—transfer, cryo-preservation, SCNT, stem cell derivation, and so forth, the embryo is no longer knowable in the "state of nature."[104] With SCNT in particular, "we can no longer say that we understand exactly when life beings, how to respect life, depending upon certain properties that might inhere in par-ticular cells or tissues."[105] If embryonic potential was not a function of intrinsic nature but of extrinsic technological choices, he argued, moral deliberation could not make legitimate recourse to assessments of the intrinsic nature of the embryo. Ontological assessment could not supply sufficient deontological clues. Therefore, he argued, the focus of reasoning had to shift away from intrinsic moral status to the costs and benefits of using embryos.

Arguments like Caplan's took for granted the background social con-ditions under which American clinical IVF practices had taken shape. They treated the de facto privatization of IVF that had taken place in the 1980s as a social fact, albeit one with clear normative implications for public policy. The large number of left-over embryos languishing in freezers were a byproduct of a process that was within the moral discre-tion of private individuals. These embryos had come into being through choices that were beyond the reach of public oversight, and their ultimate fate likewise was a matter of individual choice and private moral judg-ment. An increasing number of Americans came to believe that federally funded human embryo research could capitalize on the surplus embryos that were produced in clinical IVF without researchers or the public fund-ing that research being ethically responsible for either their creation or destruction. They were going to be destroyed anyway. They were waste. Public discourse increasingly treated the social circumstances of their cre-ation as a naturalized feature of their ontological status. They were not merely human embryos, but surplus, "left-over" human embryos. If they were going to be destroyed anyway, and the public bore no responsibil-ity for this fact, then, many argued, there was likewise no moral hazard associated with capturing some value from this waste stream. This conse-quentialist justification came to be embedded in the shorthand reference to "left-over embryos," naturalizing the contingent social arrangements that rendered them left over.[106] This justification would prove highly consequential in its own right as figures such as Senate majority leader Bill Frist, initially an adamant critic of human embryonic stem cell research shifted his position to endorse federal funding for stem cell lines created with left-over IVF embryos.

Caplan's and Charo's arguments reflected an important shift in public discourse. Since the 1970s, proponents of embryo research had used the frame of moral status to argue that the embryo did not meet the threshold for special protection. Many prominent critics of human embryo research had focused instead on the ethical meaning of the technology of IVF in human life, focusing on its purpose and the ways it might alter morally significant dimensions of human life. Richard McCormick's contributions to the EAB deliberations reflected this sensibility. McCormick's approach entailed imagining the broader human meaning of technological projects and futures in a way that the narrow focus on moral status did not.[107] Yet, by the late 1990s, debate had come to focus almost exclusively on the moral status of the embryo. As we saw in the previous chapters, much of that debate took the form of arguments over which biological features of the embryo were relevant in assessing moral status and how those (scientific) judgments should be codified in the terms of public reasoning. Critics of embryo research also focused on the frame of moral status in public debate. As a result, objections to human embryo research that were not based on the notion that the human embryo is a full person tended to get squeezed out of public view.[108] It was widely assumed that the only reason one could possibly have for opposing human embryonic stem cell research (including research uses of SCNT) was a belief in the full personhood of the human embryo.

As debate shifted away from what the embryo *is* to what embryos can be used *for*, imagined technological futures once again came to figure prominently in the debate, but without the questions of human purpose and dignity that had been associated with them in the 1960s and 1970s. Advocates of research emphasized technological benefits and predicted the specific technological futures that would be achieved if only researchers were permitted to move forward. In contrast to the earlier period, these imagined futures were not used to reflect upon the moral subtleties of human biotechnological self-transformations, but as expert predictions to stack up on the scales for weighing costs against benefits. These predictions were seen as expressions of scientific expertise to which policymakers and the public would have to defer. As such, they played a powerful role in framing the terms of public moral deliberation, even as they were offered in the language of scientific expertise and treated as morally- neutral statements of (future) fact. In a 1999 congressional hearing, Senator Arlen Specter (R-PA) asked the panel of distinguished scientists to predict the number of years before hESC research might cure the particular disease that their research addressed: "People in Congress like to have figures. . . . Let me press you on the question. . . . This business of advocacy is a very tough issue. . . . If you talk in terms of being close, and what the dollars will do, then you start to create an impetus for it. . . ." Larry Goldstein, a University of California, San Diego, stem cell biologist answered: "Maybe five to ten years, Senator, where we could see some hope [of curing Alzheimer's]."[109]

These sorts of predictions expanded the range of "facts" that had to be taken into account in public debate. As a result, scientific experts acquired a still more privileged position in shaping the terms of bioethical debate. They asserted the authority to declare what technological futures were realistic and therefore what benefits would be gained through research— and what costs would be incurred by inhibiting it. The authority to predict the future became an important corollary to the authority to declare the ontological parameters of moral sense-making.

Thus, whereas bioethicists like Caplan asserted that technological change had made ontological and, therefore, deontological, clarity untenable, scientists claimed to see clearly what future would flow from research, and what benefits would be denied were public policy to stand in the way of scientific progress. The derivation of hESCs had brought about broadened imaginations of the biomedical potential of human embryo research, with increased stakes for the many Americans who might benefit. The work of the next bioethics body to address human embryo research was subtly but significantly shaped by scientific authority via such imaginations of the technological future.

REPRESENTING REASON

The National Bioethics Advisory Commission was created by executive order of President Clinton on October 3, 1995. After the news of Dolly broke, Clinton called upon the NBAC to assess the ethical and policy dimensions of human cloning.[110] In late 1998, he also called upon the commission to examine issues associated with human embryonic stem cell research.[111]

The NBAC's deliberations on human cloning came just a few years after the Human Embryo Research Panel's recommendations elicited congressional and presidential rebukes. The NBAC attempted to avoid the HERP's missteps by foregrounding the sorts of public views that the HERP had excluded. As one commissioner explained to a Senate subcommittee, the NBAC would solicit the "widest possible range of views so that no aspect of public sentiment is left unexplored" in its study of cloning.[112] By mobilizing the full range of American pluralism, the commission promised to represent every citizen while also locating premises held in common beneath pluralistic disagreement. According to another NBAC member, public deliberation would benefit from encountering the "strongest representations" of differing positions on cloning.[113] In practice, the NBAC took this to mean soliciting religious views. Representatives of a range of religions were brought in to testify and were told to speak in explicitly theological terms.

The NBAC differed from the HERP not only in what sort of input it sought, but in how it understood that input. While the HERP had privileged reasons that were grounded in science, the NBAC treated all disagreement over embryo research as moral disagreement. The NBAC's equalizing move created an important asymmetry. Whereas the HERP had subjected all claims to the same test of reasonableness, the NBAC aproached scientific and moral questions as epistemologically separate, treating each as belonging to a distinct and nonoverlapping sphere of authority.

As a consequence, the commission ignored competing ontological representations. This is noteworthy given the significant public controversy over the biological status of the ambiguous biological entities discussed above. Indeed, the NBAC had to directly contend with these ambiguities.

After ACT revealed its human–bovine hybrid experiments, a "deeply troubled" President Clinton requested that the NBAC consider the implications of the research and report back within the week.[114]

The ACT experiment posed a problem for the NBAC's strong distinction between ontological and ethical evaluation. Using the law's familiar mode of analogical reasoning, commissioner and lawyer R. Alta Charo suggested that "part of the analysis that one would want to develop for the president could focus on what this fused cell is most like that we already know. Is it most like two non-gametic cells that are fused, or is it most like a regular human embryo, or is it most like something else?" Stanford geneticist David Cox supplied an authoritative answer: "It's new, Alta, is what it is." Yet, in responding to President Clinton, the commission expressed uncertainty about the ACT experiment while at once affirming that a (scientifically authoritative) ontological classification was an obligatory passage point into ethical analysis. According to the NBAC, it was unclear whether the "construct" was an embryo, which they defined as "an organism . . . which has the potential, if transferred to a uterus, to develop in the normal course of events into a living human being." If it was, this raised "complex and controversial" concerns. If not, the research raised no new ethical issues.[115]

By bypassing the question of what the biological entity *is*, and how this question should be resolved, the commission sidestepped the very problem of ontological politics that had given rise to the problem of "moral status" in the first place. In the NBAC's view, ethical analysis could proceed without resolving the status of the object because legitimate democratic disagreement was, by definition, disagreement over questions of values. Ontological and normative questions belonged to science and democracy, respectively. The processes of answering fact-based questions and values-based questions belonged to different deliberative communities employing different criteria of evaluation. Each could proceed independently of the other, with their respective results ultimately linked to form policy.

By erecting a strong boundary between science and democracy, the commission was able to treat all public disagreement as an expression of reasonable pluralism. Rather than simply exclude (putatively) theologically informed ontological accounts from the mix as the HERP had, the NBAC took the opposite approach. It treated accounts of ontological status that were marshaled in public debate as necessarily moral (and theological), rather than epistemic. The commission judged that if ontological questions were important in ethical debates, it was only because some system of values had attached particular meanings to them. These meanings could be dissociated from the ontological accounts and treated as yet one more moral account in the range of plural perspectives. Controversy over the embryo was a straightforward result of moral pluralism within the polity, and the NBAC's task was to discover the overlapping consensus within.

By characterizing these ontological debates as covertly moral, the NBAC bounded moral deliberation from ontological sense-making and separated problems of knowing accurately and reasoning well. As one commissioner put it, "Let's stop staring at the embryo and looking for the source of its meaning," and instead look "at its context in our lives, including how and why it was brought into creation."[116] Representing the embryo meant uncovering the pluralistic moral representations of the embryo and exposing whatever common principles lay beneath them. The disagreements that the American Fertility Society committee had traced to a public misunderstanding of the nature of the embryo and attempted to resolve by exercising technocratic authority to discipline the terms of public debate, the NBAC treated as purely moral disagreement. Moral status in the NBAC's analysis ceased to be a problem of how to relate to the embryo and instead became a problem of how to relate one person's moral convictions to the next's.

Thus, the commission abandoned the project of locating overlapping consensus in an ontological account of what an embryo is and instead gathered the "input of a group of religious scholars from diverse faith traditions whose views within and across traditions reflected the diversity found within the public as a whole."[117] Indeed, the commission instructed witnesses who were meant to represent religious perspectives to speak in explicitly theological terms. Ethicist Gilbert Meilaender was asked to represent a Protestant perspective, even though his scholarship was disciplinarily closer to bioethics than to Protestant theology. He noted that, although he had been directed to speak in explicitly theological terms, he could have made very similar arguments without drawing on Protestant theology in any way. Theologian and bioethicist Lisa Cahill was asked to present a Catholic perspective. She, too, assumed a theological idiom but noted that the NBAC's boundary construction enforced an artificial distinction between theological and secular (including scientific) reasoning. She noted that many of the Catholic arguments were grounded more in natural law theory than in Catholic dogma and as such could easily be presented in secular terms.

The commission's strategy appeared to be at odds with the ideas of public reasoning and democratic legitimacy that it explicitly endorsed. But, according to the commission, "An appropriate approach to public policy in this area is to develop policies that demonstrate respect for all reasonable alternative points of view and that focus, when possible, on the shared fundamental values that these divergent opinions, in their own ways, seek to affirm." In seeking religious perspectives, it was soliciting reasons that *diverged* from, rather than converged, on "shared fundamental values." The NBAC resolved this contradiction through three related ideas of representation. First, it treated religious accounts as the furthest removed from public views on which there was overlapping consensus. By capturing the diversity of religious views, the full range of intermediate moral views held by "the public as a whole" would be adequately represented. Religious perspectives offered, in the NBAC's view, a kind of snapshot of raw (prereasonable) pluralism. Views expressed in terms of "comprehensive doctrines" reflected the kinds of public perspectives whose advocates had not taken any steps toward translating into public reasons. Second, as noted above, it segregated representations of facts from representations of values by treating ontological disagreements as reflecting value-laden perspectives. Third, it positioned itself as serving a particular kind of representational role by performing public reasoning on the public's behalf. Its aim was to discover an incipient overlapping consensus in the picture of divergent disagreement that it had assembled. The commission proceeded as though overlapping consensus was possible, but the public had failed to achieve it on its own because it was not adequately committed to (or capable of) finding the "shared fundamental values that these divergent opinions, in their own ways, seek to affirm." This third representational move depended upon the other two. By soliciting reasons that demonstrably failed the test of being "acknowledged by all as reasons,"[118] and by designating ontological questions as being beyond—and irrelevant to—its remit, it marked out the boundaries of appropriately public reasons. The problem of society's relationship to the embryo, and the corollary question of its moral status, gave way to an ontology of right public reason. In effect, the *moral* problem of moral status became dissociated from the embryo as an entity in the world.

In soliciting theological perspectives, the NBAC made two key assumptions. First, it treated the distinction between fact and value as epistemologically unproblematic. This is remarkable not only in light of the ontologically ambiguous entities discussed above, but also because most of the witnesses grounded their ethical accounts of how the embryo should be treated in accounts of what the embryo *is* and in notions of which biological features they considered relevant to moral judgments. In short, ethical evaluations tended to be grounded in (somewhat divergent) ontological accounts. By drawing a strong boundary between fact and value, the commission absolved itself of having to deal with the problem of the right relationship between scientific authority and democratic authority. Public moral sense-making then became a procedural matter of reconciling the range of views that liberal democracy permitted.

Second, it assumed that, where there is agreement on matters of fact among experts, public disagreements must necessarily be over values, even if couched as disagreements over matters of fact. Therefore, to bring all moral views into the open, it would be necessary to translate disagreements on matters of fact into a values-based idiom. As a result, competing claims would be grounded in no authority beyond the right of individuals to hold their own moral and religious views.

With these assumptions, the NBAC set out to analyze and mediate moral disagreement. It assumed the role of translating religious (nonpublic) reasons into secular, ethical (public) reasons in order to bring them in line with the rules of public reason. The commission's stem cell report quoted political theorists Dennis Thompson and Amy Gutmann: "The construction of public policy on morally controversial matters should involve a 'search for significant points of convergence between one's own understandings and those of citizens whose positions, taken in their more comprehensive forms, one must reject.'"[119]

In Gutmann and Thompson's theory of deliberative democracy, this is a normative requirement of democratic deliberation and policy formation.

Given the fact of reasonable pluralism, a procedural means is required to move from disagreement to democratically legitimate resolution. The ideal means, they argue, is robust deliberation in which imbalances in political power and understanding are neutralized. Therefore, everyone must adhere to certain norms of engagement in the public square. In their conception of democracy, the most important norm is "reciprocity." The principle of reciprocity requires that "when citizens make moral claims in a deliberative democracy, they appeal to reasons or principles that can be shared by fellow citizens." These reasons should be "recognizably moral in form and mutually acceptable in content."[120] A claim fails the test of reciprocity when "it imposes a requirement on other citizens to adopt one's sectarian way of life as a condition of gaining access to the moral understanding that is essential to judging the validity of one's moral claims." In keeping with Rawls as discussed above, Gutmann and Thompson assert without theoretical justification that another element of reciprocity is the "plausibility" of fact claims.[121]

FOUND IN TRANSLATION

The commission sought as "wide a set of views as possible" and discerned the "points of convergence" between these views. It translated reasons that were closed to general moral understanding—explicitly theological reasons, for example—into reasons that "could be shared by fellow citizens." The role of the public bioethics body, as the NBAC saw it, was to translate nonpublic (i.e., religious) reasons into a secular, ideologically neutral, normative idiom that could, as far as possible, draw out points of consensus within the moral pluralism of the American public. The NBAC, like the HERP before it, drew a Rawlsian distinction between public and nonpublic reasons. The commission maintained that for public policy to be legitimate, it had to be grounded in "the shared fundamental values that . . . [all reasonable alternative points of view] in their own ways, seek to affirm."[122] "Reasonable" here meant simply that a moral position could be translated into a common, secular currency. For the NBAC, the appropriate limits of pluralistic representation corresponded with the limits of translation: Public policy should incorporate only those positions that can be translated into generic, common principles.

In discussion, commissioners tended to distinguish between the "religious" and the "ethical," which meant nonpublic and public reasons, respectively. Certain commissioners repeatedly commented on the difficulties of translating the former into the latter. Translation became a gatekeeping device; if commissioners could not come up with what they thought was a reasonable translation of a theological claim, they excluded it. During the cloning deliberations, Tom Murray said, "I was one of the people . . . who repeatedly asked the religiously oriented thinkers at our last meeting if they could also try to state their concerns in ways that would be accessible to those who did not necessarily share all their faith commitments. I am going to continue to do that because it is one thing to say that we should respect your belief just because you hold this belief deeply, and I think we should respect those beliefs, but it is difficult to know exactly what to do with that when one comes to making public policy."[123]

For the NBAC, translation from religious to secular reasons was not a matter of merely scratching out references to God and seeing whether the resulting sentence was still coherent. It was a means for transforming what it saw as half-formed moral declarations into rationally coherent arguments that abided by the rules of public reason, including, in particular, rational consistency. Sometimes this meant uncovering putatively tacit elements of a moral position—elements that the proponent of that position would not necessarily recognize as his or her own. For instance, the commission's report on stem cell research leaned on an argument from philosopher Ronald Dworkin about abortion. Dworkin argued that that few anti-abortion Americans genuinely believe that the conceptus is a person. Those who accept abortion in cases of rape or incest, for instance, hold moral positions that are inconsistent with a position of fetal personhood. Since anyone engaged in public moral deliberation is bound by a commitment to consistency, the only way to resolve this apparent inconsistency is to recognize that the anti-abortionist is in reality open to balancing harm to the fetus against other harms or goods.[124] The NBAC treated this discovery of openness to balancing as a "shared view" of both proponents and opponents of embryo research.[125] On this basis, the NBAC concluded that because most defenders of nascent human life were unwittingly open to balancing protection of the embryo against other goods, it would be permissible to destroy embryos in order to secure compelling therapeutic benefits. The committee described this conclusion as a "reasonable statement of the kind of agreement that could be possible."[126]

It is noteworthy that in this section of the report, the NBAC characterized opponents as conservatives and proponents as liberals, identifying arguments with a (rather simplistic) mapping of political alignments. This is the only place in the report where such language is used. The rest of the report describes people solely in terms of the specific moral positions they hold (or those which were attributed to them once the NBAC had translated them into appropriately public reasons). By attributing tacit moral positions to political constituencies—moral positions that these constituencies explicitly disavow but unwittingly hold—the NBAC discovered agreement in principle. Unbeknownst to conservatives and liberals themselves, they shared common moral ground.[127]

Thus, for the NBAC, the public ethics body was an organ of democratic deliberation grafted onto the body of existing political institutions to rectify a new kind of failure in the public square: the failure of Americans to reason properly about a morally complex technical domain. By assuming this role as guardian of public reasoning and applying its rational acuity to problems of pluralistic disagreement, the NBAC would aspire to nurture moral arguments beyond the limits of the citizen's own philosophical faculties and produce ideally democratic deliberation without relying on the polity itself to do the deliberating. Yet, equally noteworthy is the kind of reasoning that the NBAC imagined to be ideal. The commission in effect made itself a moral calculating machine. It defined the rules of the game by operationalizing the norms of public reason. Democracy would be achieved through a kind of philosophical-bureaucratic commensuration of (prereasonable) values claims by subjecting them to tests of internal consistency and translatability into a common, secular idiom.

Its approach was predicated on the notion that facts and values are self-evidently distinct and are subject to completely separate regimes of justification. The consequence was that the ontological—and moral—ambiguity of the material world was removed from the calculative picture. The subject of moral deliberation ceased to be the instrumental use of the human embryo and became the mechanical extraction of shared moral principles from the public's (nonpublic) reasoning. Knowing what was right in the light of public reason was artificially severed from the problem of right knowledge of things in the world. And the authority to declare what a thing *is* such that society's *oughts* could be made to apply to it was thereby delegated to science.

The NBAC's calculative process was built upon a balancing test whose parameters were defined by science. Because future benefits could trump public moral concerns about the embryo, the outcome of its balancing test depended upon scientific judgments of what imagined technological futures were realistic. The NBAC empowered scientific experts who were seen as able to predict the technological future to set the terms of debate. It asymmetrically subjected public concerns about embryo research to critical scrutiny without similarly interrogating scientific accounts of the future and the visions of the good with which they were inflected.

The NBAC's framing of the stakes of debate was consequential. In order to deliver on its charge of supplying policy-relevant ethical reasoning, the commission saw the need to construct reified "religious perspectives." By characterizing public disagreement as an expression of religion, it altered the focus of congressional debates over cloning. This shifted the initial focus of congressional debate away from asking which dimensions of human life ought not be objects of technological manipulation toward a divisive debate over the place of religious belief in public policymaking. Whereas there had been little reference to religion in the public debates over cloning that preceded the NBAC's cloning report, the respective roles of science and religion in public moral reasoning became an explicit focus after NBAC chose to focus on religious perspectives.[128] In the subsequent decade, many Americans came to see (and resent) the debates over embryonic stem cell research and cloning as fundamentally a battle between secular reason and religious ideology.

FROM PRINCIPLES TO POLICY

In August 2000, the Clinton administration established rules for the federal funding of research on cell lines derived from left-over IVF-derived embryos. Dickey remained in force, so in order for stem cell lines to be eligible for federal funding, they had to be derived without using federal funding. The rules also required that the embryos from which lines were derived meet certain criteria. Among these was the requirement that the embryos had been previously frozen. The purpose of this requirement was to create as much distance as possible between the creation and destruction of the embryos. Cryopreservation forced a temporal and (it was assumed) emotional distance from the process of trying to conceive. The Clinton administration judged that cryopreserved embryos were closer to the category of soon to be medical waste than potential human being.[129]

Using left-over embryos was, according to the *New York Times*, "an attempt to side-step the abortion issue" by avoiding public complicity in the private ethical decisions associated with clinical IVF.[130] Clinton commented on the guidelines, enthusiastically citing predicted benefits of hESC technology and laying out in a sentence the social contract that hESCs were coming to embody: "We cannot walk away from the potential to save lives and improve lives, to help people literally get up and walk, to do all kinds of things we could never have imagined as long as we meet rigorous ethical standards."[131]

With rules in place, the NIH moved to solicit proposals for hESC research. With the change of administration in 2001, however, this process was halted, and controversy ratcheted up.

5

CONFUSING DELIBERATION

fter George W. Bush took office in 2001, debates over human embryonic stem cell research and human cloning become a locus of major
political controversy in the United States. In this chapter, I continue
to trace the embryo debates as a site of ontological politics, describing
in particular how the joined problems of representing the embryo as
a contested object and of adequately representing public moral pluralism shifted into a question of discourse—of what language should be
employed in science, in law, and in public deliberation, underwritten by
whose ontological accounts, and grounded in what authority. As in earlier
moments, questions of what the embryo *is* remained linked with the question of what it should be called. But the stakes of the question explicitly
shifted from guaranteeing the truth-to-nature of linguistic representations to disciplining public discourse to ensure that the debate was reasonable and its conclusions democratically legitimate. Scientific experts
who claimed authority to declare correct ontological representations
extended this claim to include a custodial responsibility over the quality
of public debate. I detail efforts to reform the language employed in public
deliberation, specifically the use of the term *cloning* to refer to somatic cell
nuclear transfer (SCNT) to produce embryonic stem cells. I begin with
the President's Council on Bioethics (PCB), whose first task was to clarify
the terminology employed in discussions of cloning. I then shift focus
to a group of scientists who took up the same task as the PCB, though
with a quite different underlying claim to authority. These scientists justified their efforts to reform the terms of debate by arguing that the existing discourse was confusing and, therefore, that reasonable democratic

deliberation simply could not take place in such a context. Public debate was confused, they argued, because it was employing a terminology that, unbeknownst to those using it, failed to adequately separate facts from values. The experts proposed to reform the language by supplying terms that were accurate and value neutral, claiming that cleaned-up language would provide a common ground for reasoned public deliberation.

Though these efforts drew force from the epistemic authority of science, they were also built upon a tacit understanding of what qualified as good deliberation. Attempts to reform language were based on a vision of democracy that entailed a special role for the scientific expert as a guardian of discursive order over technically complex matters in the public sphere. In arguing that deliberation was confused, scientist-reformers claimed to see failures of public deliberation that were invisible to the public itself because the public was insufficiently knowledgeable to distinguish reason from confusion. These scientists tended to distinguish between reasonable and legitimate disagreement over moral matters that were properly problems for political discourse and unreasonable deliberation in which illusory ethical problems arose because of the failure to keep the facts of the matter separate from value-laden formulations.

As experts on matters of fact, engaged scientists claimed the authority to distinguish between (democratically corrosive) confusion and (democratically legitimate) disagreement. They claimed this authority by treating key facts as lying outside of politics, thus constructing for themselves an extra-democratic position from which they could assess the quality of public deliberation. By positioning themselves outside politics, they could claim that their interventions in public deliberation were apolitical and value neutral but, at the same time, essential for engendering robust democratic deliberation. Thus, in their efforts to reform public discourse, they advanced a vision not merely of good knowledge but of virtuous politics.

These attempted reforms amounted to more than simply another instance of experts trying to cure a perceived deficit in public understanding. In each of the moments this chapter explores, the notion that scientific knowledge stands outside of politics ended up placing knowledge at the heart of arguments over how to do democracy well. Thus, I draw attention to the subtle but critically important role that the invocation of democratic norms served in justifying expert intervention in the public sphere. Put simply, these interventions were made not merely in the name of truth, but in the name of democracy. By rendering democracy, rather than the embryo, the primarily contested object, scientific experts claimed the authority to diagnose and rectify democratic failure.

A CHANGE IN ADMINISTRATION

During the 2000 presidential campaign, human embryonic stem cell research had a relatively low profile. George W. Bush expressed opposition to research that "requires the destruction of human embryos" but did not taken a firm policy stance on federal funding specifically for human embryonic stem cells (hESCs) during his campaign. Upon entering office in early 2001, President Bush requested that the Department of Health and Human Services (HHS) conduct a new a legal review of hESC funding and of the Rabb memo, which had interpreted the law forbidding federal funding for research that harms human embryos not to extend to human embryonic stem cells. Bush gave no indication of what, if any, policy changes he would make, and the National Institutes of Health (NIH) continued to proceed under the Clinton administration regulations. In April, just as the NIH was about to begin reviewing grant applications, the administration called a halt to the process until a legal review could be completed. At that point, hESC research policy began to emerge as locus of political controversy. By June, the issue was appearing with increasing frequency in the news media. The Bush administration made it known that hESC research was being actively deliberated within the White House, with senior members of the administration divided on the issues. Between early June and early August, stem cell research developed into what the administration saw as a defining issue of the Bush presidency and a test case for how Bush would "compassionately" navigate between religious conservatism and the moderate middle on matters of domestic policy.[1]

On August 9, 2001, Bush announced his policy decision in the first prime-time televised address of his presidency. He delivered the address during his "Home to the Heartland Tour" from the terra firma of his Texas ranch. He detailed his long deliberation and conversations with "scientists, scholars, bioethicists, religious leaders, doctors, researchers, members of

Congress, my Cabinet and my friends" over the "profound ethical questions" raised by stem cell research. He had found "widespread disagreement," including over the question of whether "these frozen embryos [are] human life and therefore something precious to be protected." And he referred to the by then well-worn disagreements over what the embryo is, what it should be called, and what such ontological clarity might mean for moral sense-making and public policy:

> One researcher told me he believes this five-day-old cluster of cells is not an embryo, not yet an individual but a pre-embryo. He argued that it has the potential for life, but it is not a life because it cannot develop on its own. An ethicist dismissed that as a callous attempt at rationalization. "Make no mistake," he told me, "that cluster of cells is the same way you and I, and all the rest of us, started our lives." "One goes with a heavy heart if we use these," he said, "because we are dealing with the seeds of the next generation."[2]

The president settled upon a compromise. He decreed that federal support was acceptable for research only on already established cell lines "where the life-and-death decision has already been made." Cell lines established prior to August 9, 2001, at 9 P.M. eastern time, were eligible for federal funding.[3]

During his address, Bush also announced that he would form a President's Council on Bioethics. In the address, he named Dr. Leon Kass of the University of Chicago to chair the commission. Kass had been an important figure in the White House deliberations, speaking at length with the president and his staff as the policy was being crafted.

THE PRESIDENT'S COUNCIL ON BIOETHICS

Leon Kass had been a prominent figure in American bioethics for decades but was something of an outsider to the approaches that coalesced into mainstream bioethics beginning in the late 1970s.[4] He was often criticized by the bioethics mainstream as an irrationalist, more inclined to find wisdom in the natural order of things than to find truth in the apparatus of cold rationality.[5] His career as an ethicist and public intellectual had in many respects directly tracked the deliberations over the embryo. In the early 1970s, he had commented extensively on the emerging technology of in vitro fertilization (IVF).[6] In late 1978, he had spoken before the Ethics Advisory Board (EAB) alongside Samuel Gorovitz. Observing that IVF was a gateway into radically new possibilities for manipulating human life in the laboratory, Kass had told the board that technology cannot be easily contained, that its meanings and applications are not easily managed by social restraint, and that the logic of justification that accompanies social acceptance of a technology becomes a force in itself, difficult to resist or reverse. His account attributed a certain agency to both nature and technology, attributions that mainstream bioethics would categorically resist in favor of the notion that sociotechnical change is always a matter of choice. Testifying alongside Kass, Gorovitz had taken this line. He noted that as a skier, he found the slippery slope argument unconvincing: No slopes are truly slippery because societies, like skilled skiers, can always choose to stop.[7] This exchange between Kass and Gorovitz in many respects reflected the deep cleavages between the approaches to human embryo research that the National Bioethics Advisory Commission (NBAC) and the President's Council on Bioethics would take two decades late.

In 2001, Kass still held many of the same positions. Although an accomplished scholar, he remained an outsider to the mainstream of American professional bioethics. This, in part, can be traced to a radically different vision of both the purpose of bioethics and the forms of reasoning appropriate to it. Bioethics for Kass was an Aristotelian project of inquiring into the nature of the human and acting with prudence to ensure human flourishing, an urgent enterprise, since, in Kass's view, the human was newly endangered by its own radically novel tools of self-manipulation.[8]

For Kass, an essential feature of human life was embodied sociality, a sociality that included dialectic among its supreme abilities.[9] This was reflected in the work of the President's Council. From its charter to its membership to its discussions, robust moral deliberation became, in some respects, an end in itself for the council. In both its mandate and its practices, it eschewed the traditional emphasis in public bioethics on consensus, instead opening space for the forms of discensus and cleavage that, in Kass's view, would more robustly capture the stakes.[10] The executive order that created the council required that it

> strive to develop a deep and comprehensive understanding of the issues that it considers. In pursuit of this goal, the Council shall be guided by the need to articulate fully the complex and often competing moral positions on any given issue, rather than by an overriding concern to find consensus. The Council may therefore choose to proceed by offering a variety of views on a particular issue, rather than attempt to reach a single consensus position.[11]

The council adopted a very different model of democratic representation than had the NBAC before it. Whereas the NBAC saw itself as a mechanism for eliciting common premises out of pluralistic disagreement and deriving ethically acceptable policy options by reconstructing overlapping consensus, the council saw its contribution to policy making as being more its performance of long-duration deliberation than in the production of consensus recommendations. Kass described this approach at an early council meeting:

> It seems to me that when and if we make recommendations, and perhaps even conflicting recommendations on the policy side, it would be very helpful to the policy makers to understand as fully as we can help them to understand, the full meaning, and the full costs of doing whichever thing that they do. And that is a task for us. Not simply to speak in terms of the names of the goods which we privately defend, whether it be the life of the embryo, or the good of medical research, but to take upon ourselves individually the burden of speaking to the concerns of the others in this room, and to see whether one can somehow acknowledge and accommodate it, and learn how to grapple with it for ourselves so that we finally own all of the positions around the table, including the ones for which we would personally come down.[12]

The performance of a kind of "model moral political deliberation" would, according to Kass, be a "real contribution" to public debate, "at least to those who would care to pay attention."[13]

The council's approach to deliberation, one may note, conformed to the norm of reciprocity invoked by the NBAC. Discourse was to be civil, reasons were to be mutually intelligible, and even if disagreement was not resolved, members were expected to "own all of the positions around the table." But, for the NBAC, the role of the public ethicist was to uncover common principles in divergent positions and to translate these into "a new, firmer foundation for agreement," to act, in effect, as a surrogate for ideal, goal-directed public deliberation.[14] The council perceived a radically different role for itself. The deliberations of the council drew on the plurality of approaches represented in the room and elicited the thick discourse of ends and goods.[15] As Kass put it, the council would "take pains to locate the new biomedical developments, both with their promise and their peril, within the larger context of human life."[16]

Like the NBAC, the council affirmed that common reasoning necessarily had to be grounded in a common language. But, whereas the NBAC had sought to uncover a common moral world into which facts could be unproblematically introduced, the council considered the relationships between ontological and moral world making to be more directly linked. Moral disagreements could and often did trace to differing accounts of the material world, accounts that were represented in differing languages. According to Kass, finding a common language was itself a normatively laden deliberative activity, one that ought to find its ground in the world itself. It was "not just a matter of semantics; it is a matter of trying hard to call things by their right names; of trying to fit speech to fact as best one can."[17] Thus, the primary problem of representation for the Council was ontological rather than democratic; the council began with the question of what human cloning *is*, though unlike much of the prior deliberation, it treated this question as simultaneously factual and moral.

Yet, to engage in a discussion about what it *is*, the council found it necessary to begin with the question of what *human cloning* means. By relocating the moral questions into the ontological domain of the things themselves, the stabilizing work that had previously been done by finding facts was shifted onto the representation of meanings present in the conventions of speech. Whereas the question of what *human cloning* means (along with *embryo*, etc.) was, for Congress and the NBAC, a matter of navigating public ignorance, for the council, it was a matter of constructing a common language, and thus a shared space for moral deliberation, by building upon the nature of the biological entities themselves. Finding a common language on so divisive a matter meant stabilizing the basic discursive currency; it meant finding the right names for things.[18]

FINDING THE RIGHT TERMS

The council began its deliberations on human cloning by discussing terminology. Kass underlined the importance of finding a common deliberative language for this morally fraught and technically complex subject:

> In our area of bioethics there is an additional and crucial danger of terminological distortion . . . we should try to choose terms that most accurately convey the descriptive reality of the matter at hand. If this is well done, the moral argument can then proceed on the merits without distortion by linguistic sloppiness or chicanery.[19]

The council's discussions drew the moral and the ontological into proximity, but at the same time affirmed the fact–value distinction as a necessary ground for reasoning together. There was general agreement that the "right names" would be value-neutral facts and that these would provide the scaffolding for reasonable moral arguments. In discussion, council members repeatedly invoked the need to avoid value-laden language. At the same time, however, terms that were advanced by some as empirical descriptions, such as *organism* and *living*, were challenged by others as value-laden and prejudicial. The council found it virtually impossible to avoid straying into what some took to be moral discussion of the embryo. Concerned, council member Charles Krauthammer interrupted discussion:

> It seems to me that we ought not be having our debate on the moral aspects of cloning in this session and try to find a definition. The whole idea of trying to find a definition is a way to enable us to then have our debate in which our terms are agreed upon so I think we ought to go for the lowest common denominator and to find an adjective and a noun that work.[20]

Most council members agreed that the problem would be resolved by finding the "least common denominator." But for this group of civil, highly educated people making a good-faith effort, it was virtually impossible to arrive at that starting position. As terms were proposed, members objected that they were prejudicial, inaccurate, or both. Those most committed to finding a value-neutral language progressively proposed less and less specific'terms, including, for example, "type 1" and "type 2" cloning (though some also objected to the use of the term *cloning*).[21]

Many of the by now familiar disagreements were rehearsed. Some council members wanted to actively dissociate context and intent from the characterization of the SCNT embryo, whereas others saw these aspects as intrinsic to it. Paul McHugh advocated the term *clonote* to distinguish the product of SCNT from the IVF embryo. Although he favored research on the former but not the latter, he saw this demarcation as a morally neutral biological taxonomy.[22] Neuroscientist Michael Gazzaniga argued that the product of SCNT was merely bioengineered raw material for a future building project that could take many forms, depending on the intentions of the engineer. Describing raw materials as though they were already a finished form was a failure to fit "speech to fact":

> But for those who do not believe that, they can consider, well, what is this blastocyst? And the argument generally is, well, it is potentially a human being. . . . But an analogy helps me think about it, which is you go into a Home [Depot] . . . there are the elements for 30 homes and they have the potential of 30 homes in that Home Depot. The Home Depot burns down. The headline is not "Community Burns Down Houses"; [it is] "A Home Depot Burns Down." That is the stage those goods were at. So the notion that this blastocyst is . . . or can be something else, it is a truism. Of course, it can be.[23]

In these respects, the council's deliberations reflected many of the arguments that were already circulating in public debate. "Owning all of the positions around the table" did not resolve the question of how best to represent a neutral and shared ontology through a common conceptual and linguistic currency.

As the council reflected on the form of the ideal discourse, some members expressed skepticism that technical scientific language could serve as a value-neutral common ground. Public deliberation depended on communicative engagement, so facts had to be rendered in language that would allow public reasoning to get at relevant dimensions of normative disagreement. To some, this was a pedagogical problem. It required actively reconstructing language to address the value-laden questions of public deliberation, rather than attempting to convey putatively value-neutral technical scientific information in terms whose detail might stymie public deliberation. On this account, the role of the council was to enhance public deliberation by supplying terms of debate that captured the salient aspects, without burdening the naïve public with excessive detail. As council member Daniel Foster put it, "We ought to speak accurately but in terms that ordinary people understand. . . . When a child asks a mother where babies come from, you do not have to go into the precise description of sexual intercourse. You can simply say that this is where they come from."[24]

Indeed, a majority of council members, including proponents of SCNT research, argued that terminology ought to be constructed to take into account existing moral disagreements. Some argued that the term *cloning* should be preserved and that language should be able to accommodate the ways "moral meaning attaches [to] a contested point . . . a point that is alive in the country and alive around the table."[25] There was some ambivalence about how such representation should be accomplished. While testifying before the council, Stanford stem cell biologist Irving Weissman suggested that accuracy entailed completely disembedding language from culture. He suggested that "it is important to try to have very clean language that is free of even convention," since any conventional or contested language is already freighted with meanings and possible misunderstanding.[26] The notion that language should (or could) be free of convention might raise eyebrows, but Weissman's proposal was grounded in a semiology that had powerful purchase in the politics of the 2000s: the notion that fact claims point back to nature and are mediated by science, that values claims point to democratic pluralism, and that the fundamental foundation for doing democracy well is keeping these separate. In his remarks, Weissman repeatedly suggested to the group that they ought to postpone discussion of terminology until after he could give an extended scientific presentation.

WHO SPEAKS FIRST?

There was significant hand-wringing within the group about how scientific expertise ought to inform the council's discussion of terminology. Some suggested that before the group could "call things by their right names," they needed scientific experts to explain the nature of those things to them. Anxiety about the conditions of possibility for "fitting speech to fact" took form as questions over who should speak first, scientific experts or those tasked with moral sense-making.

In the political microcosm of the council, this concern was expressed in repeated discussions of the order of the meeting agenda. Some members thought that in order to construct a shared language, it was necessary to be educated in the technical facts of the matter first. Others thought it necessary to discuss the scientific and moral questions together before settling on a set of terms. For council member and legal theorist Robert George, the accuracy of terms was best assessed by "making sure that you get a fair representation of competing points of view without the definitions or language prejudicing it."[27] The solution was not necessarily to disembed language from moral deliberation, but to construct terms that would facilitate "fair representation." Accuracy could not be measured purely by ascertaining whether a description was true to nature. Yale law professor Stephen Carter noted that "part of the problem we are facing with definitions, and it is also a problem that we are facing with the debate about the agenda order, is that it is not obvious to everyone around the table that the fact that there is a particular scientific way of addressing the issue means that that is clearly the most accurate way of addressing the issue."[28]

Thus, the council's effort to produce a neutral, discursively held-in-common representation of "human cloning" translated into a debate over which sources of authority—epistemic or democratic—should inform the common currency of deliberation. Council members tackled the problem of representation directly by searching for the right language for reasoning together. The result of this effort provided a picture of a deliberative body confronting the coproduction of knowledge and norms in moral deliberation. At the same time, it found the dynamics of their co-constitution difficult to reconcile with the task of designating idealized, neutral and held-in-common discursive foundations for public reasoning. In short, the council's deliberation itself reveals the entwining in practice of what otherwise get marked as facts or values, and it reveals how foundational the commitment to "neutral" premises—premises grounded in the facts of the matter that are independent of moral meaning—is in U.S. political culture. In confronting this dynamic of coproduction, the council constantly felt the pressure to escape it.

The council's attempt at "calling things by their right names" demonstrates that technical knowledge can be made to order public reason only insofar as a political community is already committed to an idea of the kind of premises that *can* be held in common in public reasoning. The council refused to hand responsibility for declaring the terms of debate to science, yet it was precisely this refusal that stymied its efforts at achieving linguistic clarity. This was not because science could supply it, but because of an imagination in wider politics that the kind of accounts that are necessarily held in common are value-neutral, epistemic accounts; that is, scientific accounts. And, in social practice, to be considered scientific, accounts must be certified by scientific authority. Thus, one of the council's most illuminating insights was that designating the rightness (both epistemic and normative) of a name was linked to who is authorized to speak first. Yet, observations about their own quotidian practices and constraints—such as who is first on (and thereby sets) the agenda, and what tacit constructions of authority and right reason underwrites these practies—were largely absent from the council's formal conclusions.[29]

The council's report on cloning began with a discussion of terminology, reinscribing the notion that a common language precedes robust democratic deliberation while also supplying the basis for its legitimacy. Although the council's language avoided terms that council members found ontologically or morally prejudicial, it nevertheless contained a far more consequential ingredient, though arguably one that the council could not have rejected even if it wished to. This was the notion that robust public reasoning depends on first arriving at a morally neutral shared language. In the wider context of the human embryo research debates, moral neutrality meant scientific accuracy, which in practice meant terms certified by scientific experts. As we shall see, the scientific community used this notion to great advantage.

FINDING THE RIGHT TERMS

In September 2001, the National Research Council (NRC) issued a report titled *Scientific and Medical Aspects of Human Reproductive Cloning*. The NRC committee that authored the report explicitly limited the scope of its inquiry to matters of scientific and medical concern, excluding "ethical" dimensions.[30] The committee located responsibility for the latter with the public and made repeated calls for "a broad national dialogue on the societal, religious, and ethical issues" surrounding human reproductive cloning.[31] Yet, behind this clean (and commonsense) separation between facts and values, science and politics, the report outlined a role for scientific experts in configuring public deliberation. Affirming that ethical deliberation is the business of democracy, it recommended that public dialogue be presided over by a committee of scientific experts who would "reach out to constituencies in a systematic manner" and ensure that the debate is "structured to inform the public" of relevant matters of fact.[32]

The rationale for expert intervention was linked to the NRC committee's diagnosis of a democratic failure: the use of the phrase *human cloning* in public deliberation over embryo research. The committee claimed that "human reproductive cloning" and "nuclear transplantation to produce stem cells" are often inappropriately linked in public debate.[33] Asserting that "clarity on these issues is vitally important," the committee acknowledged that "because one method to establish new human embryonic stem cell lines uses a process very similar to the first steps in the reproductive cloning of complete humans, it is easy to understand how even a scientifically literate society could become confused about these issues."[34] The committee declared that a conceptual dissociation of these projects in public debate was imperative because, apart from overlapping first steps, these procedures are "completely different." Despite these differences, "in the popular press and other media, the term 'human cloning' has often been misleadingly applied to both this procedure and reproductive cloning whenever either is proposed to be used in a human context."[35]

The chairman of the NRC committee, Dr. Irving Weissman of Stanford University, later testified about the report before the President's Council on Bioethics. Explaining the rationale for (ostensibly) focusing exclusively on "scientific and medical aspects," he said, "Our objective was to try to report to society at large what are the facts about either reproductive cloning or nuclear transplantation to produce human pluripotent stem cells to give you and Congress and others in society that data so that you would be informed about the debate."[36] He explained that a critical component of reporting the facts was identifying a terminology that could capture the salient features, applications, and potential benefits of the science specifically *for the public*. In effect, Weissman claimed the authority to teach his interlocutors how to talk about the science: "We need to come to the right terms because after a while what this group does, what the government does, what the national societies do to change the terminology will lead to a terminology that will be learned by the [public]."[37] The NRC report was critical of terms that associated "human cloning" with "nuclear transfer to produce stem cells" because its authors considered the purposes of the two processes, as well as their end products, to be very different.

Prior to Thomson's derivation of human embryonic stem cells in 1998, discussions of human cloning had largely focused on its potential reproductive applications. However, the combination of SCNT and hESC derivation had the potential to produce tissues immunologically matched to the somatic cell donor; it also had the potential to generate stem cell lines from known phenotypes, including those of individuals suffering from heritable diseases. Given these imagined scientific and therapeutic applications, the conceptual marriage of nuclear transplantation to hESC research became a prominent feature of discussions of human cloning almost immediately after the 1998 Thomson paper. By early 2001, SCNT as a tool of stem cell culture was commonly distinguished from reproductive applications by attaching a modifier to the term *cloning*. "Therapeutic cloning," as distinct from "reproductive cloning," became the preferred formulation for ratifying this separation in both scientific and popular discourse.

These adjectival modifications of the word *cloning* actually preceded embryonic stem cells. In January 1998, Britain's Human Fertilisation & Embryology Authority (HFEA) and Human Genetics Advisory Commission (HGAC; now the Human Genetics Commission) issued a consultation paper titled "Cloning Issues in Reproduction, Science and Medicine" in order to explore regulatory dilemmas that might arise in relation to human cloning. The paper was distributed to interested organizations and the public for comment. In order to facilitate clear thinking on the different potential applications of nuclear transfer (NT), the document drew a terminological distinction based on the intended use of the technique:

> We draw the distinction between two types of cloning: on the one hand, human reproductive cloning, where the intention is to produce identical fetuses or babies; and, on the other hand, what may broadly be called therapeutic cloning, which (although not coterminous with conventional scientific usage) includes other scientific and medical applications of nuclear replacement technology.[38]

It is noteworthy that this distinction was constructed by its authors to reflect the categories of an already established regulatory regime in the United Kingdom.[39] Since the *Human Fertilisation and Embryology Act of 1990*, research on human embryos in the U.K. had been permitted up to fourteen days of development, though under regulatory supervision.[40] Before fourteen days, the embryo was considered a legitimate research object. Beyond fourteen days, it was considered to have transitioned into a different biological and legal status, exclusively inhabiting the realm of human reproduction, and was subject to very different regulatory constraints. Thus, the distinction between reproductive and therapeutic cloning inscribed a boundary constructed in British law on the product of SCNT itself. The aim was to structure ontological, normative, and regulatory questions about each application of the technique such that they reflected the categories and boundaries of the existing legal settlement.

The terminology was crafted specifically to discipline public discourse into attending to salient questions. The authors of the paper presumed that by building distinctions into the terms themselves, the terms would quiet unwarranted public debate and help "avoid confusion":

> It is important that stringent definitions be adopted and that the precise context be defined on a consistent basis to avoid . . . confusion. . . . For the purposes of clarity in this document we will use two distinct meanings of 'cloning.'"[41]

The HGAC justified its efforts to configure public discourse not by invoking technical precision, but by asserting the importance of a shared, empirical commonsense, captured in a shared language, as a foundation for robust democratic deliberation. Colin Campbell, chairman of the HGAC in 1998, argued, "If we are to encourage wider discussion of the issues, and involve lay people, we must establish a common lexicon for the purposes of this public discourse and debate." This "common lexicon" would, he argued, engender greater participation in deliberation while at once enhancing clarity.[42]

The HGAC's terminology was adopted into a very different regulatory, discursive, and political cultural environment in the United States. In the United States, human embryo research was unregulated in the private sector and ineligible for federal funding. The 1990 U.K. law, by contrast, had established a regulatory regime to govern the creation and use of human embryos, regardless of whether the source of funding was public or private. The ethical acceptability of human embryo research was, for all regulatory intents and purposes, a settled matter in Britain. Therefore, the HGAC considered SCNT a laboratory research tool that would raise few new ethical questions; it was merely another in vitro manipulation of human biological materials that had already been deemed to be below the threshold of ethical and legal protection. But, as a reproductive technology, SCNT raised new and previously unexamined ethical questions.[43]

Both therapeutic and reproductive cloning belonged in the same consultation paper because, in the view of the HGAC, they were distinct applications of the same technology. The distinction between them was intended to exclude normative questions that had already been asked and answered in the 1980s. Thus, no new public input was deemed to be required; given the regulatory distinction between reproduction and research, it made sense to the HGAC to segregate potential applications of SCNT accordingly, thus giving rise to two distinct and nonoverlapping lines of ethical deliberation.[44] Thus, the consultation paper identified what its authors considered to be the "right terms" for reasoned public debate and used them to structure deliberation.

If the uptake of terms is a measure of its success, the HGAC was extremely successful. "Therapeutic cloning" quickly became shorthand for "SCNT for stem cell derivation" in both popular and expert circles.[45] It is ironic, therefore, that this very terminology was identified by the NRC report as a primary source of confusion in U.S. public deliberation.

The NRC committee argued that the application of the term *cloning* to nonreproductive SCNT created an inappropriate linguistic association with "reproductive cloning."[46] What in the U.K. consultation document had been a terminological mechanism to "avoid confusion" and guarantee "clarity" was described by the NRC committee as "misleading." Both groups had access to the highest level of scientific expertise. No meaningful changes in scientific knowledge had emerged in the intervening years that complicated the distinction. Rather, the NRC committee was responding to the way the reproductive–therapeutic cloning distinction had been employed in public deliberation in the United States. The committee did not like what it saw.

CONFUSION AND DISAGREEMENT

The NRC committee asserted a crisp distinction between scientific and ethical matters, claiming significant authority over the former and none over the latter. It then declared it imperative that value-laden meanings be purged from technical terminology, characterizing the task of identifying and excising these meanings as one for scientific experts. This reflected the longstanding concerns of committee chairman Irving Weissman.

During an early meeting, Weissman conducted an experiment. He asked each of the distinguished experts on the NRC committee to "draw a picture of an embryo."[47] Some, according to Weissman, drew a morula, some drew a blastocyst, and some drew a fetus. None, he claims, drew what he considered to be an embryo.[48] Weissman took this as evidence of a fundamental problem for the deliberative work of the committee, and for public deliberation more generally. If a committee of scientific experts did not understand and agree on the biological referent of a basic term like *embryo*, it was very unlikely that the public did. According to Weissman, people had different things in their heads even if the same words were coming out of their mouths. This was a recipe for public confusion, particularly where the different referents that people imagined to be associated with the same term had moral significance or emotional valences attached to them.[49]

Weissman believed that reasoned deliberation depended upon beginning with clear, precise and value-neutral language, free of what he referred to as "emotional overlay."[50] Without the foundation of a shared, neutral language, deliberation would inevitably remain "confused."[51]

Weissman's efforts met with resistance. In describing the committee's initiative to clarify the language, Weissman told me,

> We tried to use neutral language. And as you might guess, the more we got devoid of emotion-bearing terms, the more I got criticized, especially from the far right, as trying to change the subject they *thought* they knew. But of course *they had the same misapprehension of terms.* Many of them believed that a fetus with a head, with budding arms and legs, was the same as an embryo.[52]

Weissman's last sentence reflects the tension between the efforts of would-be reformers of terminology to radically separate fact from value and the deeply rooted material–moral hybridity of the embryo. The notion that "a fetus with a head, with budding arms and legs [is] the same as an embryo" may be morphologically inaccurate (depending on the prior definition of an embryo), but as a morally inflected representation of the status of the embryo, it was not only commonly made, but perfectly intelligible. Indeed, there were plenty of prior examples of arguments that drew scientific distinctions (or connections) between developmental states as a way of making a moral argument—Grobstein's preembryo is but one of a wealth of examples in which a moral evaluation was embedded within a description of the facts of the matter.

Grobstein's terminology is only superior if one presumes that moral perspectives must be shaped in advance by a scientifically correct (and thus expert-certified) ontological picture—that in formulating a moral view, one must have the "period at the end of this sentence" in one's mind's eye rather than some other image of human life.[53]

Weissman's experimental demonstration of public confusion, however, was an innovation. In designating the "emotional overlay" associated with terms like *embryo* as evidence of confusion, Weissman and the NRC committee made two tacit assertions about the failed state of public deliberation. First, they implied that confusion was a state that was by its very nature invisible to the confused. Only an expert could distinguish between those who know and those who only think they know. Second, by simultaneously asserting a clear boundary between facts and values and characterizing experts who are immune from the effects of confusion as uniquely positioned to distinguish between neutral facts and values masquerading as facts, they simultaneously positioned experts as custodians of the legitimacy of democratic deliberation. In asking, "How can you use the same language when two people at the table don't even agree on the use of the term?"[54] Weissman implied that no "broad national dialogue on the societal, religious, and ethical issues" had yet taken place.[55] Nor could one take place until everyone was speaking the same language, "devoid of emotion-bearing terms."[56]

MODELING PUBLIC DELIBERATION

The NRC report was issued in early 2002. At roughly the same moment, the Bush-appointed President's Council on Bioethics began its discussion of human cloning and terminology

After a lengthy deliberation, the council settled on the terms *cloning-to-produce-children* in place of *reproductive cloning* and *cloning-for-biomedical-research* in place of *therapeutic cloning*. It also affirmed that even if the intended uses of the two products of the SCNT procedure are different, the product itself is the same in both cases: a "cloned human embryo."[57]

Weissman, in his presentation to the council, directly challenged the idea that a "cloned human" was, by criteria of scientific accuracy, the "product" of SCNT:

> The product of nuclear transplantation to produce stem cells describes the product, stem cells. You may choose to say that an intermediate step in your mind is the product, the blastocyst, *that is your choice*. I am just saying that *we tried to be as clear as possible* what the product was and we said what the product of the first was, the intent to make a human live birth by implantation, and the second to make stem cells not by implanting but by extracting cells. So the products are different.[58]

Rather, in the NRC committee's judgment, the "cloned human embryo" was a linguistic construct that was the product of a private, value-laden "choice." As language laden with preexisting moral concerns, it failed to provide the transparent ("as clear as possible") discursive starting point for robust public debate.

In his personal comments appended to the President's Council's report, neuroscientist and council member Michael Gazzaniga provided a more developed version of the same idea. Quoting Oscar Wilde's line, "A man who moralizes is usually a hypocrite," Gazzaniga argued that it "cuts to the heart of much of the problematic nature of moralization: the divide that can exist between reasoning as reflected in actions in the face of a collection of facts and reasoning grounded on little more than a cultural belief system."[59]

He went on to comment on the place of "moralization" in a pluralistic democracy:

> Of course, we are all free to have our views on everything from base-ball to embryos. This is a large part of what makes this country great. But moralizers often go much further. Frequently, they want you to conform to their views, an agenda that I find entirely disturbing, and particularly troubling, when cast in the large, as a basis for social and even scientific policy.[60]

Policy, he argued, should conform to what is shared: scientific facts, not moral views. Thus, the enemy of sound policy was public confusion—in particular confusion engendered by "moralization" masquerading as scientific representation:

> The general public gets confused around this point in a discussion [where the reproductive and therapeutic applications of SCNT are distinguished from one another]. The confusions come from a conflation of ideas, beliefs, and facts. At the core seems to be the idea, asserted by some religious groups and some ethicists, that this moment of transfer of cellular material is an initiation of life, and so is the moment when a moral equivalency is established between a developing group of cells and a human being.[61]

Public confusion was, according to Gazzaniga, the result of an unauthorized—and unwitting—"conflation of ideas, beliefs, and facts." "Moralizers" exploit confusion to make others "conform to their views." But this form of consensus is illegitimate because it is a product of confusion rather than reasoned agreement rooted in held-in-common facts.[62]

Once again, this characterization of confusion and of the corollary illegitimacy of deliberation asserted a privileged role for scientific experts in deliberative democracy, not only in setting the terms of debate, but as custodians of its quality. Gazzaniga's distinction "between reasoning as reflected in actions in the face of a collection of facts and reasoning grounded on little more than a cultural belief system"[63] was not merely epistemic, but constitutional; that is, it was not merely between knowledge and belief, but between legitimate and illegitimate forms of public reason. It positioned scientific authority as tethering public deliberation to a firm foundation in reason, as the appropriate diagnostician of when that tether has been broken, and as the regulative authority that should discipline public disagreement into "reasonable pluralism."[64]

There is no question that their interest in directing public debate toward policies that favored research motivated Gazzaniga's and Weissman's efforts. But social interests are insufficient to explain the form they took in practice. They marshaled a construction of scientific authority that was not of their invention, even if efforts like theirs did much to reinforce it. Rather, their efforts depended in turn upon the constitutional position of science in American democracy: upon the collective cultural imagination that knowledge and norms are distinct and nonoverlapping domains and upon scientific authority as an extra-political custodian of the reasonableness and legitimacy of democratic deliberation.

CHANGING THE TERMS

In the summer of 2001, Lee Silver, a professor of molecular biology at Princeton, published a commentary in *Nature* entitled "What Are Clones? They're Not What You Think They Are."[65] Silver, like Weissman and Gazzaniga, insisted that public deliberation over human cloning was compromised by confusion. He concluded with a call to action for the scientific community:

> Cloning has a popular connotation that is impossible to dislodge. We must accept that democratic debate on cloning is bereft of any meaning. Science and scientists would be better served by choosing other words to explain advances in developmental biotechnology to the public.[66]

In the following months and years, an increasingly vocal group of scientists expressed similar sentiments. In a commentary in *Science*, Bert Vogelstein and his coauthors implored the scientific community and the public alike: "Please Don't Call It Cloning." In a table listing the crucial differences between nuclear transplantation and human reproductive cloning, the authors listed the "end product" of "nuclear transplantation" as "cells growing in a Petri dish" and that of "human reproductive cloning" as "a human being."

The authors argued that terminological accuracy in public contexts cannot be guaranteed by simply adopting scientific terms in public discourse. The "shorthand expressions" employed in the "scientific dialect" are prone to misunderstanding and misapplication as they make their way to the nonscientific public, and it is the misunderstanding of the terms, not the terms themselves, that are the cause of confusion. The problem, in other words, was not with science, but with democracy. That "cloning seems to have become almost synonymous with somatic cell nuclear transfer" in public discourse demonstrated that "much confusion ha[d] arisen in the public."[67] Testifying before a Senate subcommittee, Vogelstein asserted that because of this confusion, "the term 'therapeutic cloning' . . . has become effectively useless."[68]

Note that neither Silver nor Vogelstein advocated public education as a solution to this democratic deficit. Instead, they proposed a change in terminology to purge public discourse of confusion. Vogelstein predicted that a "more careful use of terminology would help the public and lawmakers sort out the substantial difference between nuclear transplantation and human reproductive cloning."[69] This was because the terminological problem was not a problem of technical accuracy, but a conflation in public discourse of what were (in their view) technically distinct (and therefore ethically distinct) matters: the use of SCNT for laboratory research and the use of SCNT to produce a child. Vogelstein suggested that terminology itself, rather than the public's understanding of what lay behind it, would enforce (what the experts judged to be) the proper foundations for rendering public debate reasonable. As with *preembryo* in the 1980s, it was felt that new terminology would discipline public discourse into employing relevant ontological distinctions. But, in this case, Vogelstein's belief was based not solely on a judgment about what ontological insights needed to be injected into public debate, but on scientists' diagnosis that political debate had rendered perfectly good technical–ontological distinctions "useless" for public reasoning. Irving Weissman put it more strongly: "'Embryonic cloning' is the language of the extreme Christian right and other groups trying to block [the research]."[70] The solution to this problem, he felt, was to "remove emotion and put in fact" by replacing the terminology currently in use.[71]

The President's Council likewise proposed terminological reform but arrived at the opposite conclusion regarding which ontological facts of the matter should be codified in the terms of debate. In a *Wall Street Journal* commentary announcing the council report *Human Cloning and Human Dignity*, Leon Kass wrote,

> Our first goal was to clarify the terminology that confounds public discussion, beginning with "human cloning" itself. Whatever the purpose for which cloning is undertaken, the act that produces the genetic "replica" is the first step, the creation of an embryonic clone.[72]

Critics continued to criticize the term *cloning*, identifying it as a cause of public confusion. In a letter to Senator Orrin Hatch (R-UT), Nobel prizewinner and California Institute of Technology (Caltech) president David Baltimore noted that SCNT for research "is often called therapeutic although that is a terminology that many people find confusing."[73] Senator Arlen Specter (R-PA) commented in a 2001 subcommittee hearing,

> I think it is very unfortunate that the name "cloning" has been attached to what is called "therapeutic cloning," because it confuses the issue with reproductive cloning, and the appropriate scientific name . . . is somatic cell nuclear transfer.[74]

Importantly, the notion that a shared language should be grounded in a "right" ontological account transcended partisan lines. Put differently, there was wide agreement upon the constitutional imperative for public reasoning grounded in ontological correctness, even if there was significant disagreement over whose account, and thus whose terminology, was correct. Thus, even within the most overt instances of political conflict, this shared imagination of right reason reinforced the constitutional position of science—with the effect of privileging particular scientific voices.

RENDERING PUBLIC REASON

In invoking the specter of confusion, the advocates of terminological reform implied that science stood in a privileged position to judge the legitimacy of public deliberation over matters of technical complexity. They asserted that proper public deliberation depended upon keeping fact and values separate—a demarcation that the reformers characterized as being given in advance—and they simultaneously positioned themselves as uniquely able to see where this demarcation had been transgressed. In this respect, the notion of confusion invoked in these debates was different from mere ignorance. With the former concept, scientific experts claimed to be exposing a democratic deficit, rather than merely an epistemic one with secondary implications for public deliberation. Whereas ignorance implies a failure to take into account relevant facts in making moral judgments, confusion was taken as a symptom of a compromised democratic process, one that could be rectified only through exogenous, technocratic management of the terms of debate to engender (what scientific experts saw as) the right forms of public deliberation.

Importantly, advocates of reform did not see the terminology as intrinsically problematic. Their concern was not with the technical accuracy or inaccuracy of the terms themselves, but with the value-laden meanings with which terms had become encumbered in the public sphere. Indeed, the term *therapeutic cloning* was in widespread use within the scientific community, including in peer-reviewed journal publications. It was only when the scientific language "[made] its way to the non-scientific public" that there is "a potential for . . . meaning to be lost or misunderstood."[75] Thus, at issue was not the descriptive accuracy (truth to nature) of the term, but who was entitled to determine how it should be used in public reasoning.

INSTITUTING CHANGE

At the 2004 meeting of the International Society for Stem Cell Research (ISSCR),[76] the society's leadership encouraged members to stop using the term *cloning* to refer to nuclear transplantation. *Nuclear transfer* was recommended as a superior substitute. ISSCR president Leonard Zon announced that a "nomenclature task force" would be established to discuss problems with the term *therapeutic cloning*. In September 2004, the society issued a position statement to the effect that

> the inaccurate use in various public and scientific venues of various terms dealing with the production of stem cell lines by the transfer of body cell (somatic) nuclei into enucleated eggs of the same species, and the negative connotation of the commercial term "therapeutic cloning," make a change in terminology necessary.[77]

The committee encouraged its membership as well as the scientific press to adopt this change in terminology in all publications—scientific and nonscientific—and all forms of communication. This, they suggested, "will introduce scientifically accurate terminology into scientific as well as general literature and language."[78] The rationale for this action was, once again, to enhance public reasoning: "The aim of this terminology change is to provide accurate, standardized terminology that will facilitate frank scientific, ethical and public debate on stem cells and their potential for medicine."[79]

The issue of language arose again at the 2005 ISSCR meeting. During the society's Town Hall Meeting, Paul Abrams addressed the assembled group of over one hundred scientists. A physician, attorney, and biotechnology entrepreneur, Abrams proposed that the word *embryonic* should be abandoned in discussions of nuclear transfer. The term, he asserted, was politically problematic, scientifically inaccurate, and potentially confusing to the public. He insisted that stem cells derived via SCNT are not embryos, so the phrase *embryonic stem cell research* is misleading.[80] He went on to say,

> If we adopt the view that an embryo means a cell is going to implant to make a baby, and none of what we're doing is [making] cells to implant to make a baby, and we come up with different terminology, I think we will have more long-term political success.[81]

Noting the large amount of financial support given to opposition groups to write position papers against embryonic stem cell research, Abrams told his ISSCR audience, "Every time we use the word 'embryonic' we play to their frame." His comments met with an enthusiastic round of applause from the assembled scientists.[82]

In the ensuing discussion, Leonard Zon noted that the society had adopted the phrase *nuclear transfer to produce embryonic stem cells* in its official nomenclature the previous year with positive results. He approvingly cited the use of this language in a recent paper by Korean scientist Hwang Woo-Suk on the successful derivation of hESC from SCNT-derived human blastocysts—a paper that had received considerable media attention (and would receive much more in the future).[83]

CONFUSING THE PUBLIC

On December 10, 2002, Stanford University held a press conference to announce plans to establish a stem cell and cancer research institute. During the press conference, it was announced that the institute's research program would not include the production of cloned human embryos, but would include the creation of pluripotent embryonic stem cell lines through nuclear transplantation. The Associated Press published an article that called into question the choice of terminology. The article quoted Irving Weissman, director of the new institute, saying that "his planned research is 'not even close' to cloning" but noted that "many other researchers say this is a distinction without a difference." The story appeared in newspapers across the country.[84]

The university quickly responded. A Stanford spokesperson told the press, "We're not cloning embryos, and we're not going to clone embryos."[85] The university also issued a series of clarifying press releases. One invoked the authority of the NRC committee that Weissman had chaired, along with scientific societies such as the ISSCR, to dismiss as scientifically incredible the idea that this was cloning:

> Some people consider the process of generating a blastocyst by nuclear transfer to be equivalent to cloning a human embryo. Weissman pointed out that two national scientific panels that reviewed nuclear transfer—one of which Weissman chaired—considered the wording "human embryonic cloning" to be an inaccurate way to describe this procedure. These panels along with all major scientific associations call the procedure "nuclear transplantation to produce human pluripotent stem cell lines."[86]

A spokesperson for the medical center pointed to the public, as opposed to the terms themselves, as the cause of confusion: "I think the concern is that in the minds of the general public, cloning has a certain connotation. For the average person, cloning means the creation of a new life form. That is not what we're engaged in here."[87] The university posted an explanatory webpage that stated that research scientists, research organizations, and expert bodies, including the President's Council on Bioethics, had declared the term *cloned human embryo* to be "an inaccurate and misleading term."[88] Given that this was the opposite of what the President's Council had concluded, chair Leon Kass was nonplussed and sent a letter to university president John Hennessy demanding an official retraction.[89] The university apologized but held its ground on the terminological issue.[90]

A week later, Philip Pizzo, dean of the Stanford University School of Medicine, published an op-ed in the *San Jose Mercury News* in which he stated that the institute's research would involve a process called "nucleus transfer, but which has also been called biomedical or therapeutic cloning."[91] He went on to clarify the distinction:

> In this context, the word "cloning" has very different meanings to scientists and the public, which has led to confusion over the moral and ethical underpinnings of stem cell research. To the scientist, "cloning" in this context simply means creating an identical copy of a cell. *To the public, the word often means the creation of a new human life, to which the scientists at the institute and Stanford are unanimously opposed.* With the help of those in the media and the scientific community, we must work to overcome the language and definitional barriers so that all people can understand the scientific progress being made through stem cell research.[92]

Pizzo's op-ed was distributed by email to the Stanford medical school community. In a prefacing comment, Pizzo referred to the "inaccurate story from the Associated Press that Stanford was going to 'clone human embryos,' which is not true." He went on to say that "one of the lessons I've learned from all this is that the words used in stem cell research, such as 'cloning,' carry an enormous amount of impact to some who are not part of the scientific community."[93]

Pizzo's comment is an example of the way scientist-reformers used the concept of confusion to license interventions in public deliberation and, in the process, to exclude a broad category of claims. He dismissed the notion that human SCNT involved the "creation of a human life" as an instance of public confusion over a practice that "simply means creating an identical copy of a cell."[94]

These efforts to reform public discourse drew upon an imagination of democratically legitimate public reason: reason grounded in a common, value-neutral language that is common by virtue of being tethered to scientifically authorized facts. Scientists' efforts to control the terms of debate were underwritten by a commonplace so familiar that its cultural effects were hidden in plain sight: the notion that facts and values occupy distinct spheres, that they derive from wholly distinct forms of authority, and that the internal integrity of each of these spheres depends upon maintaining a strict separation between them. Facts can be trusted only insofar as they are purged of values and "ideology." Values are not subject to the test of veracity, but of right reason.

From this cultural commonplace followed another: where democracy confronts morally and technically complex matters, society, the custodian of shared values, must depend on scientific authority, the custodian of facts, to supply the picture of reality upon which moral deliberation must be grounded if it is to be robust.

In effect, scientific experts were claiming a position of cognitive authority to define the conditions of possibility for robust democratic deliberation. In analyzing epistemic authority, much scholarship in science and technology studies has shown how the stabilization of expert claims depends on a set of translational tools and forms of mediation—social, material, and epistemic—which are largely hidden when these claims are ultimately advanced as facts in the public sphere. Yet, an analysis of epistemic authority takes us only partway to accounting for the political conditions that made these scientists credible. Two elements distilled from the preceding discussion illustrate this point.

First, there was initially a substantial disjunction between the language employed by the scientific community and the terms proposed by the reformers. The primary argument advanced by the reformers was not that public discourse failed a truth-to-nature test. Rather, it was that the public had become "confused" by fact descriptions that were contaminated with (in Weissman's terms) the "emotional overlay" of values. It was therefore necessary to produce a value-free (rather than merely epistemically correct) language about scientific matters. Democracy ostensibly depended on it. It was not until critics of reform began pointing out that scientists were using the very terms that they were seeking to exile from public discourse that scientific authorities such as the ISSCR nomenclature task force took steps to reform scientific language as well. Put simply, the reform effort was *not* an attempt to disseminate knowledge deemed relevant to public moral deliberation—to "educate the public"—but an attempt to render deliberation reasonable and legitimate in spite of the public's unavoidable knowledge deficit. Their solution was to reform public discourse so that the ethically distressing prospect of "reproductive cloning" would be discursively (and thus also ontologically, conceptually, morally, and politically) segregated from "somatic cell nuclear transfer to produce pluripotent stem cells."

Thus, although reform efforts invoked a knowledge-deficit model of the public,[95] they were neither attempts to fill the deficit, nor were they motivated by the notion that public ignorance necessarily inhibited public reasoning and robust policy. Rather, in discerning public *confusion* (as opposed merely to ignorance), they diagnosed a fatal pathology in public reasoning itself that warranted intervention by scientific authorities to restore democratic deliberation to the right (and righteous) path.

Second, experts claimed not merely to provide the most trustworthy account of the facts of the matter, but also to serve in a role of which the public, no matter how well meaning, was not itself capable: discerning when public deliberation had become confused and therefore unreasonable. In effect, they positioned scientific experts not only in the role of authoritative "spokesperson for nature,"[96] but as the sole authority able to recognize and remedy democratic failure in public assessments of science and technology. Put simply, experts like Vogelstein and Weissman claimed for themselves not only the authority to assess the veracity of fact claims, but also the competency to assess the quality of democratic deliberation—and, more importantly, the authority to dictate the discursive conditions for reasoned public judgment by supplying a common language.

In advancing the concept of "confusion" to mark deliberative failure, reformers drew upon a widely shared imaginary of right public reason as grounded in a common, secular, value-neutral language, common not least because it is grounded in science. Part and parcel of this imaginary was a corollary construction of the constitutional position of science: of science as an extra-political authority that supplies the shared epistemic foundations for public moral sense-making while remaining outside the arena of politics.

6

IN THE LABORATORIES
OF DEMOCRACY

By 2004, the Bush administration's policy on stem cell research had become a locus of significant public controversy. A growing political movement characterized the federal policy as a dereliction of the administration's responsibility to the public's well-being. Critics argued that federal policies were inhibiting the biomedical innovations that would otherwise inevitably flow from public investment in research. During the first term of the Bush presidency, momentum at the national level began to coalesce into eddies of political activity at the state level where it was easier for grassroots efforts to navigate around the constraints of representative government. Between 2002 and 2007, initiatives emerged in a number of states to encourage embryonic stem cell research, including the provision of research funding. In some cases, these were legislative, but the most ambitious and controversial were ballot measures. These projects of direct democracy sought to wrest responsibility from the hands of lawmakers, making the public the direct custodian of the scientific and technological future. The architects of these initiatives saw the ballot initiative process as the ideal tool for bypassing the limitations of representative democracy. It was a means for the vox populi to speak clearly and unequivocally. Citizens could make law with the check of a box.

Of these state ballot initiatives, the most radical and ambitious by far was California's. In 2002, a political effort in California began to form that would ultimately lead to a successful ballot initiative in 2004 to allocate $3 billion over ten years to human embryonic stem cell (hESC) research in the state.[1] This was the largest state-level science funding initiative in the history of the United States. It was also an effort to reinvent the terms of political engagement around human embryo research and to rewrite the social contract among science, state, and citizen that underwrites public science. And the architects of the initiative saw it as a powerful tool to generate a univocal democratic rebuke of federal policies.

The title of the initiative reflected the unrestrained hope associated with hESC research: the "California Stem Cell Research and Cures Initiative," also known as Proposition 71. The initiative prompted a vigorous debate over the proper relationship among the citizen, the democratic state, and the structures of technoscientific innovation. In the politics surrounding the initiative, the focus of public debate shifted almost entirely away from the moral status of the human embryo to ideas of the right relationships between science and the state, between state and citizen, and among citizens in their deliberative exchanges in the public square. As a result, the initiative elicited a reassessment of the social contract with science concurrently with a reassessment of the democratic social contract—and, in particular, the norms of public reasoning that bind the polity together as a democratic public and require that certain kinds of claims be removed to the private sphere.

State stem cell referenda represented an important stage in the sequence of experiments in democracy that emerged around human embryo research. This chapter turns to these experimental sites to examine the constructions of democracy to which they contributed and the background work that went into staging it. Notwithstanding an apparently complete return of power to the people, science remained a significant locus of authority in these democratic dramas. Indeed, the constitutional position of science is particularly evident within the context of these apparently pure expressions of the democratic will, and so too in the unmediated politics of the public square that accompanied them. In this chapter and the next, I trace a series of domains in which scientific authority was deployed to designate what premises must be held in common (and what premises, by definition, cannot be) and what imaginations of public reasoning underwrite ideas of commonness. This chapter specifically follows the debates over terminology into the background machinery of direct democracy. I examine two legal cases that preceded ballot initiatives in California and Missouri. In these cases, the debates over terminology that were the subject of the previous chapter made their way into the workings of institutions whose explicit responsibility was to democracy, not science. Together, the cases demonstrate that debates over terminology touched directly on legal interpretations of fundamental democratic norms. They reveal how the custodial responsibility of science for democracy was not merely asserted by scientific experts, but was also conferred upon them by the courts. They reveal that the "constitutional" position of science within American democracy is regulative not only of the rhetoric of public reasoning, but of institutional power over the contours of democratic processes themselves.

DESIGNING THE EXPERIMENT

Following the announcement of Dolly in 1997, California began to develop its own research policy on cloning. The state enacted legislation placing a five-year moratorium on the cloning of human beings.[2] Companion legislation created an advisory body with "experts from the fields of medicine, theology, biotechnology, genetics, law, bioethics, and from the general public" to advise the legislature and the governor on research involving cloning.[3] That body, the California Cloning Commission, unanimously recommended in 2002 that the state ban "reproductive cloning" but endorse "human non-reproductive cloning" for research and stem cell derivation.[4] In response, California state senator Deborah Ortiz (D-Sacramento) introduced legislation meant to encourage hESC research in the state. The legislation explicitly endorsed the use of somatic cell nuclear transfer (SCNT) in stem cell research, while parallel legislation banned human reproductive cloning. It also established a basic regulatory framework for hESC research and required that in vitro fertilization (IVF) clinics in the state offer patients the option to donate unused embryos.[5] On September 22, 2002, Governor Gray Davis signed the legislation into law. At the signing, Davis expressed his hope that the law would help the state extend its existing strengths in biotechnology innovation to become a worldwide leader in hESC research: "With world-class universities, top-flight researchers and a thriving biomedical industry, California is perfectly positioned."[6]

For all the expressions of hope, however, California scientists still faced a major impediment to advancing their research agendas: a lack of funding. Some hESC research was taking place in California's private sector. Geron Corporation, which held exclusive licenses on the Wisconsin Alumni Research Foundation hESC patents, as well as on Ian Wilmut's nuclear transfer work at the University of Edinburgh's Roslin Institute, was based in Menlo Park, California. Some academic research was taking place with the support of private donors and foundations such as the Howard Hughes Medical Institute. But there was still an unmet appetite for more funding. Given that commercial applications of hESC research were a long way off, venture capital was not forthcoming. It was therefore generally recognized that it would take more than a friendly regulatory environment to raise the state to a position of global scientific leadership. It would take money. Ortiz thus proposed dedicating $1 billion of public funds to hESC research in California. The proposed legislation got little traction.[7]

At roughly the same time, two Hollywood couples began to hold fundraising dinners at their homes with prominent stem cell scientists, wealthy disease advocates, and public officials. They were Doug Wick and Lucy Fisher and Janet and Jerry Zucker. Both couples had children with type 1 diabetes and had been active for several years in juvenile diabetes advocacy efforts. The scientists invited to the dinners included Larry Goldstein of the University of California, San Diego, James Thomson of the University of Wisconsin, and Irving Weissman and Paul Berg of Stanford, among others. As the dinner guests discussed scientific possibilities and political strategies, they began to explore the idea of pushing for public funding at the state level. They saw an opportunity in California's unique apparatus of direct democracy: the ballot initiative.[8] A coalition formed around this project.

California's much cherished, and much maligned, ballot initiative process is its solution to the sometimes muddled politics of representative democracy. A ballot initiative allows the electorate to make law directly at the ballot box. To place an initiative on the ballot, its sponsors must simply collect 100,000 signatures. Any initiative on any topic, sponsored by any group that collects the requisite number of signatures, will be decided by popular vote. The initiative process is at the same time an occasion for public deliberation and an instrument of direct democracy.

The purpose of Proposition 71 was to "fill the critical funding gap" left by the federal government's hESC research funding policy.[9] This funding gap, the initiative claimed, "prevents the rapid advancement of research that could benefit millions of Californians."[10] The initiative would establish an institute that would use state bond proceeds to support those areas of research considered most neglected by federal policy: "pluripotent stem cell and progenitor cell research and other vital medical technologies for the development of life-saving regenerative medical treatments and cures."[11] (The text of the initiative avoided the terms *embryo* and *embryonic* altogether. It referred to "human pluripotent stem cells" rather than "human embryonic stem cells" and to left-over IVF-derived embryos as "surplus products of in vitro fertilization treatments.") The initiative provided for $3 billion in funding over ten years.

The coalition behind the initiative launched a powerful campaign that took on a variety of forms, from television advertisements featuring prominent scientists and celebrity patient advocates to academic lecture series at universities around the state. When all was said and done, the campaign spent over $26 million promoting the initiative.[12]

By the summer of 2004, as the Proposition 71 campaign picked up steam, a limited range of embryonic stem cell research had been funded with federal dollars.[13] Bush's funding policy permitted federal support of research on hESC lines created before August 9, 2001.[14] There was, however, no federal regulation of nonpublicly funded research involving human gametes or in vitro embryos as long as these activities were sufficiently insulated from federal funds. This meant that any university laboratory engaging in hESC research using nonfederally approved hESC lines had to separate the physical spaces and materials dedicated to hESC research from any research funded with federal dollars.

Though onerous and sometimes costly, these requirements had not prevented stem cell research from moving forward in California. Several universities, including Stanford, had established or were in the process of establishing centers dedicated specifically to hESC and regenerative medicine research. Much of the private sector research was based in California as well. Relative to other states, California was at or near the top in terms of total dollars from all sources spent on hESC-related research in 2003.[15] But, relative to the level of expenditure proposed by

Proposition 71, the sum total of dollars, public and private, invested in hESC research in the state was small.

Given the purported promise of hESC research, both scientific and economic, proponents of Proposition 71 maintained that California had a unique opportunity to generate an area of technological innovation and an industry that would be a source of wealth, "world-leadership" and well-being for its citizens. Indeed, Proposition 71 advocates argued that because California had a well-established history of nurturing revolutionary innovation—technoscientific as well as democratic—it was the ideal environment in which to undertake such a project.[16] With the California economy still smarting from the recent deflation of the dot-com bubble, there was eager anticipation for the next honing of the cutting edge.

FREEING FREE SPEECH

Because the California ballot initiative process allows laws to be passed by referendum, and because initiatives are often complex and difficult for the time-pressed citizen to understand (let alone read), the word choices in the text of initiatives and official voter guides can significantly affect their chances for success or failure. Since, with Proposition 71 (and other state-level legislation and referenda), voter perceptions would translate directly into law, the terminological disputes examined in earlier chapters acquired higher stakes.

The drafters of the text were very careful to use language that distanced the initiative from terms burdened with what Irving Weissman had called "emotional overlay".[17] The text of Proposition 71 avoided terms such as *embryo, preembryo*, and *embryonic*, instead referring to research on "pluripotent" cells derived from the "surplus products of in vitro fertilization treatments." It also stated that "pluripotent stem cells may be derived from somatic cell nuclear transfer." The term *cloning* appeared only in reference to reproductive cloning. SCNT was never explicitly associated with cloning, therapeutic or otherwise. Reproductive cloning was defined as "the practice of creating or attempting to create a human being by transferring the nucleus from a human cell into an egg cell from which the nucleus has been removed for the purpose of implanting the resulting product in a uterus to initiate a pregnancy."[18]

Proposition 71 advocates argued in many contexts and to many audiences that a fair vote depended on understanding the facts and that confusion with regard to facts was the enemy of democracy. Proposition 71 was an opportunity to demonstrate that the majority of the public, when given the right terms, would support hESC research funding. It was a kind of proof-of-principle democratic experiment designed to show that representative democracy had failed to reflect the public will. Advocates of hESC research hoped that Proposition 71 would transform national politics through a direct democratic rejoinder to federal policies. In the words of Daniel Perry, president of the Coalition for the Advancement of Medical Research, Proposition 71 would "rattle windowpanes in Washington."[19]

Stanford Medicine, a publication of the Stanford University School of Medicine, published a special issue dedicated to hESC research in the fall of 2004 in anticipation of the Proposition 71 vote. The feature article began with a simple conversion story of a politician by a scientist, in this case a mother by a son. The article recounted a trusting exchange in which the scientist redefined and unburdened complex terms from their "emotional overlay," transforming his mother's political position simply by enhancing her grasp of the scientific details and stakes:

> Stanford physician Michael Lyons, MD, is not a stem cell researcher. But when the Connecticut House Speaker recently called him to discuss her "cautious, maybe even negative, feelings" about a state bill that would endorse embryonic stem cell research, the Stanford genetics fellow was happy to oblige. The state lawmaker felt uneasy about portions of the bill, so Lyons patiently defined complex scientific terms, clarified the differences between this type of research and reproductive cloning, and outlined what he saw as the merits of the work. By the end of the conversation he had convinced his mom that she should support the legislation.[20]

The article gave a detailed account of this exchange to demonstrate how prejudice can give way to support once people use the "right terms." It explained that Speaker Moira Lyons of Connecticut was but one of many examples of confusion-induced negativity: "Stem cells are so small that they cannot be seen with the naked eye, yet they tend to cause mass confusion and evoke the largest of responses." And the wrong terms undermine the right moral and political positions: "Moira Lyons blames the bill's eventual failure to pass in the Connecticut House on legislators' confusion over terminology."[21]

In the months before the vote on Proposition 71, a legal battle took place in California to prevent a repeat of the Connecticut failure. It occurred quietly and behind the scenes, far from the raucous politics of the public stem cell debate. The suit was brought by three of the architects of Proposition 71 against a small coalition of Proposition 71 opponents.[22] They challenged the text in the General Election State Ballot pamphlet provided by the state to educate voters on the ballot initiatives.[23]

Because ballot measures are often complex, the state tries to provide resources to the citizen to understand, evaluate, and deliberate over the content of the measure. To this end, the state provides voters with a ballot pamphlet that includes summaries of the initiatives and the principal arguments for and against. Rather than attempting to construct a neutral and balanced assessment of all sides of the issue, however, the state makes use of the weights and counterweights of adversarial politics. It commissions the initiative's strongest proponents and strongest critics to formulate the arguments for and against.[24] Given that these arguments are understood as political speech, opinions are expressed, and value-laden arguments are made. The only limits on the process are that arguments should contain no "false and misleading" statements.[25]

Another very similar suit was brought in Missouri roughly a year later in conjunction with a Missouri referendum on stem cell research. The case concerned a challenge to the official summary produced by the Missouri secretary of state. The summary of the measure explained that the initiative would "ban human cloning."

The primary question before the court in both cases was not whether a specific claim was true or false, but whether the challenged claim consisted of value-neutral, factual speech, and thus was subject to misrepresentation, or value-laden political speech, and thus the very stuff of the democratic process. If the claim was the former, it would misinform voters and cause a miscarriage of democracy—votes cast might reflect confusion rather than informed choice. If the claim was the latter, it represented political speak—the apex of first amendment protection. Thus, in each case, the court was, in effect, required to make a judgment about public reason—about how the language of science should be spoken in the public square in order to bring about robust and legitimate democracy. In this capacity, the courts were tasked with determining what qualifies as evidence for informed political judgment. At stake was the most basic procedural expression of democracy—the right to vote, and to vote meaningfully. In what follows, I compare the two lawsuits and show how the efforts to reform language became a focal point as custodianship for hESC policy was given directly to the public. The lawsuits demonstrate how efforts to reform public speech became contests over expert authority where the very legitimacy of the democratic process was seen as dependent upon scientific certification of the terms of public reasoning.

CALIFORNIA: PUTTING REFORM TO THE TEST

In late July 2004, three of the chief architects of Proposition 71—Paul Berg, Stanford Nobel laureate; Larry Goldstein, stem cell scientist from the University of California, San Diego; and Robert Klein, patient advocate and primary author of Proposition 71—filed a petition alleging that the "No-on-71" section of the General Election State Ballot pamphlet contained "false and misleading" statements. The plaintiffs identified themselves as citizens, experts, and stakeholders:

1. Petitioner PAUL BERG, Ph.D. is a registered California voter and California taxpayer. Petitioner Berg is a Nobel Laureate Professor of Cancer Research at Stanford University.

2. ROBERT N. KLEIN is a registered California voter and a California taxpayer. Petitioner Klein is the father of a son who has juvenile diabetes, and is the son of a mother who has Alzheimer's disease.

3. Petitioner LARRY GOLDSTEIN is a registered California voter and California taxpayer. Petitioner Goldstein is a university professor and a research scientist working on understanding and treating human disease.

Pursuant to the California election code, the petition requested the court to "prevent the publication of false or misleading information" in the ballot pamphlet. The law designates that such petitions will be granted only upon clear and convincing proof that the copy in question is clearly "false, misleading or inconsistent with the requirements of this code," or if mistakes were made in the printing of a voter pamphlet.[26]

The petition identified a number of statements as false and misleading. Among these was the header of the opposition's "rebuttal argument":

"Stem Cell Research? Yes! Human cloning? No!"

The petitioners argued that "this statement is false and misleading because Proposition 71 prohibits the use of Institute funds for human reproductive cloning which is also illegal under state law."[27] They also objected to the text in the rebuttal paragraph that argued that "the perfection of embryo cloning technology . . . will increase the likelihood human clones will be produced."[28] Petitioners argued,

> This statement is false and misleading because under Proposition 71 there will not be any 'embryo cloning technology' that will 'increase the likelihood that human clones will be produced' because human cloning is banned in California both by the initiative and existing state law.[29]

The "No-on-71" defendants responded that the petitioners were drawing a false distinction between "cloning" and SCNT to produce stem cells:

> What the petitioners would have this court ignore is the fact that *both* of these techniques begin with nuclear transfer into an unfertilized egg and the cloning of a human embryo. . . . The result is a cloned embryo, in other words a human clone.[30]

The defendants engaged in the same form of boundary work as the petitioners, claiming that their language reflected an ontological (and thus scientific) fact of the matter and that the petitioners' intervention was both scientifically irresponsible and antidemocratic. It was an attempt "to camouflage that inescapable scientific reality" that nuclear transfer results in the creation of a cloned embryo—which can be implanted in a uterus or from which stem cells can be derived.[31] The challenged statements, they argued, were "neither false nor misleading" but were "grounded on and reflected solid science."[32] The the suit was, the defendents declared, an effort to "suppress the facts, mislead voters, and stifle any robust argument."

While fact speech is regulated by the California election code, first amendment protection is "'at its zenith" in the initiative process because "it involves interactive communication involving political change."[33] Therefore, according to California's interpretation of this constitutional standard, in order to limit speech around the initiative process, evidence must be so "clear and convincing" as to "command the unhesitating assent of every reasonable mind."[34]

These provisions also comport with the basic premise of deliberative democratic theory that the fact–value distinction is foundational for producing clear articulations of contentious, value-laden questions. Value speech must be enhanced and protected, whereas fact claims must be stabilized (or marked as uncertain) in advance so that democratic deliberation focuses on the forms of value disagreement that are appropriate to it.[35] I have argued above that the notion of confusion advanced in critiques of the term *cloning* is consistent with this view of the fact–value distinction. The advocates of terminological reform whom I discussed in the previous chapter too affirmed a fact–value boundary; only they claimed that confusion was the result of the lay citizen's inability to separate neutral, scientific facts from value-laden evaluations (or "emotional overlay") in discussions of cloning because they were confused by the technical complexity of the issue. Therefore, the authority to diagnose public confusion in order to safeguard the legitimacy of public reasoning, they implied, must be delegated to scientific experts. The California election code reflects the same foundational presumptions of a discernable boundary between facts and values—between fact speech, which can be false and misleading, and political speech. In practice, however, drawing this boundary becomes a question of who is authorized to speak for the epistemic "view from nowhere" and distinguish it from situated political views, and thus who becomes the custodian of the distinction between fact and value and the political arrangements that rely upon this distinction. It is the question that the President's Council on Bioethics confronted in determining which experts should be first on the agenda to guide the process of fitting "speech to fact."

Thus, the California court encountered claims about the ontology of a biological entity—the product of SCNT—and corollary claims about the profound stakes for democracy of getting the ontological account correct. Judge Gail Ohanesian was asked to distinguish fact claims from value claims and, as such, to distinguish between democracy-subverting confusion and democracy-enhancing disagreement. If the anti–Proposition 71 arguments were determined to be fact claims, they would be subject to evaluation by scientific experts for their veracity. Were they to fail, they would be suppressed. If they were determined to be political speech, however, they would be the very stuff of democratic deliberation. As such, they would deserve protection as expressions of the most essential and precious American liberty. Thus, the court was required to rule on the nature of the speech, not on the veracity of particular fact claims, and as such, on a normative problem of democratic legitimacy, not an epistemic problem of scientific correctness. But the judge herself, as a layperson, was of course subject to the very problem that motivated efforts to reform the language: confusion. The plaintiffs argued that the legal standard that the falsity of the cloning claims should "command the unhesitating assent of every reasonable mind" could not be applied by just anyone. What made minds "reasonable," in this instance, was, they asserted, deference to scientific judgment.

Each side marshaled a set of experts to testify to its reading of the facts. Professor Irving Weissman of Stanford testified for the petitioners. Supplying a short declaration and a long curriculum vitae as evidence of his expertise, he presented himself as an authorized spokesperson for the facts as they present themselves in the Petri dish:

Scientists can extract the precursors of embryonic stem cells from blastocysts, or clusters of cells, created by transferring the nucleus of a cell into a human oocyte. . . . In both cases the blastocysts are destroyed after the embryonic stem cells are extracted, and neither process results in a 'human embryo clone'; it results in an embryonic stem cell line.[36]

This position was yet more explicitly laid out in the declaration of Evan Snyder, director of the Program in Stem Cell and Regenerative Biology at the Burnham Institute in La Jolla, California. Snyder identified the two forms of embryonic stem cell research: the extraction of embryonic stem cells from the "surplus product of in vitro fertilization" and the "extract[ion of] embryonic stem cells from blastocysts, or clusters of cells, created by transferring the nucleus from a cell into an unfertilized egg." Agreeing with Weissman's conclusion, he stated that neither process creates a "human embryo clone." He went on to testify that Stanford and the International Society for Stem Cell Research had officially changed the terminology they use because "the terms 'embryo cloning' and 'cloned embryo' are imprecise and misleading."[37]

Declarations on behalf of the opposition argued that the termino-logical distinctions advanced by the plaintiffs were attempts at political manipulation masquerading as scientific expertise and that they subverted genuine deliberation by sowing confusion. Physician Rex Greene testified that "although the authors and proponents of Proposition 71 use different names for somatic cell nuclear transfer and reproductive cloning, these are medically and scientifically the same procedure. . . . SCNT is the scientific name for the procedure popularly known as 'cloning.'"[38] Journalist Wesley Smith argued that the distinction drawn by the petitioners was a "subter-fuge." While the purposes of the two processes may differ, "once the cloned embryo comes into existence, there are no further acts of cloning," though "there may be different fates for the embryo that now exists."[39]

The argument that seems to have convinced the court was made by cell biologist Stuart Newman. Newman was in some respects an unlikely ally to the "No-on-71" coalition. Given his stronger ties to the progres-sive left than the conservative right, Newman's support was considered a "shot in the dark" by the defense. Newman's contribution is remarkable because it was the only declaration submitted by a scientist that did not simply make a descriptive claim about the facts of the matter backed up by an extensive CV. Newman departed from the presumption that the stakes turned on "fitting speech to fact." He instead marshaled a piece of social evidence—namely, the record of scientific practice—that opened the black box of scientific representation to reveal the social conventions and interests within.

Newman testified that "until Stanford University decided in the last year to stop using the terms 'embryo cloning' and 'cloned embryos' to describe the technique of producing human embryos by nuclear transfer and the products of the technique, these were the names used virtually exclusively by scientists for these items."[40] "Cloned embryos," he maintained, was still the "term of art in this field."[41] Citing the only piece of empirical evidence included in any declaration on cloning terminology, Newman indicated that a search on the Medline database revealed forty-two uses of the phrase in the past year, including in the title of an editorial by no less an expert than Ian Wilmut, the scientist responsible for cloning Dolly. At the same time, Newman invoked the authority of science to discount the authority of the plaintiffs' experts:

> Whether or not a scientist intends to implant a cluster of cells does not determine whether or not it is an embryo. If it is a cluster of liver cells, for example, the intention to implant it does not make it an embryo. Correspondingly, if it is a blastocyst capable of giving rise to embryo stem cells, the lack of intention to implant it does not cause it not to be an embryo. To believe that the material nature of a biological entity changes depending on the intention of the investigator is an example of magical thinking, which is antithetical to modern science.[42]

With this invocation of the nature of the thing-in-itself, Newman did something no other witness on either side had done. Whereas all other witnesses had claimed to be making extra-political truth claims, Newman dismantled the notion that science sits outside of politics by suggesting that truth claims (though not truth itself) are the product of social practices and changeable linguistic conventions. And whereas the others had presented technical scientific language as an unmediated representation of the natural facts, Newman placed science on the side of social action, invoking the essential nature of the material entity as having a higher ontological authority than the scientific representations of it.

It is remarkable that Newman was the only witness in the proceeding to treat language as nominal and grounded in social convention, but it is equally noteworthy that his constructivist account of language was grounded in an even deeper realism than was advanced by others.

To challenge others' authority, he did not argue that he was more credible or knew better. Instead, he argued that their fact claims were mixtures of the natural and the social and, as such, closer to the ideology-laden super-stitions of "magical thinking" than the enlightened objectivity of "modern science." Thus, even as he located specific scientific claims within a social (and thus political) field, he invoked the idea of "modern science" to do so. Though one can only speculate about what ultimately influenced the court's judgments, it is notable that the imaginary of science as an extra-political source of authority remained intact even where the credibility of particular scientists was challenged. Indeed, it remained the measure against which expert claims were judged to be true to fact or merely politi-cal speech.

Newman's was an empirically grounded argument the judge could understand. She ruled that the "cloning" language was political speech and should therefore remain unchanged. The Proposition 71 opponents won in the courts, but not at the polls.

MISSOURI: THE EXPERIMENT REPRODUCED

In 2005, a coalition of Missouri-based pro–hESC research advocates, referred to as the "Missouri Coalition for Lifesaving Cures," became alarmed at state-level legislative efforts to outlaw all human SCNT research. They drafted a ballot initiative that would, among other things, prevent the enactment of such legislation. The purpose of the initiative was to protect any hESC or SCNT research conducted in the state of Missouri and to lay the groundwork for encouraging more of it.

The Missouri case differs from the California case in instructive ways. First, it played out in a much more conservative political environment. Second, in Missouri, the secretary of state is responsible for drafting the ballot title and summary using politically neutral language that is meant to be unbiased and purely informational. In contrast to California, where the ballot pamphlet explains a measure by offering politically opposing viewpoints, the purpose of the ballot summary in Missouri is to pro-vide the voter with a neutral account of the initiative in straightforward language. The secretary of state plays the role of the neutral arbiter of language. Third, unlike in California, the challenge to the term *cloning* was brought by an anti–hESC research organization on the grounds that it was being used in a misleading way by the secretary of state.

The official ballot summary for Constitutional Amendment 2 as prepared by Secretary of State Robin Carnahan read as follows:

> Shall the Missouri Constitution be amended to allow and set limitations on stem cell research, therapies, and cures which will:
>
> 1. ensure Missouri patients have access to any therapies and cures, and allow Missouri researchers to conduct any research, permitted under federal law;
> 2. ban human cloning or attempted cloning;
> 3. require expert medical and public oversight and annual reports on the nature and purpose of stem cell research;
> 4. impose criminal and civil penalties for any violations; and
> 5. prohibit state or local governments from preventing or discouraging lawful stem cell research, therapies and cures?[43]

The text of the amendment stipulated that "no person may clone or attempt to clone a human being," and defined human cloning as follows:

> "Clone or attempt to clone a human being" means to implant in a uterus or attempt to implant in a uterus anything other than the product of fertilization of an egg of a human female by a sperm of a human male for the purpose of initiating a pregnancy that could result in the creation of a human fetus, or the birth of a human being.[44]

A group called "Missourians Against Human Cloning" filed a suit against the secretary of state. They were represented by a pro-life legal organization called the Bioethics Defense Fund, which requested that the court amend the summary statements in the following way:

> 1. ~~ensure Missouri patients have access to any therapies and cure, and~~ allow Missouri researchers to conduct any research, permitted under federal law;

2. ban human cloning or attempted cloning *to produce children*;
3. *allow human cloning for biomedical research*;
4. require expert medical and public oversight and annual reports on the nature and purpose of *embryonic* stem cell research;
5. impose criminal and civil penalties for any violations; and
6. prohibit state or local governments from preventing or discouraging lawful *embryonic* stem cell research, therapies and cures?[45]

The purpose of the suit was to change the language to emphasize that if the amendment were to pass, human embryo research, including SCNT, would proceed and be newly protected. The primary claim of voter deception was over statement 2: "ban human cloning or attempted cloning."

Like the pro-research plaintiffs in California, the Missouri plaintiffs, represented by the conservative Bioethics Defense Fund, built their case upon the notion that the democratic process depends upon accurate epistemic representations. The purpose of the lawsuit, they declared, was not to adjudicate value-laden questions, but to ensure that the democratic process was built upon a scientifically firm foundation. They wrote,

> This case is not about when human life begins or how to define personhood. Neither is this case about whether embryonic stem cell research or human cloning is good public policy. Plaintiffs' challenge to the Official Ballot Title is about one thing: *the deception of Missouri voters. This case is about honesty in both science and the democratic process.*[46]

The defense responded that there is deception only if the language is factually inaccurate—and, they argued, it was not. Furthermore, they proposed changes using terms that were "not readily understood by the Missouri public" and not defined, namely "human cloning or attempted cloning to produce children" and "human cloning for biomedical research." Therefore, the defense argued "their proposal does nothing but confuse."[47]

The plaintiffs rejoined that the defendants were "attempting to redefine the term 'cloning.'" Because most Missourians were opposed to "human cloning," and few would discover the unconventional definition of the term in the text of the initiative, they were likely to unwittingly vote in favor of a law that did precisely the opposite of what they thought. It was like "stating that the proposed initiative bans hunting in Missouri, but defines hunting as only applying to animals larger than elephants."[48]So, the question before the court was whether the language of the summary would deceive voters and was therefore "insufficient" to the needs of democracy. In marshaling evidence, however, both sides approached the case as a problem of the accuracy of technical scientific language—and they both brought in scientific experts to give evidence.

SPEAKING TRUTH TO POWER

Disputes over ballot titles in Missouri are common. However, they almost never involve the presentation of evidence. Usually, the judge serves as a discerning reader—standing in for the reasonable citizen—by assessing the summary in relation to the initiative text. However, in this instance, the judge decided that expert testimony should be presented because the case dealt with a complex technical matter. Thus, in admitting evidence, the judge affirmed that for a scientific description to be "fair and sufficient" for good politics, it must be certified by science. In effect, because science was at issue, the judge set aside his own powers of reasoning—his own ability to stand in for the lay voter and make sense of the text—and instead deferred to expert reasoning.

At trial, scientific experts were called by both sides. Maureen Condic, a developmental biologist from the University of Utah and a pro-life Catholic critic of embryo research, testified that "cloning" in common scientific speech refers to the process of SCNT, regardless of the ultimate product of the process—whether embryo, stem cell, fetus, or baby.

Experts for the defense, William Neaves of the Stowers Institute and Douglas Melton of Harvard University, both disagreed with Condic, testifying that the term "cloning" was not commonly used in scientific contexts to refer to SCNT. Neaves stated that the terms "reproductive" and "therapeutic cloning" are "principally used in popular articles . . . scientists do not typically use those terms."[49] Several months earlier Neaves had published a letter in *Science* commenting on public misunderstanding of the term "clone." In his commentary, he drew a strong distinction between confusion on facts and disagreement over values, asserting that science could address confusion without interfering with politics, and that it was imperative that it do so. By keeping the facts straight, science would enhance politics: "We have no illusions that more exact terminology will quiet disputes about when life begins and what research is permissible. We do believe that accurate language will result in clearer debates and will not so routinely mislead the uniformed."[50]

In his testimony, Neaves again drew a distinction between factual descriptions that belong to the expert and moral judgments that belong to public deliberation. He asserted authority over the former, but not the latter:

> It is important to help people understand exactly what the source of these cells is. . . . If someone has a moral objection to that, then their opinion is as good as anyone else's. And it is not my intention to do anything other than say these are the facts. And then it's your responsibility in the context of your faith tradition and values and philosophy to decide whether this is something you support or oppose.[51]

Neaves was repeating a version of the account of right public reason that appears throughout the episodes I have analyzed: To be robust, public deliberation must be grounded in a scientifically authorized common language, and, therefore, scientific experts should order public discourse around technically complex issues. Put simply, to fulfill its duties, democracy needs to be guided by experts. This idea of the role of scientific expertise in shaping public reasoning is by now familiar. In this instance, however, scientific experts were not merely acting on their political interests and drawing on their rhetorical credibility in a wider social field. They were expert witnesses, supplying resources to the court to execute its custodial responsibility for democracy itself. In positioning a scientifically certified common language as the prerequisite for true democracy, Neaves positioned scientists as the proper custodians of both knowledge and democratic politics, and he claimed this role on ostensibly epistemic grounds. Thus, scientific expertise, offered in the setting of the court, became evidence for (or against) rightly performed democracy.

In a way, the Missouri trial was a microcosmic performance of this democratic theory. Judge Byron Kinder unreflexively adopted the role of the nonexpert citizen, interrupting the examination of witnesses to ask his own questions. Explaining himself to the assembled litigants, he said, "It has nothing to do with what I have to do here. I rarely get to ask questions about somatic cell nuclear transfer."[52] At such moments, the judge acted as the figure of the citizen who depends upon a unidirectional flow of information from science, unconditioned by surrounding politics. Despite taking place in as overtly a political setting as can be imagined, in these brief interludes, the judge's questions affirmed the notion that the scientific expert was a mouthpiece of nature, a purveyor of evidence rather than a politically embedded person. Even where an expert was connected to an explicitly political organization, the judge affirmed the political neutrality of scientific expertise and drew a sharp distinction between the social identity of the expert and the extra-political authority of his expertise. For instance,

PLAINTIFF COUNSEL: I believe in your deposition last Friday you testified that Harvard is a member of the Coalition for the Advancement of Medical Research,[53] correct?

THE COURT: Counselor, you're stretching it a little far. You're dealing with a man who sat in part of the McCarthy hearings when I was a policeman in Washington, D.C. Guilt by association was not going to sell then, it's not going to sell now. I mean, you might ask what church he belongs to and ask what their position is. *These things speak for themselves.*[54]

The trial judge ruled in favor of the defendants by letting the ballot text stand.

Invoking a different sort of positivism than had been deployed in the trial, the appellate court affirmed the ruling.[55] The court explained that, because the initiative defined *human cloning*, the use of the term in the title summary by definition could not be inaccurate:

One of the purposes of the initiative is to ban human cloning, a term it defines. The Secretary of State's summary states that the initiative would "ban human cloning and attempted cloning." The summary accurately describes what the initiative says it will do.[56]

"Our role is not to act as political arbiter between opposing viewpoints," the opinion explained. Any assessment of the politically contested meaning of the term would require the court to overstep the limits of its authority by straying into politics: "To [choose between the two definitions] would edge us toward a review of the merits of the initiative itself."[57]

Judge James M. Smart, Jr., wrote a separate opinion in which he argued that the question of terminological accuracy was neither here nor there. He noted, "There is no dispute in this case about the biological facts."[58] Nevertheless, he argued, the right of voters not to be misled requires that the language be clarified, because "this case is about a phrase that has become a shibboleth of both sides of the debate about somatic cell nuclear transfer."[59] The fact that this phrase entered the ballot process already embedded in political controversy created a unique "climate of uncertainty as to the meaning of the phrase."[60]

Smart's dissent was right in its reasoning but wrong in claiming there was "no dispute . . . about the biological facts." Indeed, what is most noteworthy about this story, and crystallized most clearly in the two cases, is that the responsibility for engendering circumstances of free and equal deliberative democratic engagement was appropriated by scientific experts. They capitalized on the imagination, deeply embedded in American political culture, that scientific knowledge stands outside of politics to assert custodial responsibility over the machinery of democracy. Drawing on the commonsense notion that reasoned deliberation requires a common language, they claimed that the language of "cloning" was invisibly but perniciously prejudiced by minority values and thus undermined the conditions for legitimate democratic judgment. When this account was tested in the crucible of the courtroom, what had emerged as a political strategy to shape terms of epistemic representation took the form of formal expertise supplied in the name of safeguarding democracy itself.

This pair of courtroom dramas played out outside of the public eye. Indeed, they went essentially unnoticed in the extensive media coverage about each of these initiatives. Yet, in these moments, the very discursive staging upon which democracy itself would be performed was being constructed. At stake was an imagination of rightly ordered democracy that depended upon right knowledge—where the conditions of possibility for the robust exercise of democratic judgment required corollary prior judgments about how the polity should know, speak, disagree, and deliberate when exercising its duties of citizenship.

That these cases took the form of technical disputes over fact representations and contests over expert credibility reflects the constitutional position of science in the American democratic imagination. The authority of science here depended on more than scientists' claims to special knowledge. That authority was not sui generis but was conferred upon scientific experts. The experts required the court to construct its own dependency upon science in executing its role. Law privileged science because science seemed to offer it resources in the task of defining the limits—and the foundations—of legitimate politics. The expert testimony heard in these cases functioned not merely as authoritative accounts of natural facts, but as evidence for an informed polity—a polity that was constructed as requiring the right kind of access to properly authorized knowledge to make politically legitimate judgments. At stake was the question of "who knows best," but these stakes derived not from some general imperative to achieve true-to-nature epistemic representations, but from a very specific normative commitment to the notion that the foundations of public reasoning, and of the democratic judgments that follow from it, should be grounded in a shared, prepolitical picture of the natural world.

Therefore, these moments cannot be explained away as reflecting naïve failures to see that epistemic representations are always already political. In their own way, each case demonstrates the privileged place of the idea of neutral knowledge in American political culture and the court as one site where this privilege is bestowed and reinscribed. Even in the California ballot pamphlet's explicitly adversarial construction of the terms debate, scientific knowledge was treated as separate from politics. In Missouri's supposedly politically neutral ballot summary, the meaning of the language was grounded variously in a scientific positivism (linguistic constructions are grounded in empirical representations of nature) and a legal positivism (the law is self-referential, transparent, and internally coherent). The primary claims in both cases were normative; namely, that inaccurate language compromises democracy. And, in both cases, each side marshaled scientific experts to resolve this dilemma. Both sides in both cases proceeded on the assumption that to safeguard political institutions, politics must be grounded in held-in-common premises.

Furthermore, both sides in each case advanced a tacit theory in which reasoned deliberation depended upon a common, value-neutral language, authorized by nature, that was immune to contestation and supplied in advance. Scientific authority was important, but it took the cooperation and the machinery of the court to transform expert pronouncements into evidence for the fairness and sufficiency of a democratic project.

Thus, even though the California and Missouri ballot initiatives reflected a rejection of representational government and recourse to the "general will" as the authority of last resort—policy made by a raw, unmediated, public majority—it was precisely in these direct-democratic moments that scientific authority stepped in. Scientific experts intervened invisibly and behind the scenes to put democratic politics in order.

7

RELIGION, REASON, AND THE POLITICS OF PROGRESS

This chapter turns to the politics of the public square, focusing in particular on California's Proposition 71 and the ways imagined technological futures figured in notions of progress, reason, and the public good. In the months leading up to the November 2004 election, the primary focus of public debate shifted from the moral (and ontological) status of the embryo to the idea that the state's responsibility to ensure the well-being of its citizens requires that it both support science and protect it from "political interference." I focus in particular upon how a cultural narrative of struggle between regressive religion and progressive technoscience shaped the politics of the California initiative.

Religion figured centrally in the California politics, although not primarily because representatives of religious groups were prominent in the political debates (they were not), nor because arguments marshaled against the initiative drew on religious perspectives (they did not). Rather, it was the proponents, not the opponents, of the initiative who tended to invoke religion. They did so in order to characterize the motivations of opponents as religious in origin to thereby mark them as democratically illicit. Advocates for the initiative referred to religious identity (whether actual or attributed) to characterize anti-research objections as contravening the norms of public reasoning. This move tended to close down political debate by marking arguments as expressions of intrinsically private individual beliefs and therefore as nonpublic reasons. Support for the initiative came to mean opposition to what was seen as an inappropriate intrusion of (private) religion into (public) reason.

If religion was used to mark citizens' claims as private, science served the opposite purpose. Science was seen as a source of right reason, but also as a driver of progress and source of future public benefits. Research promised future security and well-being. Indeed, in the California politics, the therapeutic potential of human embryonic stem cell (hESC) research was framed as a forgone conclusion—cures would come, and they would come quickly, unless politics stood in the way. Scientific research was therefore seen as an intrinsic public good and an essential ally of the state in delivering on its responsibilities to the lives in its care. I argue that the figure of science as a purveyor of technological futures produced more than an instrumental relationship between science and the state. The notion of a social contract between state and citizen was rearticulated around the imagined technological future that scientists claimed was latent in the potential of the embryonic stem cell. Ideas of the rights and entitlements of citizens came to encompass access to the technological future and to the kind of democracy that would bring it into being.[1]

In the previous chapters, I argued that accounts of democracy were constructed around the notions that science underpins public reason by providing a shared and prepolitical language and that public reason elevates scientific experts to a privilege political position. Here, I build upon that insight to demonstrate how notions of scientific authority and democratic legitimacy are coproduced through imaginations of science as a source of beneficial technological futures and as an institution of liberal democracy. In the politics of Proposition 71, and indeed within U.S. stem cell politics more broadly, science was figured not only as an epistemic authority that could safeguard public reasoning against confusion, but as an essential agent of the state in delivering on responsibilities of government.

RELIGION AS A CONVERSATION STOPPER

Religion played an important role in the politics of the Proposition 71 campaign, both in the formation of coalitions and in political discourse. Religion was routinely invoked in arguments about the place of science in democracy, as well as in arguments about the forms of deliberation and public reason that ought to inform the democratic process. Religion was deployed to demarcate the public from the private and to distinguish between reasons that could be universally entertained (if not necessarily agreed with) and reasons that were barred because they were inaccessible to anyone not already committed to the underlying premises.

The figure of religion was prominent in the political rhetoric that emerged around the California initiative. Yet, very few prominent political actors explicitly identified themselves or their arguments as religious. Instead, it was the advocates of the initiative who tended to bring up religion, primarily to characterize opposition to hESC research and to science in general as a product of religious ideology. Proponents built on this characterization as emblematic of what they identified as the norms of American liberal democracy, norms that keep private religious belief out of democratic politics. Proposition 71 advocates associated opposition to research funding with cultural resistance to science. Opposition was viewed as unenlightened and anti-progressive. It was characterized as a rejection of the norms of secular public life and, as such, could have no source but a premodern theocratic impulse to privilege religious ideology over the democratic institutions of the liberal state. The flipside of this frame was the notion that those committed to a politics of public reason were necessarily also committed to the secular authority of science. If so committed, advocates argued, one simply could not have any good reason for opposing hESC research—or, therefore, the initiative. Within this frame, science and technology were associated with liberal democratic institutions by virtue of standing together as the twin pillars of secular public life.

Certain influential strands of contemporary political theory support the notion that the boundary between universal (scientific) knowledge and individual (religious) belief is constitutive not only of notions of science but also of public reason. They privilege the distinction between public and private reasons and the corollary separation in democratic deliberation of common knowledge from individual belief.[2] As I have discussed in prior chapters, an influential line of thought that builds upon John Rawls's concept of "public reason" argues that an essential requirement for democracy is civilized restraint in the giving of reasons in democratic deliberation. Religious reasons are the quintessential example of nonpublic reasons.[3]

Richard Rorty made this argument on pragmatic grounds. In his essay "Religion as Conversation Stopper," Rorty argued that the central achievement of the Enlightenment had been the secularization of public life. In a liberal democracy, religion must remain private; it should take no part in the activities of the public square. "At the heart of the Jeffersonian compromise," he states, is an effort "to limit conversation to premises held in common."[4] The introduction of religious discourse, or indeed any discourse that claims to have access to a "source of moral knowledge" into public, democratic space, gums up the deliberative machinery. The thrust of this argument is pragmatic, geared toward a workable politics rather than foundational principles: "The main reason religion needs to be privatized is that, in political discussion with those outside the relevant religious community, it is a conversation-stopper."[5]

Rorty's argument reflects a cultural commonplace that religious views and secular public reasoning are incompatible. The corollary is that authoritative scientific knowledge, by contrast, supplies premises held in common. Thus, this knowledge necessarily serves as a foundation for reasonable engagement by virtue of its universality and value neutrality. Private beliefs corrode public reasoning, whereas epistemic correctness is exemplary of the forms of reasoned agreement to which democracy aspires.[6]

In deliberative democratic theory, this notion is elevated from armchair social theory to a normative truism. The sociological hypothesis that religion is a conversation stopper becomes a prescriptive norm of public reasoning. As we saw with the Human Embryo Research Panel (HERP) and the National Bioethics Advisory Commission (NBAC), when put into practice, this idea becomes regulative. It is used to discipline discourse into predefined constructions of right reason. It produces asymmetries in political authority, most notably between (what gets marked as) science and nonscience. This is because it incorporates a tacit presumption of how scientific knowledge is constituted (free rational reflection on matters of knowledge inevitably produce consensus; i.e., epistemic correctness), and this in turn is seen as a model for how public reasoning ought to work.[7]

Religion was indeed a conversation stopper in the Proposition 71 politics, but not in the way that Rorty predicted. Rather, it was the very assumption that religion was at odds with both science and democratic politics that caused conversations to stop. Social actors tended to mark criticisms of the initiative as motivated by religious views, thereby closing down conversations about substantive critiques and refocusing them on the question of whether the reasons that critics were offering were appropriate for public debate. One common move was to assert that a given claim was motivated by religious reasons, challenging the legitimacy of the claim as an acceptable public reason (versus a privately held belief) without addressing the merits of the claim itself. Another was to assert that scientific cresearch necessarily produced benefits that were intrinsically *public* benefits, with the implication that any opposition could therefore be motivated only by private (ideological) views. Finally, and perhaps most consequentially, critics of Proposition 71 worked hard to avoid being labeled as religiously motivated, even as proponents of the measure characterized all opposition as religious. One consequence of this was that many genuine concerns about the measure went unheard and unspoken.

Because Rorty's argument is purely pragmatic (the norm is justified only if the sociological thesis is correct), it offers a useful heuristic for examining whether the presumed social dynamics that also underwrite Rawlsian assumptions about public reasoning actually hold in practice. I argue that not only do they not hold, but that what closes down democratic deliberation are precisely the Rawlsian assumptions about what makes it open. That is, the norms of public reason that deliberative democratic theorists judge to be the necessary conditions of possibility for "free and equal" democratic deliberation are instead deployed in social life to write off arguments as irrelevant to public decision making. Proposition 71 offers an interesting case because its most politically active critics identified with the secular Left rather than the religious Right.

ABORTIVE POLITICS

In the spring of 2004, the "Yes-on-71" coalition began to collect signatures to put the initiative on the ballot. News of the effort began to circulate, and an opposition coalition began to form. The opposition coalition was small, and its political efforts met with very limited success.

Its total campaign spending amounted to only one percent of the "Yes-on-71" campaign.[8] While the Proposition 71 campaign spent tens of millions of dollars on television commercials and campaign literature, the opposition coalition produced no television or radio ads. Neverthe-less, the efforts of this coalition deserve detailed attention because they demonstrate the complexities of the ways the politics of abortion figured in relation to Proposition 71 and the ways religion was seen as informing political arguments.

The groundwork of opposition was laid by the California Catholic Conference (CCC), the official voice of California's Catholic bishops in matters of public policy.[9] The CCC is active in many policy areas, joining with actors on the Right on some issues and the Left on others. For this reason, CCC communications director Carol Hogan had contacts across the political spectrum. She recognized that a broad coalition would be critical to have credibility with voters: "We were looking for people who would not be identified as pro-life . . . if you get identified with being pro-life then it's very easy for the other side to write you off as nuts."[10] The CCC retained the services of a political consultant who advised that political pluralism was the best strategy. If an opposition campaign uni-fied perspectives from across the political spectrum, it would give cred-ibility to the argument that partisan ideology lay more on the pro-71 side than the anti.[11]

The CCC hosted a meeting in June 2004 to lay the foundations for an anti-71 effort. Hogan invited the Center for Genetics and Society (CGS) to attend. CGS is an Oakland, California–based civil society organization concerned with the governance and responsible use of the new human genetic and reproductive technologies and one of just a few left-leaning civil society organizations with this focus in the United States.[12] Formed in 2001, the CGS was a relatively young organization. Prior to Proposition 71, the CGS had intentionally avoided addressing human embryo research because of its association with abortion politics. The organization's lead-ership felt that the credibility of its progressive Left critique of emerging technology would be undermined by any apparent association with pro-life positions, no matter how false the appearance.[13]

In fact, since it had been founded in 2001, the CGS had made every effort to avoid issues associated with human embryo research. The CGS leadership had encountered such difficulty in establishing the credibility of the organization among progressives that it felt it was essential to avoid issues that might appear to associate the CGS with pro-life positions. The CGS's credibility among pro-choice organizations was tenuous. Its efforts to carve out a space for critique of human reproductive biotechnologies in Left politics was, in the words of CGS cofounder Marcy Darnovsky, "a long slog."[14] In the early days of the organization, its leaders sought to establish connections with pro-choice groups. But, in detailing their issues of concern, which related primarily to distributive justice and exploitation of women by the assisted reproductive technologies industry, the CGS gained little traction with pro-choice organizations. Given criticisms of these technologies by the Right, pro-choice organizations saw calls for constraints as just further efforts to limit reproductive freedoms. As a result, these organizations had adopted almost libertarian positions on reproductive and genetic technologies. Indeed, in the late 1990s, Planned Parenthood was well on its way to endorsing human reproductive cloning as a reproductive right until the scientific community spoke out against it. The CGS therefore found its closest allies not in organizations focused on reproductive freedoms, but in women's groups focused on social issues, especially organizations for women of color.[15]

Given these challenges, the organization steered clear of the hESC controversy in order to avoid any abortion politics taint. According to Jesse Reynolds, former project director on biotechnology accountability at the CGS, "We really wanted to avoid the embryo. That can't be stated clearly enough. Because as long as the embryo wasn't an issue, we could talk to our natural [liberal and progressive] allies."[16] Yet, perceptions of the CGS's natural political allies were often beyond CGS control, shaped instead by mainstream political imaginations of the necessary linkages between skepticism of the promises of human biotechnology and religion-inflected right-wing politics. Indeed, the CGS had great difficulty developing an identity as a Left-progressive organization. In its early days, the organization found itself almost invariably associated in press accounts with political actors on the right. In 2003, one of its goals was to achieve press coverage in which the phrase "strange bedfellows" did not appear.[17]

With Proposition 71, however, the CGS was in a bind. The leadership felt it would be nearly impossible, and irresponsible, not to take a position.

Accordingly, the CGS drafted a strong opposition statement to Proposition 71 early in the summer of 2004 but sat on it for several months. The organization did not publicly oppose Proposition 71 until mid-September, and even then it sought primarily to distance itself from the efforts of other opponents, including the CCC.[18] The CGS chose to take a public position only after a major organization, the California Nurses Association (CNA) came out against Proposition 71 in late September 2004. A large organization with significant sway in matters of California health policy, the CNA supported reproductive freedoms and was generally seen as left leaning. When it did speak out, the CGS made a conscious strategic decision to avoid associating with any pro-life organizations.[19] This was in spite of friendly relations with the CCC and significantly overlapping policy positions, even if grounded in very different normative views. In the wider public imagination, such a convergence was so inconceivable that standing together was politically untenable.

Despite the CGS's resistance, a small number of pro-choice progressive Left activists joined the opposition effort. Primary among these was Diane Beeson, a sociology professor at California State University, East Bay. Beeson tried to assemble a small group of similarly disposed individuals to attend the CCC meeting, but all refused to attend a meeting at the offices of a pro-life organization. She was similarly unsuccessful in convincing left-leaning feminists to lend their names to the anti-71 effort, in spite of their opposition to the measure in private. One notable exception was Judy Norsigian of the Boston-based women's health group Our Bodies Ourselves. Norsigian was moved by the argument that the scientific projects to be supported by Proposition 71, most notably human somatic cell nuclear transfer (SCNT), would require a large number of human oocytes, which would thus lead to the exploitation of young women. The large amount of money involved and the perceived lack of appropriate oversight suggested to Norsigian a situation where exploitation was a real risk.[20]

Beeson rejected what she saw as a simplistic pro-life–pro-choice division and joined the CCC-led effort. Beeson recalls that, of the roughly twenty-five people in attendance, she was the only one who was not a "religious conservative."[21] In fact, her impression was incorrect, though it is indicative of how all actors tended to parse positions in terms of religious motivation. A number of the attendees who became members of the coalition had no particular religious background or motivation let alone official association. One such person was Rex Greene, a pro-choice obstetrician whom Hogan knew through their collaborative efforts against physician-assisted suicide. Hogan recruited Greene as a valuable ally "because he could not be pigeonholed as a pro-lifer."[22] The coalition that resulted from the meeting assumed a name that distanced it as much as possible from any recognizably pro-life or religious platform: Doctors, Patients & Taxpayers for Fiscal Responsibility (DPTFR).

DPTFR's efforts to give opposition to Proposition 71 credibility among Left-progressives met resistance at almost every turn. The pro-life opposition to embryonic stem cell (ESC) research had elicited de facto support for embryo research among pro-choice organizations. Support of Proposition 71 from organizations such as Planned Parenthood was sufficient to render the authenticity of any progressive expressions of opposition suspect. The markers of left and right affiliations were deployed swiftly and definitively.

One example comes from Beeson's testimony at a health committee hearing on Proposition 71 held on September 15, 2004. The hearing was held in San Diego, one of the centers of California biotechnology. The hearing included testimony from several patient advocates and several senior stem cell scientists. Parkinson's advocate Greg Wasson argued that it was the responsibility of the state of California to rectify the failure of the Bush administration to fund embryonic stem cell research. He characterized the federal policy as the product of an "administration that has ignored science and all its potential in favor of politics and religious extremism."[23] Beeson, who testified alongside pro-choice physician and DPTFR president Vincent Fortanasce, challenged the notion that the religious Right was the sole source of opposition. She told the committee,

> Today I represent not only myself but a growing alliance of pro-choice, progressive and liberal scholars, attorneys, and others working to defeat Proposition 71. We support public funding of stem cell research, including embryonic stem cell research, provided it is conducted responsibly with appropriate transparency and oversight. However, we find that Proposition 71 falls short on these and other counts. We cannot let Bush's irrational restrictions push us to the opposite extreme.[24]

Senator Deborah Ortiz (D-Sacramento), who chaired the committee, interrupted Beeson, expressing incredulity and demanding that she identify pro-choice organizations who were opposing the initiative. Beeson, somewhat flustered, indicated that, given their lack of funding, the opponents were not yet organized beyond an alliance of like-minded individuals. Ortiz, threatening to cut short Beeson's testimony demanded again that she identify "pro-choice groups" opposed to Proposition 71. Ortiz concluded,

> Planned Parenthood is a strong supporter of every piece of legislation I've ever done. They're a supporter of this initiative. . . . For the record, I just want to let you know, every pro-choice group I've worked with throughout my political career, over 12 years now, have all been aware of this in the legislative process . . . and in fact are part of the favorable campaign.[25]

DPTFR must have had anti-abortion motivations, Ortiz suspected, since it had funding from the Catholic Church. Fortanasce, DPTFR president, strongly denied this:

DR. FORTANASCE: That is not true at all.
CHAIRWOMAN ORTIZ: Okay.
DR. FORTANASCE: That's a misstatement.
CHAIRWOMAN ORTIZ: Okay.
DR. FORTANASCE: I am pro-choice.
CHAIRWOMAN ORTIZ: I appreciate that.
DR. FORTANASCE: Please correct yourself.
CHAIRWOMAN ORTIZ: I'm not going to correct myself. We know that you're funded by the Catholic Church.[26]

Media reporting on the Proposition 71 campaign contributed to the notion that opposition to the initiative derived from religion. Reporters routinely sought comments from representatives of religious organizations for anti–Proposition 71 perspectives and generally characterized opposition as religious, rarely acknowledging critics from the Left.[27] Beeson, though one of the more prominent figures in the opposition campaign, received relatively little media attention. Both she and fellow Left-feminist Tina Stevens, who became a more prominent figure in the opposition efforts when she became a signatory to the "No-on-71" arguments in the ballot handbook, found that their handful of interactions with the media primarily involved expressions of incredulity from the reporter. Stevens recalled one interaction in which the reporter asked her, "So you're a Democrat? Are you really pro-choice?"[28]

The media's insistence on the abortion-politics frame extended beyond the handful of hard-to-categorize progressives like Beeson. In early June 2004, as news of the Proposition 71 effort was emerging, Carol Hogan gave a one-hour interview to *CBS Evening News*. She discussed the full range of the California bishops' concerns about the initiative, ranging from the just distribution of resources to governance to uncertainty about the therapeutic promise of the science. During the interview, she made a single statement about the Catholic Church's teaching on the inviolability of the human embryo, but this was the only statement that appeared in the broadcast.[29] Hogan resolved to stop making statements about the sanctity of the embryo, but she found that reporters became quite frustrated with her silence. She recalled the following exchange that took place in the summer of 2004:

> The reporter said, "I thought you guys believe in the sanctity of life." I said, "We do." He said, "Well, can you tell me the Church's position on it?" I said, "No." He said, "But I already have my story written, I just need a quote from you." I said, "You're not going to get it from me." I was just tired of being pigeonholed like we're parrots and that's all we're going to say.[30]

The religious framing that was applied to the Proposition 71 opposition is significant for several reasons. First, efforts to apply (or avoid) the religious label heavily shaped the politics of the campaign. Second, and more important, by characterizing opposition to the initiative as motivated by private religious belief, proponents constructed the initiative as a referendum on the sorts of reasons that should inform public policy, particularly regarding science and technology. The boundary work that distinguished science from religion was at once a demarcation of democratic institutions, and the goods they serve, from private interest and ideology.

SCIENCE AS LIBERAL DEMOCRACY

Science and technology studies scholar Thomas Gieryn has described how scientists' accounts of what science is tend to be constructed by reference to what it is not. They tend to describe its attributes in terms of the boundaries that separate and distinguish science from other social activities.[31] This sort of boundary work was on full display in public debates around Proposition 71. Although scientists and other actors did construct accounts of science that sought to preserve its autonomy and privileged identity, they also engaged in such boundary work to locate scientific authority within a wider normative and political imagination of secular public life. The figure of religion was invoked to exemplify nonscience, but also non-public reason. In this way, science and democracy were allied, whereas religious views (or those that were marked as such) were constructed as being at odds with both. By constructing religion as being at odds with the "publicness" of both science and democracy, scientific rationality and democratic public reason were seen as essentially and necessarily linked. Each was dependent on the other, and together they were unified in the secular project of tolerating, but limiting the public role of, the religious. By marking opposition to hESC research as necessarily religion-derived, political actors thereby characterized rejection of the public authority of science—and the visions of progress it offered—as a contravention of the norms of liberal democracy.

By constructing opposition to Proposition 71 as religiously motivated, advocates implied that the public good and the democratic institutions responsible for protecting it had been captured by private, religious interests. Democracy itself was at stake in the Proposition 71 project, they asserted, because threats to democratic institutions were playing out most forcefully through the anti-liberal opposition to hESC research.

For instance, in a commentary on hESC research policy and politics, Stanford bioethicist Ernle Young lamented,

> In a pluralistic society such as ours, no single set of moral certainties, ideological convictions or religious beliefs ought to pre-empt, let alone prevail over, other points of view. Yet this seems to be happening. We are

witnessing a resurgence of religious conservatism wielding political power to an unprecedented extent. The future not only of stem cell research, but also of all our democratic freedoms may well be at stake.[32]

Young's essay appeared in a special issue of *Stanford Medicine* in the fall of 2004.[33] The issue was dedicated to hESC science and politics, with a special focus on Proposition 71. The cover image depicted the "great divide" that separated the religious opposition to hESC research from the enlightened community of support—a large army of identical, bible-brandishing preachers stood opposite a small, diverse group of white-coat-clad scientist-physicians holding aloft laboratory instruments.[34] The image and the majority of the articles in the issue characterized the political battle over Proposition 71 as a struggle between the anti-modern, anti-democratic forces of religion and the enlightened, secular democratic forces of science. They characterized the federal policy as a throwback to premodern battles that had been fought and won centuries ago. In the words of Philip Pizzo, dean of Stanford Medical School,

> Today stem cell research remains embattled in the United States. We are once again watching science pitted against political ideology. As a physician and a citizen, I am deeply troubled by what is occurring. It's as if we have entered a time warp, and are spectators at the Inquisition's reading of charges against Galileo for his view of the solar system.[35]

At the same time, Pizzo expressed faith in the public sphere as the locus of a rational, democratic, common sense, which, if given the opportunity, could distinguish the liberal potential of science from the tyranny of religious irrationalism: "Yet I am an optimist. I believe in the common sense of the American people and am convinced that science will triumph over ideology."[36]

This narrative persisted well after the 2004 election. In February 2006, Robert Klein, who had spearheaded Proposition 71 and would later oversee the funding institution that it created, reflected on the initiative process before a large audience at the Goldman School of Public Policy at the University of California, Berkeley. He told the audience that Proposition 71 had been more than an effort to fund embryonic stem cell research. Rather, its purpose was to demonstrate that "ideological fringe groups cannot shut down every scientifically or medically mandated program in this country that they disagree with."[37] He described how California's leadership in this area had initiated similar efforts in other states. Indeed, during the campaign, many proponents argued that Proposition 71 would establish more than an isolated public program. They argued that it was a democratic experiment to demonstrate that the public goods of science and technology could not be denied by a religious minority on the basis of private ideological views. Scientific and democratic progress, in their view, moved in lock-step.

This narrative first catalyzed the Proposition 71 initiative and later was reinscribed by it. In 2002, Senator Ortiz held a hearing on stem cell research at the Salk Institute for Biological Studies in La Jolla to explore the possibility of public funding of stem cell research in California. Dr. David Gollaher, president of the California Healthcare Institute, an advocacy organization for California's biomedical industry, characterized the cultural import of such an effort. Pointing out that "much of the opposition is rooted in a set of particular religious worldviews," he offered a historical morality tale to show that the force of scientific progress would inevitably overcome the barriers of (what was putatively) religious resistance:

> We also need to recognize that historically religion has not been the hand-maiden of science and scientific progress. . . . Religion has had a particularly hard time dealing with sexual and reproductive issues, whether it's contraception, etc. Now, on the left is someone you all know—Galileo. On the right is Pope Paul the Fifth, who's not much remembered, except in his role in the Inquisition and the containment, if you will, of Galileo's astronomical ideas. It's worth noting that the ideas, I suppose, were slowed down a bit, but in the larger scheme of things, they weren't stopped.[38]

The risks associated with the emerging biotechnology were more likely to play out in the legislature, he suggested, than in the laboratory: "When you take cultural anxiety and you graft it onto partisan politics, you have very ugly offspring."[39]

Nobel laureate and Stanford biologist Paul Berg similarly invoked Galileo in his criticism of the Bush policy and his campaign efforts in favor of Proposition 71.[40] He saw the opposition to public support of ESC research as "a threat, particularly when it's based on ideology or religion."[41] To Berg, this ideological interference demanded a renewed commitment to the social contract between science and the state. A reassessment of the obligations of democracy to science likewise called into question the terms of the social contract between the state and its citizens:

> The debate has reopened the question of the proper relationship between science and society; indeed those who purport to speak for society. This is not an issue for stem cell biologists alone but for all scientists, for when science is attacked on ideological grounds, its integrity is threatened.[42]

The framing of opposition as religiously based had two related consequences. First, Proposition 71 politics became an episode in the ongoing American narrative of the struggle between science and religion—between the modernizing forces of Enlightenment reason expressed in democratic institutions and a premodern, theocratic impulse. In this narrative, science and democracy were cut from the same cloth and equally threatened by the intrusion of (private) religious perspectives into public space. Second, it helped proponents to characterize the measure as serving an unequivocal public good. The asymmetry that Berg and others saw between the precedent of recombinant DNA research, where time and clear thinking had ostensibly defused the politics,[43] and hESCs, where the politics were intractable, showed that the problem was not merely a matter of bringing politics into alignment with science; it was a matter of reforming (and secularizing) politics. This argument represented a significant departure from the idea that the failures of the public square were simply a result of public confusion, and it was one of the primary rationales for making the Californian public direct custodians of hESC policy. As Ortiz put it,

> Once persons have that information and they refuse to listen [to the science] or they refuse to listen to those who know the policy area better than themselves, then we simply can't call them ignorant. We can just simply call them ideologues.[44]

Through the construction of those who refused scientific authority as ideologues, science was constructed as free of such ideology. Science was constructed as the measure of what political public reasoning should aspire to be. As an epistemic authority, it offered the promise of value neutrality and thus an even, discursive playing field upon which citizens could mount their (publicly reasonable) moral arguments. As an institution, science represented the form of deliberative engagement and reasoned agreement that seemed to those who bought into its promise of progress to be precisely what was deficient in politics, and thus what was standing in the way of progress. In this way, the forms of boundary work that were marshaled to mark a claim or political identity as nonscience were at the same time used to mark it as nonpublic; that is, a violation of the norms of political engagement and of the social contract between state and citizen.

A SECULAR SOTERIOLOGY

The Proposition 71 case helps bring to the surface how central imaginations of technological potential were in constructing the constitutional position of science. Science and democracy were framed as allied, both in realizing a secular, liberal political order and in bringing about the forms of progress appropriate to that order. Progress, in this debate, meant technological progress—the cures that scientists promised would arrive as soon as democracy got its house in order. Getting democracy's house in order meant re-establishing the secular foundations of democratic politics; that is, purging religion from public reasoning.

The politics surrounding Proposition 71 exhibited a familiar and culturally powerful imaginary of secularization.[45] This imaginary, codified by the social sciences as the "secularization thesis," presumes that modernization necessarily and inevitable entails a gradual separation of values spheres. In this imaginary, secular knowledge and reason (of which science is seen as exemplary) disenchant the world and displace religion from public life. Some scholars have turned a critical lens on "formations of the secular" as constitutive features of modernity.[46] Rejecting the secularization thesis as an inevitable and teleological feature of modernization, they have taken notions of the secular itself as an object of interrogation.[47] Science figures centrally in the idea of secularization. In what Charles Taylor has called the "subtraction story," religion is displaced from the authoritative space that it used to occupy by advancing scientific knowledge.[48] Taylor and others argue that the idea of secularization is itself an expression of a historically situated and culturally particular social imaginary.[49] They demonstrate that "the secular is made, not simply found."[50] They have begun to demonstrate how secularity is not a natural result of modern life, but a normative posture within in; it is not an inevitable outcome of either scientific progress or the secularization of politics. One implication is that proponents of the secularization thesis have overestimated the significance of science and technology in shaping public meaning and moral imagination.

Yet, the body of scholarship that has critiqued the secularization thesis has nevertheless consistently left the figure of science itself uninterrogated. Insofar as science figures at all in these accounts, it is generally an autonomous domain that is associated with modernity, but not interrogated in a constructivist mode as an institutional expression of it. Technology too is generally figured as a kind of extra-social outgrowth of advances in knowledge and technique. As a consequence, this scholarship overlooks the politically privileged position of science as a constitutive element of the "social imaginary" of which secularization is an expression, and, therefore, so too the dynamics whereby the constitutional position of science is linked to a secular imagination of progress. Although the debates over stem cell research are but one example among many, they reveal how normative notions of secularity—for instance the notion that liberal politics cannot function unless comprehensive doctrines are checked at the door—are linked to notions of scientific authority.

As we have seen, scientific authority informs ideas of right public reason in American political culture. As a result, U.S. democracy defers to scientific authority, which thereby acquires the power to shape the terms of debate—that is, the putatively given-in-advance and universally shared epistemic foundations for deliberation over values questions. The politics surrounding Proposition 71 bring to light an additional dimension of the constitutional position of science. They show how public accounts of the right ordering of politics were constructed in deference not only to scientific accounts of nature, but to technoscientific accounts of progress. Thus, science was authorized to shape public reasoning not only because it claimed to see the material reality underlying moral judgment, but because it could putatively see the way to a better future. In this way, scientific authorities could claim a privileged position, both in adjudicating between good and bad reasoning and in orienting democratic judgment toward desirable futures.

My aim is not to expose scientists' accounts of the potential of hESC research as incredible. Indeed, many actors criticized scientists' predictions as overhyped. Rather, it is to observe with other scholars that scientific promises about technological futures have important social effects in shaping political, economic, and, I would add, moral relations.[51] In contemporary public life, secular visions of social progress are often visions of technological innovation. In stem cell politics, public discourse that privileges scientific predictions of the technological future also underwrite the authority of science to imagine the good and to define the political and moral commitments appropriate to achieving progress. The promise of science-driven progress was seen as necessarily linked to a commitment to science as a secular authority, and thus to similarly secular political norms.

In this sense, the politics of Proposition 71 (and hESC research in general) were shaped not merely by a social imaginary of secularization, but by a socio*technical* imaginary of secular progress: a vision of technological progress that was simultaneously a vision of secular political order.[52] Science was linked to secularity. Secularity was linked to political institutions that reflected and enforced a separation between secular (public) reason and (private) religious belief. Those political institutions were in turn linked to social progress. Social progress (that is, reduced suffering, increased security, and enhanced human well-being) was seen as a function of technological progress. And, completing the circle, technological progress was constructed as a natural and inevitable expression of the secular institution of science, at least insofar as it was set free by (secular) politics.

For those who imagined progress in this way, the integrity of that circle required that (what was marked as) religion be written out of it. Advocates of research characterized democracy as deficient insofar as it stood in the way of scientific progress, and they diagnosed its deficiencies as the consequence of an inadequate separation of facts from values, knowledge from belief, and public from private, all of which were subsumed within the the frame of the intrusion of religion into secular public life. A commitment to secularity was seen as a commitment to science, and vice versa, and those commitments were in turn seen as requirements for achieving (technological) progress. Thus, political imaginations of the boundary between the secular and the religious—and between public and private spheres—were simultaneously imaginations of knowledge, of expertise, and of the rightful place of science among institutions of government.

These commitments privileged accounts of technoscientific innovation as an engine of progress and a source of public benefit. They also shaped corollary ideas of the rights and entitlements of citizens and the responsibilities of the state to the lives in its care.[53]

NEW SOLIDARITIES

While advocates of stem cell research had made their interest in research funding clear, there was initially no similarly self-evident rationale for the average California citizen to commit his or her tax dollars to such an effort. Public science funding in the United States has historically been almost exclusively the domain of the federal government.[54] While the case for the national value of scientific research seems to be compelling to most Americans, the same reasons do not necessarily apply to large-scale, state-level funding. Indeed, the generic advocacy of science familiar in federal politics was not nearly so present at the state level. Nor had California yet experienced the fragmented politics of disease-specific advocacy that shapes the politics of federal biomedical research funding.

Instead, a novel form of politics emerged, grounded in an imagination of collective vulnerability to disease that mirrored the generic pluripotentiality of the embryonic stem cell. Because the hESC was said to contain the potential to cure a broad array of diseases, the Proposition 71 initiative could claim to serve the well-being of Californians in general and thus to unify them as a political collective. The normal federal politics of disease-specific interests vying for a larger piece of the funding pie gave way in California to a discourse of generic public interest in hESC research. The diversity of diseases that stem cell research would address offered hope to the diversity of disease sufferers, unifying them into a single interest group that included everyone who was suffering—or would someday suffer—from disease. Thus the predicted therapeutic potential of hESC research became the basis for describing the bodies of all Californians as potential beneficiaries of the initiative. Advocates claimed that research supported by Proposition 71 could cure more than 70 different diseases and disabilities. A majority of Californian families, it was argued, had at least one member who could already benefit from a stem cell–derived cure immediately, and many more would benefit in the future as they developed diseases.[55] Indeed, every citizen could potentially benefit because every citizen was potentially sick. The essential infirmity of the citizen's body thus became the basis for a kind of imagined community of vulnerable bodies, bound together by the same vulnerabilities, fears, needs, dependencies, interests, and hopes.[56]

Critics of hESC advocacy, both nationally and in California, frequently pointed out that cures remained hypothetical. In 2004, no therapies had yet been developed with hESCs, and no human clinical trials were planned. Some critics accused scientists of overstating the potential of hESCs and exploiting the desperation of the sick and suffering for cures to their ailments. In this context, the rhetoric of hope played a prominent role in advocacy for Proposition 71. It also played an important role in mediating uncertainty about the potential of hESC research.

In a series of television ads commissioned by the "Yes-on-71" campaign, scientists emphasized the medical promise of stem cell research. Nobel laureate Paul Berg described stem cell research as "an important scientific and medical breakthrough."[57] Irving Weissman promised, "The chances of diseases to be cured by stem cell research are high, but only if we start."[58] University of California, San Francisco, diabetes expert Jeff Bluestone said of the potential of stem cell research to cure type 1 diabetes, "I'm absolutely confident in saying this will happen."[59]

Proposition 71 advocates presented the initiative not as a campaign merely for science, but a campaign for cures. The official website of the "Yes-on-71" campaign promised cures even in the web address itself (www.curesforcalifornia.com).[60] The homepage declared, "Stem cell research can provide breakthrough treatments and cures for diseases and injuries that affect millions of Californians." It included rotating profiles of individuals with diseases under the title of "Stories of Hope."

Profiled individuals pleaded with voters to "help my family find a cure" and expressed confidence that "the most probable future cure is through stem cell research."[61] Dominating the first page of the "Yes-on-71" voter pamphlet, a large-text header announced, "Stem Cell Research: Breakthrough Cures of Diseases that Affect Millions of People."[62] Proponents frequently referred to stem cell research as a "medical breakthrough."[63] A pediatric endocrinologist told Katie Couric of NBC's *Today* show that stem cell research would be the "the next big breakthrough" in diabetes medicine after the discovery of insulin seventy-five years earlier.[64] Stem cell research was compared with the smallpox and polio vaccines and other transformative developments in the history of medicine. These expressions of confidence in a technological future tended to treat uncertainty as political rather than scientific. Suggestions that science was being "impeded by ideology" and "misguided research regulations" asymmetrically minimized scientific uncertainty while ascribing to voters the ability to bring about cures at the ballot box.[65] Passing Proposition 71 would "break the political logjam and turn the hope for new cures into reality."[66] The path to cures for "over 70 different diseases and injuries" was being blocked by the pathologies of politics, but it was a disease that democracy could ostensibly cure.

Television ads featuring disease sufferers emphasized the hope they derived from the promise of stem cell research. They spoke in generic terms about the difficulty of living with disease and the urgency to find cures, making little or no reference to specific diseases. The ads presented vulnerability to disease as a risk common to all citizens. A multiple sclerosis (MS) patient and mother of a child with a spinal cord injury warned, "Injury, disease, it can happen to anybody."[67] In another ad, a young woman with MS stated, "Every person's got at least one person in their family who's dealing with something like this."[68] Christopher Reeve, the actor who had played Superman and later suffered a spinal cord injury, said that by voting for Proposition 71, "you could save the life of someone you love."[69] A man with Parkinson's disease said, "We all are exposed and potentially patients of these diseases."[70]

While this imaginary of vulnerability was used to engender public support for therapeutic research, it was the promises of the broad technological potential of the embryonic stem cell that transformed the human fact of disease risk into a shared political identity. The pluripotentiality of the cell metaphorically unified the plural causes of citizens' suffering. Irving Weissman told *NBC News* that, with sufficient funding, scientists could make hESC lines that "represented each and every human disease."[71]

But, if the cell could unify the polity through its generic technological potential, the incipient public goods harbored within it could be realized, advocates argued, only if the institutions of government could be made to act in the name of the public interest in biomedical progress. At public events, citizen-patients frequently presented their own conditions as consequences of risks and vulnerabilities that were shared by every citizen. People who were wheelchair bound or had overt symptoms of disease often spoke out at public hearings and campaign events as representatives not of specific ailments but simply of the sick—present and future. The campaign framed these individuals as standing in for the public by exemplifying a universal public interest. Their diseases and disabilities represented the public's shared vulnerability and collective interest in bringing about biomedical progress.

Forcefully arguing that hESC research was a collective good, a woman speaking from her wheelchair told the California Senate Health Committee, "You are the future with [sic] these diseases." With the imaginary of common vulnerability, advocates and scientists together sought to transform specific disease-focused advocacy into generic support for hESC research and characterized support for research as a duty of the democratic state to its citizens. As Ortiz put it at the September 2004 Health Committee hearing, "We owe it to the 128 million Americans who suffer from chronic disease to invest in cures and better treatments."[72]

In this way, technological potential also became a metaphor for democratic representation—and thus for the appropriately public nature of the research enterprise. As biologist Hans Keirstead told the California Senate Health Committee, federal restrictions had de facto limited the genetic diversity of hESC cell lines and the range of diseases that could be modeled and studied, thereby rendering significant segments of the public unrepresented. Referring to the stem cell lines eligible for federal funding, he said, "These are wealthy, white, infertile stem cells."[73]

Proposition 71 had the most powerful effect on national electoral politics not through its procedural model of democratic intervention, but through the sociotechnical imaginary of a polity unified by universal vulnerability to disease. The construction of the citizen that this imaginary underwrote came to circulate throughout the country and in the process was further refined. It engendered a solidarity that, in part, contributed to shifts in political power in other states and in the U.S. Congress after 2004.

The notion that disease vulnerability is universal to all citizens not only figured support for stem cell science as in the public interest, but became the basis for a generic construction of the citizen, and thus of the duties of the state entailed by the social contract between state and citizen. This was captured in a powerful 2006 campaign ad used to target Republican House incumbents in districts ranging from upstate New York to Virginia to Indiana. In the ad, a teenage boy, a little girl, and a middle-aged woman describe health conditions that lie in their futures. The boy begins, "Next summer I'm going on a camping trip with my friends. I'll be in a car accident, and I'll be paralyzed for the rest of my life." The woman follows: "In twenty years, I'll have Alzheimer's. I won't recognize my husband or my kids." Finally, the little girl: "Next week, my mommy and daddy are going to find out I have diabetes." Displaying a picture of the targeted congressman, the boy tells the viewer that he voted against federal funding for stem cell research. The woman: "Why did Congressman Walsh bet my life that he knows best?" The girl: "How come he thinks he gets to decide who lives and who dies?" Finally, the boy, the girl, and the woman recite in order, "Maybe I'm your grandson," "Maybe I'm your little girl," and "How do you know I'm not you?"[74]

Sick bodies played a critical role in the staging. The promised technological future transformed disability into a rights claim upon the state and one's fellow citizens: a right to access a biomedical future in which disparities in health and well-being would be overcome through technological innovation. Disease became a marker of this right. It was common practice for everyone—not only patients, but also researchers, celebrities, politicians, and interested citizens—to refer to instances of disease in their lives or families before declaring the right of access to future cures. Suffering bodies thus were made to represent a political failure, a dereliction of duty of the state to fulfill a basic obligation, and an obligation of the polity to right this wrong.

Observers of contemporary biomedicine have observed the ways in which novel forms of social relations and social movements emerge out of new medical articulations of disease or novel loci of biotechnological intervention.[75] New scientific and technological specifications of disease or risk simultaneously specify "new terms of inclusion of life itself into the body politic."[76] In this case, the imagined future of therapeutic specificity was construed as generic technological potential—and thus a politically unifying source of hope—in the present. The politics of stem cell research constructed the promise of participation in a biological future as contingent upon achieving sufficient political solidarity in the present to demand that the state open the way to that future. The human embryonic stem cell became a technology not for constituting novel disease communities, but for collectivizing fragmented biomedical interests into a collective political identity. The figure of "the public" came to be defined by a putatively universal interest in biomedical innovation, and by corollary political relationships and responsibilities of citizens in the present. Thus, more than an instrumental relationship between science and the state was at stake in this imagination of innovation as an unequivocal public good. Rather, it reflected a constitutional alignment where a concept of the rights of the governed to particular technological futures was directly tied to the social contract between science and the state.[77]

The notion that the state bears such duties of care is not new in itself. From medical licensing to public health to the regulation of drugs and devices, the vulnerability of the body to disease has long been a focus of American state action.[78] However, the stem cell controversy in general, and Proposition 71 in particular, represent a noteworthy moment for several reasons. First, the politics of Proposition 71 elevated access to technoscientific innovation from the interest of specific minority disease groups to the status of a generic public good. And it figured the machinery of technoscientific innovation as an essential partner of the state in fulfilling its obligations to its citizens.

Second, stem cell politics elevated the position of technoscience in the political imagination to *the* site though which the state should act to protect the health of its citizens. The solution to vulnerability was cure, not care. Indeed, given the fact that Proposition 71 would displace funds from programs like Medicaid, the public was putting a not insignificant number of its public health eggs in the innovation basket.[79] Thus, the politics of Proposition 71 figured biomedical innovation as a mode of governance and a mechanism of distributive justice. The initiative treated innovation as the right governmental response to the suffering of the marginal. Present financial and technological resources could only mitigate disease, not eliminate it. Research could instead produce cures, eliminating the cause of people's suffering in the future.[80]

HEALING THE ECONOMY

In the politics of the initiative, unmet medical needs were by no means invisible. As we have seen, the voices and bodies of the sick and disabled played an important role in the campaign for Proposition 71. The immediate social and economic costs of inadequate healthcare in California also figured prominently in the politics of the initiative. Yet, the promised therapeutic potential of hESC research underwrote a notion of welfare in which the most equitable allocation of resources to address the needs of the sick entailed investment in future cures over present care. Indeed, advocates of the initiative were unrestrained in their visions of the forms of health that research would bring about. The pathologies of unequal access to healthcare would itself be addressed by hitching the wagon of public health to the engine of innovation. Robert Klein, who drafted the initiative, predicted that "the state of California will gain jobs, new tax revenues, and intellectual property revenues to pay back the taxpayers, along with huge health care savings if the knowledge just allows us to mitigate these critical diseases."[81] A "Yes-on-71" campaign pamphlet detailed the reduced healthcare costs and the boost to California's economy that would result from the initiative.[82] The cost and inefficacy of the medicine of today, and thus the insufficiency of existing resources to care for everyone, were imagined to be problems of the interim, limited to the interval of time between public investment in research and the cure-alls that would flow from it. Whereas public dollars allocated to care could do little more than mitigate the effects of disease in the present, allocated to research and innovation, they could banish the causes of disease—both biological and economic—once and for all.

Advocates promised that the pluripotentiality of the embryonic stem cell would generate curative technologies, but also economic returns that would ramify, refilling public coffers and trickling down to all socioeconomic sectors. The "Yes-on-71" campaign commissioned an economic forecast of what Proposition 71 might reasonably be expected to produce for the state. Written by Stanford health policy professor Laurence Baker, the report predicted $6.4 billion to $12.6 billion in revenues and health-care cost savings during the bond payback period—a 120 percent to 236 percent return. The portion generated by state royalty revenues was estimated to be in the range of $537 million to $1.1 billion.[83] Referring to the forecast, Klein and others argued that Proposition 71 was an investment, not an expenditure, of public funds.[84] They assured voters that great rewards would be reaped from this investment.

Klein frequently pointed out that the research would be funded not by tax dollars but by bond debt and could not negatively impact the state's finances for at least five years.[85] In an arrangement not unlike the interest-only balloon mortgages that were at the same time fueling the California real estate boom (and would drive the global economy to near meltdown four years later), Proposition 71 stipulated that the interest on the bond issues would be paid out of the proceeds of bond sales for the first five years. According to Klein, not only was Proposition 71 a morally responsible project, it was a fiscally responsible one. The potential of the stem cell included the power to lift the California economy out of the economic doldrums that followed the dramatic burst of the dot-com bubble.[86] The stem cell was the seed of society's future well-being—biomedical, economic, and political. All that was needed was the political will to unlock its potential. Support for scientific inquiry joined with the engines of private capital would, advocates predicted, bring about significant public benefit in the form of increased tax revenue, reduced healthcare costs, and delivery of therapies to those least able to afford them.

Proposition 71 proponents pointed to California's history as a powerhouse of high-tech innovation and argued that California was uniquely positioned to undertake the Proposition 71 venture. Funding hESC research would further reinforce the state's elite position within the global economy by writing a new chapter in California's high-tech history.

Failure to fund would tie researchers' hands and cause California to lose out on the next adventure at the cutting edge.

Senator Deborah Ortiz was among the proponents of this imagined economic future. At a Health Committee hearing in September 2004, Ortiz said, "When you move away the ideological, ethical, moral debates, this is about economic development in one of the strongest industries not just in this state but in the nation. And California has made its mark, and it ought not to lose that standing."[87] David Gollaher, president of the California Health Institute, a consortium of several hundred California biotech companies, approvingly chimed in:

> California has already built, over the past twenty-five years, a vast, complex infrastructure that includes basic science, venture capital, commercial development in marketing companies, and all the supporting casts essential to transforming advanced scientific discoveries into products that can help patients. An idea in a laboratory is not nearly enough, and the fruits of successful experiments in places like UC Irvine or the Burnham Institute aren't nearly enough to develop a product through the Food and Drug Administration to become available to patients around the world.[88]

This was an oft-repeated refrain both before and after the campaign. California would succeed not only because it had the scientific expertise but also the industrial infrastructure to rapidly transform public dollars into public health via therapeutic innovation.

Some Proposition 71 proponents used the recombinant DNA revolution as a model for the way history might reasonably be expected to repeat itself.[89] They expected that the potency of the stem cell unlocked with public funding would drive a multitude of specialized industries and commercial products. Evan Snyder, director of the program in stem cell biology at the Burnham Institute in San Diego predicted, "This is going to be the stem cell center of the world, not just the country." Investors seemed to agree.[90] In late October 2004, as polls showed that Proposition 71 would likely pass by a wide margin, shares in stem cell–based biotechnology companies posted significant gains.[91] Between October 11 and November 2, the stock value of both Geron Corporation and Aastrom

Biosciences (now Vericel Corporation) increased by 25 percent, and that of StemCells Inc. appreciated by nearly 250 percent.

When Proposition 71 passed, many expressed excitement over California's financial future. One especially enthusiastic commentator eschewed the future conditional for the present indicative in an editorial entitled "State Economy Gets a Boost."[92] Fiona Hutton, spokesperson for the "Yes-on-71" campaign, predicted, "You'll see new biotech clusters emerging and new jobs created. In terms of economic benefit, there's new tax revenues, royalty revenues that arise from the discovery, and potential reduction in health care costs."[93]

INNOVATING BEYOND RISK

Every element of the Proposition 71 vision was predicated on the notion that science's linear forward march is inevitable but for the inhibitory effects of law and politics. What it means for society to protect and care for life was reframed around imagined technological futures and the imperative to realize them. Supporting science was framed as a matter of life and death. And the scientific experts that claimed the authority to see what futures were possible—and what futures might be foreclosed—also claimed the authority to judge what society's duties to protecting human life demand. As Stanford stem cell biologist Irving Weissman put it, anyone responsible for inhibiting stem cell research is "responsible for the lives that have been lost in the window of time that was available."[94]

Advocates of the initiative characterized its critics as failing to honor the social contract with science and, in so doing, as undermining the democratic social contract itself, polluting public institutions and the democratic commitment to the common good with private interests and religious ideologies. In this framing, scientific authority retained a privileged—indeed constitutional—position, as an arbiter of public reasoning and as an agent capable of fulfilling the promise of progress. According to Dr. David Gollaher, president of the California Healthcare Institute, science could deliver therapeutics not only to aging bodies, but to democracy itself. It was imperative "to encourage . . . right thinking and accurate thought that can be transplanted into the body politic to make it . . . behave best for its own health."[95]

The presumption that cures were inevitable and the benefits to society unequivocal cast opposition to the initiative as an expression of beliefs that have no place in public space. As Qualcomm founder Steve Altman, who contributed $300,000 to the Proposition 71 campaign, put it, "The only reason I can justify that people are taking this position is that they don't have kids with diseases. Otherwise, how can you say, 'I'm against this?' . . . I don't want their religious beliefs imposed on me and my kids."

This imaginary of common risk generated a (Californian) "cosmopolitan moment," in which citizens were bound together by the imperative to reorder public institutions to minister to risk.[96] Yet the risk for this "risk society" was not a catastrophic future, but the catastrophic possibility that that future might not happen. Political obligations—and failures—of the present were diagnosed in terms of an imagined technological future. Proposition 71 made risk out of politics, rather than politics out of risk. Scientific knowledge and promissory technological futures configured imaginations of the right relationships not only between science and the state, but also between the state and its citizens. The presumption that therapeutic benefits would inevitably flow from public investment in hESC research reconfigured imaginations of citizenship, including of the moral interests and identities that warranted political recognition. This imagination of risk and benefit figured the state as responsible for supporting science in order that its citizens might reap these benefits.

This "social contract for science" reflects entrenched notions of the social benefits of scientific research and encodes corollary imaginations of the right relationships between science and the state, in particular the forms of deference to scientific authority necessary for the state to meet its obligations to enhance public well-being.[97] The California case shows that the stakes were more than instrumental and organizational. Imagined as an agent for realizing a better future, science was also seen as an agent of governance.

In this particular experiment in democracy, the promise of the technological future captured the public imagination. On November 2, 2004, Proposition 71 was passed in a landslide victory, earning fifty-nine percent of the vote.

Science played a constitutive role—and claimed a constitutional position—in giving shape to California's remarkable experiment in democracy. Yet, whereas democratic institutions are essentially contested by design, and the allocations of power encoded in the social contract between the state and its citizens are explicit and perpetually unsettled, the balance of power between science and democracy in the politics of stem cell research was not subject to the same constitutional correctives. Although the power of the vote was in the hands of the people, experts claimed the authority to imagine the good on their behalf. Scientific experts' constructions of right reason and predictions of technological futures were taken as authoritative and incontestable. They became the invisible scaffolding surrounding apparently unscripted public debate, molding the repertoire of meaning and moral imagination available to the project of deliberative democracy.

The debates around Proposition 71 were apparently limited to a singular question of science policy, but more was at stake. They were also about the responsibilities of a democracy to its citizens and of the rightful place of science in governance. Those responsibilities certainly embraced the task of making provision for the sick and suffering, but they were not limited to it. They also embraced the task of imagining and aspiring to collective visions of the good. Yet, the very idiom of moral imagination was not, in the end, supplied by democracy. And in authorizing experts to imagine the future, the repertoire of democratic imagination was correspondingly attenuated.

8

THE LEGACY OF EXPERIMENT

On june 20, 2007, George W. Bush vetoed the *Stem Cell Research Enhancement Act*. It was only the third veto of his presidency but the second veto of a bill to authorize federal funding of research on newly derived embryonic stem cell lines. In his veto message, Bush suggested that the bill was not only morally unacceptable but scientifically unwarranted: "Technical innovation" funded under his administration was "opening up new possibilities for progress without conflict or ethical controversy," raising the prospect of "new discoveries that could transform lives."[1]

He was referring to recent advances in reprogramming adult somatic cells into an embryonic stem cell–like state, in effect producing pluripotent cell lines without "having to destroy human life."[2] In August 2006, a paper from the laboratory of Japanese cell biologist Shinya Yamanaka described a technique to reprogram mouse fibroblasts, starting a race to make the same technique work in human cells.[3] On November 20, 2007, nine years after embryonic stem cells first made international headlines, two research groups announced successes in reprogramming human somatic cells into "induced pluripotent stem cells" (iPSCs), cells that behaved like human embryonic stem cells (hESCs) but were not derived from human embryos.[4] One was led by Yamanaka, the other by James Thomson, whose lab had first cultured human embryonic stem cells.

These cells were heralded as a scientific solution to moral disagreement. The *New York Times* predicted that their discovery would "quell the ethical debate."[5] The Family Research Council (FRC), a Washington-based pro-life organization, issued a press release with the headline "New

Studies End Debate on Embryonic Stem Cell Research."[6] Harvard stem cell biologist Douglas Melton declared them "ethically uncomplicated," and James Thomson predicted, "A decade from now, [the divisive stem cell debate] will be just a funny historical footnote."[7]

In 2012, Yamanaka was awarded the Nobel Prize in Physiology or Medicine jointly with John Gurdon, two years after Robert Edwards had won it for his pioneering work on in vitro fertilization (IVF). Forty years earlier, Gurdon had successfully cloned a frog using a somatic cell.[8] His work represented one of the first experimental successes in engineering unprecedented forms of embryonic life. Some quipped that this was a Nobel Prize in ethics, awarded for the experiment that had opened the way to ethically disconcerting manipulations of life and for the experiment that had neutralized their moral threat.[9] Yamanaka's research had indeed been inspired in part by his own ethical uneasiness about human embryo research. When he had once stared through a microscope at some human embryos slated for research use, he had thought about his own daughters and resolved to find another way.[10]

Critics of human embryo research declared that the iPSC advances vindicated the ethical restraint of the Bush administration policy and the relationship among science, state, and society that it reflected. FRC president Tony Perkins declared, "This demonstrates what pro-lifers have been saying since the beginning. It is never necessary to compromise ethics by destroying life in order to achieve scientific aims."[11] For the White House, the iPSC success was taken as an experimental confirmation that democratic politics had a place at the laboratory bench. The experiments demonstrated that the "politicization of science," a phrase often invoked to decry the Bush stem cell policy and the administration's posture toward science more generally, could produce ethically superior innovation. According to Karl Zinsmeister, director of the White House Domestic Policy Council, the president's "drawing of lines on cloning and embryo use was a positive factor in making this come to fruition."[12] Crediting the Bush policy, Zinsmeister discerned a lesson of history. Through experimentation in the laboratory, duly constrained by principled ethical limits, science would find a way: "If you set reasonable parameters and offer a lot of encouragement and public funding, science will solve [the] dilemma."[13]

Yet, as this book has demonstrated, the embryo research debates were never only about science; thus, neither could they be resolved by it. They were about the right relationship between science and democracy and the modes of public reasoning appropriate to governing our technological future. Indeed, the claim that reprogramming represented a technical solution to ethical disagreement was yet another instance where the question of which scientific projects comport with democratically articulated moral imaginations was transmuted into a scientific idiom, rendering scientists custodians of the terms of debate by treating ethical questions as secondary to (expert assessments of) the sufficiency or insufficiency of a technology.

Beginning in 2007, researchers rapidly adopted reprogramming and the cell lines it generated. Yet, both before and after human iPSC lines had been created and evaluated, a powerful chorus of voices from the scientific community rejected the notion that reprogramming rendered the moral disagreement at the heart of the stem cell controversy moot. In early 2007, in a letter to the congressional sponsors of the legislation Bush would later veto, prominent Harvard biologists declared that it was a "misuse and misunderstanding" of their research to find in it promising alternatives to destroying human embryos. Declaring with authority that "the White House ha[d] gotten it wrong," they made the familiar shift in idiom to scientifically authoritative (though wildly speculative) claims about the technological future. "The overwhelming consensus of the scientific and medical community is that embryonic stem cell research holds the greatest potential to cure diseases and end the suffering of millions."[14]

Within a few years, however, as scientific practices began to drift away from ethically contentious human embryo research, these sorts of statements would become less common. Years have passed, and none of the cures that were predicted have materialized, even though much important scientific work has been accomplished. Neither has research progressed along the promised linear path from bench to bedside. California's largest investments have shifted away from the domains of embryonic stem cell research that proponents of Proposition 71 promised would cure its citizens to clinical trials involving a modest range of therapies that in most cases have little or no connection to embryonic stem cells, and for which there was no particular need for public investment.[15]

As ever, scientists could not predict the technological trajectory of research with any special degree of accuracy. Like most of the history of science, stem cell biology has followed a more meandering course with much more quotidian breakthroughs and frictions than the rhetoric of the 2000s anticipated. Indeed, the medical effects of such predictions have probably been felt most not from the fruits of the research they underwrote, but by patients—so-called "stem cell tourists." Believing in the promises and the corollary claims that it is not science but political opposition and regulatory inefficacy that have made cures slow in coming, these patients have sought questionable stem cell therapies from those who capitalize on that potent combination of scientific credibility and the desperation of the sick.[16] While such interventions in people's bodies are undertaken only at the margins of biomedicine,[17] the politics of the human embryo research debates in the 2000s were shaped by—and did much to fuel— a similar cocktail of credibility and desperation.

Hype is a ubiquitous element of contemporary biotechnology. Speculative promising has become an obligatory and quotidian feature of grant proposals, pitches for venture capital, and political justifications for investments in research. The "political economy of hype" configures the allocations of resources that shape the landscapes of "biocapital."[18] Yet, not even in genomics has such easy promising coalesced into the messianic narrative that took shape around human embryonic stem cell research. Nor have the putative blockages to the promised future elsewhere been taken as so self-evident. Whereas the day-to-day coursing of capital flows through the capillaries of the biosciences are pumped by investors who parse scientific publications and patent filings for hints of a blockbuster to be, in the embryonic stem cell controversy, the promise of stem cell research elicited more than speculative investment in pursuit of the promise of profit. It elicited a reimagining of the social contract between science and the state, but also between the state and its citizens. And it became a locus of profound disagreement about modes of public reasoning appropriate to rendering judgments about society's obligations to human life. The contours of debate were configured at every level by the cultural authority of science, from the promise to act where government's institutions were powerless—to cure and not merely care—to supplying the terms of public reasoning.

Recall, for instance, the exchange at a congressional hearing in early 1999, just a few months after hESCs had first been cultured, at which Senator Arlen Specter schooled a group of scientists in the art of promising. He repeatedly asked the panel of distinguished scientists to predict the number of years before hESC research might cure the particular disease that their research addressed. They repeatedly demurred. He pressed them, requesting that they predict so that the stakes could be clear: "People in Congress like to have figures. . . . Let me press you on the question . . . this business of advocacy is a very tough issue. . . . If you talk in terms of being close, and what the dollars will do, then you start to create an impetus for it. . . ." Larry Goldstein, a University of California, San Diego, faculty member who would later become deeply involved with the Proposition 71 initiative picked up on the rules of this game: "Maybe five to ten years, Senator, where we could see some hope [of curing Alzheimer's]."[19]

These sorts of claims were made many times over, and with increasing confidence and regularity in the subsequent years. They were celebrated by the millions of Americans whose diseases stood to be cured and suffering ended, and they were derisively dismissed by the millions of others who opposed the research, sometimes with similarly speculative counterclaims about the potential of adult stem cell research as the scientifically superior avenue.[20] Both endorsement and critique turned on the questions of what technological future lay in the offing and whose epistemic authority would underwrite such prediction.[21] Claiming authority entailed drawing sharp lines between objective expertise and personal religious beliefs, pure science and impure politics.

These competing accounts of what futures were possible and plausible ought not be explained away as expressions of political ideology masquerading as science. Neither should they be caricatured as science playing politics by indulging in disingenuous hype for its own strategic gains. Such explanations may well be accurate as far as they go, but they are not adequate to understand the true stakes of this debate, for they reify science as an extra-political institution, a transcendent source of authority that can test the credibility of claims in the public square against value-neural knowledge. But science and democracy, perhaps the two greatest achievements of modernity, are human institutions. And, as I have demonstrated, the imaginations of enlightenment and the projects of progress

they encode are mutually constituted. Thus, such explanations of interests and false representations are but the surface contours of the political
landscape, mere signs and symptoms of our modes of responding to the
challenge of governing our biotechnological future.

This study has sought to map some of this landscape and offer a more
thoroughgoing diagnosis of what animates our modes of response. It has
offered a history of the debates surrounding human embryo research as a
lens through which to observe the development of new norms, practices,
and institutions of deliberation for contending with morally and technically complex problems in the biosciences. It has traversed one of the
longest and most contentious controversies in the history of biotechnology. It is a controversy that continues to unfold, with more chapters yet
to be written and more deeply challenging problems yet to be confronted.

Indeed, even in the weeks and months before this book went to print, a
new series of experiments in democracy have begun to unfold. The sudden
arrival of powerful techniques of gene editing, such as clustered regularly
interspaced short palindromic repeats (CRISPR/cas-9), have elicited a
wave of international concern about the powers of control over human life
that these technologies portend. Central among these concerns are their
application to human embryos. In early 2015, an experiment to genetically
modify a disease-causing gene was conducted by a Chinese laboratory.[22]
That experiment elicited a statement from a group of elite scientists and
ethicists calling for a moratorium on reproductive applications of
gene editing in humans. These worries notwithstanding, there is significant excitement about—and support for—using this technology to alter
the genomes of future children. Still more exciting for many researchers,
however, are the wide range of experimental opportunities that gene editing offers for studying human development in human embryos. The first
application for research involving embryo editing was recently approved
by the UK Human Fertilization and Embryology Authority, and that
research has commenced. This experiment and others like it promise to
reveal the genetic and epigenetic processes that direct human embryogenesis. They will do so by interfering with genes implicated in embryogensis
and observing the effects.[23]

These developments happen to coincide with the advent of new techniques for culturing human embryos in vitro up to the threshold of

gastrulation. Before these techniques were developed, it had not been technically possible to maintain morphologically intact human embryos in vitro beyond about eight days post-fertilization. In one of the first studies to exceed this threshold, researchers cultured embryos to nearly fourteen days, at which point they ended the experiments in deference to the fourteen-day rule.[24] This newfound ability to test the fourteen-day rule—the most widely adopted and well-established limit to human embryo research in the world—has led to immediate calls to revise it. Harvard stem cell biologist George Daley has suggested that the "achievements in the lab may be grounds for re-examining the limit."[25] Janet Rossant, an eminent figure in development biology, has suggested that improvements of these techniques that make it possible to culture human embryos through gastrulation "would again raise the question of where to place the ethical limits on human embryo development in vitro."[26] Several bioethicists, one of whom helped draft international guidelines that reaffirm the limit, maintain that "these advances . . . put human developmental biology on a collision course with the 14-day rule."[27] They advocate for revising the rule, arguing that it was never intended as a fixed and firm limit, but rather as a policy compromise that would be revisited as science progressed. It is a remarkable claim that a rule—codified as law in numerous jurisdictions—requires revision simply because it is now possible to break it. More remarkable, however, is the assertion that:

> Revisiting the 14-day rule might tempt people to try to rationalize or attach the philosophical coherence of the limit as an ethical tenet grounded in biological facts. This misconstrues the restriction. The 14-day rule was never intended to be a bright line denoting the onset of moral status in human embryos. Rather, it is a public policy tool designed to carve out a space for scientific inquiry and simultaneously show respect for the diverse views on human embryo-research.[28]

As I have shown, when the Ethics Advisory Board (EAB) first proposed a fourteen-day limit, it was explicitly unprincipled and arbitrary because it was intended simply to cohere with existing regulations. The EAB treated it as more of a clarification of the relationship of the recommendations to existing rules than as an ethical judgment, and accordingly gave it little weight. It was proposed because any other rule would have required ethical justification rather than mere deference to existing law. Yet over a period of decades, arguments were built as a bulwark to underwrite the credibility of the fourteen-day limit in the U.S. debates. Far from constructing it as a "public policy tool," the bodies that advanced these arguments maintained precisely that it was a "bright line denoting the onset of moral status in human embryos." Still more importantly, the very notion that they could discern such a bright line, notwithstanding significant dissent from the wider public, depended precisely on the notion that they could produce publicly reasonable "ethical tenet[s] grounded in biological facts," and that those tenets could and should be adopted by society because they were exemplary of right public reason. In short, the fourteen-day rule derived its credibility not only from scientific constructions of salient biological fact, and not only from the claim that the rule is grounded in the clarity of right reason. It derived its credibility from corollary constructions of deficiencies of democracy—deficiencies that authorized the parties who declared this limit to speak for society even as they limited opportunities for deliberation and dissent. Thus, it is correct that the limit is "relatively arbitrary."[29] But it is so precisely because it was grounded in forms of authority that were exempted from public scrutiny, and thus from mechanisms of democratic correction that can render the exercise of political power legitimate rather than arbitrary.

Between powers of genetic control and capacities to sustain developing embryos in vitro for longer periods, an enormous research horizon has been opened. As Ali Brivanlou, the senior author on one of the studies that cultured embryos to nearly fourteen days, puts it, "every hour as we move forward in development is a treasure box for me."[30] Yet, so too have the range and complexity of ethical challenges expanded, and with them the urgency to build more robust capacities for deliberation and governance. Scientists are once again turning their eye toward the IVF industry and the surplus embryos it has created as a source of research materials. Yet the very same scientists are now worrying over the fact that this industry is a readymade pathway for applying the techniques they will develop to human lives at their inception.

Notwithstanding the notion that new technologies demand novel modes of evaluation lest society's norms lag behind, the debates that are unfolding today are profoundly shaped by the sensibilities, practices, and imaginations that emerged out of the experiments in democracy that preceded them. A growing chorus of voices is declaring that CRISPR will revolutionize the ability to shape human life at its earliest stages. The technique portends a new chapter in the history of biotechnology, offering unprecedented power to modify life to satisfy human needs and desires. Prominent scientists are worrying over the advent of this technology and the prospects of genetic enhancement and eugenic control that it raises. They have called for international guidelines to govern human applications of gene-editing technology: The technical possibility of human gene editing makes ethical deliberation urgent. As the magazine *Science* stated in announcing CRISPR as the 2015 breakthrough of the year, "For better or worse, we all now live in CRISPR's world."[31]

Yet, the world into which this technology has arrived was decades in the making.[32] It was wrought no less in the arenas of public moral reasoning than in the laboratories of the life sciences. And the contours of our practices, norms, and political commitments that have crystalized though the debates over human embryo research will shape the future in which these new technologies unfold. Governing that future well will require asking questions that too easily go unasked, attending to ethical concerns that are too easily occluded, and drawing upon the richest repertoire of human moral imagination, since in the end it is human life—material, social, political and moral—that is at stake.

Recent scientific developments have already elicited renewed debate about how ethical stakes should be imagined and addressed, including by whom, and in what terms. In December 2015, the U.S. National Academy of Sciences joined hands with the Chinese Academy of Sciences and the UK Royal Society to host an "International Summit" on Human Gene Editing to explore ethical dimensions of these powerful technologies.[33] Among the most immediate ethical issues associated with human germline gene editing is the vast number of human embryos that would be consumed in the myriad experiments researches are now contemplating. Yet in a "summit" with hundreds of experts, where virtually every session ended before everyone who wished to could speak, the session that focused on genetic editing of human embryos for research purposes made essentially no mention of public uneasiness and closed twenty minutes

early because no one had anything more to say. That a locus of public concern so significant that it was at the forefront of U.S. politics only a decade
ago elicited only silence within such a meeting is a symptom of a failure
of both science and democracy. For insofar as questions are foreclosed,
conversations stopped, and moral uncertainties left unacknowledged, the
robustness of our institutions of governance are attenuated. Yet it is these
institutions and experts that U.S. society relies upon to chart a "prudent
path forward" into the biotechnological future.[34]

At the center of this task of governance is the question of how we imagine the future—in what terms, how narrowly or broadly, how inclusively
or exclusively of alternative and dissenting imaginations? *Governance*, for
all its vagueness, is an apt word for this task. It is a nautical term that in
its ancient meaning meant to steer. If we think of governance as steering
the ship, we need to ask what trajectory we are on and sailing onward
toward what uncharted future. Who is navigating at the helm, and with
what instruments? The question of how we should navigate is fundamentally a democratic one. In orienting ourselves to a technological future,
we as a society assume postures in the present—toward ways of knowing,
ways of reasoning, and ways of experimenting with our techniques of nav-
igation. Imagined technological futures come and go, but it is these postures, embedded in institutions and codified as precedents, that become
durable features of our world.

The role of science in American democratic judgment has become a
lightning rod and a cause of political division in domains that extend
well beyond the focus of this study. Seen as a source of transcendent
knowledge that demands deference in the ways we order our collective
social life, science comes to stand in for normative political imaginations,
for visions of how we ought to navigate the challenges of our world. In
his first inaugural address, President Barack Obama declared that his
administration would "restore science to its rightful place."[35] In issuing
an executive order "removing barriers to responsible scientific research
involving human stem cells" by reversing the Bush administration's policy, he declared, "We make scientific decisions based on facts, not ideology."[36] Yet, to call such a decision "scientific" denigrates the convictions
of many citizens, even as it constructs the right course for our society as
unambiguous. In constructing the rightful place of science as at the helm,

steering the ship, democracy shirks its own responsibilities of governance, displacing an excessive, unwarranted, and illegitimate burden onto the shoulders of science.

The moral stakes of human embryo research have been almost universally acknowledged: The power to control and manipulate human life at its earliest stages opens the way to futures that sooner or later run afoul of human dignity. In the U.S. debates, this problem was confronted as a matter of balancing predicted biomedical benefits against the present violation of many Americans' deeply held moral views. Yet, I have argued that is has also been a problem of knowledge—of accounting for what it is we are balancing, be it the chances for a promised technological future or the instrumental use of forms of life that defy easy sorting into already morally marked ontological categories. In this sense, it is also a problem of expertise: Moral questions were shaped by notions of who knows and thus who is best able to assess and balance the range of reasons, and therefore to load the scales of judgment with precision. Thus, it is also a problem of delegation and deference: of authorizing the few to stand in for the many, with corollary privileging of particular voices and silencing of others. And, therefore, it is a problem of public reasoning: of commitments—whether intentional or unwitting—to problem framings, to tacit rules of public deliberation, and to allocations of authority to declare what is right, necessary, and good. Finally, it is a problem of democracy: of seeking robustness in our collective work of moral imagination, of tempering the confidence in promises of future progress with circumspection and humility in the present, thereby taking responsibility for the technological worlds we bring into being and the forms of life we thereby produce.

The numerous sites of democratic experiment that this study has examined each sought to address challenges—epistemic, moral, and political—that strained existing American institutions of governance. Taken together, they reveal an important insight: the history of American imaginations of the forms of public reason adequate to contend with morally complex problems in the biosciences have taken shape around a notion of democracy that privileges the role of scientific authority in supplying the terms—and thus the parameters—of public moral reasoning. In conclusion, I draw together the several threads of analysis behind this claim.

BETWEEN PUBLIC AND PRIVATE

The boundary between public and private was fundamental to the contro-versies and the settlements that emerged around human embryo research. The meanings of this distinction are multiple but related: between science as a public undertaking and a private activity; between public and private reasoning; between state and market; between the public role of citizens and the freedoms of privatized belief; and between public and private material infrastructures of biological production. In the case of human embryo research, normative, institutional, and political demarcations between public and private came to be inscribed in the material and insti-tutional configurations in which human embryos were produced and used.

Clinical IVF in the United States was shaped by constitutional articula-tions of the right relationships between the state and its citizens, particu-larly vis-à-vis sex and reproduction. The Supreme Court holdings in cases like *Griswold v. Connecticut* and *Roe v. Wade* had constructed reproduc-tive practices as private, outside the moral and regulatory authority of the state. These constitutional norms were reinterpreted by early commenta-tors on IVF, including the EAB, to include technologically assisted repro-duction. It was within this relatively recently recognized space of private liberty that individuals sought medical services in which human embryos were brought into existence in vitro. Because private actors were left to sort out their own rules of the game, IVF emerged as a consumer good. By the late 1980s, policymakers found it necessary to defer to what had become a de facto right of individual access and contemplated intervention only in the name of protecting the newly formed class of IVF consumers from being sold a false bill of goods. Because there was no investment of federal dollars in any activities involving research on human embryos, the status of the embryo itself received no direct scrutiny. It figured as but one ele-ment in the provision of a service. As IVF was naturalized as just another form of reproductive practice, it was simultaneously assimilated into the category of moral choices that are the prerogative of the private citizen.

As we have seen, the consequences of this arrangement were material as well as moral. The institutional demarcation between public and private circulated along with the embryo: in the allocation of ethical responsibility between autonomous consumers and the structures of scientific research; in the distinction between public reason and private belief in evaluation of the embryo's moral status; and in the regulatory and market conditions that produced surplus embryos in the first place. In terms of policy and practice, the question of the moral status of the human embryo was devolved to individual citizens and thereby naturalized to technoscientific, legal, and political orders.

During the 1980s, many practices took root in the United States that subsequently shaped the deliberations over public support for human embryo research. With the routinized practices of superovulation, multiple fertilizations, and cryopreservation, each driven by the desire of service providers to deliver the most competitive product to their customers (the highest rates of pregnancy at the lowest price), excess embryos became an inevitable byproduct of clinical IVF. By the turn of the twenty-first century, hundreds of thousands of human embryos sat frozen in laboratories across the country.

This embryonic surplus became a background social fact in debates about publicly funded research. The IVF industry in effect provided the infrastructure to supply human embryos as research material while holding the circumstances of their creation outside the limits of public moral responsibility (a situation that contrasted markedly with circumstances in other countries, such as Germany and Britain).[37] This infrastructure was private in many senses. It was embedded in market relations between private parties; it was located in the private space of clinical medicine, beyond the research of public regulatory authorities or the norms of research governance; and it was morally privatized, whereby judgments about the propriety of its techniques were left to individuals.

These arrangements came to be normalized in practice and naturalized in the very existence of the reservoir of embryos. Thus, the de facto inclusion of IVF under a constitutionally defined norm of privacy in the 1980s generated the material and moral circumstances in which human embryo research seemed acceptable to many Americans who were otherwise opposed to creating embryos for research. The embryos would be destroyed anyway, so why not use them for research? This distinction between public and private came to be inscribed in the hybrid ontological-legal construction of the status of the human embryonic stem cell. It could be a resource for public science because it was onto-logically distinct from the embryo from which it was derived; it could therefore quietly slip over the high wall that had been erected to sepa-rate the realm of private reproductive choice from the moral and politi-cal meaning of public science.

Yet, even if the fact that embryos were produced and destroyed in pri-vate space was seen by some as unburdening public institutions of respon-sibility for these practices, the prospect of federal funding for embryo research forced society to confront the question of how it should relate to developing human life in the laboratory. This question represents an important departure from related concerns about abortion. There is no question but that the human embryo research debates were politically, conceptually, and institutionally entangled with U.S. abortion politics from their inception. However, my analysis has challenged the notion that the embryo research controversy was abortion politics by other means. Whereas the abortion debates focused largely on the constitutional limits of state power to regulate individual action, and on society's obligations to the human fetus in utero, with human embryo research, the moral status of the human embryo became a collective problem, one that only became more complex as the range of morally problematic biological entities expanded to human–animal chimera, cloned embryos, and other ambigu-ous entities. With the focus on the moral status of the embryo came the question of how the polity should make sense of such novel products of the laboratory and about the role of scientific knowledge in public reasoning.

The contours of public bioethical debate that took shape around human embryo research are one of the most consequential legacies of the experi-ments in democracy that this study has examined. The embryo debates elevated a "bioethical" problem to a level of sustained public visibility and political controversy that is unprecedented. This in turn gave rise to sensibilities and approaches that have come to be codified in practices of bioethics, in institutions of democratic government, and in the ever-evolving social contract between science, the state, and its citizens. The status of scientific knowledge—and, therefore, expert authority—shaped how lines were drawn between shared premises and individual beliefs. The problematic of the moral status of the embryo opened an arena of onto-logical politics wherein epistemic and normative judgments—and, thus, scientific and democratic authority—were coproduced. Embryo loss and twinning are two examples of biological features of the embryo that were repeatedly invoked to dismiss claims of its moral status (for instance, the notion that if an embryo can become two embryos, it is not yet an individual, and therefore cannot yet be a person). This line of thinking positioned scientific knowledge as prior to and a prerequisite for moral judgment. It thereby also positioned scientific knowledge as a source of public authority, supplying the common foundations of debate. This notion that science speaks first in the sequence of reasoning was profoundly consequential for the contours of public deliberation. It underwrote the notion that insofar as one held moral views that did not comport with scientific accounts, one's views were necessarily limited to the prerogative of the liberal individual to believe what he or she will in private but inappropriate to the sorts of reasons that can be offered in public deliberation. Science stood for quintessentially public reasons. As actors in the debates asserted scientific authority over the terms of debate ever more vigorously, disagreement came to be seen as division between secular knowledge and religious belief. This construction of what is within—and outside of—the shared normative space of public reason is deeply integrated into the contours of contemporary American bioethics, yet it goes essentially unacknowledged and unexamined within this consequential domain of thought. As such it is uncritically incorporated into the ways institutions of governance in American science and technology understand the normative stakes of the problems they confront and the forms of democracy appropriate to addressing them. The effects of this construction extend into territories well beyond human embryo research.

Accordingly, the primacy given to scientific voices is consequential not only for technical and ontological understanding, but for the very configuration of imaginations of public good and public reason abroad in contemporary public life. Given the embryo's potential as a technoscientific object, the goods at stake expand from the constitutional protection of individual privacy to the public good of (anticipated) technological innovation and cures. Imagined technological futures, seen as an inevitable outcome of research if politics and public could only be made to fall into line, shaped the notions of the state's primary responsibilities and the claims citizens could make on it. In the stem cell debates, promises of cures positioned science as a source of public goods and as a de facto institution of governance, capable of securing and enhancing human life in ways that the state on its own could not. Thus, science became a custodian of the future not only in its putative capacity to generate it, but also by declaring what futures are realistic, what stands in their way, and thus what must be done now to ameliorate the politics of the present in the name of a better future.

Given the biological complexity of embryonic forms and their derivatives, the problem of how to understand the object of deliberation, and in what terms to talk about it, likewise emerged as a foundational democratic problem. Public deliberation became dependent upon knowledge, and thus on the epistemic authority of science, even as some sought to set limits to scientific activities. Thus, deep-seated disagreements over the moral status of developing human life, longstanding in the abortion debates, transmuted into disagreement over what forms of knowledge are necessary for democratic deliberation, who has the authority to define matters of fact, and what language should be employed in public reasoning.

I want to emphasize that this role was as much delegated to scientific authorities as it was appropriated by them. Faced with divisive disagreement and vexing ethical questions, people of all political stripes sought to wrap their positions in the mantel of scientific authority. The turn to science was seen as a turn away from politics. When such moves were challenged, it tended to be by characterizing them as politicizations of science. Indeed, that accusation was regularly hurled by voices from both the Right and the Left. Yet in making these moves and countermoves, both factions were affirming an imaginary of ideal democratic deliberation wherein public reasoning is grounded in—and must defer to—authoritative scientific knowledge.

In this sense, the authority of science was rendered a resource for circumscribing raw politics into *reasonable* pluralism. Put differently, science was called upon not merely to play an instrumental role by serving up whatever knowledge was deemed relevant to ethical deliberation, but a constitutional role by serving as arbiter and custodian of the reasonableness and thus the legitimacy of democratic deliberation. The role accorded to scientific authority was underwritten by—and, in turn, reinforced—notions of what distinguishes (secular) public reason from private (moral and religious) belief. By constructing science as standing outside of politics and offering a "view from nowhere," knowledge became a resource for narrowing the range of reasoned public moral disagreement.

STANDING IN

Embryo research was an important site for the emergence of public bioethics. From the mid-1970s, the federal government increasingly asserted public authority over the ethical parameters of biomedical research. While this wrought changes in certain areas, for instance in regulation over research involving human subjects, no single issue remained as persistently controversial and perpetually unsettled as the limits of permissible research on human embryos. Professional bioethics was unsuccessful in its attempts to lay claim to this issue. While bioethicists successfully established jurisdiction over (and discursive rationalization of) a number of other research domains, they could not successfully shift the embryo out of the space of public controversy. Nevertheless, the embryo research controversy was a major force in making the public ethics body a new appendage of the democratic state and a mechanism for exercising particular forms of democratic authority over—as well as deference to—science.

The bioethics bodies that this book has examined all confronted a similar problem. Americans hold a plurality of moral views about human embryo research and related areas, such as cloning. Because these bodies were tasked with standing in for the wider public, this "fact of simple pluralism" could not be dismissed, even when individual members of these bodies advocated particular views. Instead, each of these bodies set about to narrow the diversity of public views into what they saw as the range of *reasonable* pluralism.

Each of these bodies constructed an account of how it could stand in for the public by reasoning on the public's behalf. Each body groped for ways to legitimate its representational role in a way that sought to overcome the limitations and failures of the bodies that proceeded it. With the notable exception of the President's Council on Bioethics (PCB), these bodies tended toward a greater emphasis on process and consensus, even as they expanded the range of perspectives they claimed to adequately represent. Bodies such as the Human Embryo Research Panel (HERP) and the National Bioethics Advisory Commission (*NBAC*) discovered overlapping consensus by constructing accounts of public reason that narrowed the range of public views that had to be taken into account. The President's Council rejected the mandate for consensus, but sought the foundations for a shared language in an appraisal of the nature of the controversial biological entities and techniques themselves.

Each approach responded to the failures of the prior effort by constructing new accounts of how to adequately represent moral pluralism and identify premises held in common. The EAB was skeptical of its ability to stand in for the public. Rather than seek to winnow down pluralism into reasonable pluralism, it instead qualified its ethical judgments as "legitimately controverted." In response to the EAB's restraint and deference to moral pluralism, the American Fertility Society (AFS) Ethics Committee adopted a technocratic approach, treating scientific knowledge as necessarily prior to ethical judgment, at least if that judgment is to be publicly reasonable.

In light of criticisms of the term *preembryo* and wary of being accused of rhetorical obfuscation, the HERP offered a full-blown theory of public reason that would accommodate the strategy of ontological refinement of public discourse that the AFS committee had employed but grounded it in an explicit democratic theory. Drawing on a Rawlsian account of public reason, the panel drew the circle of reasonable pluralism, placing science at its center. In so doing, the panel dismissed the relevance of (what it considered to be) religion-inflected perspectives to public ethical reasoning and excluded them from its deliberations. The panel was chastised for excluding voices that were critical of human embryo research, particularly religious ones. Its approach elicited significant pushback from members of Congress and, ultimately, a legislative ban on federal funding for human embryo research.

The NBAC, seeking to avoid the missteps of the HERP, solicited explicitly religious arguments. In keeping with mainstream bioethics' approach of boiling down diverse views into common morality principles, it sought to extract overlapping moral consensus from the range of public views by discovering the (ostensibly) shared moral commitments that lie beneath political disagreement. To this end, the NBAC solicited explicitly religious views and subjected them to a translation test. It treated as reasonable only those arguments that its members felt could be translated into a common currency of secular public reason. By assuming this translational role, the NBAC constructed itself as an organ of public reason, capable of discovering common premises beneath apparent moral disagreement—premises that were unknown even to those who unwittingly held them—thereby transmuting unreasonable public debate into reasoned democratic deliberation conducted by proxy.

The President's Council on Bioethics reacted against the NBAC's strategy of generating consensus by reducing distinct moral views into an attenuated least common denominator. For the council, the primary role of the ethics body was not to produce consensus, but to exemplify robust debate, accepting dissensus as a potentially necessary means of achieving the fullest possible moral articulations. It too sought to represent robust public reasoning, but by deliberating about the moral questions directly, as if a miniature, enlightened public sphere, rather than attempting to rationalize existing disagreement.

In their efforts to circumscribe pluralism into reasonable pluralism, these bodies made recourse to scientific authority, though in different ways; for instance, as an exemplar of public reason and thus as a standard against which to judge conflicting claims, or in order to bracket questions as epistemic, thereby removing explicitly value-laden ontological disagreements from the range of ethical questions that must be entertained.

For the Ethics Advisory Board in 1978, the (recently described) high rate of natural embryo loss was a means for assigning responsibility to amoral nature, thus shrinking the ground for moral disagreement. For the American Fertility Society Ethics Committee, the term *preembryo* was proposed to discipline public discourse into taking account of relevant facts—facts that the committee took to demonstrate that notions of preembryonic personhood were untenable without recourse to theology and thus the realm of private belief. For the National Institutes of Health (NIH) Human Embryo Research Panel, scientific descriptions of the embryo were taken as exemplary of public reasons and became the measure against which other reasons were tested. For the National Bioethics Advisory Commission, ontological questions were treated as within the remit of science and wholly distinct from ethical deliberation.

This allowed the NBAC to treat all disagreements about the nature of the embryo (and related biological entities) as moral disagreements. As such, they could be subjected to philosophical scrutiny and translated, where possible, into a common currency of secular public reason. Translation became a gatekeeping device. When the NBAC's philosophers could not rearticulate theologically inflected views in secular terms, the "residue" was excluded. The President's Council on Bioethics saw robust ontological appraisals, codified in a shared language—"calling things by their right names"—as the common ground for reasoned deliberation.

The powerful role that these accounts of public reason accorded scientific authority is evident in the way scientists appropriated the President's Council's project of supplying the terms of debate. Exploiting the notion that science stands outside politics and speaks in value-neutral terms, these scientists claimed the authority to reconstruct the common language of public discourse in the name of inoculating democracy against the corrosive effects of public confusion and thereby safeguarding the legitimacy of democratic judgment. They went so far as to mediate the ostensibly unmediated infrastructure of direct democracy to ensure that the state-sanctioned language would be science sanctioned, all in the name of safeguarding the democratic process. Thus, even when disagreement was to be resolved through popular vote—that most pure mechanism of procedural democracy—public debate was shaped around an idea of public reason in which values deliberation must defer to scientific accounts.

I have demonstrated how ethics bodies and other actors justified their claims to stand in for the public by tethering democratic legitimacy to scientific authority. Problems of moral disagreement were resolved by invoking an idea of an extra-political, scientific "view from nowhere." This depended in turn on constructing an account of democracy that relied on scientific knowledge in a particular way—whether as a common premise given in advance (as for the EAB and the AFS committee); as exemplary of public reason (as for the HERP); as the custodian of questions that could be purged from (and thus disregarded in) public values debate (as for the NBAC); as a neutral starting point for finding a common language (as for the PCB); or as a discursive ordering device to guarantee that disagreement is resolved in a legitimately democratic manner (as in California and Missouri). Thus, notions of democratic representation were coproduced with notions of what is known, who knows it, and how it should be known. The notion that knowledge stands outside politics had a profound *political* effect because that claim was used to underwrite accounts of political representation, of public reason, and of the role of science in guaranteeing the legitimacy of democratic processes.

CONSTITUTIONAL KNOWLEDGE

Justice is the first virtue of social institutions, as truth is of systems of thought. A theory however elegant and economical must be rejected or revised if it is untrue; likewise laws and institutions no matter how efficient and well-arranged must be reformed or abolished if they are unjust. . . . Being first virtues of human activities, truth and justice are uncompromising.[38]

Thus begins John Rawls's famous *A Theory of Justice*, perhaps the most influential book in American political theory of the twentieth century. The statement defines the scope of his philosophical project: the development of an image of justice to ground the rightness of social institutions as robustly as reality tethers knowledge to truth. Yet, read as a reflection of political culture, these bedrocks of truth and justice are themselves rooted in a prior constitutionalism: an imaginary of right social order that seeks security in the notions that truth is uncompromising because it is independent of the contingencies of social life and that justice is uncompromising because it is a foundational commitment of political society to make it so. Rawls's bifurcation of spheres—of truth and justice, knowledge and norms, modern science and political modernity—is grounded in the assumption that this bifurcation is given in advance. It is a cosmological assumption that the "starry heavens above" and the "moral law within" are bounded by their respective rules of reason and that the teleological unfolding of reason in social life will reflect these orderings of the world.[39] Yet these categories—truth and justice—are themselves refractions of the core, aspirational institutions of secular modernity: science and law. The presumptive givenness of their separatist logic is itself a normative commitment. Indeed, it is first a normative commitment, and only secondarily an epistemological one, and, as such, it is not amenable to merely epistemological critique.[40] It is grounded in an imagination of right reason wherein "rightness" is simultaneously an aspiration to be true to the world as we know it and as we wish it to be.[41]

The short sentences quoted above are virtually all the thought Rawls gives to the right ordering of knowledge in his lengthy treatment of justice. Yet, right knowledge is a fundamental ingredient in his account of right public reason. Indeed, we can look to Rawls's own idealized constitutional moment, the original position, to see this at work. Rawls's "parties in the original position" sit behind a "veil of ignorance" that prevents them from knowing what particulars of social, cultural, and material circumstance define their individual interests. Like a perfect jury, they represent the "everyman." They reason as the everyman would reason about his own interests, thereby eliminating disparity by universalizing interests. Yet, the condition of possibility for Rawls's original position is epistemic: ties in the original position have perfect knowledge of the world they inhabit and thus of the causal effects of pursuing their interests in particular ways. The veil of ignorance functions as a means to right moral reasoning only insofar as it is stitched to a veil of knowledge. Put differently, the universalizability of normative insight is predicated on that insight being grounded in universal knowledge. As Rawls conceives it, without knowledge, the veil of ignorance would only produce prejudice.

My purpose in analyzing Rawls is not to critique his philosophical account. Perfect knowledge of the world is perhaps no more and no less unimaginable than rational egos disembedded from and unshaped by a socio-material world. Rather, my purpose is to observe how these idealized imaginations of right reason (and corollary constructions of right institutional orders) touch down in the social world. The bioethics bodies that deliberated over human embryo research refracted Rawls's constitutional bifurcation in various ways. Indeed, in different ways, they each sought to constitute themselves as a microcosmic community of reason that could reason as the wider public could not. Particularly instructive are those instances where bioethics bodies such as the HERP and the NBAC drew on Rawls's idea of public reason and constructed themselves as occupying a role not unlike the parties in the original position—disembedded from their own social positions, reasoning for a wider social world in the way that citizens of that world would reason were they to be emancipated from the tunnel vision of their particular subject positions. Noteworthy, too, is the way each of these bodies held up a veil of knowledge. Right knowledge (which in practice meant scientifically certified claims) underwrote their various ways of claiming to perform right public reason. Like the veil of ignorance, the veil of knowledge separated these committees from the wider social world. Unlike the veil of ignorance, which renders individuals ignorant of their interests in order to make their reasoning universal, the veil of knowledge attributes ignorance to the external social world, placing those behind the veil in a privileged position of reason.

As I have shown, these moves are not innocent. They are not mere expressions of deference to given-in-advance spheres of knowledge and norms, even if their proponents understand them as such. Rather, they assert an unacknowledged—and unratified—constitutionalism in order to position the authorities that speak for those spheres as constitutionally authorized arbiters of public reason. If we bracket the constitutional creation myth of Rawls's truth–justice distinction, and instead ask what imaginary it codifies and what regulative effect that imaginary has on social life, we see a world in which knowledge and normative orders are profoundly coproduced. We see accounts of secular reason that violate the very norms of critical reflexivity and provisionality that they claim to espouse.

Numerous actors in the embryo debates declared the public incompetent to think for itself. From behind the veil of knowledge, these actors claimed not only to be able to see what the public did not see, but also how the public *could not* reason. That is, they claimed to be able to see what constraints prevented people from participating in public moral reasoning, notwithstanding the fact that those people were often speaking loudly and seeking to be heard. These claims to privileged reason underwrote the HERP's dismissiveness of public expressions of concern (the "hate mail") and the exclusion of those moral idioms it deemed to be unreasonable. They similarly underwrote the NBAC's apparent inclusiveness of public perspectives insofar as it required that its witnesses speak in an explicitly theological idiom, not withstanding witnesses' protests that they could make the same arguments in secular terms. The NBAC asserted its own authority to discern public reasons in religion-inflected utterances and to consign to the waste bin of mere talk those accounts that did not pass the test.

What is remarkable about this exercise of authority is not that it was exercised—after all, asymmetrical power is an inevitable feature of political life. What is remarkable is that these asymmetries were underwritten by frequent and near-universal declarations that public bioethical debate was urgent and that participation must be—and, indeed, was—inclusive. Yet the same actors who made these declarations marked many public voices as unreasonable, and thus ineligible, for political recognition. They marked particular moral idioms as violating the norms of civility because those who spoke in those idioms refused to defer to discursive proscriptions that were asserted in the name of science. These moves reflect a modern fundamentalism, yet one that is invisible because it bears the labels of liberty and progress. It is a confidence in the sufficiency of an imagination of reason wherein the freedom to participate in political deliberation requires that citizens first be emancipated from the constraints of confusion (and thus unwitting unreason) by deferring to authorized knowledge.

Such a construction of political participation is evident in the work of the most recent U.S. public bioethics body, the Presidential Commission for the Study of Bioethical Issues. The commission is chaired by Amy Gutmann, a political theorist and leading scholar of deliberative democracy. As *Nature* has described her, Gutmann is a scholar "whose work deals with . . . using reasoned argument to depolarize politics."[42] The fingerprints of Gutmann's philosophical expertise are all over the work of the Presidential Commission. Under her leadership, the commission has given deliberative democracy pride of place, affirming it as a "pillar" of public bioethics. Like others that have preceded it, the commission's approach has emphasized the norms of Rawlsian public reason.

This ongoing experiment in democracy has thus far confirmed the argument of this book. While systematically affirming the role of public deliberation in governing the technological future, the commission has at the same time advocated for measures to discipline public discourse to comport with the strictures of scientific judgments. For instance, in its evaluation of synthetic biology, the commission recommended a "publicly accessible fact-checking mechanism" to correct false facts in public and media discourse in order to facilitate reasoned deliberation and improve "public perception and acceptance of emerging technologies."[43] The commission offered "playing god" and "creating life" as examples of the sorts of discourse that such fact checking would hold in check. Thus, the commission that has most explicitly celebrated deliberative democracy has unreflexively called for modulating public debate to limit the range of discourse and problem framings that are (in its view) appropriate to public ethical deliberation, and it has relied upon the authority of science to do so. Scientific authority over matters of fact becomes, in the commission's approach, the authority to hold in check the range of debate, disciplining public discourse to comport with scientifically authorized constructions of what promises can be made, what risks warrant worry, and what technological futures are plausible, desirable, and good. That the commission that celebrates democratic deliberation calls on science to set limits on public debate, and that it fails to recognize this move as violating its own commitment to deliberative democracy, reveals the privileged yet unrecognized role that scientific authority plays in contemporary imaginations of right public reason.[44]

Put into practice in the cases I have examined, ideas of public reason have uncritically elevated the role of scientific authority in determining which voices are heard or silenced, and in privileging particular constructions of representativeness, democratic legitimacy, and the good. The ideal of reasoned deliberative engagement between free and equal citizens was used to discipline public reasoning while exempting the institution of science from the same tests of legitimacy to which democracy was itself subject. By ignoring the coproduction of knowledge and norms, democratic theory has at once facilitated and occluded moves that are profoundly consequential in structuring power and authority. This study has demonstrated the unexpected and surprising results of this under-theorization for practices of bioethical deliberation in contemporary governance of science and technology.

The stakes are high. These are sites where modernity's powerful imaginaries touch down, orienting our technological aspirations and our ethical postures. They are sites where the basic normative vocabularies that inform the democratic imagination take shape, ordering our most fundamental commitments to human life. They are also moments of secularization, where certain repertoires of public moral imagination are codified as right and appropriate to public reason, even as other moral idioms are excluded from the thereby impoverished public sphere. The teleological narrative of secularization, like its cousin concept, scientific progress, is too easily naturalized to an imaginary of modernity's inevitable forward march. Yet in interrogating the workings of a social world that is ostensibly carried along by these forces of history, we see that these forces are, in fact, enacted in the practices of that social world. Understanding these processes and the imaginaries that underwrite them therefore becomes an urgent political task.

One critical element of this task is to attend to the remarkable absence of science in contemporary theories of politics. Science and democracy are the defining achievements of secular modernity. As an essentially contested enterprise, democracy demands that we perpetually interrogate political authority by refusing the power of government as natural or given in advance. Yet, this critical project is incomplete if we fail to interrogate the forms of power that likewise reside in modernity's other defining institution. To this end, we must attend to the constructions of reason that define the social contract between science and democracy, and to the constitutional position of science in arenas of collective moral sense-making.

Science and technology occupy a powerful, indeed constitutional, position in contemporary democracy. Yet, they are not in the conventional pantheon of institutional power. As such, they tend to escape our notice as sites of political authority. In the face of vexing moral questions and divisive political disagreement, scientific knowledge seems to offer a univocal "view from nowhere," dissolving dissent by reducing the range of reasons that democracy must entertain. We imagine science as outside the arena of politics and, as such, capable of shouldering responsibilities of political judgment whose weight we would rather not bear, judgments that we would rather have rendered by the faceless authority of fact than through our own far less powerful, but far more personal, voices.

This book has traversed but a handful of experiments in democracy's wide laboratory. Yet, it is within such experiments that reorderings of our world—both moral and material—take shape. They give form to the contours of imagination and constructions of rightness upon which human futures are built. And, as sites of interrogation, they reveal what questions go systematically unasked, what moral articulations are consistently silenced, and what imaginaries are quietly codified in our political and technological regimes. They are sites where modernity's flight from ambivalence at once confronts and refuses its limits, where confidence in its conception of right reason forecloses alternative moral imaginations.[45] It is in such moments of ambivalence, when the fabric of sociotechnical order frays and tears, that we can see through to the warp and weft of our world, and so too to the skeins of power and authority out of which it is woven.

Where these threads of social order entwine our deepest moral commitments, they cannot—and ought not—be tied off into neat philosophical knots. Neither should they be simplified to cohere with our fickle imaginations of progress. The greatest virtue of democracy—and its most fragile achievement—is a social order in which visions of progress and the good are products of collective imagination. As custodians of our own modes of public reasoning, we are likewise custodians of the futures they engender. These responsibilities demand that our images of right reason perpetually remain projects of critical reflection.

Faced with the provisionality of political life, we look to science as the agent of transformation: that revolutionary force whose inevitable unfolding determines our lives to come. Yet, notions of right knowledge and the technological futures of which it foretells are sites of moral imagination. They refract images of righteous authority, of the deficiencies of life in the present, and of the politics of a redeemed future. The sociotechnical orders that emerge out of the legacies of experiment are worlds of our own making, and so too they bear the mark of our frailties. It is we who bring them into being, no less in the laboratories of democracy than in the esoteric spaces of science. Only by acknowledging the infirmities of our aspirations to perfected reason, not least the ways we press science into a position of transcendent authority, can democracy come to occupy its rightful place, shouldering due responsibility in ordering our technological future.

NOTES

INTRODUCTION

1. For instance, beginning in the mid-1960s, Nobel laureate Joshua Lederberg wrote a regular column in the *Washington Post* entitled "Science and Man," exploring a wide range of issues at the nexus of science, technology, and society. John H. Evans, *Playing God? Human Genetic Engineering and the Rationalization of Public Bioethical Debate* (Chicago: University of Chicago Press, 2002); Gordon Wolstenholme, *Man and His Future* (Boston: Little, Brown, 1963).

2. Henry K. Beecher et al., "A Definition of Irreversible Coma. Report of the Ad Hoc Committee of the Harvard Medical School to Examine the Definition of Brain Death," *JAMA* 205, no. 6 (1968): 337–40.

3. Margaret Lock, *Twice Dead: Organ Transplants and the Reinvention of Death* (Berkeley, CA: University of California Press, 2001).

4. Harry M. Marks, *The Progress of Experiment: Science and Therapeutic Reform in the United States, 1900–1990* (Cambridge: Cambridge University Press, 2000).

5. David J. Rothman, *Strangers at the Bedside: A History of How Law and Bioethics Transformed Medical Decision Making*, 2nd ed. (Piscataway, NJ: Aldine Transaction, 2003).

6. Henry K. Beecher, "Ethics and Clinical Research," *New England Journal of Medicine* 274, no. 24 (1966): 1354–60.

7. Laura Stark, *Behind Closed Doors: IRBs and the Making of Ethical Research* (Chicago: University of Chicago Press, 2011).

8. Susan Wright, *Molecular Politics: Developing American and British Regulatory Policy for Genetic Engineering, 1972–1982* (Chicago: University of Chicago Press, 1994); Herbert Gottweis, *Governing Molecules: The Discursive Politics of Genetic Engineering in Europe and the United States* (Cambridge, MA: MIT Press, 1998).

9. J. Benjamin Hurlbut, "Remembering the Future: Science, Law, and the Legacy of Asilomar," in *Dreamscapes of Modernity: Sociotechnical Imaginaries and the Fabrication of Power*, ed. Sheila Jasanoff and Sang-Hyun Kim (Chicago: University of Chicago Press, 2015), 126–51.

10. Sheila Jasanoff, "Introduction: Rewriting Life, Reframing Rights," in *Reframing Rights: Bioconstitutionalism in the Genetic Age*, ed. Sheila Jasanoff (Cambridge, MA: MIT Press, 2011), 1–28.

11. I follow John Evans's (2002, 34) definition of public bioethical debate as "social elites . . . debat[ing] over what society should do about a problem such as [human genetic engineering.]" However, while his analysis focuses on professional bioethicists as the key players in that category of elites, mine looks to other elites as well, particularly scientists.

12. J. Benjamin Hurlbut, "Limits of Responsibility: Genome Editing, Asilomar, and the Politics of Deliberation," *Hastings Center Report* 45, no. 5 (2015): 11–14.

13. For a detailed study of the place of human embryo research within the broader context of embryology, and in the related conceptions of life that informed ethical evaluations, see Jane Maienschein, *Whose View of Life? Embryos, Cloning, and Stem Cells* (Cambridge, MA: Harvard University Press, 2005).

14. Centers for Disease Control and Prevention, "Assisted Reproductive Technology Surveillance—United States, 2000," *Morbidity and Mortality Weekly Report* 52, no. SS09 (August 29, 2003): 1–16.

15. David I. Hoffman et al., "Cryopreserved Embryos in the United States and Their Availability for Research," *Fertility and Sterility* 79, no. 5 (2003): 1063–69.

16. Geoffrey P. Lomax and Alan O. Trounson, "Correcting Misperceptions about Cryopreserved Embryos and Stem Cell Research," *Nature Biotechnology* 31, no. 4 (April 2013): 288–90.

17. James A. Thomson et al., "Embryonic Stem Cell Lines Derived from Human Blastocysts," *Science* 282, no. 5391 (November 6, 1998): 1145–47.

18. Dolly the sheep was the first mammal to be cloned using a somatic cell. A somatic cell (i.e., a fully differentiated cell) was taken from a cell line derived from a mammary gland cell of a sheep. An oocyte (i.e., egg cell) from another sheep was enucleated (the pronuclei were removed), and the somatic cell was injected into the enucleated oocyte. The oocyte was then chemically and electrically activated. Through a still incompletely understood process, the somatic cell genome was "reprogrammed" into a de-differentiated state. This process of "somatic cell nuclear transfer" produced an artificially reconstructed embryo that was genetically identical to (i.e., a clone of) the sheep who supplied the somatic cell. Dolly demonstrated that mammalian somatic cells could be reprogrammed and that genetically identical clones of adult mammals could therefore be produced. In principle, if this could be done with a sheep, it could be done with a human. Ian Wilmut et al., "Viable Offspring Derived from Fetal and Adult Mammalian Cells," *Nature* 385, no. 6619 (February 27, 1997): 810–13.

19. A few representative texts from scientists, theologian-ethicists and others: Paul Ramsey, *Fabricated Man: The Ethics of Genetic Control* (New Haven: Yale University Press, 1970); Leon R. Kass, "Making Babies: The New Biology and the Old Morality," *The Public Interest*, no. 26 (1972): 18–56; Gordon Wolstenholme, *Man and His Future* (Boston: Little, Brown, 1963); Hermann Joseph Muller, *Man's Future Birthright: Essays*

on *Science and Humanity* (Albany: SUNY Press, 1973); Amitai Etzioni, *Genetic Fix* (New York: Macmillan, 1973). On dignity, see Gaymon Bennett, *Technicians of Human Dignity: Bodies, Souls, and the Making of Intrinsic Worth* (New York: Fordham University Press, 2015).

20. This change reflects what John Evans has described as the "thinning" of public bioethical debate. I attend in particular to the role of ontological accounts and, thus, scientific knowledge, in this process. Evans, *Playing God?*

21. On the relationship between biological knowledge and moral evaluation, see Jane Maienschein, *Embryos Under the Microscope* (Cambridge, MA: Harvard University Press, 2014).

22. My use of the concept follows Jasanoff's. See Sheila Jasanoff, "Making the Facts of Life," in *Reframing Rights: Bioconstitutionalism in the Genetic Age*, ed. Sheila Jasanoff (Cambridge, MA: MIT Press, 2011). Annemarie Mol's use of the concept is different. It explores the political meaning of the multiplicity of realities revealed by actor-network theory. My use instead attends to the coproduction of epistemic and normative accounts, where questions of ontology are raised and contested precisely because they are seen as necessary to settle in order to arrive at corollary normative answers. The ontological is, in this respect, reopened by politics of normative sense-making, not by analytically opening the black box to reveal the actual multiplicity of a putatively singular reality. See Annemarie Mol, "Ontological Politics. A Word and Some Questions," *The Sociological Review* 47, no. S1 (May 1, 1999): 74–89.

23. cf. Sheila Jasanoff, "The Idiom of Co-Production," in *States of Knowledge: The Co-Production of Science and Social Order* (London: Routledge, 2004), 1–13.

24. I use phrases like *early human life* in a purely descriptive, not morally evaluative, sense. I do so without a naïve aspiration to "neutral" language. In the human embryo research debates, one's choice of words to refer to the embryo has come to be seen as morally (and politically) laden. Indeed, it is. One main area of focus in this book is on the battles over terminology and over who has the authority to declare which terms are "correct" and which are prejudicial. I take no position on the question of which terms are the right ones, except to show that the notions of neutrality and rightness are thoroughly political. Indeed, my aim is to illuminate how language itself came to be such a significant locus of disagreement and which competing imaginations of right reason informed those disagreements. My analysis will show that there is no given-in-advance neutral language, because the very notion of what constitutes neutrality—and who is in a position to declare it—is deeply entangled with normative notions of how political life ought to be ordered. One consequence is that the whole linguistic repertoire in this domain— including the terms that I myself use—are always already politically inflected and subject to contestation. My project is not to take a position on which terms are the right ones, but rather to step back from the dynamics of these disagreements to illuminate what is at stake in them. Therefore, I ask the reader to bear with me and check the impulse to discover my ethical views in my choice of terms, just as I trust, in turn, that my reader

will attempt, as I have, to step back from the welter of political disagreement to see what unnamed and unnoticed commitments are at stake in the very impulse to expose value judgments masquerading as neutral matters of fact.

25. This was the National Commission for the Protection of Human Subjects of Biomedical and Behavioral Research, which was created by the *National Research Act* in 1974. I claim that this was the first public bioethics body, but there were other committees charged with addressing ethical issues in research. These, however, were ad hoc committees convened to address specific administrative and regulatory questions. They were, for the most part, politically invisible and did not have the broad remit of the National Commission. See Stark, *Behind Closed Doors*; Frazier Benya, "Biomedical Advances Confront Society: Congressional Hearings and the Development of Bioethics, 1960–1975" (Ph.D. dissertation, University of Minnesota, 2012).

26. There are a number of excellent histories of the development of bioethics. However, most of them take for granted the distinction between epistemic and normative questions and thus the boundary between science and ethics. As a result, most scholarship on (and, for that matter, in) bioethics has attended to intra-bioethical debates over the appropriate moral philosophical frameworks in which to contend with bioethics problems on behalf of wider society. They have for the most part not examined the role that scientific authority has played in shaping the contours of ethical deliberation. This book seeks to fill that gap. Rothman, *Strangers at the Bedside*; Albert R. Jonsen, *The Birth of Bioethics* (New York: Oxford University Press, 2003); M. L. Tina Stevens, *Bioethics in America: Origins and Cultural Politics* (Baltimore: Johns Hopkins University Press, 2000); Stark, *Behind Closed Doors*; Evans, *Playing God?*; John Evans, *The History and Future of Bioethics: An Unorthodox Sociological View* (Chicago: University of Chicago Press, 2013).

27. Evans, *Playing God?*; Evans, *The History and Future of Bioethics*.

28. The ELSI program of the Human Genome Project (HGP) was a major federal investment in bioethics. The HGP allocated five percent of its total budget to the ELSI program. On this program and its legacy, see Hilgartner, Prainsack, and J. Benjamin Hurlbut, "Ethics as Governance in Genomics and Beyond," in Felt et al., *The Handbook of Science and Technology Studies*, 4th ed. (Cambridge, MA: MIT Press, 2016): 823–51. On its place within the governance of biotechnology, see Sheila Jasanoff, *Designs on Nature* (Princeton: Princeton University Press, 2005).

29. Jasanoff, *States of Knowledge*.

30. Thomas F. Gieryn, "Boundary-Work and the Demarcation of Science from Non-Science: Strains and Interests in Professional Ideologies of Scientists," *American Sociological Review* 48, no. 6 (December 1983): 781–95.

31. On the principle of symmetry, see David Bloor, *Knowledge and Social Imagery* (Chicago: University of Chicago Press, 1991), 7ff. For a collection of studies that are exemplary of this approach to coproduction, see Jasanoff, *States of Knowledge*. For a coproductionist analysis that attends specifically to science and technology as sites of future-oriented, aspirational imaginations of the good, particularly as codified in political institutions and

practices, see Jasanoff and Kim, *Dreamscapes of Modernity*. For a compendium of some of Jasanoff's most important work, see Sheila Jasanoff, *Science and Public Reason* (London: Routledge, 2012).

32. Jasanoff, *Designs on Nature*.

33. John Rawls, *Political Liberalism*, 2nd ed. (New York: Columbia University Press, 2005), xvii.

34. Sheila Jasanoff, *Science at the Bar: Law, Science, and Technology in America* (Cambridge, MA: Harvard University Press, 1995); Sheila Jasanoff, "Science and the Statistical Victim: Modernizing Knowledge in Breast Implant Litigation," *Social Studies of Science* 32, no. 1 (February 2002): 37–69.

35. Amy Gutmann and Dennis Thompson, *Democracy and Disagreement* (Cambridge, MA: Belknap, 1998); James S. Fishkin, *When the People Speak: Deliberative Democracy and Public Consultation* (New York: Oxford University Press, 2009).

36. Jason Chilvers and Matthew Kearnes, eds., *Remaking Participation: Science, Environment and Emergent Publics* (Abingdon, Oxon: Routledge, 2015).

37. Amy Gutmann and Dennis Thompson, "Deliberating about Bioethics," *Hastings Center Report* 27, no. 3 (June 1997): 38–41.

38. Presidential Commission for the Study of Bioethical Issues, "New Directions: The Ethics of Synthetic Biology and Emerging Technologies" (Washington, DC, December 2010), http://bioethics.gov/cms/sites/default/files/PCSBI-Synthetic-Biology-Report -12.16.10_0.pdf.

39. Lisa M. Lee, Mildred Z. Solomon, and Amy Gutmann, "Teaching Bioethics," *Hastings Center Report* 44, no. 5 (September 1, 2014): 10–11.

40. For a discussion of this issue in relation to Gutmann and the Presidential Commission, see Hurlbut, "Remembering the Future."

41. Sheila Jasanoff, "In a Constitutional Moment: Science and Social Order at the Millennium," in *Social Studies of Science and Technology: Looking Back, Ahead, Volume 23 of the Sociology of the Sciences Yearbook*, ed. Bernward Joerges and Helga Nowotny (Dordrecht, Netherlands: Springer, 2003), 166.

42. Jasanoff, *Designs on Nature*, 255–71.

43. Jasanoff, *Science at the Bar*.

44. Jasanoff, *Science and Public Reason*.

45. On imaginaries, see Jasanoff and Kim, *Dreamscapes of Modernity*.

46. John Rawls, *A Theory of Justice: Original Edition* (Cambridge, MA: Belknap, 2005); Rawls, *Political Liberalism*; John Rawls, *The Law of Peoples: With "The Idea of Public Reason Revisited"* (Cambridge, MA: Harvard University Press, 2001).

47. Michel Callon, Pierre Lascoumes, and Yannick Barthe, *Acting in an Uncertain World: An Essay on Technical Democracy* (Cambridge, MA: MIT Press, 2009).

48. Looking to practice is a foundational analytic move in STS. Here, I attend symmetrically to the production of politics and the production of knowledge, consistent with the idea of coproduction.

49. Joshua Cohen, "Democracy and Liberty," in *Deliberative Democracy*, ed. Jon Elster (New York: Cambridge University Press, 1998), 186, my emphasis.

50. John Rawls, *Justice as Fairness: A Restatement* (Cambridge, MA: Harvard University Press, 2001), 27.

51. Ibid.

52. Gutmann and Thompson, *Democracy and Disagreement*, 55.

53. Rawls, *Justice as Fairness*, 92.

54. Ibid., 116.

55. Ibid., 117.

56. Cohen, "Democracy and Liberty," 199.

57. Rawls, *Justice as Fairness*, 92.

58. After nearly a century of social analysis of processes of scientific judgment, this claim is axiomatic for STS. Science does not exist independent of the social community that develops, debates, and accepts scientific accounts. For obvious reasons, Rawls treats the political "community of reason" as filled with people and governed by rules of engagement. Symmetrically, the same applies to the "thought communities" and "thought styles" of science and to the knowledge that they produce. Ludwik Fleck, *Genesis and Development of a Scientific Fact* (Chicago: University of Chicago Press, 1981).

59. Rawls, *Justice as Fairness*, 27.

60. Michael Polanyi. "The Republic of Science: Its Political and Economic Theory." *Minerva* 1, no. 1 (1962): 54–73.

61. Harry Collins and Robert Evans, *Rethinking Expertise* (Chicago: University of Chicago Press, 2007); Callon, Lascoumes, and Barthe, *Acting in an Uncertain World*.

62. Indeed, it is a *sociotechnical* imaginary. cf. Jasanoff and Kim, *Dreamscapes of Modernity*.

63. Cohen, "Democracy and Liberty," 193:"We can work out the content of the deliberative democratic ideal and its conception of public reasoning by considering features of such reasoning in the idealized case and then aiming to build those features into institutions."

64. Jürgen Habermas, *Toward a Rational Society: Student Protest, Science, and Politics*, trans. Jeremy J. Shapiro (Boston: Beacon, 1971).

65. Ibid.; Jürgen Habermas, *The Theory of Communicative Action* (Cambridge: Polity, 1986).

66. Sheila Jasanoff et al., eds., *Handbook of Science and Technology Studies* (New York: Sage, 1995); Edward J. Hackett et al., eds., *The Handbook of Science and Technology Studies*, 3rd ed. (Cambridge, MA: MIT Press, 2007).

67. Thomas F. Gieryn, *Cultural Boundaries of Science: Credibility on the Line* (Chicago: University of Chicago Press, 1999).

68. Bloor, *Knowledge and Social Imagery*.

69. Bruno Latour, *Science in Action: How to Follow Scientists and Engineers through Society* (Cambridge, MA: Harvard University Press, 1987).

70. Sheila Jasanoff, *The Fifth Branch: Science Advisers as Policymakers* (Cambridge, MA: Harvard University Press, 1994).

71. Steven Shapin and Simon Schaffer, *Leviathan and the Air-Pump* (Princeton: Princeton University Press, 1989).

72. Jasanoff, *Designs on Nature*; Yaron Ezrahi, *The Descent of Icarus: Science and the Transformation of Contemporary Democracy* (Cambridge, MA: Harvard University Press, 1990).

73. Bruno Latour, "Give Me a Laboratory and I Will Raise the World," in *Science Observed: Perspectives on the Social Study of Science*, ed. Karin Knorr-Cetina and Michael Mulkay (London and Beverly Hills: Sage, 1983).

74. Jasanoff and Kim, *Dreamscapes of Modernity*.

75. Chris Mooney, *The Republican War on Science* (New York: Basic Books, 2005).

76. Put differently, this is a distinction between *verstehen* and *erklären*. The latter has a purposive dimension insofar as correct explanation implies clarity also about what one should do. Understanding, by contrast, is the territory of critique. Its project is reflection that "humiliates" overconfidence in a settled notion of correctness—that is, that brings back into view the forms of historically situated consciousness within which we construct accounts of transcendent secular authority. *Verstehen* is as much an ethical project as an epistemic one, since its project is to elicit and confront the ethos from within which we give accounts of the good. I take this to be the core critical project of coproductionist STS. Such critique has an essential role to play in enhancing political practices of reasoning and world-making. It is in the service of a project of public reason that is "born of civility, willing to engage with unpalatable viewpoints, with honesty to acknowledge its own provisionality and courage to confront radical disbelief." Jasanoff, *Science and Public Reason*, 281. cf. Sheila Jasanoff, "Technologies of Humility: Citizen Participation in Governing Science," *Minerva* 41, no. 3 (2003): 223–44.

77. Michel Foucault, "Nietzsche, Genealogy, History," in *The Foucault Reader*, ed. Paul Rabinow (New York: Pantheon, 1984), 76–100.

78. Jasanoff, "The Idiom of Co-Production."

1. NEW BEGINNINGS

1. Paul Ramsey, *Fabricated Man: The Ethics of Genetic Control* (New Haven: Yale University Press, 1970).

2. Gordon Wolstenholme, *Man and His Future* (Boston: Little, Brown, 1963); Hermann Joseph Muller, *Man's Future Birthright: Essays on Science and Humanity* (Albany: SUNY Press, 1973).

3. Indeed, conversations among prominent biologists like Huxley, Haldane, Joshua Lederberg, and others about the human technological future in the 1960s were almost always also explicitly conversations about the political norms and institutions necessary to guide that future.

4. See, for example, Congress, Senate, Subcommittee on Health, National Advisory Commission on Health, Science and Society: *Hearings on S.J. Res. 75*, 92nd Cong., (November 9, 1971); Congress, Senate, Subcommittee on Health, Committee on Labor and Public Welfare, *Quality of Health Care—Human Experimentation, Part 1–3*, 93rd

Cong., (February 21–23, March 6–8, 1973); cf. Frazier Benya, "Biomedical Advances Confront Society: Congressional Hearings and the Development of Bioethics, 1960–1975" (Ph.D. dissertation, University of Minnesota, 2012).

5. Robert G. Edwards and David J. Sharp, "Social Values and Research in Human Embryology," *Nature* 231, no. 5298 (May 14, 1971): 87–91.

6. John Rock and Miriam F. Menkin, "In Vitro Fertilization and Cleavage of Human Ovarian Eggs," *Science*, n.s., 100, no. 2588 (August 4, 1944): 105–07.

7. Jane E. Brody, "Egg Fertilized Outside the Body; Aid to Infertile Women Foreseen," *New York Times*, March 4, 1966.

8. "Scientists Grow a Human Embryo," *New York Times*, January 14, 1961.

9. Min Chueh Chang, "Fertilization of Rabbit Ova In Vitro," *Nature* 184, no. 4684 (1959): 466–67.

10. Robert Edwards began work on human IVF five years after Chang's success with rabbits.

11. Yu-Chih Hsu, "Post-Blastocyst Differentiation In Vitro," *Nature* 231, no. 5298 (May 14, 1971): 100–102.

12. Robert G. Edwards and Patrick C. Steptoe, "Control of Human Ovulation, Fertilization and Implantation," *Proceedings of the Royal Society of Medicine—London* 67, no. 9 (1974): 932–36. Among other possible applications of IVF, Edwards listed an improved understanding of the modes of action of contraception, improvements in the efficacy of the rhythm method, the development of effective intrauterine devices (IUDs) and other contraceptives, and the development of a detailed analysis of genetic disorders in early human embryos through the study of cleaving embryos in vitro.

13. Edwards and Sharp, "Social Values and Research in Human Embryology."

14. Joseph F. Fletcher, *The Ethics of Genetic Control: Ending Reproductive Roulette* (Garden City, NY: Anchor, 1974); Paul Ramsey, *Fabricated Man: The Ethics of Genetic Control* (New Haven: Yale University Press, 1970).

15. John H. Evans, *Playing God? Human Genetic Engineering and the Rationalization of Public Bioethical Debate* (Chicago: University of Chicago Press, 2002).

16. Ramsey, *Fabricated Man*, 32–33.

17. U.S. House, Committee on Science and Astronautics, *Panel on Science and Technology: International Science Policy*, January 26–28, 1971, 342. HRG-1971-SAH-0008. Text in LexisNexis, Congressional Hearings Digital Collection.

18. John B. Gurdon, "The Transplantation of Nuclei Between Two Species of Xenopus," *Developmental Biology* 5 (1962): 68; John B. Gurdon, "The Developmental Capacity of Nuclei Taken from Intestinal Epithelium Cells of Feeding Tadpoles," *Development* 10, no. 4 (1962): 622.

19. U.S. House, Committee on Science and Astronautics, *Panel on Science and Technology*, 343.

20. Ibid., 344.

21. "Genetic Engineering in Man: Ethical Considerations," *JAMA* 220 (May 1, 1972): 721. The editorial was most likely authored by Paul Ramsey.

22. J. B. S. Haldane, *Daedalus; or, Science and the Future. A Paper Read to the Heretics, Cambridge, on February 4th, 1923*, 6th impression (London: K. Paul, Trench, Trubner, 1925).

23. Aldous Huxley, *Brave New World* (1932; repr., New York: HarperCollins, 1998).

24. Gregory Pincus and Ernst V. Enzmann, "Can Mammalian Eggs Undergo Normal Development In Vitro?" *Proceedings of the National Academy of Sciences of the United States of America* 20, no. 2 (February 15, 1934): 121–22.

25. Daniel J. Kevles, *In the Name of Eugenics: Genetics and the Uses of Human Heredity* (1985; repr., Cambridge, MA: Harvard University Press, 1995), 189–90.

26. Frank Zala, "Homes Will Be Made of Metal; And Clothing New Each Day," *Washington Post*, April 28, 1935.

27. Editorial, "Conception in a Watchglass," *New England Journal of Medicine*, October 21, 1937. Howard Jones has speculated that this editorial was written by John Rock. See also Joshua Cohen et al., "The Early Days of IVF Outside the UK," *Human Reproduction Update* 11, no. 5 (2005): 445.

28. "NBC Evening News for Wednesday, July 26, 1978: Test Tube Birth", Vanderbilt Television News Archive, http://tvnews.vanderbilt.edu/program.pl?ID=499896.

29. *Chicago Tribune*, July 27, 1978.

30. "Welcome, Louise Brown," *Chicago Tribune*, July 28, 1978.

31. "Conceiving the Inconceivable," *New York Times*, July 28, 1978.

32. Leon R. Kass, "The New Biology: What Price Relieving Man's Estate?" *Science*, n.s., 174, no. 4011 (November 19, 1971): 779–88.

33. Ethics Advisory Board, *Transcript of the Fourth Meeting: Proceedings of the Ethics Advisory Board Held at Boston, Massachusetts, on October 13, 1978* (Washington, DC; Springfield, VA: U.S. Department of Health, Education, and Welfare; Office of the Secretary, 1978), available through the National Technical Information Service; Leon R. Kass, "Ethical Issues in Human In Vitro Fertilization, Embryo Culture and Research, and Embryo Transfer," a paper prepared for the Ethics Advisory Board, 1978, appendix to *HEW Support of Research Involving Human In Vitro Fertilization and Embryo Transfer.* (Washington, DC: Department of Health, Education and Welfare, 1979).

34. Marc Lappé, "Ethics at the Center of Life: Protecting Vulnerable Subjects," *Hastings Center Report* 8, no. 5 (October 1978): 11–13.

35. Ibid.

36. For an excellent discussion of how this discursive reorientation took place, see Evans, *Playing God?*

37. Paul Weindling, "The Origins of Informed Consent: The International Scientific Commission on Medical War Crimes, and the Nuremberg Code," *Bulletin of the History of Medicine* 75, no. 1 (2001): 37–71.

38. Laura Stark, *Behind Closed Doors: IRBs and the Making of Ethical Research* (Chicago: University of Chicago Press, 2011).

39. Henry K. Beecher, "Ethics and Clinical Research," *New England Journal of Medicine* 274, no. 24 (1966): 1354–60.

40. Benya, "Biomedical Advances Confront Society."

41. David J. Rothman, *Strangers at the Bedside: A History of How Law and Bioethics Transformed Medical Decision Making* (Piscataway, NJ: Transaction, 2003), 169–76.

42. Public Law (P.L.) 93-348.

43. Ibid., section 202(a).

44. L. Lawn and R. A. McCance, "Ventures with an Artificial Placenta. I. Principles and Preliminary Results," *Proceedings of the Royal Society of London, Series B, Biological Sciences* 155, no. 961 (April 10, 1962): 500–509; M. Pavone-Macaluso, "An Artificial Placenta," *Lancet* 280, no. 7256 (September 22, 1962): 608–9; Björn Westin, Rune Nyberg, and Göran Enhörning, "A Technique for Perfusion of the Previable Human Fetus," *Acta Paediatrica* 47, no. 4 (1958): 339–49.

45. Westin et al., "A Technique for Perfusion of the Previable Human Fetus."

46. P. A. J. Adam et al., "Oxidation of Glucose and DB-OH-Butyrate by the Early Human Fetal Brain," *Acta Paediatrica* 64, no. 1 (1975): 17–24.

47. Roe v. Wade, 410 U.S. 113 (1973).

48. Willard Gaylin and Marc Lappé, "Fetal Politics," *Atlantic Monthly* 235, no. 5 (May 1975): 66; Maggie Scarf, "The Fetus as Guinea Pig," *New York Times*, October 19, 1975.

49. P.L. 93-348, section 213; see also 39 Fed. Reg. 30962 (August 27, 1974), 30925–1286.

50. National Commission for the Protection of Human Subjects of Biomedical and Behavioral Research, *Report and Recommendations: Research on the Fetus*, HEW Publication No. (OS) 76-127 (Washington DC: Department of Health, Education, and Welfare, 1975).

51. Ibid., 63.

52. Ibid., 62.

53. Ibid., 63.

54. Ibid., 70.

55. Ibid., 67.

56. Ibid., 69, 76.

57. *Griswold v. Connecticut*, 381 U.S. 479 (1965); *Roe v. Wade*, 410 U.S. 113 (1973).

58. National Commission for the Protection of Human Subjects of Biomedical and Behavioral Research, *Report and Recommendations: Research on the Fetus*, 53–59.

59. J. Benjamin Hurlbut, "Promising Waste: Biobanking, Embryo Research, and Infrastructures of Ethical Efficiency," *Monash Bioethics Review* 33, no. 4 (December 2015), 301–24.

60. National Commission for the Protection of Human Subjects of Biomedical and Behavioral Research, *Report and Recommendations: Research on the Fetus*, 69.

61. 38 Fed. Reg. 31739 (November 16, 1973), 31661–747.

62. Ibid., 31738.

63. Ibid. Under products of in vitro fertilization, the study group stated, "No research involving implantation of human ova which have been fertilized in vitro shall be approved until the safety of the technique has been demonstrated as far as possible in sub-human primates, and the responsibilities of the donor and recipient 'parents' and of research institutions and personnel have been established. Therefore, no such research may be conducted without review of the Ethical Review Board."

64. 39 Fed. Reg. 30648 (August 23, 1974), 30648.

65. 40 Fed. Reg. 33529 (August 8, 1975), 33529.

66. James C. Gaither, personal communication, telephone, July 8, 2009.

67. United States Department of Health, Education, and Welfare, *HEW Support of Research Involving Human In Vitro Fertilization and Embryo Transfer: Report and Conclusions* (Washington, DC: Department of Health, Education, and Welfare, 1979).

68. Gaither, personal communication.

69. Ethics Advisory Board, *Transcript of the First Meeting: Proceedings of the Ethics Advisory Board* (Washington, DC; Springfield, VA: U.S. Department of Health, Education and Welfare; Office of the Secretary, 1978), available through the National Technical Information Service.

70. Gaither, personal communication.

71. U.S. House, Subcommittee on Health and the Environment of the Committee on Interstate and Foreign Commerce, *In-Vitro Fertilization: Oversight* (August 4, 1978), 91ff. HRG-1978-FCH-0030. Text in LexisNexis, Congressional Hearings Digital Collection.

72. United States Department of Health, Education, and Welfare, *HEW Support of Research Involving Human In Vitro Fertilization and Embryo Transfer*, 100.

73. Gaither, personal communication.

74. Ibid.

75. Ethics Advisory Board, *Ethics Advisory Board Meeting VII: In Vitro Fertilization and Clinical Trials*, vols. 1–2 (Washington, DC; Springfield, VA: U.S. Department of Health, Education and Welfare; Office of the Secretary, 1979), available through the National Technical Information Service. For example, Hamburg: "It's not simply balancing ethical concerns, but is a kind of meshing of the conflicting values to some extent, in the sense that we're not saying it's okay to do it. We're saying, if it should be done, if it were to be done, it would be ethically justifiable only under certain specified conditions. And therefore, I think we are restricting the grounds for ethical acceptability; and in so doing, are trying to some extent to accommodate the different values that enter into this picture."

76. United States Department of Health, Education, and Welfare, *HEW Support of Research Involving Human In Vitro Fertilization and Embryo Transfer*, 100.

77. Ethics Advisory Board, *Transcript of the Third Meeting: Proceedings of the Ethics Advisory Board Held at Bethesda, Maryland, on September 15, 1978* (Washington, DC; Springfield, VA: U.S. Department of Health, Education and Welfare; Office of the Secretary, 1978), available through the National Technical Information Service, 1978.

78. Patrick C. Steptoe and Robert G. Edwards, "Birth After the Reimplantation of a Human Embryo," *Lancet* 312, no. 8085 (August 12, 1978): 366.

79. Gaither, personal communication.

80. Ethics Advisory Board, *Transcript of the Third Meeting*.

81. Ibid.; Ethics Advisory Board, *Transcript of Meeting IV of the Ethics Advisory Board* (Washington, DC; Springfield, VA: U.S. Department of Health, Education and Welfare; Office of the Secretary, 1978), available through the National Technical Information Service.

82. This is in contrast to the process of superovulation and multiple egg retrieval, which later became standard practice in clinical IVF.

83. Ethics Advisory Board, *Transcript of the Third Meeting*; Ethics Advisory Board, *Ethics Advisory Board Public Hearing on In Vitro Fertilization and Embryo Transfer, Kansas City, Missouri* (Washington, DC; Springfield, VA: U.S. Department of Health, Education and Welfare; Office of the Secretary, 1978), available through the National Technical Information Service.

84. For example, see Ethics Advisory Board, *Ethics Advisory Board Meeting V (Public Hearing)* (Washington, DC; Springfield, VA: U.S. Department of Health, Education and Welfare; Office of the Secretary, 1978), 19, available through the National Technical Information Service.

85. Anne McLaren and John D. Biggers, "Successful Development and Birth of Mice Cultivated In Vitro as Early Embryos," *Nature* 182, no. 4639 (1958): 877–78.

86. John D. Biggers, "In Vitro Fertilization, Embryo Culture and Embryo Transfer in the Human," a paper prepared for the Ethics Advisory Board, 1978; Ethics Advisory Board, *Transcript of the Third Meeting*.

87. Biggers, "In Vitro Fertilization, Embryo Culture and Embryo Transfer in the Human," a paper prepared for the Ethics Advisory Board, 10, citing Joëlle G. Boué and André Boué, "Chromosomal Anomalies in Early Spontaneous Abortion," *Current Topics in Pathology [Ergebnisse Der Pathologie]* 62 (1976): 193–208; Henri Leridon, "Les Accidents Chromosomiques de la Reproduction," ed. André Boué and Charles Thibault *Demographie des Echers de la Reproduction*, (Paris: INSERM, 1974); C. J. Roberts and C. R. Lowe, "Where Have All the Conceptions Gone?" *Lancet* 305, no. 7905 (March 1, 1975).

88. "NBC Evening News for Wednesday, July 26, 1978: Test Tube Birth."

89. Ibid.

90. Ethics Advisory Board, *Ethics Advisory Board Meeting V (Public Hearing)*, 307.

91. Ethics Advisory Board, *Transcript of the Third Meeting*, 53: "If human IVF and ET are considered to be research, a well-developed set of ethical standards for the conduct of research can applied. Review mechanisms for federally supported research have been carefully worked out and codified in regulations. If, on the other hand, IVF and ET are considered to be innovative therapy for infertility, and if federal funds are not directly involved, one may be confronting the private practice of medicine. Ethical standards apply here too, but they are somewhat different from those in the research setting. The patient's right of privacy, especially in personal matters like reproduction, becomes an important consideration, as does the physician's right to recommend a treatment on the basis of his or her best clinical judgment. Review procedures for therapy are much less well worked out. When review occurs, it is usually retrospective rather than prospective. From a legal standpoint, the federal government may have very little handle on innovative therapy. Responsibility for the oversight of such therapy rests primarily with the state and/or professional organizations."

92. Ethics Advisory Board, *Ethics Advisory Board Meeting VI: In Vitro Fertilization and Fetoscopy*, vols. 1–2 (Washington, DC; Springfield, VA: U.S. Department of Health,

Education and Welfare; Office of the Secretary, 1979), 130, available through the National Technical Information Service.

93. Ibid.

94. Joëlle. G. Boué and André. Boué, "Chromosomal Anomalies in Early Spontaneous Abortion."

95. United States Department of Health, Education, and Welfare, *HEW Support of Research Involving Human In Vitro Fertilization and Embryo Transfer*, 1–2.

96. Ethics Advisory Board, *Transcript of the Third Meeting*, 43ff; LeRoy Walters, "Ethical Issues in Human In Vitro Fertilization and Research Involving Early Human Embryos," a paper prepared for the Ethics Advisory Board, 1978.

97. LeRoy Walters, personal communication, telephone, June 23, 2009; Gaither, personal communication; Charles McCarthy, personal communication, telephone, June 17, 2009.

98. National Commission for the Protection of Human Subjects of Biomedical and Behavioral Research, *The Belmont Report: Ethical Principles and Guidelines for the Protection of Human Subjects of Research*, HEW Publication No. (OS) 78-0012-78-0014 (Washington, DC: Department of Health, Education, and Welfare, 1978).

99. United States, National Commission for the Protection of Human Subjects of Biomedical and Behavioral Research. The Belmont Report: Ethical Principles and Guidelines for the Protection of Human Subjects of Research. DHEW Publication, no. (OS) 78-0012-78-0014. (Bethesda, MD: The Commission, 1978.)

100. Tom L. Beauchamp and James F. Childress, *Principles of Biomedical Ethics*, 1st ed. (New York: Oxford University Press, 1979).

101. National Commission for the Protection of Human Subjects of Biomedical and Behavioral Research, *Report and Recommendations: Research on the Fetus*, 62.

102. The Belmont principles assume that the research subject is a human subject and offer no means for differentiating between moral kinds.

103. John H. Evans, *The History and Future of Bioethics: A Sociological View* (New York: Oxford University Press, 2012). Evans has further argued that bioethical deliberation could be made more robust by drawing upon the range of "thick" views held by the wider public. My analysis suggests a complication in this approach insofar as this would transgress not only the "jurisdictional authority" of bioethics but that of science as well.

104. Ethics Advisory Board, *Transcript of the Third Meeting*, 139–45.

105. Ibid. See especially 7–45, 75–139.

106. Ibid., 77–80.

107. Ibid., 139–49. One of the primary purposes of the proposed Soupart study was to understand the mechanisms behind fertilization with the hope that this new knowledge would lead to new contraceptive technologies.

108. Ethics Advisory Board, *Ethics Advisory Board Meeting V (Public Hearing)*, 404ff.

109. Ibid., 404.

110. Ibid., 426.

111. Ibid., 411.

112. McCarthy, personal communication.

113. Ibid.

114. Timothy Lenoir, *The Strategy of Life: Teleology and Mechanics in Nineteenth-Century German Biology* (Chicago: University of Chicago Press, 1989); Jane Maienschein, *Embryos Under the Microscope* (Cambridge: Harvard University Press, 2014).

115. David Albert Jones, *The Soul of the Embryo: An Enquiry into the Status of the Human Embryo in the Christian Tradition* (London: Continuum, 2004).

116. Pius IX, *Apostolicae sedis moderationi*, October 12, 1869.

117. Catholic Church, *Donum Vitae: Instruction on Respect for Human Life in Its Origin and on the Dignity of Procreation; Replies to Certain Questions of the Day* (London: Catholic Truth Society, 1987).

118. Ethics Advisory Board, *Ethics Advisory Board Meeting VII*, 129 (my emphasis).

119. Ibid., 130.

120. Ibid., 132.

121. United States Department of Health, Education, and Welfare, *HEW Support of Research Involving Human In Vitro Fertilization and Embryo Transfer*, 101 (my emphasis).

122. Ibid., 107.

123. Gaither, personal communication.

124. Robert G. Edwards and Patrick C. Steptoe, "A Matter of Life," in *A Matter of Life: The Story of a Medical Breakthrough* (London: Hutchinson, 1980), 186.

125. Ethics Advisory Board, *Transcript of the Third Meeting*, 70–71. For example, Walters stated, "When one gets to later embryonic development, let's say after the completion of implantation which would normally occur in utero, after about 14 days, let's say, then I think an additional issue arises which is the kind of equal treatment issue, and that is an early embryo that is in utero receives protection, at least legally, under current National Commission recommendations and under current HEW regulations. Unless this board were to develop some standards for that stage, the embryo in the laboratory situation of exactly the same age would not be subject to similar protection. I think that is an issue that at least needs to be raised, whether some kind of equal protection standard should be developed from 14 days on."

126. For the definitions of *fetus* and *pregnancy* in the regulations promulgated in light of the national commission recommendations, see 40 Fed. Reg. 33529 (August 8, 1975), 33529. For a discussion of comments on the definitions, see 39 Fed. Reg. 30651 (August 23, 1974), 30651, and 42 Fed. Reg. 2792 (January 13, 1977), 2792.

127. 39 Fed. Reg. 30651 (August 23, 1974), 30651.

128. United States Department of Health, Education, and Welfare, *HEW Support of Research Involving Human In Vitro Fertilization and Embryo Transfer*, 100.

129. Ibid., 66.

130. "While it is true that, on the basis of available evidence, the possibility of increased fetal risk associated with human in vitro fertilization cannot be excluded, it is not general practice in this country to interfere with the reproductive options facing couples who may be at increased risk for having abnormal offspring." Schulman made virtually the same statement in his testimony before a congressional subcommittee on August 3, 1978.

131. Ethics Advisory Board, *Ethics Advisory Board Meeting VII*, 142–43.

132. Ethics Advisory Board, *Transcript of the Fourth Meeting*, 232–42.

133. And history would repeat itself. Richard Seed reemerged briefly in the late 1990s and caused a national stir by expressing his intention to clone a human being (see chapter 4).

134. Gaither, personal communication.

135. Stark, *Behind Closed Doors*.

136. McCarthy, personal communication.

137. P.L. 95-622, codified at 45 U.S.C. Ch. 6A.

138. "HEW to Cut Off Funding for Ethics Advisory Board," *Hastings Center Report* 10, no. 1 (February 1980): 2–3; Gaither, personal communication; U.S. House, Subcommittee on Human Resources and Intergovernmental Relations, Committee on Government Operations, *Medical and Social Choices for Infertile Couples and the Federal Role in Prevention and Treatment* (testimony of Barbara Mishkin) (July 14, 1988), 148ff. HRG-1988-OPH-0045.

139. U.S. House, Subcommittee on Human Resources and Intergovernmental Relations, Committee on Government Operations, *Medical and Social Choices for Infertile Couples and the Federal Role in Prevention and Treatment* (testimony of Barbara Mishkin), 148ff.

2. PRODUCING LIFE, CONCEIVING REASON

1. Walter Sullivan, " 'Test-Tube' Baby Born in U.S., Joining Successes Around the World," *New York Times*, December 29, 1981.

2. *Consumer Protection Issues Involving In Vitro Fertilization Clinics: Hearing Before the Subcommittee on Regulation and Business Opportunities of the Committee on Small Business, House of Representatives*, 100th Cong. (June 1, 1988). HRG-1988-SMB-0011.

3. Ibid., 100.

4. Centers for Disease Control and Prevention, "Assisted Reproductive Technology Surveillance—United States, 2000," *Morbidity and Mortality Weekly Report* 52, no. SS09 (August 29, 2003): 1–16.

5. A Bill to Provide that Human Life Shall Be Deemed to Exist from Conception, S. 158, 97th Cong. (1981); A Bill to Provide that Human Life Shall Be Deemed to Exist from Conception, H.R. 900, 97th Cong. (1981).

6. *The Human Life Bill: Hearings Before the Subcommittee on Separation of Powers of the Committee on the Judiciary*, United States Senate, 97th Cong. (April 23, 24; May 20, 21; June 1, 10, 12, 18, 1981). HRG-1981-SJS-0032.

7. The Human Life Bill, 1981.

8. Ibid., 16.

9. Ibid., 8.

10. Ibid., 9.

11. Ibid.

12. Ibid., 48.

13. Ibid., 13.

14. Ibid., 8–25.

15. Ibid., 49.

16. Ibid.

17. Ibid., 1044.

18. Ibid., 243.

19. Ibid., 244.

20. Ibid., 889.

21. Ibid., 75ff.

22. At the blastocyst stage, the embryo forms a hollow sphere with a clump of cells on the inner face of that sphere. That clump of cells is called the inner cell mass (ICM) and ultimately gives rise to the body of the fetus. The sphere is called the trophoblast and gives rise to the "extra-embryonic" tissues, which includes the yolk sac and placenta. It remains a matter of scientific debate whether the blastocyst-stage human embryo is organized beyond this binary differentiation; for instance, whether it has internal axes around which the cells are oriented or whether there is further differentiation within the ICM and trophoblast cell populations. It is also unclear whether cells migrate between these sites, though it is clear that the two populations of cells are in communication with each other and that this relationship is essential to normal development.

23. Clifford Grobstein, "External Human Fertilization," *Scientific American* 240, no. 6 (1979): 57–67; see also Clifford Grobstein, *From Chance to Purpose: An Appraisal of External Human Fertilization* (Reading, MA: Addison-Wesley, 1981); Clifford Grobstein, "The Moral Uses of 'Spare' Embryos," *Hastings Center Report* 12, no. 3 (June 1982): 5–6; Clifford Grobstein, Michael Flower, and John Mendeloff, "External Human Fertilization: An Evaluation of Policy," *Science*, n.s., 222, no. 4620 (October 14, 1983): 127–33; Clifford Grobstein, "The Early Development of Human Embryos," *Journal of Medicine and Philosophy* 10, no. 3 (1985): 213–36.

24. Grobstein, "The Moral Uses of 'Spare' Embryos," 6; Grobstein et al., "External Human Fertilization"; Grobstein, *From Chance to Purpose*.

25. Grobstein, "The Moral Uses of 'Spare' Embryos," 6.

26. The Human Life Bill, 75.

27. Ibid., 76.

28. Michel Callon, "Some Elements of a Sociology of Translation: Domestication of the Scallops and the Fishermen of St Brieuc Bay," *Power, Action and Belief: A New Sociology of Knowledge* 32, no. S1 (1986): 196–233.

29. Thomas Nagel, *The View from Nowhere* (New York: Oxford University Press, 1989).

30. *Roe v. Wade*, 410 U.S. 113, 181 (1973): "When those trained in the respective disciplines of medicine, philosophy and theology are unable to arrive at any consensus, the judiciary, at this point in the development of man's knowledge, is not in a position to speculate as to the answer."

31. Grobstein, "External Human Fertilization"; Grobstein, *From Chance to Purpose*; Grobstein, "The Moral Uses of 'Spare' Embryos"; Grobstein, et al., "External Human

Fertilization"; Grobstein, "The Early Development of Human Embryos"; Clifford Grobstein, "Biological Characteristics of the Preembryo," *Annals of the New York Academy of Sciences* 541, no. 1 (October 27, 1988): 346–48; Clifford Grobstein, "Public Policy Aspects of Assisted Reproduction. Fifth World Congress, IVF and Embryo Transfer," *Annals of the New York Academy of Sciences* 541, no. 1 (October 27, 1988): 679–82; Clifford Grobstein, "A New Agenda for the Status of the Unborn," *Bulletin of the American Academy of Arts and Sciences* 43, no. 8 (May 1990): 16–23.

32. U.S. Department of Health, Education, and Welfare, Ethics Advisory Board, *HEW Support of Research Involving Human in Vitro Fertilization and Embryo Transfer: Appendix* (Washington, DC: U.S. Government Printing Office, 1979).

33. It should be noted that Grobstein's and Rosenberg's boundary work was built on the same epistemological premises. These premises were as follows: Insofar as questions about a material entity cannot be answered in scientific terms, they are by definition metaphysical. In a liberal democracy, such questions belong to the individual citizen. They are the responsibility of the state only insofar as it is the job of the state to protect the freedom of religious expression. But, when questions are formulated such that science can begin to address them, they have by definition entered a common epistemic space and can begin to be a legitimate arena for state action. Science makes things public even as it wrests authority over answers from the individual citizen and places it in the hands of the scientific expert.

34. "Miracle in Norfolk," *Washington Post*, December 31, 1981.

35. "Test-Tube Babies—Whatever Next?" *Lancet* 318, no. 8258 (December 5, 1981): 1265–66.

36. Walter Sullivan, "'Test-Tube' Baby Born in U.S., Joining Successes Around the World," *New York Times*, December 29, 1981.

37. U.S. Congress, Office of Technology Assessment, *Infertility: Medical and Social Choices*, OTA-BA-358 (Washington, DC: U.S. Government Printing Office, May 1988).

38. Robert G. Edwards et al., "Preliminary Attempts to Fertilize Human Oocytes Matured In Vitro," *American Journal of Obstetrics and Gynocology* 96, no. 2 (1966): 192–200.

39. Lindsay Gruson, "First American 'Test Tube' Twins Are Born on L.I.," *New York Times*, March 25, 1983.

40. Howard W. Jones, Jr. et al., "The Program for In Vitro Fertilization at Norfolk," *Fertility and Sterility* 38, no. 1 (1982): 14–21; Howard W. Jones, Jr. et al., "On the Transfer of Conceptuses from Oocytes Fertilized In Vitro," *Fertility and Sterility* 39, no. 2 (1983): 241–43; Themis Mantzavinos, Jairo E. Garcia, and Howard W. Jones, "Ultrasound Measurement of Ovarian Follicles Stimulated by Human Gonadotropins for Oocyte Recovery and In Vitro Fertilization," *Fertility and Sterility* 40, no. 4 (1983): 461–65; Jairo E. Garcia et al., "Advanced Endometrial Maturation After Ovulation Induction with Human Menopausal Gonadotropin/Human Chorionic Gonadotropin for In Vitro Fertilization," *Fertility and Sterility* 41, no. 1 (1984): 31–35; Anna Pia Ferraretti et al., "Serum Luteinizing Hormone During Ovulation Induction with Human Menopausal Gonadotropin for In Vitro Fertilization in Normally Menstruating Women," *Fertility and Sterility* 40, no. 6 (December 1983): 742–47.

41. Howard W. Jones, "The Ethics of In Vitro Fertilization—1982," *Fertility and Sterility* 37, no. 2 (1982): 146–49.
42. Howard W. Jones, personal communication, telephone, June 19, 2009.
43. Mary Warnock, *Report of the Committee of Inquiry into Human Fertilization and Embryology* (London: Her Majesty's Stationery Office, 1984).
44. Jones, personal communication.
45. Ibid.
46. November 7, 1984, letter, reprinted in American Fertility Society, *Ethical Considerations of the New Reproductive Technologies* (Birmingham, AL: American Fertility Society, 1986), iii.
47. LeRoy Walters, Personal communication, telephone, June 23, 2009.
48. Jones, personal communication; Walters, personal communication.
49. Jones, personal communication.
50. American Fertility Society, *Ethical Considerations of the New Reproductive Technologies*, 31S.
51. Ibid., 26S.
52. See chapter 1.
53. LeRoy Walters, personal communication, email, September 13, 2009.
54. American Fertility Society, *Ethical Considerations of the New Reproductive Technologies*, 26S–28S.
55. Warnock, *Report of the Committee of Inquiry into Human Fertilization and Embryology*, 65.
56. Ibid., 60.
57. Ibid.
58. Ibid., 66.
59. Sheila Jasanoff, *Designs on Nature: Science and Democracy in Europe and the United States* (Princeton: Princeton University Press, 2005).
60. Andrew Huxley, "Research and the Embryo," *New Scientist* 106, no. 1451 (April 11, 1985): 2.
61. Patricia Spallone, *Beyond Conception: The New Politics of Reproduction* (Granby, MA: Bergin & Garvey, 1989), 53.
62. Jones, personal communication. Howard Jones and Anne McLaren had been in close communication over this period as colleagues and friends. There was significant communication across the Atlantic, including Jones's multiple visits to the U.K. during and after the Warnock deliberations. The AFS ethics committee was aware of the developments in British politics, as well as the concerns of experts such as Huxley that opposition to human embryo research was largely a function of public misunderstanding. Nevertheless, according to Jones, the term *preembryo* was coined independently and almost simultaneously by the AFS ethics commitee and the VLA. In fact, Jones's recollection is only partially correct. The earliest use of a variant of the term *preembryo* that I have come across was in Grobstein's 1979 article (Grobstein, "External Human Fertilization"). However, Grobstein used the term more as a descriptive adjective in a discussion of moral status than as a technical scientific term. He described

the pregastrulation conceptus as a "cellular" precedent of the "embryo" and therefore as "preembryonic." Therefore, "the stages involved [in IVF] are not only prepersons, they are preembryos." This is the only instance where Grobstein used this term prior to the AFS ethics committee report in 1986. In its use of the term, the report disavowed precisely the sort of morally evaluative demarcations that Grobstein had intended in 1979. It became a (putatively) strictly scientific discernment.

63. Anne McLaren, "Embryo Research," *Nature* 320, no. 6063 (1986): 570. (Emphasis added.)

64. David Davies, "Embryo Research," *Nature* 320, no. 6059 (1986): 208; McLaren, "Embryo Research." On empiricism in British civic epistemology, see Jasanoff, *Designs on Nature.*

65. McLaren, "Embryo Research."

66. Royal College of Obstetricians and Gynaecologists (RCOG), "Report of the RCOG Ethics Committee on In Vitro Fertilization and Embryo Replacement or Transfer" (London: RCOG, 1983).

67. Huxley, "Research and the Embryo."

68. Human Fertilisation and Embryology Act, 1990 (U.K.).

69. Michael Mulkay, "The Triumph of the Pre-Embryo: Interpretations of the Human Embryo in Parliamentary Debate over Embryo Research," *Social Studies of Science* 24, no. 4 (1994): 611–39; Jasanoff, *Designs on Nature* (Princeton: Princeton University Press, 2005).

70. Jasanoff, *Designs on Nature*, 152–53.

71. Quoted in ibid., 154.

72. American Fertility Society, *Ethical Considerations of the New Reproductive Technologies*, 26S.

73. Ibid., 27S.

74. Ibid., vii.

75. Ibid., 29S.

76. Charles McCarthy, personal communication, June 17, 2009: "I think it was looking for some consistency that would be scientifically accurate and meaningful to the public. And we were concerned about embryos precisely because of the difference between this developing entity before and after twelve or fourteen days. And we thought use of the term *embryo* was technically misleading. We're talking about these cells at an earlier stage than that. And we thought, 'Well, *preembryo* covers them all,' and that might be the term of art that would be least misleading and still meaningful to the public. Some said we can be more precise than that, but others said if we're more precise, the public won't know what we're talking about. *Embryo* was in common use at the time, so *preembryo* should have been pretty clear."

77. Jones, personal communication.

78. American Fertility Society, *Ethical Considerations*, 28S. Though, on this point, the report is somewhat ambiguous. The distinction between the preembryo to be transferred and the preembryo for laboratory research is made very explicit at several points in the report. Elsewhere, the report speaks of "respect" owed to the preembryo generically, at one point grounding this in the "symbolic" meaning that the preembryo has for some people (30S).

Nevertheless, throughout the report it is clear that the preeembryo as such does not deserve anything approximating the full respect due a human person because it is not yet an individual human being. Insofar as it is due respect, it is out of respect for those who see it as symbolically meaningful.

79. Ibid., 30S.

80. Jones, personal communication.

81. Sandra Holmes, *Henderson's Dictionary of Biological Terms*, 9th ed. (New York: Van Nostrand Reinhold, 1986), 426.

82. For example, Gina Kolata, "Ethical Guidelines Proposed for Reproductive Technology," *Science*, n.s., 233, no. 4770 (September 19, 1986): 1255; *Hecht v. Superior Court*, 16 Cal. App. 4th 836; *Davis v. Davis*, S.W.2d 588, 592–3 (1992).

83. Editorial, "IVF Remains in Legal Limbo." *Nature* 387 (1987): 87.

84. John D. Biggers, "Arbitrary Partitions of Prenatal Life," *Human Reproduction* 5, no. 1 (January 1, 1990): 1–6.

85. C. Ward Kischer and Dianne Nutwell Irving, *The Human Development Hoax* (printed by the authors, 1997); Dianne Nutwell Irving, "Philosophical and Scientific Analysis of the Nature of the Early Human Embryo" (Ph.D. dissertation, Georgetown University, 1991).

86. The suit was over custody of frozen embryos following divorce. The trial court ruled, "The term 'preembryo' is not an accepted term and serves as a false distinction between the developmental stages of a human embryo," and on this basis ruled that the contested embryos were not property and awarded temporary custody to the mother to give her an opportunity to transfer the embryos and bring them to term. The decision was reversed on appeal as the court found the father to have a constitutional right not to procreate against his will. Much turned on the term *preembryo*. (*Davis v. Davis*, 1989 Tenn. App. LEXIS 641 [Tenn. Cir. Ct., September 21, 1989]). The Tennessee Supreme Court noted, "Semantical distinctions are significant in this context, because language defines legal status and can limit legal rights. Obviously, an 'adult' has a different legal status than does a 'child.' Likewise, 'child' means something other than 'fetus.' A 'fetus' differs from an 'embryo.' There was much dispute at trial about whether the four- to eight-cell entities in this case should properly be referred to as 'embryos' or as 'preembryos,' with resulting differences in legal analysis." (*Davis v. Davis*, 842 S.W.2d 588, 592–3 [1992].)

87. Research Involving Pregnant Women or Fetuses, 45 CFR 46.204(d).

88. Health Research Extension Act of 1985, P.L. No. 99-158 (November 20, 1985).

89. *Medical and Social Choices for Infertile Couples and the Federal Role in Prevention and Treatment: Hearing Before a Subcommittee of the Committee on Government Operations, House of Representatives*, 100th Cong. (July 14, 1988), 231. HRG-1988 -OPH-0045.

90. Ibid., 160–62.

91. Ibid., 163–64. The AAAS, however, was less concerned that HHS have the "best available" ethics advice and more concerned that individual research proposals that raised ethical hackles be given case-by-case review. In a response letter, the AAAS argued that applying principles to a specific case can be "troublesome." Case-by-case review

conducted in the open would overcome the problem of applying general principles (ibid., 165).

92. In re Baby M, 107 NJ 49 (1986). A year later, the New Jersey Supreme Court reversed the decision but left Baby M in the custody of the Sterns.

93. *Life* 10, no. 6 (June 1987).

94. *Alternative Reproductive Technologies: Implications for Children and Families; Hearing Before the Select Committee on Children, Youth, and Families*, 100th Cong. (May 21, 1987), 2.

95. Ibid.

96. Ibid., 51.

97. Ibid., 56.

98. *Medical and Social Choices for Infertile Couples and the Federal Role in Prevention and Treatment*, 165.

99. U.S. Congress, Office of Technology Assessment, *Infertility*. This report was requested by Representative Weiss in 1985.

100. Ibid., 15.

101. *Consumer Protection Issues Involving In Vitro Fertilization Clinics*, 23.

102. Ibid., 2.

103. Ibid., 27.

104. Ibid., 2, 18.

105. Ibid., 17, 28, 29; *Medical and Social Choices for Infertile Couples and the Federal Role in Prevention and Treatment*, 32. The AFS ethics committee had concluded that IVF was no longer an experimental therapy but that, if conducted by unproven clinicians who had not yet demonstrated their competency in generating pregnancies, it ought to be considered experimental. Many insurance companies were inclined to consider it experimental and elective and thus not covered. The AFS concern with characterizing the procedure as nonexperimental had as much to do with opening up a larger market of consumer-patients through insurance coverage as facilitating general public acceptance. The 1988 and 1989 hearings were in part intended to address the question of whether the procedure ought to be covered by Medicare, Medicaid, and Veterans Affairs (VA) insurance.

106. *Consumer Protection Issues Involving In Vitro Fertilization Clinics*, 27.

107. Ibid., 29.

108. *Medical and Social Choices for Infertile Couples and the Federal Role in Prevention and Treatment*, 2.

109. *Consumer Protection Issues Involving In Vitro Fertilization Clinics*, 24.

110. Ibid., 160.

111. *Medical and Social Choices for Infertile Couples and the Federal Role in Prevention and Treatment*, 29.

112. 53 Fed. Reg. 35232 (September 12, 1988), 35191–35282.

113. Organizations such as the United States Conference of Catholic Bishops and National Right to Life expressed strong opposition to anything that would lead to the experimental use of human embryos, including a reconstitution of the EAB.

In November 1988, George H. W. Bush was elected president, and on March 1, 1989, Louis W. Sullivan replaced Otis R. Bowen as secretary of HHS. The project of reconstituting the EAB seemed to have been dropped, partly as a result of fierce opposition from some pro-life organizations and partly as a result of the shuffle associated with the change in administration, though I do not have sufficient documentary evidence to detail how the project was dropped and by whom.

114. Human Fetal Tissue Transplantation Research Panel, Consultants to the Advisory Committee to the Director, National Institutes of Health, *Report of the Human Fetal Tissue Transplantation Research Panel* (Bethesda, MD: National Institutes of Health, 1988).

115. Research Freedom Act of 1990, H.R. 5456, 101st Cong. (1990).

116. National Institutes of Health Revitalization Amendments of 1992: Veto Message from the President of the United States, H. Doc. No. 102-349.

3. REPRESENTING REASON

1. Christopher Chen, "Pregnancies after Human Oocyte Cryopreservation," *Annals of the New York Academy of Sciences* 541, no. 1 (October 27, 1988): 541–49; J. Testart et al., "Human Embryo Freezing," *Annals of the New York Academy of Sciences* 541, no. 1 (October 27, 1988): 532–40; A. M. Junca et al., "Factors Involved in the Success of Human Embryo Freezing. Does Cryopreservation Really Improve the IVF Results?," *Annals of the New York Academy of Sciences* 541, no. 1 (October 27, 1988): 575–82; B. Lassalle, J. Testart, and J. P. Renard, "Human Embryo Features That Influence the Success of Cryopreservation with the Use of 1,2 Propanediol," *Fertility and Sterility* 44, no. 5 (November 1985): 645–51.

2. Douglas M. Saunders et al., "Frozen Embryos: Too Cold to Touch? The Dilemma Ten Years On," *Human Reproduction* 10, no. 12 (1995): 3081–85.; Jacqueline Lornage et al., "Six Year Follow-up of Cryopreserved Human Embryos," *Human Reproduction* 10, no. 10 (1995): 2610–16.

3. Thomas F. Banchoff, *Embryo Politics: Ethics and Policy in Atlantic Democracies* (Ithaca, NY: Cornell University Press, 2011).

4. Memorandum of January 22, 1993—Federal Funding of Fetal Tissue Transplantation Research 3 CFR, 1993 Comp., 724; Memorandum of January 22, 1993—Privately Funded Abortions at Military Hospitals 3 CFR, 1993 Comp., 722; Memorandum of January 22, 1993—The Title X "Gag Rule" 3 CFR, 1993 Comp., 723; Memorandum of January 22, 1993—Importation of RU-486 3 CFR, 1993 Comp., 724.

5. National Institutes of Health Revitalization Act of 1993, Pub. L. No. 103-43, § 121(c), 107 Stat. 122 (1993), repealing 45 C.F.R. § 46.204(d).

6. "Health and Human Services Policy for Protection of Human Subjects Research," Federal Register 59, No. 104 , June 1, 1994, Rules and Regulations, 28276.

7. Martin. J. Evans and Matthew H. Kaufman, "Establishment in Culture of Pluripotential Cells from Mouse Embryos," *Nature* 292, no. 5819 (July 9, 1981): 154–56.

8. Robert G. Edwards, "Human Conception In Vitro: New Opportunities in Medicine and Research," in *In Vitro Fertilization and Embryo Transfer*, ed. Alan Trounson and Carl Wood (Edinburgh: Churchill Livingstone, 1984), 111–30.

9. National Institutes of Health (NIH) Human Embryo Research Panel, Meeting Transcript, March 14, 1994, 50.

10. Ibid.

11. Edwards, "Human Conception In Vitro."

12. NIH Human Embryo Research Panel and the NIH, *Report of the Human Embryo Research Panel* (Bethesda, MD: National Institutes of Health, 1994).

13. Yu-Chih Hsu, "Post-Blastocyst Differentiation in Vitro," *Nature* 231, no. 5298 (May 14, 1971): 100–102.

14. This is essentially twinning produced by micromanipulation.

15. NIH Human Embryo Research Panel, Meeting Transcript, February 2, 1994, 30.

16. Ibid., 30–32.

17. Ibid., 31.

18. Ibid., 32.

19. This assumption was, of course, incorrect. The report also attributes its own rationale for the fourteen-day limit to the EAB. Referring to a pair of articles from the early 1970s that offered theological arguments for why fourteen days is significant, the report asserts, "Some of the discussion material and papers prepared for the Ethics Advisory Board presented a similar view and persuaded members of that body to adopt a fourteen-day limit in their 1979 report." While it is true that Charles Curran made similar arguments in his testimony before the EAB, the fourteen-day limit was selected purely out of pragmatic deference to the existing federal regulations. (See the discussion of this issue in chapter 1.)

20. NIH Human Embryo Research Panel, Meeting Transcript, March 14, 1994, 81.

21. Ibid., 80.

22. Patricia King: "So with the fourteen days, there's nothing magical about fourteen days, other than the fact it became a proxy. One of the issues I think we need to ask, because it's not a moral question, is the question of the need for the proxy, and whether there is in fact a need for a proxy that had to be fourteen days. If there is, can you come up with something better than fourteen days? That's a public policy, not a moral question. That is a monitoring. That is a question of can we keep track of what is going on. So I want to add that to what he's put on the table."

23. Green reiterated and strengthened this claim repeatedly after he served on the HERP. See Ronald M. Green, *The Human Embryo Research Debates: Bioethics in the Vortex of Controversy* (Oxford: Oxford University Press, 2001); Ronald M. Green, "Part III. Determining Moral Status," *American Journal of Bioethics* 2, no. 1 (2002): 20–30; Ronald M. Green, "The Ethical Considerations," *Scientific American* 286, no. 1 (January 2002): 48.

24. NIH Human Embryo Research Panel and the NIH, *Report of the Human Embryo Research Panel*, 48.

25. Ibid., 38.

26. NIH Human Embryo Research Panel, Meeting Transcript, March 14, 1994, 121.

27. NIH Human Embryo Research Panel and the NIH, *Report of the Human Embryo Research Panel*, 39.

28. NIH, *Transcript of the Sixty-Ninth Meeting of the Advisory Committee to the Director* (Bethesda, MD: National Institutes of Health, 1994), 68. As Green later explained to the NIH ADC, "It is not our role to decide which of [the public's views about moral status] is correct. Instead, we saw ourselves working under constraints appropriate to those who help inform public policy. This means that we had to confine our thinking to public modes of reasoning and to those aspects of the debate that are relevant to a pluralistic society."

29. Green wrote the initial draft of the chapter on moral status in the panel's report (chapter 3). The version that appears in the final report is an only slightly modified version of Green's original draft. See Green, *The Human Embryo Research Debates*, 70.

30. NIH Human Embryo Research Panel and the NIH, *Report of the Human Embryo Research Panel*, 39.

31. John Rawls, *Political Liberalism*, 2nd ed. (New York: Columbia University Press, 2005).

32. John Rawls, *Collected Papers*, ed. Samuel Richard Freeman (Cambridge, MA: Harvard University Press, 1999), 326: "In public questions, ways of reasoning and rules of evidence for reaching true general beliefs that help settle whether institutions are just should be of a kind that everyone can recognize." Rawls explicitly developed "the idea of public reason" only in 1993 in *Political Liberalism*. However, the concept is a further working out of the idea of "publicity," which was foundational for his earlier work, *A Theory of Justice*.

33. John Rawls, *A Theory of Justice: Original Edition* (Cambridge, MA: Belknap, 2005).

34. Rawls, *Political Liberalism*.

35. Note that this construction of the disciplining function of the public bioethics body is in keeping with Cohen's notion that by building norms of public reason into the design of political institutions, those institutions can *stand in* for a deliberative public while also reshaping political culture to comport with the norm of public reason. Joshua Cohen, "Democracy and Liberty," in *Deliberative Democracy*, ed. Jon Elster (New York: Cambridge University Press, 1998), 193: "We can work out the content of the deliberative democratic ideal and its conception of public reasoning by considering features of such reasoning in the idealized case and then aiming to build those features into institutions."

36. Ronald M. Green, "Conferred Rights and the Fetus," *The Journal of Religious Ethics* 2, no. 1 (Spring 1974): 55–75.

37. Ronald M. Green, "Toward a Copernican Revolution in Our Thinking About Life's Beginning and Life's End," *Soundings* 66, no. 2 (1983): 152–73.

38. Ibid., 158.

39. NIH Human Embryo Research Panel and the NIH, *Report of the Human Embryo Research Panel*, 47.

40. Ibid.; NIH, *Transcript of the Sixty-Ninth Meeting of the Advisory Committee to the Director*, 69: "The preimplantation embryo's lack of developmental individuation," as evident in twinning and chimerism, "make it questionable to talk about an individual human being at this stage of development."

41. Here, the panel was following Green's lead. Note that the tacit priority that is given to "hard evidence" over value-laden public reasons mirrors Rawls (see the discussion of Rawls in the introduction). Green, "Toward a Copernican Revolution in Our Thinking About Life's Beginning and Life's End," 160: "Before concluding that an entity is a person (and hence fully protectable) we presumably wish to be shown good reasons for doing so. It follows that mere surmise and undefended opinion cannot be allowed to dictate our reasoning. We want some hard evidence, or if this is not available, some convincing argumentation. . . ."

42. NIH, *Transcript of the Sixty-Ninth Meeting of the Advisory Committee to the Director*, 68.

43. Ibid., 70. Emphasis added.

44. Rawls, *A Theory of Justice*; Rawls, *Political Liberalism*.

45. NIH Human Embryo Research Panel, Meeting Transcript, March 14, 1994, 120.

46. Ibid., 121.

47. NIH Human Embryo Research Panel and the NIH, *Report of the Human Embryo Research Panel*, 36: "Moral positions emphasizing genetic identity or developmental potential offer a definitive standpoint on the status of the embryo, but they create paradoxes in logic and run counter to many widely accepted practices, including use of the intrauterine device and other contraceptive methods that work by preventing implantation."

48. NIH, *Transcript of the Sixty-Ninth Meeting of the Advisory Committee to the Director*, 35–6. Most public involvement was limited to the forms required by law under the *Administrative Procedures Act*. Muller told the ADC, "A major aspect of our work involved consultation with the public. Special efforts were made to broaden public awareness of, and participation in, the panel's work. The requisite Federal Register notices were published. Press releases were issued. Public comment solicitations were mailed to over 200 organizations." Forty-six statements were made during the meeting's public comment periods.

49. NIH Human Embryo Research Panel, Meeting Transcript, February 3, 1994, 95.

50. For instance, Muller referred to the large volume of correspondence received by the panel, most of which was critical, as "the hate mail."

51. NIH, *Transcript of the Sixty-Ninth Meeting of the Advisory Committee to the Director*, 39.

52. NIH Human Embryo Research Panel, Meeting Transcript, February 3, 1994, 95. For example, "Again, we're being asked to do something quite specific and quite complicated, and the degree to which a public that has hitherto not focused on this topic can be helpful is questionable. I think there's a tremendous amount in the way of public information and education that our report can engender, but I don't quite know how you reach out to people who haven't thought about it and say, we need to hear from you right away on this if you have any thoughts."

53. NIH Human Embryo Research Panel, Meeting Transcript, March 14, 1994, 128: ". . . one
     of the rights we have is freedom of speech. I would always defend freedom of speech.
     But freedom of speech does not mean that all speech is equal, because some speech is
     pure, absolute nonsense. And if you're going to give somebody who says something that
     is irrational the opportunity to say it, you have the opportunity immediately to point
     out that it is nonsense, so that the right to make an expression does not mean that that
     expression has the status of truth or the equal of other expressions."

54. NIH Human Embryo Research Panel, Meeting Transcript, February 2, 1994.

55. I found no correspondence lauding the panel's work in the NIH Office of the Director
     archive. A tremendous amount of the HERP-related archival material consists of
     letters criticizing human embryo research and the panel—what Muller referred to as
     "the hate mail."

56. Patricia A. Turner, "To Senator Nancy Kassebaum," March 7, 1994, 131505, NIH Office of
     the Director.

57. Daryl A. (Sandy) Chamblee, "To Senator Nancy Kassebaum," March 18, 1994, 131505,
     NIH Office of the Director; Green, *The Human Embryo Research Debates*, 5. Green cites
     the same letter as evidence that the panel membership was balanced and appropriately
     selected. He notes that the Human Fetal Tissue Transplantation Research Panel
     included pro-life members in an attempt to avoid allegations that the membership was
     stacked. This was counterproductive, Green suggests, because it resulted in a lack of
     consensus in the final recommendations that "probably weakened the panel's ultimate
     recommendations." Chamblee's and Green's accounts offer two examples of why an
     account of the human embryo research debates that maps perspectives in terms of
     political positions on abortion is insufficient. Rather, the political contours of debate were
     shaped by notions of the role of expertise (including "ethical" expertise) in producing
     democratically representative public reason. The capacity of the expert to give "true"
     representation to matters of public concern allowed for corollary accounts of political
     representation, whereby problems of political inclusion could be addressed through
     expert representations. While these include epistemic representations—for example,
     of what the embryo is—they also included representations of proper public reasons.
     Indeed, as the many examples marshaled in this book demonstrate, the correctness of
     epistemic representations was often judged in terms of the norms of public reason; that is,
     the degree to which particular ontological constructions reflected and engendered right
     public reasoning. An imaginary of perfected politics shaped notions of how natural facts
     should be discursively represented.

58. Turner, "To Senator Nancy Kassebaum."

59. Chamblee, "To Senator Nancy Kassebaum."

60. Daryl A. (Sandy) Chamblee, "To Harold Varmus, NIH Director, Re: Congressional
     Contact on Human Embryo Research Panel," March 24, 1994, NIH 131641, NIH Office of
     the Director.

61. NIH, *Transcript of the Sixty-Ninth Meeting of the Advisory Committee to the Director*,
     Statement of Nannerl Keohane, 96.

62. NIH, *Transcript of the Sixty-Ninth Meeting of the Advisory Committee to the Director*, 97.

63. NIH, *Transcript of the Sixty-Ninth Meeting of the Advisory Committee to the Director*, Statement of Bernard Lo, 86.

64. NIH, *Transcript of the Sixty-Ninth Meeting of the Advisory Committee to the Director*, Statement of Gail Cassell, 149.

65. NIH, *Transcript of the Sixty-Ninth Meeting of the Advisory Committee to the Director*, Statement of Patricia King, 96.

66. NIH, *Transcript of the Sixty-Ninth Meeting of the Advisory Committee to the Director*, Statement of Westly Clark, 105.

67. NIH, *Transcript of the Sixty-Ninth Meeting of the Advisory Committee to the Director*, 108–09. Emphasis added.

68. NIH, *Transcript of the Sixty-Ninth Meeting of the Advisory Committee to the Director*, Statement of Steven Schenker, 127.

69. NIH, *Transcript of the Sixty-Ninth Meeting of the Advisory Committee to the Director*, Statement of Ronald Green, 121.

70. NIH, *Transcript of the Sixty-Ninth Meeting of the Advisory Committee to the Director*, 137.

71. Ibid., 111.

72. Ibid., 113. Emphasis added. Green was referring to what the EAB referred to as "embryo loss," the hypothesis that a significant number of embryos do not proceed beyond gastrulation.

73. Ibid., 113–14.

74. Ibid., 45.

75. Personal communication, undisclosed party, telephone, January 5, 2016.

76. NIH Human Embryo Research Panel and the NIH, *Report of the Human Embryo Research Panel* (Bethesda, MD: National Institutes of Health, 1994): 9.

77. National Institutes of Health, *Transcript of the sixty-ninth Meeting of the Advisory Committee to the Director*, 1994, 138.

78. Ibid., 139.

79. Ibid., 148–49.

80. Ibid., 157–58.

81. Ibid., 158.

82. Parthenogenesis involves activating an unfertilized egg to develop into an embryo-like structure).

83. Chamblee, "To Senator Nancy Kassebaum."

84. John Dornan et al., "To Harold Varmus, Re: Human Embryo Research Panel," June 16, 1994.

85. Harold Varmus, "To Dornan et al., Re: Dornan Letter of 6/16/1994," June 21, 1994.

86. John Dornan et al., "To Harold Varmus, Re: Letter of 6/21/1994," September 19, 1994.

87. Harold Varmus, "To Dornan et al., Re: Letter of 9/19/1994," November 8, 1994.

88. John Dornan, "To Harold Varmus, Re: Letter of 11/8/1994," November 15, 1994.

89. Harold Varmus, personal communication, in-person interview, April 4, 2008; Stephen S. Hall, *Merchants of Immortality: Chasing the Dream of Human Life Extension* (New York: Mariner Books, 2005), 115–20; Harold Varmus, *The Art and Politics of Science* (New York: W. W. Norton, 2009), 206.

4. CLONING, KNOWLEDGE, AND THE POLITICS OF CONSENSUS

1. Ian Wilmut et al., "Viable Offspring Derived from Fetal and Adult Mammalian Cells," *Nature* 385, no. 6619 (February 27, 1997): 810–13.

2. James A. Thomson et al., "Embryonic Stem Cell Lines Derived from Human Blastocysts," *Science* 282, no. 5391 (November 6, 1998): 1145–47.

3. "Sheep in Scotland," accessed August 31, 2009, http://www.nfus.org.uk/facts _whatweproduce.asp?ID=170; "Population of Scotland, Statistics of Scottish City Population: Official Online Gateway to Scotland," accessed August 31, 2009, http://www .scotland.org/about/fact-file/population/.

4. Wilmut et al., "Viable Offspring Derived from Fetal and Adult Mammalian Cells."

5. Virtually genetically identical, because mitochondrial DNA would differ. Nuclear DNA would, in principle, be identical, though epigenetic differences and the possibility of mutations in the somatic cell or mosaicism in the patient (genetic differences between different cell lineages in the body of the patient) could result in some genetic differences.

6. James A. Thomson et al., "Embryonic Stem Cell Lines Derived from Human Blastocysts," *Science* 282, no. 5391 (November 6, 1998): 1145–47.

7. Thomas P. Zwaka and James. A. Thomson, "A Germ Cell Origin of Embryonic Stem Cells?" *Development* 132, no. 2 (2005): 227–33; J. Silva and A. Smith, "Capturing Pluripotency," *Cell* 132, no. 4 (2008): 532–36.

8. Michael J. Shamblott et al., "Derivation of Pluripotent Stem Cells from Cultured Human Primordial Germ Cells," *Proceedings of the National Academy of Sciences* 95, no. 23 (1998): 13726; Harriet S. Rabb, General Counsel, Office of the Secretary, Department of Health and Human Services, "Memorandum to Harold Varmus, M.D., NIH Director: Federal Funding for Research Involving Human Pluripotent Stem Cells," January 15, 1999.

9. James A. Thomson et al., "Isolation of a Primate Embryonic Stem Cell Line," *Proceedings of the National Academy of Sciences of the United States of America* 92, no. 17 (1995): 7844–48.

10. Robert G. Edwards, "Human Conception In Vitro: New Opportunities in Medicine and Research," in *In Vitro Fertilization and Embryo Transfer*, ed. Alan Trounson and Carl Wood (Edinburgh: Churchill Livingstone, 1984), 111–30.

11. David Perlman, "Embryonic Research Brings Great Hopes; Cell Studies May Yield Variety of Cures Within Next 10 Years," *San Francisco Chronicle*, November 6, 1998.

12. Paul Recer, "Steps Taken Toward Growing Organs," *Associated Press*, November 5, 1998.

13. Thomson et al., "Embryonic Stem Cell Lines Derived from Human Blastocysts," 1147.

14. For instance, it was unclear whether the low efficiency was the result of technical limitations or because of biological heterogeneity in the donor cells. Given differences among mammalian species, there were plenty of reasons to believe that the technique would not work in primates and that, even if it would, it would take require significant experimental work and adjustment first. Indeed, within a few years, one prominent biologist, Gerald Schatten, declared with some certainty that SCNT would not and could not work in humans because of certain idiosyncrasies of primate somatic cells.

Simerly, Calvin, et al. "Molecular Correlates of Primate Nuclear Transfer Failures." *Science* 300, no. 5617 (April 11, 2003): 297.

15. Human Cloning Research Prohibition Act, H.R. 922, 105th Cong. (1997); Human Cloning Prohibition Act, H.R. 923, 105th Cong. (1997). A bill essentially identical to H.R. 923 had been introduced by Senators Bond, Byrd, and Ashcroft in the Senate (S.368).

16. *Biotechnology and the Ethics of Cloning: How Far Should We Go? Hearing Before the Committee on Science, Subcommittee on Technology,* U.S. House of Representatives, 105th Cong. (March 5, 1997). HRG-1997-SCI-0008. Text in LexisNexis, Congressional Hearings Digital Collection.

17. Ibid., 2.

18. Ibid., 5, 39, 40, 44.

19. U.S. Senate, Committee on Labor and Human Resources, *Scientific Discoveries in Cloning: Challenges for Public Policy.* Text in LexisNexis, Congressional Hearings Digital Collection. March 12, 1997. HRG-1997-LHR-0005.

20. U.S. Senate, Committee on Labor and Human Resources, *Scientific Discoveries in Cloning,* 4.

21. *Biotechnology and the Ethics of Cloning,* 55.

22. U.S. Senate, Committee on Labor and Human Resources, *Scientific Discoveries in Cloning,* 31.

23. *Cloning: Legal, Medical, Ethical and Social Issues. Hearing Before the Subcommittee on Health and Environment of the Committee on Commerce,* 105th Cong. (February 12, 1998), 27. HRG-1998-COH-0002. Text in LexisNexis, Congressional Hearings Digital Collection.

24. U.S. Senate, Committee on Labor and Human Resources, *Scientific Discoveries in Cloning,* 25.

25. Ibid., 3.

26. Ibid., 5.

27. A Bill to Prohibit the Use of Federal Funds for Human Cloning Research, S.368, 105th Cong. (February 27, 1997).

28. U.S. Senate, Committee on Labor and Human Resources, *Scientific Discoveries in Cloning,* 6.

29. Ibid., 25.

30. *Diamond v. Chakrabarty,* 447 U.S. 303 (1980).

31. *Cloning,* 31.

32. Ibid.

33. *Biotechnology and the Ethics of Cloning,* 1.

34. Sheila Jasanoff, "Making Order: Law and Science in Action," in *Handbook of Science and Technology Studies,* 3rd ed., ed. Edward J. Hackett et al. (Cambridge, MA: MIT Press, 2007), 761–86.

35. cf. J. Benjamin Hurlbut, "Remembering the Future: Science, Law, and the Legacy of Asilomar," in *Dreamscapes of Modernity: Sociotechnical Imaginaries and the Fabrication of Power,* ed. Sheila Jasanoff and Sang-Hyun Kim (Chicago: University of Chicago Press, 2015), 126–51.

36. U.S. Senate, Committee on Labor and Human Resources, *Scientific Discoveries in Cloning*, 27.

37. Ibid., 23.

38. *Biotechnology and the Ethics of Cloning*, 5.

39. U.S. Senate, Committee on Labor and Human Resources, *Scientific Discoveries in Cloning*, 5.

40. *Biotechnology and the Ethics of Cloning*, 33.

41. U.S. Senate, Committee on Labor and Human Resources, *Scientific Discoveries in Cloning*, 2.

42. Ibid., 3.

43. Ibid., 57.

44. Ibid., 28.

45. With "normal science" I am, of course, evoking the kind of unexceptional, quotidian, within-the-paradigm science to which Thomas Kuhn first applied the term. Yet I wish to draw attention to the normative and political role that the idea of such normal science plays in public debate about science and technology. Normal science implies scientific practices that are governed according to internal scientific norms. Normal science is self-regulating science. Seen on an epistemic level, it is "normal" science because it reflects the held-in-common commitments that are the conditions of possibility for shared knowledge-making. But on a normative and political level, the idea of normality also underwrites a claim to scientific sovereignty and simultaneously externalizes responsibility for normative transgression by constructing it as abnormal, and thus outside the bounds of normal science by definition. T. S. Kuhn, *The Structure of Scientific Revolutions* (Chicago, IL: University of Chicago Press, 1996 [1962]).

46. Ted Koppel and Chris Bury, "Cloning Humans: Method or Madness?" *Nightline*, January 7, 1998. (LexisNexis Transcript 98010701-j07).

47. *Cloning*, 93.

48. Ibid., 3.

49. Ibid., 22.

50. See chapter 1.

51. Ethics Advisory Board, *Transcript of the Fourth Meeting: Proceedings of the Ethics Advisory Board Held at Boston, Massachusetts on October 13, 1978* (Washington, DC; Springfield, VA: U.S. Department of Health, Education, and Welfare; Office of the Secretary, 1978), available through the National Technical Information Service.

52. *Cloning*, 3–4.

53. Ibid., 7.

54. Ibid., 8.

55. Ibid., 7.

56. Ibid., 3.

57. Ibid., 58.

58. *Biotechnology and the Ethics of Cloning*, 38.

59. H.R. 922 banned the application of the SCNT technique to human biological materials.

60. *Cloning*, 74.

61. Ibid., 69. Emphasis in the original.

62. H.R. 922.

63. For example, *Cloning*, Statement of Representative Brian P. Bilbray (D-CA), 10.

64. Douglas Johnson, National Right to Life Committee Legislative Director, "Letter from NRLC to U.S. House of Representatives Against Greenwood Clone-and-Kill Bill," July 25, 2001, accessed February 12, 2016, http://www.nrlc.org/federal/killingembryos /letterongreenwood/.

65. *Cloning*, 18.

66. Ibid., 19.

67. Ibid.

68. Ibid., 20.

69. Richard M. Doerflinger, personal communication, in-person interview, June 5, 2009.

70. *Cloning*, 117; National Right to Life Committee, "Human Cloning Legislation in Congress: Misconceptions and Realities," updated September 13, 2005, accessed January 5, 2010, http://www.nrlc.org/federal/killingembryos/cloningmisconceptions/.

71. *Cloning*, 89.

72. Ibid., 50.

73. Ibid., 60.

74. Ibid., 91.

75. Ibid 92.

76. Gearhart's embryonic germ cells had been derived from aborted fetal tissue in compliance with federal regulations and, as such, posed no new legal questions.

77. See chapter 3.

78. The Balanced Budget Downpayment Act, Pub. L. No. 104-99, Sec. 128 (January 26, 1996).

79. Rabb, "Memorandum to Harold Varmus, M.D., NIH Director," 2.

80. Ibid.

81. Ibid., 3.

82. J. Benjamin Hurlbut, "Promising Waste: Biobanking, Embryo Research, and Infrastructures of Ethical Efficiency," *Monash Bioethics Review* 33, no. 4 (December 2015), 301–24.

83. Sherley v. Sebelius, 704 F. Supp. 2d 63 (D.C. Cir. 2010). This question was the subject of a lawsuit years later that temporarily shut down federal funding of human embryonic stem cell research.

84. Former NIH director Bernadine Healy, who presided over the fetal tissue research rulemaking process under the George H. W. Bush administration, had offered a very similar assessment of Dickey before hESCs existed. Bernadine Healy and Lynn Sargent Berner, "Con: A Position Against Federal Funding for Human Embryo Research: Words of Caution for Women, for Science, and for Society," *Journal of Women's Health* 4, no. 6 (1995): 609–13.

85. *Stem Cell Research: Special Hearing Before the U.S. Senate, Subcommittee on Labor, Health and Human Services, and Education Appropriations, Committee on Appropriations*, 105th Cong. (January 29, 1999): 147. HRG-1998-SAP-0028. Text in LexisNexis, Congressional Hearings Digital Collection.

86. In experimental animals, SCNT-derived embryos experienced problematic gene expression patterns because SCNT did not completely strip the somatic cell nucleus of its epigenetics. They were therefore often dysfunctional, frequently disordered, and rarely could give rise to a live born organism if transferred to a receptive uterus. When a pregnancy could be established, the fetus tended to exhibit bizarre syndromes and often killed the mother during pregnancy. The statistical arguments that had been used to distinguish the preembryo from the embryo became even more pronounced in the case of the SCNT-derived embryo.

87. Paul R. McHugh, "Zygote and 'Clonote'—The Ethical Use of Embryonic Stem Cells," *New England Journal of Medicine* 351, no. 3 (July 15, 2004): 209–11.

88. *Stem Cell Research: Special Hearing Before the U.S. Senate, Subcommittee on Labor, Health and Human Services, and Education Appropriations, Committee on Appropriations*, 105th Cong. (December 2, 1998). HRG-1998-SAP-0028. Text in LexisNexis, Congressional Hearings Digital Collection.

89. Though others later proposed conceptually analogous strategies, ACT's bovine–human hybrids were the first laboratory attempt at a biological workaround to moral and legal research impediments.

90. Several years later, William Hurlbut, a bioethicist and member of the President's Council on Bioethics, made a similar proposal. See William Hurlbut, Personal Statement, President's Council on Bioethics, in Leon R. Kass, *Human Cloning and Human Dignity: The Report of the President's Council on Bioethics* (New York: PublicAffairs, 2002).

91. That is, cow eggs.

92. Kass, *Human Cloning and Human Dignity*.

93. Rick Weiss, "A Cloning Claim's Controversies; Massachusetts Firm Says It Created Embryo Out of Human, Cow Cells," *Washington Post*, November 13, 1998.

94. Nicholas Wade, "Researchers Claim Embryonic Cell Mix Of Human and Cow," *New York Times*, November 12, 1998.

95. Others wondered how such an experiment could have passed ethical review. The research was carried out at the University of Massachusetts by Jose Cibelli, an ACT scientist, Amherst, supported by ACT funding. The proposal had received only administrative review by the university's institutional review board because Cibelli was using his own cells and self-experimentation did not require review. (Weiss, "A Cloning Claim's Controversies"; Wade, "Researchers Claim Embryonic Cell Mix Of Human and Cow.")

96. "Biotech Company Says Nuclear Transfer Research Blocked by Policy Confusion," *Reuters Health Medical News*, November 13, 1998.

97. *Cloning, 2001: Special Hearing Before a Subcommittee of the Committee on Appropriations*, U.S. Senate, 107th Cong. (December 4, 2001). Text in LexisNexis, Congressional Hearings Digital Collection.

98. Ibid.

99. U.S. Senate, Committee on Labor and Human Resources, *Scientific Discoveries in Cloning*.

100. As the final section of this chapter demonstrates, the NBAC would adopt a similar position, though by bracketing ontological questions altogether.

101. U.S. Senate, Committee on Labor and Human Resources, *Scientific Discoveries in Cloning*.

102. R. Alta Charo, "Every Cell Is Sacred: Logical Consequences of the Argument from Potential in the Age of Cloning," in *Cloning and the Future of Human Embryo Research*, ed. Paul Lauritzen (New York: Oxford University Press, 2001).

103. *Stem Cell Research*, 37.

104. Glenn McGee and Arthur L. Caplan, "What's in the Dish?" *Hastings Center Report* 29, no. 2 (April 1999): 36–38.

105. *Stem Cell Research*, 37.

106. There is nothing inevitable about these arrangements. Many countries in which IVF is in wide use do not produce left-over embryos.

107. See chapter 1.

108. Leon Kass is one prominent figure who was critical of instrumental uses of human life not because he believed in the full moral status of the embryo, but out of a commitment to the idea of human dignity.

109. Stem Cell Research: Special Hearing Before the U.S. Senate, Subcommittee on Labor, Health and Human Services, and Education Appropriations, Committee on Appropriations, 105th Cong. (January 12, 1999):113 HRG-1998-SAP-0028. Text in LexisNexis, Congressional Hearings Digital Collection.

110. Wilmut et al., "Viable Offspring Derived from Fetal and Adult Mammalian Cells." *Nature* 380, no. 6569 (March 7, 1996): 64–66.

111. James A. Thomson et al., "Embryonic Stem Cell Lines Derived from Human Blastocysts," *Science* 282, no. 5391 (November 6, 1998): 1145–47.

112. *Cloning*, 36.

113. *Biotechnology and the Ethics of Cloning*, 26.

114. William J. Clinton, "Letter to Harold Shapiro, Chair, National Bioethics Advisory Commission," November 14, 1998, in NBAC, *Ethical Issues in Human Stem Cell Research* (NBAC: Rockville, MD, 1999), 90–91.

115. Harold T. Shapiro, "Letter to President Clinton," November 20, 1998, in NBAC, *Ethical Issues in Human Stem Cell Research*, 91–92.

116. NBAC. *Thirty-First Meeting of the National Bioethics Advisory Commission Transcript* (Northbrook, IL: Eberlin Reporting Service, 1999), 228 (Holtzman).

117. NBAC, *Ethical Issues in Human Stem Cell Research*, 4.

118. Joshua Cohen, "Democracy and Liberty," in *Deliberative Democracy*, ed. Jon Elster (New York: Cambridge University Press, 1998), 186.

119. NBAC, *Ethical Issues in Human Stem Cell Research*, 51.

120. Amy Gutmann and Dennis Thompson, *Democracy and Disagreement* (Cambridge, MA: Belknap, 1998), 57.

121. Ibid., 56.

122. NBAC, *Ethical Issues in Human Stem Cell Research*, 51.

123. NBAC, *Meeting of the National Bioethics Advisory Commission Transcript* (Arlington, VA: Eberlin Reporting Service, 1997), 12.

124. Ronald M. Dworkin, *Life's Dominion: An Argument About Abortion, Euthanasia, and Individual Freedom* (New York: Knopf, 1993).

125. NBAC, *Ethical Issues in Human Stem Cell Research*, 52.

126. Ibid.

127. Ibid., 52–53.

128. For instance, *Ethics and Theology: A Continuation of the National Discussion on Human Cloning, Hearing before the Committee on Labor and Human Resources, Subcommittee on Public Health and Safety*, U.S. Senate, 105th Cong. (June 17, 1997) S-HRG-105-128. Text in LexisNexis, Congressional Hearings Digital Collection.

129. This effort to distance public science from morally controversial private choices was analogous to the "fetus-to-be-aborted" of the *Research on the Fetus* report of the National Commission for the Protection of Human Subjects of Biomedical and Behavioral Research. See chapter 1.

130. Nicholas Wade, "New Rules on the Use of Human Embryos in Cell Research," *New York Times*, August 24, 2000.

131. "Remarks by the President upon Departure for New Jersey," as made available by the White House Press Office, August 23, 2000.

5. CONFUSING DELIBERATION

1. Undisclosed White House official, personal communication, in-person interview, November 17, 2011.

2. President George W. Bush, "Remarks by the President on Stem Cell Research," as made available by the White House Press Office, August 9, 2001.

3. Ibid.

4. John H. Evans, *Playing God? Human Genetic Engineering and the Rationalization of Public Bioethical Debate* (Chicago: University of Chicago Press, 2002).

5. Leon R. Kass, "The Wisdom of Repugnance: Why We Should Ban the Cloning of Humans," *New Republic* 216, no. 22 (1997): 17–26. This criticism has been made especially of his notion of "the wisdom of repugnance," which is often glossed as the "yuck factor." Bioethicist Arthur Caplan formulated the latter phrase, even though it is often associated with Kass.

6. Leon R. Kass, "Babies By Means of In-Vitro Fertilization: Unethical Experiments on the Unborn," *New England Journal of Medicine* 285, no. 21 (1971): 1174.

7. Ethics Advisory Board, *Transcript of the Fourth Meeting: Proceedings of the Ethics Advisory Board Held at Boston, Massachusetts on October 13, 1978* (Washington, DC; Springfield, VA: U.S. Department of Health, Education, and Welfare; Office of the Secretary, 1978).

8. Leon R. Kass, *Toward a More Natural Science* (New York: Simon & Schuster, 2008).

9. A view he articulated in Leon Kass, *The Hungry Soul: Eating and the Perfecting of Our Nature* (Chicago: University of Chicago Press, 1999).

10. On consensus in bioethics, see Jonathan D. Moreno, *Deciding Together: Bioethics and Moral Consensus* (New York: Oxford University Press, 1995); on ethical closure, see Tom L. Beauchamp, "Ethical Theory and the Problem of Closure," in *Scientific Controversies: Case Studies in the Resolution and Closures of Disputes in Science and Technology*, ed. H. Tristram Engelhardt, Jr., and Arthur L. Caplan (Cambridge: Cambridge University Press, 1987).

11. George W. Bush, Executive Order 13237, Creation of the President's Council on Bioethics, November 28, 2001. Kass had a direct hand in formulating the charter. (Leon R. Kass, personal communication, telephone, December 11, 2009.)

12. President's Council on Bioethics, "Closing Remarks," Transcripts, January 18, 2002, accessed January 5, 2010, http://www.bioethics.gov/transcripts/jan02/jan18close.html.

13. Ibid.

14. Quotation from Thomas Nagel, Moral Epistemology," in *Society's Choices: Social and Ethical Decision Making in Biomedicine*, ed. Ruth Ellen Bulger, Elizabeth Meyer Bobby, and Harvey V. Fineberg (Washington, DC: National Academy Press, 1995), 211.

15. Council members, personal communication. Criticisms of the council notwithstanding, the members were quite diverse in their views and on the ethical questions the council addressed, but also in personal political views.

16. President's Council on Bioethics, "Welcome and Opening Remarks," Transcripts, February 13, 2002, accessed January 5, 2010, http://www.bioethics.gov/transcripts/feb02/feb13open.html.

17. Ibid.

18. In this respect, the council's affirmed that a common language provides the discursive conditions for the possibility of reasoned deliberation. At the same time, however, the council insisted on a substantive normative idiom that was in many respects a direct reaction against the thinning effects of the Rawlsian idea of public reason. In this respect, the PCB was an equivalent deliberative experiment to the bodies that had preceded it, but one that applied the thick, communitarian notion that "the good" should be a collective cultural articulation, rather than procedurally produced through thinning discourse down into (Rawlsian) public reasons, with its primary preoccupation that no one's toes get stepped on. To push the metaphor a bit too far, in the Rawlsian approach, when in public, one hides whatever moral feet one stands on in constructing a private comprehensive doctrine, so one does not step on others' toes. In the council's communitarian approach, it was the duty of the collective to assess whether a moral account had "legs" and to "make it walk" by laboring to construct a collective account of "the good."

19. The quote was part of the working paper that framed the council's discussion of terminology. It was retained in the final report. President's Council on Bioethics, in Leon R. Kass, *Human Cloning and Human Dignity: The Report of the President's Council on Bioethics* (New York: PublicAffairs, 2002), 43.

20. President's Council on Bioethics, "Session 1: Human Cloning 4: Proper Use of Language," Transcripts, February 13, 2002.

21. Ibid.

22. Ibid. For example,

DR. McHUGH: I am concerned that *we have already made decisions when we begin these definitions. . . . They are distinct as 'zygote' and 'clone' in the way they came about and in their essence fundamentally* and that *from those essences different ways of handling* are going to—different ways of managing [are] going to occur.

PROF. MEILAENDER: If you could keep that synthesized totipotent cell that is a clone alive for four weeks, what would you call it?

DR. McHUGH: That is an interesting question. I had not thought about what I would call it . . . a synthesized embryo.

PROF. MEILAENDER: If you could keep it alive for nine months, what would you call it?

DR. McHUGH: Well, that is the issue that comes with the eventual use of these products.

PROF. MEILAENDER: No.

DR. McHUGH: For which we are eventually going to want to speak.

PROF. MEILAENDER: No, it is the issue about what capacities it has from the start.

23. President's Council on Bioethics, "Session 6: Human Cloning; 8: Ethical Issues in 'Therapeutic/Research' Cloning," accessed January 5, 2010, http://www.bioethics.gov /transcripts/feb02/feb14session6.html.

24. President's Council on Bioethics, "Session 1: Human Cloning; 4: Proper Use of Language," Transcripts, February 13, 2002.

25. Ibid., comment of Gilbert Meilaender.

26. Ibid.

27. President's Council on Bioethics, "Session 6: Human Cloning; 3: Policy Issues and Research Cloning," Transcripts, January 18, 2002.

28. President's Council on Bioethics, "Session 1: Human Cloning; 4: Proper Use of Language," Transcripts, February 13, 2002.

29. Kass, *Human Cloning and Human Dignity*.

30. This thereby affirmed a distinction between two putatively separate domains of expertise and the values spheres to which they corresponded (see introduction). This move to delimit the reach of scientific authority and refrain from weighing in on "ethical issues" actually underwrites the authority to supply the epistemic conditions of possibility for ethical evaluation—the staging upon which ethical reasoning will be performed, and by which it will be constrained. These constraints are extremely consequential.

31. Committee on Science, Engineering, and Public Policy, *Scientific and Medical Aspects of Human Reproductive Cloning* (Washington, DC: National Academy Press, 2002).

32. Ibid., 5.

33. SCNT involves transferring a somatic cell nucleus into an enucleated oocyte. The resulting embryo can be transferred to a uterus (as with Dolly) to develop into an offspring that is genetically essentially identical to the somatic cell donor. In the late 1990s, this process came to be called "reproductive cloning." Alternatively, the embryo can be used in laboratory research, including for embryonic stem cell derivation, which prevents further development of the embryo itself. An embryonic stem cell line derived from an SCNT-derived blastocyst will be genetically identical to the somatic cell donor.

In the late 1990s, this use of SCNT, as a precursor to possible medical application, was commonly referred to as "therapeutic cloning" in both scientific and popular discourse.

34. Committee on Science, Engineering, and Public Policy, *Scientific and Medical Aspects of Human Reproductive Cloning*, xi–xii.

35. Ibid., 9. The extended quotation explains the rationale behind this fundamental distinction: "In nuclear transplantation to produce stem cells, cells are isolated from the blastocyst four to five days after the procedure, and the cells are used to make a stem cell line for further study and clinical applications. Neither the blastocyst nor the stem cells are ever placed into a uterus. Moreover, as described in chapter 2, human stem cells do not have the capacity to form a fetus or a newborn animal. Nevertheless, in the popular press and other media, the term 'human cloning' has often been misleadingly applied to both this procedure and reproductive cloning whenever either is proposed to be used in a human context."

36. President's Council on Bioethics, "Session 2: Human Cloning; 5: National Academies' Report, *Scientific and Medical Aspects of Human Reproductive Cloning*," Transcripts, February 13, 2002.

37. Ibid.

38. The Human Genetics Advisory Commission and the Human Fertilisation and Embryology Authority, *Cloning Issues in Reproduction, Science and Medicine*, December 1998.

39. Colin Campbell, "A Commission for the 21st Century," *The Modern Law Review* 61, no. 5, Human Genetics and the Law: Regulating a Revolution (September 1998): 598–602.

40. Human Fertilisation and Embryology Act, 1990 (U.K.).

41. The Human Genetics Advisory Commission and the Human Fertilisation and Embryology Authority, *Cloning Issues in Reproduction, Science and Medicine*.

42. Campbell, "A Commission for the 21st Century."

43. Sarah Parry, "The Politics of Cloning: Mapping the Rhetorical Convergence of Embryos and Stem Cells in Parliamentary Debates," *New Genetics and Society* 22, no. 2 (2003): 145–68.

44. Campbell, "A Commission for the 21st Century."

45. A search of LexisNexis full-text of English-language news sources shows 81 uses in 1998, 145 in 1999, 617 in 2000, 1,910 in 2001, and 2,179 in 2002.

46. Committee on Science, Engineering, and Public Policy, *Scientific and Medical Aspects of Human Reproductive Cloning*.

47. Irving Weissman, personal communication, in-person interview, June 1, 2009.

48. Ibid. *Embryo* for Weissman meant a conceptus post-implantation when the germ layer has begun to differentiate. This is the definition given in the edition of *Dorland's Medical Dictionary* that he had used as a medical student.

49. Ibid.

50. Ibid.; President's Council on Bioethics, "Session 2: Human Cloning; 5: National Academies' Report, *Scientific and Medical Aspects of Human Reproductive Cloning*."

51. Weissman, personal communication; President's Council on Bioethics, "Session 2: Human Cloning; 5: National Academies' Report, *Scientific and Medical Aspects of Human Reproductive Cloning*."

52. Weissman, personal communication.

53. NIH Human Embryo Research Panel and the NIH, *Report of the Human Embryo Research Panel* (Bethesda, MD: National Institutes of Health, 1994): 9. See chapter 3.

54. Weissman, personal communication.

55. Committee on Science, Engineering, and Public Policy, *Scientific and Medical Aspects of Human Reproductive Cloning.*

56. Weissman, personal communication.

57. Kass, *Human Cloning and Human Dignity: An Ethical Inquiry.* The discussion of the moral status of the cloned human embryo that appears elsewhere in the report suggests that the council found it necessary to retain a singular term for the product of SCNT, regardless of its ultimate use, because it saw this entity as a relevant locus of ethical deliberation. Given a set of existing moral concerns, *cloned human embryo* seemed to belong in the linguistic repertoire.

58. President's Council on Bioethics, "Session 2: Human Cloning; 5: National Academies' Report, *Scientific and Medical Aspects of Human Reproductive Cloning.*

59. Kass, *Human Cloning and Human Dignity,* 290.

60. Ibid.

61. Ibid., 292.

62. Ibid.

63. Ibid., 290.

64. John Rawls (see discussion on Rawls in the introduction).

65. Lee M. Silver, "What Are Clones?," *Nature* 412, no. 6842 (July 5, 2001): 21, doi:10.1038/35083650.

66. Ibid.

67. Bert Vogelstein et al., "Genetics. Please Don't Call It Cloning!" *Science* 295, no. 5558 (February 15, 2002): 1237, doi:10.1126/science.1070247.

68. *Cloning, 2001: Special Hearing Before a Subcommittee of the Committee on Appropriations,* U.S. Senate, 107th Cong. (December 4, 2001), 26. HRG-2001-SAP-0010. Text in LexisNexis, Congressional Hearings Digital Collection.

69. Vogelstein et al., "Genetics. Please Don't Call It Cloning!"

70. Kim Vo, "Outspoken Perspective," *San Jose Mercury News,* July 6, 2003.

71. Ibid.

72. Leon R. Kass, "Stop All Cloning of Humans for Four Years," *Wall Street Journal,* June 11, 2002.

73. 107th Cong. 2nd Sess. May 2, 2002, *Congressional Record,* S.3635.

74. *Cloning, 2001: Special Hearing Before a Subcommittee of the Committee on Appropriations,* 2.

75. Vogelstein et al., "Genetics. Please Don't Call It Cloning!"

76. The ISSCR was formed in 2002 by scientists working internationally in the field of stem cell biology to facilitate the exchange of scientific information both among scientists and with the public. From its inception, the ISSCR dedicated a substantial portion of its efforts to public education and political action. The ISSCR also provided

strategic opportunities for leading researchers (many of whom also became public figures) to coordinate their efforts to influence public deliberation and policy.

77. International Society for Stem Cell Research, "Nomenclature Statement," September 27, 2004, http://www.isscr.org/press_releases/nomenclature.htm.

78. Ibid.

79. Ibid.

80. Erika Check Hayden, personal communication, July 9, 2009.

81. Erika Check, "Stem Cell Conference: Nature News," *Nature News*, June 24, 2005, http://www.nature.com/news/2005/050620/full/news050620-14.html.

82. Hayden, personal communication.

83. Ibid.; Hwang et al., "Patient-Specific Embryonic Stem Cells Derived from Human SCNT Blastocysts," *Science* 308, no. 5729 (June 17, 2005): 1777–83. Hwang's results turned out to be falsified, leading to one of the most public and scandalous cases of scientific fraud in modern memory.

84. Paul Elias, "Stanford University Announces Human Embryonic Stem Cell Project," *Associated Press*, December 10, 2002.

85. Rick Weiss, "Stanford May Clone Human Embryos; New Center's Work Could Have Big Impact," *Washington Post*, December 11, 2002.

86. Office of Communications & Public Affairs, Stanford University School of Medicine, "News Conference Clarifies Future Stem Cell Activities at Stanford Office of Communications & Public Affairs—Stanford University School of Medicine," 12/11/02, accessed January 28, 2008, http://med.stanford.edu/news_releases/2002/december/future_stem_cell.html.

87. David Curtin, "Stanford Cloning" (unpublished article, submitted to the *National Catholic Register*), January 8, 2003.

88. Office of Communications & Public Affairs, Stanford University School of Medicine, "Q&A on the Institute for Cancer/Stem Cell Biology and Medicine," *Stem Cell Q&A*, accessed December 10, 2002, http://mednews.stanford.edu/stemcellQA.html.

89. President's Council on Bioethics and Diane Gianelli, "Press Release," December 19, 2002.

90. Office of Communications & Public Affairs, Stanford University School of Medicine, "Statement Regarding the President's Council on Bioethics," December 19, 2002, http://med.stanford.edu/news_releases/2002/december/bioethics-statement.html.

91. Philip Pizzo, op-ed, "Public Needs to Understand Cloning in Research Context," *San Jose Mercury News*, December 17, 2002.

92. Pizzo, "Public Needs to Understand Cloning in Research Context." Emphasis added.

93. "Dean's Newsletter Bulletin: OpEd Piece on Cancer/Stem Cell Biology Institute," *Dean's Newsletter*, December 19, 2002.

94. Pizzo, "Public Needs to Understand Cloning in Research Context."

95. Brian Wynne, "Knowledges in Context," *Science, Technology, & Human Values* 16, no. 1 (January 1, 1991): 111–21, doi:10.2307/690044.

96. Bruno Latour, *Science in Action: How to Follow Scientists and Engineers Through Society* (Cambridge, MA: Harvard University Press, 1987).

6. IN THE LABORATORIES OF DEMOCRACY

1. Proposed Law: Proposition 71 (California Stem Cell Research and Cures Act) (2004).

2. California S.B. 1344 (Human Cloning) (Johnston, Chapter 688, Statutes of 1997).

3. S.C.R. 39 (Johnson) (2003).

4. California Advisory Committee on Human Cloning, *Cloning Californians: Report of the California Advisory Committee on Human Cloning.* (Sacramento, CA: California Department of Health Services, 2002).

5. California S.B. 253 (Ortiz, Chapter 789, Statutes of 2002).

6. Mark Martin, "Davis OKs Stem Cell Research; California Is First State to Encourage Studies," *San Francisco Chronicle,* September 23, 2002.

7. California S.B. 765; California S.B. 778.

8. Paul Berg, personal communication, June 1, 2009; Larry Goldstein, personal communication, October 14, 2005; Wesley Smith, personal communication, June 1, 2009; Irving Weissman, personal communication, June 1, 2009.

9. Proposed Law: Proposition 71 (California Stem Cell Research and Cures Act), section 2.

10. Proposed Law: Proposition 71 (California Stem Cell Research and Cures Act).

11. Ibid.

12. Data from California Secretary of State, Cal-Access, Campaign Finance, July 19, 2002, http://cal-access.ss.ca.gov/Campaign/Committees/Detail.aspx?id=1260661&session=2003&view=expenditures.

13. President's Council on Bioethics, *Monitoring Stem Cell Research,* 2004.

14. "Remarks by the President on Stem Cell Research," as made available by the White House Press Office, August 9, 2001.

15. Robin R. Young, *Stem Cell Market Analysis and Forecast 2005–2015* (Wayne, PA: RRY Publications, 2006).

16. California State Senate. *Proposition 71: Stem Cell Research, Funding, Bonds. Initiative Constitutional Amendment and Statute* (San Diego, CA: California State Senate, 2004). Transcript available at http://senweb03.senate.ca.gov/committee/standing/health/PROP_71_INIATIVE_TRANSCRIPT.doc.

17. See discussion in chapter 5.

18. Proposed Law: Proposition 71 (California Stem Cell Research and Cures Act).

19. Michelle L. Brandt, "The Great Stem Cell Divide: The Science and Politics of Stem Cell Research," *Stanford Medicine* 21, no. 2 (Fall 2004): 16.

20. Ibid., 13.

21. Ibid.

22. Berg, personal communication. Indeed, it was so much behind the scenes that Paul Berg, one of the three plaintiffs, has no recollection whatsoever that it even took place. "It's the first I've heard of it," he told me when I showed him the complaint filed in his name.

23. *Berg v. Shelley*, CA Sup. Court, Sac. County, Case No. 04CS01015.

24. Sheila Jasanoff, *Designs on Nature: Science and Democracy in Europe and the United States* (Princeton: Princeton University Press, 2005). This approach is consistent with Jasanoff's observations of an American "civic epistemology."

25. CA gov. code 88006, elections code 9092, 13314.

26. Ibid.

27. Brief of Petitioner for Writ of Mandate, *Berg v. Shelley*, CA Sup. Court, Sac. County, Case No. 04CS01015, filed July 28, 2004, 11.

28. Ibid., 13.

29. Ibid.

30. Brief, Opposition of Real Parties in Interest to Petition for and Alternative Writ of Mandate/Order to Show Cause, *Berg v. Shelley*, CA Sup. Court, Sac. County, Case No. 04CS01015, filed Aug. 2, 2004, 13.

31. Ibid., 14.

32. Ibid.

33. *Buckley v. Am. Constitutional Law Found.*, 525 U.S. 182, 186 (1999).

34. In re Jost, 117 Cal. App. 2d 379 (1953).

35. Amy Gutmann and Dennis Thompson, *Democracy and Disagreement* (Cambridge, MA: Belknap, 1998), 46.

36. Declaration of Irving Weissman, M.D., Ph.D., *Berg v. Shelley*, CA Sup. Court, Sac. County, Case No. 04CS01015, filed Aug. 3, 2004.

37. Reply Declaration of Evan Snyder, *Berg v. Shelley*, CA Sup. Court, Sac. County, Case No. 04CS01015, filed Aug. 3, 2004. Imprecise and misleading to the nonexpert, that is. These changes in terminology were intended to address public confusion that derived from a putative misunderstanding of the meanings of the terms that gave them a certain "emotional overlay." The terms were not intrinsically imprecise, but had, according to the experts' judgments, become so in their usage in the public sphere (see chapter 5): "[Two panels convened by the National Academies] chose not to use the words 'embryo' and 'cloning' because of confusion in the public over their meaning. In scientific terms, all stages of development from fertilization up to organ development constitute the embryonic period. However, most people asked to draw an embryo instead draw a fetus with head, limbs, eyes and other identifiably human traits. Likewise, scientists use the word 'cloning' every day to describe how they isolate genes; how cancer cells develop from a single cancer stem cell; or to characterize the progeny of a single blood-forming stem cell, or bacterium or virus. But to most people the word 'cloning' conjures up images of mad scientists producing fully grown human clones. For this reason, both National Academies panels chose to use language that accurately and dispassionately describes the nuclear transplantation technique. This language was also supported in a *Science* article written by the presidents of the National Academies of Science and of the Institute of Medicine." (Office of Communication & Public Affairs, Stanford University School of Medicine, "Q&A on the Institute for Cancer/Stem Cell Biology and Medicine," accessed December 10, 2002, http://mednews.stanford.edu/stemcellQA.html.)

38. Declaration of H. Rex Greene, M.D., In Opposition, *Berg v. Shelley*, CA Sup. Court, Sac. County, Case No. 04CS01015, filed Aug. 2, 2004.

39. Declaration of Wesley J. Smith, In Opposition, *Berg v. Shelley*, CA Sup. Court, Sac. County, Case No. 04CS01015, filed Aug. 2, 2004. Smith was a vocal critic of "phony" terminology, though largely by turning reformist arguments on their heads: The pro-research lobby "refuses to use accurate definitions and make lucid arguments," causing confusion, but it "isn't about to let facts get in the way" of its political goals. (Wesley J. Smith, *Consumer's Guide to a Brave New World* [New York: Encounter Books, 2004], 73).

40. Declaration of Stewart A. Newman, Ph.D., In Opposition, *Berg v. Shelley*, CA Sup. Court, Sac. County, Case No. 04CS01015, filed Aug. 2, 2004.

41. Ibid.

42. Ibid.

43. Ballot Measure Constitutional Amendment 2 (The Missouri Stem Cell Research and Cures Initiative), Missouri, 2006. Emphasis added

44. Ibid. This is, of course, a much broader definition than the definition of *reproductive cloning* put forward by the National Academies as it is not limited to an embryo produced through SCNT but includes any embryo or embryo-like entity produced through any means other than IVF using human gametes.

45. Brief of Petitioner at 3, *Missourians Against Human Cloning v. Carnahan Cole Count*. Cir., MO. Case No. 05AC-CC01108, filed Jan. 17, 2006.

46. Ibid., 1.

47. Transcript of Trial, *Missourians Against Human Cloning v. Carnahan Cole Count*. Cir., MO. Case No. 05AC-CC01108, January 19, 2006: 11.

48. Ibid., 86.

49. Ibid., 136.

50. William H. Danforth and William B. Neaves, "Using Words Carefully," *Science* 309, no. 5742 (September 16, 2005): 1815–16, doi:10.1126/science.309.5742.1815.

51. Transcript of Trial, *Missourians Against Human Cloning v. Carnahan Cole Count*. Cir., MO. Case No. 05AC-CC01108, January 19, 2006, 117.

52. Transcript of Trial, *Missourians Against Human Cloning v. Carnahan Cole Count*. Cir., MO. Case No. 05AC-CC01108, 122. Emphasis added.

53. The Coalition for the Advancement of Medical Research is a pro–stem cell research political advocacy organization.

54. Transcript of Trial, *Missourians Against Human Cloning v. Carnahan Cole Count*. Cir., MO. Case No. 05AC-CC01108, 173. Emphasis added.

55. *Missourians Against Human Cloning v. Carnahan Cole Count*. Cir., MO. Case No. 05AC-CC01108, 190 S.W.3d 451 (2006).

56. Ibid., 17.

57. Ibid., 1.

58. Ibid., 23.

59. Ibid., 18.

60. Ibid., 43–44.

7. RELIGION, REASON, AND THE POLITICS OF PROGRESS

1. It was, in short, a bioconstitutional moment. With the concept of bioconstitutionalism, Jasanoff and others have elaborated the powerful but largely tacit role that science plays in configuring the normative relationship between state and citizen, including in shaping imaginations of both the state's responsibilities to the lives in its care, and of the very nature of those lives. Sheila Jasanoff, ed., *Reframing Rights: Bioconstitutionalism in the Genetic Age* (Cambridge, MA: MIT Press, 2011).

2. Amy Gutmann and Dennis Thompson, "Deliberative Democracy Beyond Process," *Journal of Political Philosophy* 10, no. 2 (June 2002): 153; Amy Gutmann and Dennis Thompson, *Democracy and Disagreement* (Cambridge, MA: Belknap, 1998); John Rawls, *Political Liberalism*, 2nd ed. (New York: Columbia University Press, 2005).

3. Rawls, *Political Liberalism*.

4. Richard Rorty, "Religion as a Conversation Stopper," in *Philosophy and Social Hope* (New York: Penguin, 1999).

5. Ibid.

6. The classic statement of this view is Michael Polanyi, "The Republic of Science: Its Political and Economic Theory," *Minerva* 1, no. 1 (1962): 54–73.

7. John Rawls, *A Theory of Justice: Original Edition* (Cambridge, MA: Belknap, 2005), 586. It is the sort of reasoning Rawls imagines for the original position. The parties in the original position are disconnected from social position and cultural identity so that the kinds of reasoning they employ in making judgments about right social relations are not colored by creed: "Among the essential features of this situation is that no one knows his place in society, his class position or social status, nor does anyone know his fortune in the distribution of natural assets and abilities, his intelligence, strength and the like. We shall even assume that the parties do not know their conceptions of the good or their special psychological propensities. The principles of justice are chosen behind a veil of ignorance."

8. Data from California Secretary of State, Cal-Access, Campaign Finance, July 19, 2002, http://cal-access.ss.ca.gov/Campaign/Committees/Detail.aspx?id=1260661&session=20 03&view=expenditures, accesed July 19, 2009.

9. Carol Hogan, personal communication, in-person interview, December 29, 2008; Diane Beeson and Tina Stevens, personal communication, in-person interview, June 20, 2008.

10. Hogan, personal communication.

11. Ibid.; Beeson and Stevens, personal communication.

12. Hogan, personal communication; "CGS: Center for Genetics and Society," accessed July 31, 2009, http://www.geneticsandsociety.org/.

13. Marcy Darnovsky and Jesse Reynolds, personal communication, in-person interview, December 22, 2008.

14. Ibid.

15. Ibid.

16. Ibid.

17. Ibid.

18. Ibid.

19. Ibid.

20. This concern proved well founded. In 2013, the state legislature passed a law allowing Proposition 71 funds to go toward purchasing human eggs at market rates. The bill was vetoed by Governor Jerry Brown.

21. Beeson and Stevens, personal communication.

22. Hogan, personal communication.

23. *Implementation of Proposition 71, the Stem Cell Research and Cures Initiative: Joint Informational Hearing of the Senate Health Committee, Senate Subcommittee on Stem Cell Research, Assembly Health Committee* (Sacramento, CA: Senate Publications, 2004), 11.

24. *Implementation of Proposition 71, the Stem Cell Research and Cures Initiative: Joint Informational Hearing of the Senate Health Committee, Senate Subcommittee on Stem Cell Research, Assembly Health Committee.*

25. Ibid.

26. Ibid.

27. See, for example, Paul Elias, "Stem Cell Research Measure Contested," *Associated Press*, September 9, 2004; Paul Elias, "Initiative Would Provide $3 Billion for Stem Cell Work," *Associated Press*, September 18, 2004; Paul Elias, "Political Insider Emerges as Stem Cell's Biggest Patron," September 16, 2004; "CBS Evening News for Thursday, June 3, 2004: Inside Story (Hollywood & Stem Cell Research)" (CBS, June 3, 2004), Vanderbilt Television News Archive, http://tvnews.vanderbilt.edu/program.pl?ID=756810.

28. Beeson and Stevens, personal communication.

29. "CBS Evening News for Thursday, June 3, 2004: Inside Story (Hollywood & Stem Cell Research)"; Hogan, personal communication.

30. Hogan, personal communication.

31. Thomas F. Gieryn, "Boundary-Work and the Demarcation of Science from Non-Science: Strains and Interests in Professional Ideologies of Scientists," *American Sociological Review* 48, no. 6 (December 1983): 781–95.

32. Ernle Young, "To Be or Not to Be," *Stanford Medicine* 21, no. 2 (Fall 2004).

33. Also discussed in the previous chapter.

34. Guy Billout, *The Great Divide*, cover illustration for *Stanford Medicine* 21, no. 2 (Fall 2004).

35. Philip Pizzo, "Letter from the Dean," *Stanford Medicine* 21, no. 2 (Fall 2004).

36. Ibid.

37. Robert Klein, "A Conversation on Stem Cell Research" (lecture, Goldman School of Public Policy, University of California, Berkeley, Berkeley, CA, February 8, 2006).

38. California State Senate Committee on Health and Human Services *The Impact of California's Stem Cell Policy on the Biomedical Industry* (La Jolla, CA: Salk Institute for Biological Studies, May 10, 2002).

39. Ibid.

40. Paul Berg, "Stem Cells: Shades of Galileo" (lecture, Clark Center, Stanford University School of Medicine, Stanford, CA, May 2, 2005).

41. Quoted in Ceci Connolly, "California Puts Stem Cells to a Popular Vote," *Washington Post*, October 25 2004.

42. Paul Berg, "California Speaks Out on Stem Cells" (lecture, Princeton, NJ, April 15, 2005).

43. J. Benjamin Hurlbut, "Remembering the Future: Science, Law, and the Legacy of Asilomar," in *Dreamscapes of Modernity: Sociotechnical Imaginaries and the Fabrication of Power*, ed. Sheila Jasanoff and Sang-Hyun Kim (Chicago: University of Chicago Press, 2015), 126–51.

44. *The Impact of California's Stem Cell Policy on the Biomedical Industry*.

45. Sheila Jasanoff and Sang-Hyun Kim, eds., *Dreamscapes of Modernity: Sociotechnical Imaginaries and the Fabrication of Power* (Chicago: University of Chicago Press, 2015). Charles Taylor has called this a social imaginary. I argue below that it is a sociotechnical imaginary.

46. Charles Taylor, *A Secular Age* (Cambridge, MA: Belknap, 2007).

47. Ibid.; Philip Gorski et al., eds., *The Post-Secular in Question: Religion in Contemporary Society* (New York: NYU Press, 2012); Manav Ratti, *The Postsecular Imagination: Postcolonialism, Religion, and Literature* (New York: Routledge, 2014).

48. Taylor, *A Secular Age*.

49. Charles Taylor, *Modern Social Imaginaries* (Durham, NC: Duke University Press, 2003).

50. Craig Calhoun et al., *Rethinking Secularism* (New York: Oxford University Press, 2011), 20.

51. Michael A. Fortun, *Promising Genomics: Iceland and deCODE Genetics in a World of Speculation* (Berkeley: University of California Press, 2008); Kaushik Sunder Rajan, *Biocapital: The Constitution of Postgenomic Life*. (Durham, NC: Duke University Press, 2006).

52. Jasanoff and Kim, *Dreamscapes of Modernity*. Sociotechnical imaginaries are "collectively held, institutionally stabilized, and publicly performed visions of desirable futures, animated by shared understandings of forms of social life and social order attainable through, and supportive of, advances in science and technology."

53. In this respect, the notion that science and technology are loci of both secular authority and social progress is bioconstitutional as well as biopolitical. That is, it reflects an aspirational, normative ordering of institutions in the care of life, and not only an administrative one. Foucault draws attention to configurations of power in the governance of life, yet his concept of biopolitics does not fully embrace the dynamics of social hope or the moral imaginations of progress that inhabit, and also give form to, projects of governing life in contemporary science and technology. On bioconstitutionalism, see Jasanoff, *Reframing Rights*. On biopolitics, see Michel Foucault, *The History of Sexuality*, vol. 1, *An Introduction*, trans. Robert Hurley (New York: Vintage, 1990).

54. David H. Guston and Kenneth Keniston, eds., *The Fragile Contract: University Science and the Federal Government* (Cambridge, MA: MIT Press, 1994); Daniel S. Greenberg, *Science, Money, and Politics: Political Triumph and Ethical Erosion* (Chicago: University of Chicago Press, 2001).

55. California State Senate, *Proposition 71: Stem Cell Research, Funding, Bonds. Initiative Constitutional Amendment and Statute* (San Diego, CA: California State Senate, September 15, 2004).

56. Benedict Anderson, *Imagined Communities: Reflections on the Origin and Spread of Nationalism*, rev. ed. (London: Verso, 1991).

57. "Stanford—Nobel Interview" ("Yes-on-71" campaign television advertisement, 2004).

58. "Dr. Irving Weissman" ("Yes-on-71" campaign television advertisement, 2004).

59. "Bluestone" ("Yes-on-71" campaign television advertisement, 2004).

60. The site is now defunct and the URL has been taken over by an organization offering a diet scheme. The version of the site that was up during the week before the 2004 election is archived at https://web.archive.org/web/20040308035040/http://www.curesforcalifornia.com/site/PageServer

61. Homepage of the "Yes-on-71" campaign website, "California Stem Cell Research & Cures Initiative," www.curesforcalifornia.com, August 25, 2004.

62. Paid for by the "Yes on 71" Coalition for Stem Cell Research and Cures, "Support Stem Cell Research, Yes-on-71."

63. California State Senate, *Proposition 71: Stem Cell Research, Funding, Bonds. Initiative Constitutional Amendment and Statute.*

64. "The Today Show" (NBC, October 26, 2004).

65. Ken Garcia, "Needless Research Limits Hit Home," *San Francisco Chronicle*, July 19, 2004.

66. "Dr. Paul Berg" ("Yes-on-71" campaign television advertisement, 2004).

67. "June and Leilani" ("Yes-on-71" campaign television advertisement, 2004).

68. "Candace Coffee" ("Yes-on-71" campaign television advertisement, 2004).

69. "Christopher Reeve—Reeve Foundation" ("Yes-on-71" campaign television advertisement, 2004).

70. "Scott and Lenore" ("Yes-on-71" campaign television advertisement, 2004).

71. "NBC Nightly News," October 13, 2004.

72. *Implementation of Proposition 71, the Stem Cell Research and Cures Initiative: Joint Informational Hearing of the Senate Health Committee, Senate Subcommittee on Stem Cell Research, Assembly Health Committee.*

73. Ibid.

74. The ads were funded by a Democratic political action committee (PAC) called Majority Action. The identical ad was used against six different candidates. The sections with the candidates' pictures and names were separately shot, with the remainder of the ad being identical in the six campaigns. The organization's goal was to "to promote and build a progressive majority agenda in the U.S. House of Representatives." The complete script of the ad is as follows (though it is far more powerful to watch than to read):
TEENAGE BOY: Next summer, I'm going on a camping trip with my friends. I'll be in a car accident, and I'll be paralyzed for the rest of my life.
MIDDLE-AGED WOMAN: In twenty years, I'll have Alzheimer's. I won't recognize my husband or my kids.

GIRL: Next week, my mommy and daddy are going to find out I have diabetes.

WOMAN: This is my congressman.

GIRL: James Walsh.

BOY: He voted against federal funding for stem cell research.

WOMAN: Is he a doctor?

BOY: Is he a scientist?

WOMAN: Why did Congressman Walsh bet my life that he knows best?

BOY: Help me.

GIRL: Help me.

WOMAN: Who knows? Maybe I'm your mother.

BOY: Maybe I'm your grandson.

GIRL: Maybe I'm your little girl.

WOMAN: How do you know I'm not you?

BOY: Stem cell research could save lives. Maybe yours, or your family's. Someone you love. Only, Congressman Walsh said no.

GIRL: How come he thinks he gets to decide who lives and who dies? Who is he?

One version of the ad is available at *Stem Cell Ad Against James Walsh* (2007), accessed July 24, 2009, http://www.youtube.com/watch?v=EBobHMq-ixI.

75. Paul Rabinow, *Essays on the Anthropology of Reason* (Princeton: Princeton University Press, 1996); Adriana Petryna, *Life Exposed: Biological Citizens After Chernobyl* (Princeton: Princeton University Press, 2002); Steven Epstein, *Impure Science: AIDS, Activism, and the Politics of Knowledge* (Berkeley: University of California Press, 1996); Nikolas Rose, *The Politics of Life Itself: Biomedicine, Power, and Subjectivity in the Twenty-First Century* (Princeton: Princeton University Press, 2006); Adele E. Clarke et al., "Biomedicalization: Technoscientific Transformations of Health, Illness, and U.S. Biomedicine," *American Sociological Review* 68, no. 2 (April 2003): 161.

76. Nikolas Rose and Carlos Novas, "Biological Citizenship," in *Global Assemblages: Technology, Politics, and Ethics as Anthropological Problems*, ed. Aihwa Ong and Stephen J. Collier (Malden, MA: Blackwell, 2005), 439–63.

77. In this sense, the "social contract for science" is also implicated in contemporary re-imaginings of the social contract between the state and its citizens. Science occupies a constitutional position not only as an regulative authority for public reasoning—as I have discussed in prior chapters, but as source of imaginations of the future that mediate the political, or, better, bioconstitutional relationships between state and citizen. On bioconstitutionalism see Jasanoff, *Reframing Rights*.

78. Paul Starr, *The Social Transformation of American Medicine* (New York: Basic Books, 1982); Charles E. Rosenberg, *Our Present Complaint: American Medicine, Then and Now* (Baltimore: Johns Hopkins University Press, 2007).

79. This trade-off of care in the present for cures in the future was made explicit in discussions before and after Proposition 71 passed. In a 2005 hearing, as mechanisms for the just distribution of anticipated benefits from research were being debated, Deborah Ortiz made reference to "the public who not only are waiting for cures but are also footing the

bill for this research and who may be faced with critical healthcare programs that they rely upon today being further cut in order to finance the bonds and this research that may not benefit them." "Implementation of Proposition 71: Options for Handling Intellectual Property Associated with Stem Cell Research Grants," Joint Informational Hearing of the Senate Health Committee, Senate Subcommittee on Stem Cell Research Oversight, Assembly Health and Assembly Judiciary Committees, Monday, October 31, 2005.

80. For a powerful analysis of this promise and its failings, see Ruha Benjamin, *People's Science: Bodies and Rights on the Stem Cell Frontier* (Stanford: Stanford University Press, 2013). For an excellent study of the constructions of "good science" that underwrote the California stem cell initiative and the missed opportunities to render it more inclusive, deliberative and robust, see Thompson, Charis. *Good Science: The Ethical Choreography of Stem Cell Research.* Cambridge, MA: MIT Press, 2013.

81. PBS News Hour, "California Places Stem Cell Research Proposition on Ballot," October 27, 2004, accessed April 19, 2008, http://www.pbs.org/newshour/bb/politics-july-dec04 -stemcell_10-27/.

82. Paid for by the "Yes-on-71" Coalition for Stem Cell Research and Cures, "Support Stem Cell Research, Yes-on-71."

83. Laurence Baker, "Economic Impact Analysis: Proposition 71, California Stem Cell Research and Cures Initiative" (Bruce Deal Managing Principle Analysis Group, Inc., September 14, 2004).

84. Larry Goldstein, personal communication via telephone, October 14, 2005. According to Larry Goldstein and many of the most active proponents of Proposition 71, "This is an investment, not an expenditure."

85. This was argument he continued to make after the election as well. See, for example, Klein, "A Conversation on Stem Cell Research."

86. Tapan Munroe, "State Economy Gets a Boost," *Contra Costa Times*, December 5, 2004.

87. California State Senate, *Proposition 71: Stem Cell Research, Funding, Bonds. Initiative Constitutional Amendment and Statute.*

88. Ibid.

89. Bernadette Tansey, "Proposition 71; Stem Cell Initiative Aids State," *San Francisco Chronicle*, November 4, 2004.

90. Andrew Pollack, "Measure Passed, California Weighs Its Future as a Stem Cell Epicenter," *New York Times*, November 4, 2004.

91. Antonio Regaldo and David P. Hamilton, "Ballot Initiative on Stems Cells Gives Some Biotech Stocks Lift," *Wall Street Journal*, October 26, 2004.

92. Munroe, "State Economy Gets a Boost."

93. Brent Hopkins, "Line Forms for Prop 71 Money," *Daily News of Los Angeles*, November 4, 2004.

94. *NBC Nightly News*, July 27, 2004.

95. *The Impact of California's Stem Cell Policy on the Biomedical Industry.*

96. Ulrich Beck, *World at Risk*, trans. Ciaran Cronin (Cambridge: Polity, 2009).

97. Guston, *Between Politics and Science.*

8. THE LEGACY OF EXPERIMENT

1. *Veto—S. 5 (Pm 18) Message from the President of the United States Returning Without My Approval S. 5, The Stem Cell Research Enhancement Act of 2007.*

2. Ibid.

3. Kazutoshi Takahashi and Shinya Yamanaka, "Induction of Pluripotent Stem Cells from Mouse Embryonic and Adult Fibroblast Cultures by Defined Factors," *Cell* 126, no. 4 (August 25, 2006): 663–76.

4. Junying Yu et al., "Induced Pluripotent Stem Cell Lines Derived from Human Somatic Cells," *Science* 318, no. 5858 (December 21, 2007): 1917–20; Kazutoshi Takahashi et al., "Induction of Pluripotent Stem Cells from Adult Human Fibroblasts by Defined Factors," *Cell* 131, no. 5 (November 30, 2007): 861–72. However, the question of whether iPSCs were equivalent to hESCs was extremely contentious for several years. Still largely unresolved, the question has fallen by the wayside. In 2015, the vast majority of research involving human pluripotent stem cells uses reprogrammed cell lines, not lines derived from human embryos.

5. Gina Kolata, "Scientists Bypass Need for Embryo to Get Stem Cells," *New York Times*, November 21, 2007, http://www.nytimes.com/2007/11/21/science/21stem.html?_r=1.

6. Family Research Council, "Press Release: New Studies End Debate on Embryonic Stem Cell Research," November 20, 2007.

7. Melton, quoted in Kolata, "Scientists Bypass Need for Embryo to Get Stem Cells"; Thompson, quoted in Gina Kolata, "Man Who Helped Start Stem Cell War May End It," *New York Times*, November 22, 2007, http://www.nytimes.com/2007/11/22/science/22stem.html.

8. John B. Gurdon, "The Developmental Capacity of Nuclei Taken from Intestinal Epithelium Cells of Feeding Tadpoles," *Development* 10, no. 4 (1962): 622.

9. Julian Savulescu, "Yamanaka Wins Nobel Prize for Ethics," *Practical Ethics*, October 8, 2012, accessed July 3, 2015, http://blog.practicalethics.ox.ac.uk/2012/10/yamanaka-wins-nobel-prize-for-ethics/.

10. "When I saw the embryo, I suddenly realized there was such a small difference between it and my daughters. . . . I thought, we can't keep destroying embryos for our research. There must be another way." Quoted in Martin Fackler, "Risk Taking Is in His Genes," *New York Times*, December 11, 2007.

11. Quoted in Family Research Council, "Press Release: New Studies End Debate on Embryonic Stem Cell Research."

12. Quoted in Sheryl Gay Stolberg, "Method Equalizes Stem Cell Debate," *New York Times*, November 21, 2007, http://www.nytimes.com/2007/11/21/washington/21bush.html?ref=science.

13. Quoted in Michael Abramowitz and Rick Weiss, "A Scientific Advance, a Political Question Mark," *Washington Post*, November 21, 2007, accessed January 11, 2010, http://www.washingtonpost.com/wp-dyn/content/article/2007/11/20/AR2007112001909.html.

14. Douglas A. Melton, Kevin Eggan, and Chad Cowan, "Letter to Mike Castle and Diana DeGette," January 10, 2007.

15. California Institute for Regenerative Medicine, "Funding Clinical Trials," accessed May 6, 2015, https://www.cirm.ca.gov/our-progress/funding-clinical-trials.

16. Indeed, so-called stem cell tourism became a major concern of the ISSCR in the late 2000s as patients who were sold on the promise of stem cell research and impatient for the results have sought out therapies whose value is suspect at best. This was a concern not least because the ISSCR saw the rise of negative health outcomes as a political vulnerability that would tarnish the credibility of the scientific community's claims. It is worth recalling that the same patients had been enrolled as political spokespersons for the imperative of research funding, particularly in the California initiative.

17. Insoo Hyun, "Therapeutic Hope, Spiritual Distress, and the Problem of Stem Cell Tourism," *Cell Stem Cell* 12, no. 5 (May 2, 2013): 505–07.

18. Kaushik Sunder Rajan. *Biocapital: The Constitution of Postgenomic Life.* (Duke University Press, 2006).

19. *Stem Cell Research: Special Hearing Before the U.S. Senate, Subcommittee on Labor, Health and Human Services, and Education Appropriations, Committee on Appropriations,* 105th Cong. (January 12, 1999):113 HRG-1998-SAP-0028. Text in LexisNexis, Congressional Hearings Digital Collection.

20. Kathryn Jean Lopez, "The Truth About Stem Cells: An Interview with Dr. David Prentice," *National Review,* February 26, 2001, accessed February 12, 2016, http://www.catholiceducation.org/en/science/ethical-issues/the-truth-about-stem-cells-an-interview-with-dr-david-prentice.html.

21. Shane Smith, et al., "Adult Stem Cell Treatments for Diseases?" *Science* 313, no. 5786 (July 28, 2006): 439.

22. Puping Liang, Yanwen Xu, Xiya Zhang, Chenhui Ding, Rui Huang, Zhen Zhang, Jie Lv, et al. "CRISPR/Cas9-Mediated Gene Editing in Human Tripronuclear Zygotes." *Protein & Cell* 6, no. 5 (May 2015): 363–72.

23. Ewen Callaway, "UK Scientists Gain Licence to Edit Genes in Human Embryos." *Nature* 530, no. 7588 (February 1, 2016): 18.

24. This was in deference to the International Society for Stem Cell Research (ISSCR) and U.S. National Academies Guidelines for stem cell research, both of which have adopted the fourteen-day limit. The ISSCR reaffirmed the fourteen-day limit just as this experiment was made public. But in a summary of its recommendations, the ethics Members of the ethics task force indicated that they intend for the limit to be subject to change as "science and social priorities evolve." Jonathan Kimmelman et al. "Policy: Global Standards for Stem-Cell Research." *Nature* 533, no. 7603 (May 12, 2016): 313.

For the ISSCR guidelines that were applied in this experiment, see International Society for Stem Cell Research. Guidelines for the Conduct of Human Embryonic Stem Cell Research, Version 1 (ISSCR, Northbrook, IL, 2006). For the National Academies guidelines, see National Research Council Human Embryonic Stem Cell Research Advisory Committee, Board on Life Sciences, Board on Health Sciences Policy, National Research Council, and Institute of Medicine. *Final Report of the National Academies' Human Embryonic Stem Cell Research Advisory Committee and 2010 Amendments to the National Academies' Guidelines for Human Embryonic Stem Cell Research* (National Academies Press, 2010). For the experiments themselves, see Alessia Deglincerti, Gist F. Croft, Lauren N. Pietila, Magdalena Zernicka-Goetz, Eric D. Siggia, and Ali H. Brivanlou. "Self-Organization of the in Vitro Attached Human Embryo." *Nature* 533, no. 7602 (May 4, 2016): 251–54.; Shahbazi, Marta N., Agnieszka Jedrusik, Sanna Vuoristo, Gaelle Recher, Anna Hupalowska, Virginia Bolton, Norah M. E. Fogarty, et al. "Self-Organization of the Human Embryo in the Absence of Maternal Tissues." *Nature Cell Biology* 18, no. 6 (May 4, 2016): 700–708.

25. Sara Reardon, "Human Embryos Grown in Lab for Longer than Ever before." *Nature* 533, no. 7601 (May 4, 2016):16.

26. Janet Rossant. "Human Embryology: Implantation Barrier Overcome." *Nature* 533, (May 4, 2016): 183.

27. Insoo Hyun, Amy Wilkerson, and Josephine Johnston. "Embryology Policy: Revisit the 14-Day Rule." *Nature* 533, no. 7602 (May 4, 2016): 170.

28. Ibid.

29. Sara Reardon, "Human Embryos," 16.

30. Ibid.

31. John Travis, "Making the Cut," *Science* 350, no. 6267 (December 18, 2015): 1456–57.

32. Benjamin J. Hurlbut, "Limits of Responsibility: Genome Editing, Asilomar, and the Politics of Deliberation." *Hastings Center Report* 45, no. 5 (2015): 11–14.

33. National Academies of Sciences, Engineering, and Medicine, "International Summit on Human Gene Editing," December 1–3, 2015, accessed February 15, 2016, http://www .nationalacademies.org/gene-editing/Gene-Edit-Summit/index.htm. It is notable that the national academies that convened the meeting gave it a label—a "summit"—that denotes an international gathering of political leaders authorized by their polities to negotiate the terms of future international order and did so without inviting any systematic reflection on their own democratic authority or remit.

34. B. D. Baltimore, Paul Berg, Michael Botchan, Dana Carroll, R. Alta Charo, George Church, Jacob E. Corn, et al. "A Prudent Path Forward for Genomic Engineering and Germline Gene Modification." *Science* 348, no. 6230 (2015): 36–38.

35. Barack Obama, "President Barack Obama's Inaugural Address," The White House, January 21, 2009, accessed February 19, 2015, http://www.whitehouse.gov/blog /inaugural-address.

36. Barack Obama, "Remarks of the President—as Prepared for Delivery—upon the Signing of Stem Cell Executive Order and Scientific Integrity Presidential Memorandum," The White House, Office of the Press Secretary, March 9, 2009, http://www.whitehouse.gov /the_press_office/Remarks-of-the-President-As-Prepared-for-Delivery-Signing-of -Stem-Cell-Executive-Order-and-Scientific-Integrity-Presidential-Memorandum.

37. Thomas F. Banchoff, *Embryo Politics: Ethics and Policy in Atlantic Democracies* (Ithaca, NY: Cornell University Press, 2011); Sheila Jasanoff, *Designs on Nature: Science and Democracy in Europe and the United States* (Princeton: Princeton University Press, 2005).

38. John Rawls, *A Theory of Justice.* (Belknap Press of Harvard University Press, 2005): 3–4.

39. Immanuel Kant, *Critique of Practical Reason*. Translated by Mary Gregor. (Cambridge: Cambridge University Press, 2015): 129

40. Bruno Latour, *We Have Never Been Modern* (Cambridge, MA: Harvard University Press, 1993). I have Bruno Latour in mind. Latour is right that the nature–society distinction is a constitutional fundamental for modernity. But we are very much modern precisely because this constitutionalism reflects a secular account of—and aspiration to—moral rightness. Purification is not a merely epistemological move, and thus neither is it an epistemically obligatory one. Purification, insofar as it is undertaken, is done in the name of a moral imagination of purity: of the right orderings of the world—orderings to which our ways of knowing and being are urged to aspire. Thus, modernity's "flight from ambivalence" is not a flight from hybrid nature–cultures, since not only are such hybrids ubiquitous in modern life, they are also consciously constructed. (Indeed, *preembryo*, *cloning, public reason*, and *moral status* are but a few examples of such consciously crafted hybrids that appear in this study alone.) Rather, it is a flight *toward* an idea of perfected reason, an idea that comes to order and regulate social life precisely by virtue of the fact that it is moral. Thus, the boundary between fact and value is not an epistemological mistake, a myth of modernity that can be unmasked by inviting the nonhumans back into social life. The boundary is an artifact of secular commitments to the project of reason, a reason in which truth refuses to tolerate the infirmities of an all-too-human subjectivity and in which justice, because it cannot make recourse to any exterior cosmology, must be wholly located within the conventions of social life. In a modest way, this study has sought to show how epistemic and normative orders are coproduced, not in spite of the fact–value distinction, but by virtue of it, and by virtue of the aspiration to rightness that underlies it. The challenge, then, is not to expose the specificity and contingency of those sociotechnical imbroglios we call "facts," but to see the ways in which our imaginaries of rightness order the worlds we bring into existence—and to thereby "humiliate" our overly confident convictions of moral rightness in order to open the space for a wider, if more provisional, repertoire of moral imagination. On humility, see Sheila Jasanoff, "Technologies of Humility: Citizen Participation in Governing Science," *Minerva* 41, no. 3 (2003): 223–44. On ambivalence, see Zygmunt Bauman, *Modernity and Ambivalence* (Cambridge: Polity, 1993).

41. Sheila Jasanoff, *Science and Public Reason* (Abingdon, Oxon: Routledge, 2012).

42. Vicki Brower, "US Bioethics Commission Promises Policy Action," *Nature* 462, no. 7273 (2009): 553.

43. Presidential Commission for the Study of Bioethical Issues, *New Directions: The Ethics of Synthetic Biology and Emerging Technologies* (Washington, DC: Presidential Commission for the Study of Bioethical Issues, December 1, 2010), 4.

44. For a more extensive discussion, see J. Benjamin Hurlbut, "Remembering the Future: Science, Law, and the Legacy of Asilomar," in *Dreamscapes of Modernity: Sociotechnical Imaginaries and the Fabrication of Power*, ed. Sheila Jasanoff and Sang-Hyun Kim (Chicago: University of Chicago Press, 2015), 126–51.

45. Bauman, *Modernity and Ambivalence*.

INDEX

Aastrom Biosciences (now Vericel Corporation), 259–60
abortion: as amoral, 52; constitutional right to, 51; contraceptive devices as proxies for moral status of embryos, 119, 315n47; fetal viability and elective, 51–52; germs cells from human fetuses, 137–38, 321n76; and human embryo research, 49, 97, 103, 158, 159–60, 177, 276; politics, 10, 31–32, 238–43, 276; and public-private boundary, 51, 274; and question of personhood, 117; and reconstitution of EAB, 102–3, 311n113; and status of fetus for purposes of protection, 50–51
Abram, Morris, 77
Abrams, Paul, 204
Advanced Cell Technology (ACT), 162–63, 169, 322n95
Advisory Committee to the Director (ACD) of the NIH, 109, 124–26
Alexander, Duane, 112, 128
"Alternative Reproductive Technologies, The: Implications for Children and Families" (Select Committee on Children, Families, and Youth), 98–100
Altman, Steve, 261
American Association for the Advancement of Science (AAAS), 97, 310n91

American Fertility Society (AFS; now the American Society for Reproductive Medicine): and Brown, Louis, 56, 59; definitions, 89, 308n62; findings, 89–90; formation, 87–88; and fourteen-day boundary, 114, 115; and "preembryo," 34, 93–96, 309n76; request to reconstitute EAB, 97; technocratic approach, 280; voluntary standards for IVF industry, 107
animals: cloned, 135–37; first cloned, 6, 158, 292n18; IVF, 42; in vitro culture and embryo transfer of, 59–60
Antinori, Severino, 147
assisted reproductive technology (ART), 5–6. See also in vitro fertilization (IVF)
Associated Press, 138
Australia, 87, 108

Baby M case, 98, 311n92
Baker, Laurence, 258
ballot initiatives, 212, 214, 216, 224, 226. See also Proposition 71 (California)
Baltimore, David, 202
Barnard, Christiaan, 48
Beecher, Henry, 48
Beeson, Diane, 240, 241–43
Belmont Report, 65, 66, 69, 77, 303n102
Berg, Paul, 212, 217–19, 246–47, 252, 330n22

Biggers, John D., 59–60, 96
bioconstitutionalism, 233n1
bioethics: decontextualist, 53, 65, 66, 67; defining, 11; development of, 11, 294n26; expertise claims in matters of moral judgment, 12; as having jurisdiction over value-laden dimensions of research, 9; as mechanism of governance and delimiter of public debate, 12; problem of defining the parameters of ethically acceptable research as political, 10; and science, 9; sensibilities and approaches from human embryo research codified in practices of, 276–77; sociotechnical change as matter of choice, 183
biologic status, 89, 95
Biomedical Ethics Advisory Committee, 97
biomedical research post World War II, 3
biotechnology: constitutional transformations engendered by, 17, 18; as determinant of bioethical debate, 145, 249–50; federal policy should defer to and lag behind, 140–46; hopes for, industry in California, 211; and hype, 266; inability to contain easily, 183; as measure of progress, 248, 249–50; as misunderstood and feared by public, 40–41, 75, 143–44, 151, 297n3; as pillar of secular liberal democracy, 235; and previability–viability distinction of human fetus, 52; as primary object of moral evaluation in IVF, 63–64; products of, versus techniques used by, 146, 148–49, 153, 176; as public benefit and right, 146, 234, 256; and secularization theory, 249, 250, 335n53
Bloor, David, 13
Bluestone, Jeff, 252
Bok, Sissela, 71
"Bokanovsky's process," 45

Bond, Kit, 140
Bowen, Otis R., 97, 102, 103, 312n113
Brave New World (Huxley, Aldous), 45
Brewer, Herbert, 45
Brinkley, David, 45
Brivanlou, Ali, 270
Brown, George, 143
Brown, Jerry, 334n20
Brown, John, 1
Brown, Lesley, 1, 46
Brown, Louise: birth and reporting of, 1, 39, 45–46; and EAB, 56, 59
Brown, Sherrod, 148, 149
Bush, George H. W., 103, 104, 312n113
Bush, George W.: and federal funding for hESC research, 181–82, 213; and iPSCs, 264; responses to research restrictions, 209 (See also Proposition 71 [California]); veto of bill for funding newly derived embryonic stem cell lines, 263

Cahill, Lisa, 170–71
Califano, Joseph, 54–55, 56, 76
California, 211, 213–14. See also Proposition 71 (California)
California Catholic Conference (CCC), 238, 240–41, 243
California Cloning Commission, 211
California Nurses Association (CNA), 240
California Stem Cell Research and Cures Initiative. See Proposition 71 (California)
Campbell, Colin, 194
Canada, 87, 89
Caplan, Arthur, 101, 102, 164–65, 324n5
Capron, Alexander, 77
Carnahan, Robin, 224
Carr, Elizabeth, 86, 87
Carter, Jimmy, 54
Carter, Stephen, 189
Cassell, Gail, 124

Catholicism: CCC and Proposition 71, 238, 240–41, 243; faith and reason in, 68; and Galileo, 245; moral status of embryo, 69–70; United States Conference of Catholic Bishops, 154, 155, 159–60, 311n113

CBS Evening News, 243

Center for Genetics and Society (CGS), 238–40

Chamblee, Daryl A. (Sandy), 122–23, 128, 316n57

Chang, M. C., 42

Charo, R. Alta, 113, 144, 164, 169

Chicago Tribune, 45–46

Cibelli, Jose, 322n95

civic epistemologies, 13, 17–18, 331n24

Clinton, Bill: benefits of hESC, 177; and federal funding of fetal tissue research, 108; and HERP, 130; and NBAC, 139, 168, 169; use of excess embryos for research, 159

"cloned human embryo," 197–98, 205–6, 222

cloning: first animal, 6, 292n18; frogs, 43–44; and nuclear transplantation, 136–37, 191–93, 198, 327n35; of primates, 136–37, 139, 318n14; SCNT procedure, 136, 292n18. *See also* human cloning; National Bioethics Advisory Commission (NBAC)

"Cloning Issues in Reproduction, Science and Medicine" (HFEA & HGAC, United Kingdom), 193–95

clonotes, 187

Cohen, Joshua, 23, 26, 296n63, 314n35

"Commission on Health, Science and Society" proposal, 48

Condic, Maureen, 226

Connecticut, 215–16

consent, informed: and previable fetus research, 49, 50, 52; respect for persons principle as foundation, 65–66, 303n102; and in vitro human embryo, 53

constitution: function of, in democracy, 17; public reason as essential, 22; transformations engendered by science and technology, 17, 18

constitutional position of science: biomedical innovation as a mode of governance and mechanism of distributive justice, 256–57; in courts, 230; as custodian of reasonableness, 199–200; defining, 19–20; as extra-political authority, 208, 211; privileged position in democracy, 26; and rights to particular technological futures, 256, 337n77; and secularization, 249; and technoscientific accounts of progress, 249–50; as universal, secular authority, 27

constructivism, 24, 28

coproduction: core critical project of, 297n76; in deliberations of PCB, 189–90; of knowledge and norms, 27; as methodological approach, described, 13–14

Couric, Katie, 253

court cases: Missouri, 216–17, 223–29; Proposition 71 (California), 216–23, 330n22

Cox, David, 169

CRISPR, 268, 271

cryopreservation techniques, 6, 105, 107–8, 110, 177

Curran, Charles, 68–70, 73, 313n19

Daley, George, 269

Darnovsky, Marcy, 239

Davis, Gray, 211

decontextualist bioethics, 53, 65, 66, 67

deliberative democratic theory, 20–22, 27, 172–73, 236, 314n35. *See also* Rawls, John

democracy: ballot initiatives, 212, 214, 216, 224, 226; citizen participation in deliberations through practices of, 119–20; as delimited by ethical issues, 12;

democracy (*continued*)
    disagreements over values as legitimate,
       169, 170, 172; ethical deliberation as
       task for, 191; fundamental elements of,
       17; need for commonly understood
       language, 94, 230, 309n76; normative
       issues as in realm, 169, 170, 172; problem
       of defining concerns of public, 150;
       public bioethics bodies in, 15, 175,
       282–83, 284–88; public reason in,
       21–23, 26, 116, 296n63; as reactive to
       technoscientific change, 140–46; as real
       issue of Proposition 71, 244–46; religion
       as private and out of realm of debate in,
       235, 236; responsibilities to citizens, 262;
       responsibility to answer metaphysical
       questions in, 307n33; theories of, as
       culturally situated artifacts, 21; value-
       laden speech in, 216–17, 225, 231. *See
       also* public bioethics debate; science in
       American democracy
Department of Health, Education, and
    Welfare (HEW; now the Department
    of Health and Human Services):
    IVF regulations, 53–54; regulation of
    human subjects research, 48. *See* Ethics
    Advisory Board (EAB)
Department of Health and Human Services
    (HHS; formerly Department of Health,
    Education, and Welfare): and fetal
    tissue transplantation research, 103–4;
    legal review of hESC funding and Rabb
    memo, 181; reconstitution of EAB,
    96–97, 102–3, 311n113
Diamond v. Chakrabarty (1980), 141
Dickey, Jay, 130
Dickey–Wicker amendment (1995), 157–58,
    159, 160, 176, 321nn83–84
diversity, public reason as delimiter of, 22–23
Doctors, Patients & Taxpayers for Fiscal
    Responsibility (DPTFR), 241, 242
Dodd, Chris, 140

Doerflinger, Richard, 99, 159–60
Dolly (cloned sheep), 6, 135–36, 158, 292n18
Donahoe, Patricia, 111
Dornan, Robert K., 129
Dreamscapes of Modernity (Jasanoff and
    Kim), 335n52
Dworkin, Ronald, 174

East, John P., 82
ectogenesis, 44, 72
Edwards, Robert G., 73; and culturing
    primordial stem cells from in vitro
    human embryos, 138; and EAB, 58, 59;
    and Howard Jones, 87; intended IVF
    applications, 43, 298n12; Louise Brown,
    42; Nobel Prize, 264; value of human
    embryo research, 111
Ehlers, Vernon, 139, 148, 152, 154, 319n15
Ellis, Gary B., 101, 102
embodied sociality, 183
embryogenesis: EAB report, 63; and gene
    editing, 268; HERP approached as
    continuum, 315; *Human Life bill*
    testimony, 81; and research on in vitro
    embryos, 67; Warnock report, 92
embryos
    confusion with fetuses, 196
    early research uses, 5–6
    excess: allowed to be donated for research
       in California, 211; from IVF techniques,
       6, 87, 110; as matter of individual choice
       and private moral judgment, 165; as
       morally neutral, 52–53; as research
       materials, 275
    genetic manipulation concerns, 46–47
    inevitability of regulation of in vitro
       human, 85–86
    as laboratory artifacts, 164–65
    loss of, 59, 60–61, 62, 63
    moral status of, 8–10, 104–5, 293n20;
       biological features as informing, 8–10;
       Catholic position on, 69–70; concept

of respect for persons applied, 70–72, 323n108; as dependent on consequences of use, 164–65; as dissociated from, as entity, 171–72, 275; EAB and, 34, 63–65, 66–72; as human subjects, 62; individuality as criterion for, 68; IVF and use of abortifacient contraceptive devices as proxies for, 119, 315n47; public-private boundary and, 75, 78; SCNT products and, 162–64
preimplantation versus postimplantation, 83–84, 306n22
produced for research, 67–68
products of SCNT as, 153–58, 160–63, 322n86, 322nn89–91
terminology for, 91, 112–13, 157–58, 195–96, 327n48
See also fourteen-day limit for research on embryos; human embryo research; in vitro fertilization (IVF); preembryos
embryo transfer (ET): in animals, 59–60; early efforts, 42; ethical standards for, as therapy versus as research, 302n91; grant application to EAB for IVF without, 56–57; moratorium urged, 44
"equality principle," 52, 97
erklären, 297n76
ethical, legal, and social implications (ELSI) research, 12, 294n28
"Ethical Review Boards," establishment of federal, 54, 300n63
ethics: as acted upon by science, 19–20; as collective judgments about the good, 9; defining issues of, 11–12; democracy as delimited by, 12; private versus public spheres, 53; science of, versus deciding what is ethical, 55. See also bioethics
Ethics Advisory Board (EAB): comparison of in vitro to in vivo ovulation, 59–64; conclusions, 57–58, 65, 72–75, 76–77, 301n75; and consensus building, 57; deliberations framework, 58;

formation, 54–55, 56; fourteen-day embryo research rule, 74, 78, 269–70; and funding of IVF and ET research, 56–57, 302n91; IVF without ET, 56–57, 69–70; moral status of embryo produced by IVF, 34, 63–65, 66–72; needed to protect consumers, 102; reconstitution attempts, 97, 99, 100–103, 311n113; requests to implement recommendations, 99; role, 33, 41, 55–56, 99–100; safety of IVF, 58–59, 75, 304n130; as skeptical of role as public stand-in, 280; termination, 77–78
Ethics Committee of AFS. See American Fertility Society (AFS; now the American Society for Reproductive Medicine)
eugenics, 44–45, 268, 271
Evans, John: bioethics bodies narrow parameters of public debate, 12; claims of expertise by bioethicists, 12; defining public bioethical debate, 292n11; EAB transition to frame of principlism, 66, 303n103; "thinning" of public bioethical debate, 293n20

"fabricated man," visions of, 40
facts: abortion as amoral, 52; and beginning of human life, 83; coproduction of norms and, 27; crafting of right, 29; disputes over representations of (See court cases); as product of community of reason, 24, 296n58; public disagreements about, 172; role in politics, 227; science as provider of, 9, 23–24, 28, 30, 169–70, 230, 278; as truth, 283–84; values versus, 21, 24, 26, 175–76, 198–99, 207, 219–21, 282, 342n40
Family Research Council (FRC), 263–64
federal government as deferring to and lagging behind science, 140–46
fetus as defined in regulations, 73

federal government (*continued*)
funding: all forms of research on in vitro human embryos, 108–9; ELSI project, 294n28; fetal tissue research, 103–4, 108; hESC research, 181; human cloning research, 139, 319n15; human embryo research, 10, 101, 130; innovative therapy versus research, 302n91; prioritization of, biomedical research, 56–57, 302n91; research on aborted embryos from in vivo reproduction, 158; research on cell lines from excess embryos, 176–77; research on excess embryos from IVF, 157, 159, 165; research only on cell lines established by 8/9/2001, 181; research using human pluripotent stem cells, 158–59
IVF as consumer issue, 100–102, 104, 311n105
legislative response to Dolly, 140
pregnancy as defined by, 74
as providing oversight only for abuses of self-governing norms of science, 145–46
and regulation of IVF, 53–54, 98–100, 101, 300n63
states' responses to restrictions on hESC (*See* Proposition 71 [California])
See also specific acts and regulations; specific departments
Feinstein, Diane, 148, 153–54
Fertility and Sterility, 96
Fetal Tissue Research Panel, 108
fetus: confusion with embryos, 196; as defined in federal regulations, 73. *See also* abortion; human fetal research; National Commission for the Protection of Human Subjects of Biomedical and Behavioral Research
"fetus-to-be-aborted" versus "fetus-to-go-to term," 50–51, 52
Fisher, Lucy, 212
FitzGerald, Kevin, 155

Fortanasce, Vincent, 241, 242
Foster, Daniel, 188
fourteen-day limit for research: HERP retention of, 113–15; as move from biological to moral status, 270; primitive streak as demarcation, 90, 92, 118, 315n40; revision of, called for, 269–70, 340n24; in U.K., 193; in in vitro culture, 72–74, 78, 89–90, 92, 111–12, 304n125, 313n22
France, 108
Fredrickson, Donald, 56
free speech, and California Proposition 71, 216, 217–21, 330n22
Frist, Bill, 139–40, 144, 154, 166

Gaither, James, 54–59, 72, 75, 76
Galileo, 245
Ganske, Greg, 156–57
Gazzaniga, Michael, 187, 198–99
Gearhart, John, 137–38, 321n76
gene editing, 268, 271–72, 342n33
General Election State Ballot (for California Proposition 71) court case, 216, 217–23, 330n22
George, Robert, 189
Germany, 108
germ cells, 321n76
Geron Corporation, 212, 259–60
Gieryn, Thomas, 244
Goldstein, Larry, 167, 212, 217–19, 267, 338n84
Gollaher, David, 246, 259, 260–61
Gorovitz, Samuel, 183
Green, Ronald: background, 114; boundaries of life dismantled by SCNT, 163; embryogenesis as continuum, 115, 313n23; ethicist as arbiter of right public reason, 115, 119, 121, 316n57; HERP report, 314n29; and pluralistic approach of reasonableness, 115, 117, 314n28, 315n21; and public concerns about research, 124, 125, 126, 127; and reflective equilibrium, 119

Greene, Rex, 221, 241

Griswold v. Connecticut (1965), 51, 274

Grobstein, Clifford, 83–86, 89–90, 94, 196–97, 307n33, 308n62

Gurdon, John, 43–44, 264

Gutmann, Amy, 16, 172–73, 287

Habermas, Jürgen, 26, 27

Haldane, J. B. S., 40, 44–45

Hamburg, David, 55, 301n75

Hammond, Charles B., 87

Harkin, Tom, 140, 141

Harris, Patricia, 76, 77

Hastert, Dennis, 99–100

Health Research Extension Act (1985), 97

Healy, Bernadine, 321n84

Henderson's Dictionary of Biological Terms, 96

Hodgen, Gary D., 98–99

Hogan, Brigid, 113, 114

Hogan, Carol, 238, 241, 243

Howard Hughes Medical Institute, 212

Hsu, Yu-Chih, 42

Hughes, Mark, 109

human cloning: Antinori claims, 147; in California, 211; defined in Missouri ballot issue, 224, 332n44; facts reported in *Scientific and Medical Aspects of Human Reproductive Cloning*, 191–92; federal funding of research, 139, 319n15; issues of defining term, 150, 151, 152, 154, 185, 189–90; and IVF, 44; and legislative response to Dolly, 139–40; public misunderstanding of, 226–27; public opposition to and legislation to prevent, 149–50; SCNT confused with, 191–93, 198, 200, 205–6, 326n33, 327n35

Human Cloning and Human Dignity (PCB), 201

human embryonic stem cell (hESC) research: California legislation to encourage, 211; as curer of diseases, 251–54, 257–58, 265, 266–67, 340n16; federal funding for,

176–77, 181, 213; first cultured cell lines, 137–38; forms, 221; and immortality of cell lines, 158; and iPSCs, 263–64, 265, 339n4; opposition to, as contravention of norms of democracy, 244–48; overview of questions raised, 134–35; present versus future health care, 256–57, 337n79; and public-private boundary, 275–76; SCNT derived cells lines as producing embryos, 155; and social contract for science, 256, 337n77; terminology used, 155–57; using nonfederal funds, 213. *See also* Proposition 71 (California)

human embryo research: and abortion, 49, 97, 103, 158, 159–60, 177, 276; background, 6, 292n18; beginning of, 47; effects of National Commission for the Protection of Human Subjects of Biomedical and Behavioral Research on, 52–53; effects on bioethics, 276–77; and excess embryos, 6, 110, 159; federal funding for, 10, 101, 130, 157, 158, 159, 165; in fetal tissue transplantation, 103–4, 108; fourteen-day boundary, 74, 78, 113–15, 269–70, 340n24; frame of debate, 5, 7–10, 19, 293n20, 293n22; and gene editing, 271; in other nations, 108; privatization of, 78; safety conditions necessary for human subjects research applied to, 109. *See also* American Fertility Society (AFS); Ethics Advisory Board (EAB); Human Embryo Research Panel (HERP)

Human Embryo Research Panel (HERP): claim of legitimacy, 121–22; as example of public reason in practice, 130–31; focus on excess embryos from cryopreservation, 110; formation, 34, 109, 122; and fourteen-day boundary, 113–15; and hESC, 138; IVF and use of abortifacient contraceptive devices,

Human Embryo Research Panel (*continued*)
    119, 315n47; moral status frame, 112–13;
    and NBAC, 168; overview of, 109–10;
    pluralistic approach, 115–18, 314n28;
    and political realities, 129–30; problems
    defining embryo, 112–13; and public
    involvement, 119–23, 285, 315n48,
    315n50, 315nn52–53; reasoning used,
    117–18, 315nn40–41; recommendations,
    109, 123–27, 129; and reflective
    equilibrium, 118–20; science as definer
    of parameters of debate, 281; science at
    center of reasonable pluralism, 280
*Human Fertilisation and Embryology Act of
    1990* (United Kingdom), 92, 193, 194
Human Fertilisation & Embryology
    Authority (HFEA), 193–95
human fetal research, 49, 50, 52, 97. *See also*
    human embryo research
Human Fetal Tissue Transplantation
    Research Panel, 316n57
Human Genetics Advisory Commission
    (HGAC; now the Human Genetics
    Commission), 193–95
Human Genome Project (HGP), 12, 294n28
human life. *See* personhood
Human Life Bill, 80–86
human parthenogenesis, 128–29
human pluripotent stem cells, federal
    funding of research using, 158–59
human subjects research: beginning of
    concerns, 47; history of abuse, 3, 48;
    and IVF, 58, 62; minimal-risk standard,
    50–51; necessity of, 50; oversight failures,
    41; previable human fetal research,
    49, 50, 52; questions of stewardship,
    3–4; and respect for persons principle,
    65–66, 303n102; safety conditions
    applied to human embryo research, 109
Human Subjects Working Group of
    the Recombinant DNA Advisory
    Committee, 97

human transformation technologies, 43
Hutton, Fiona, 260
Huxley, Aldous, 45
Huxley, Andrew, 91, 92
Huxley, Julian, 40
Hwang Woo-Suk, 204, 329n83

immunotherapy, 137, 318n5
individual autonomy/liberty/rights: and
    abortion, 51–52; and determination
    of beginning of human life, 85, 86,
    306n30; and excess embryos, 165; and
    innovative therapy, 74–75, 302n91;
    and IVF, 274; and protections owed to
    incipient human life, 10; respect for
    persons principle as foundation, 65–66,
    302n102; Supreme Court decisions on
    state intervention versus, 51
individuality, as criterion for moral status of
    embryo, 68
induced pluripotent stem cells (iPSCs),
    263–64, 265, 339n4
infertility, as IVF target, 43, 298n12
Infertility: Medical and Social Choices (Office
    of Technology Assessment), 100–101
International Society for Stem Cell Research
    (ISSCR), 203–4, 240n16, 328n76,
    340n24
in vitro fertilization (IVF): as analogous to
    in vivo reproduction, 59–64, 70, 75;
    California legislation to offer donation
    of unused embryos, 211; as consumer
    issue, 100–102, 104, 274–75, 311n105;
    and cryopreservation, 6, 105, 107–8,
    110, 177; dystopian images of, 61; EAB
    conclusions of ethical acceptability,
    57–58, 301n75; early efforts, 42;
    embryos from, as laboratory artifacts,
    67–68, 164–65; ethical standards for,
    107, 302n91; as eugenics tool, 44–45;
    federal funding research on excess
    embryos from, 159, 176–77; federal

regulation, 53–54, 98–100, 101, 300n63; first public bioethics body to assess, 41; first successful human, 1; fourteen-day boundary, 72–74, 89–90, 92, 111–12, 113–14, 269, 304n125, 313n22; grant application to EAB for, without ET, 56–57; inefficiency of, and loss of embryos, 59, 60–61, 62; initial countries regulating, 87; as medical miracle, 45–46; moral status of embryo produced by, 63–65, 66–72, 119, 165–66, 315n47, 323n108; moratorium urged, 44; as "playing God," 43, 44; privatization of, 75–76, 78, 275; as proxy for moral status of embryos, 119, 315n47; public ethical assessment of, and National Commission for the Protection of Human Subjects of Biomedical and Behavioral Research, 53; and public-private boundary, 274; safety concerns, 58–59, 75, 304n130; as slippery slope, 46–47, 183; and superovulation, 6, 59, 87, 137, 302n82, 323n106; as therapy for infertility and not research, 5, 43, 60–62, 74–75, 298n12, 302n91; as widespread practice, 79–80, 86, 97, 100–101, 107, 311n105

in vivo reproduction: federal funding of research on aborted embryos, 158; IVF as analogous to, 59–64, 70, 75; loss of embryos, 60, 61, 63

Irving, Diane, 156–57

IVF. See in vitro fertilization (IVF)

Jaenisch, Rudolf, 160–61

Jasanoff, Sheila: bioconstitutionalism, 233n1; civic epistemologies, 17–18, 331n24; constitutional transformations engendered by science and technology, 17; and coproduction, 13; courts as constructing boundary between science and law, 14–15; importance

of preembryo concept, 92–93; public reason, 18; sociotechnical imaginaries, 335n52

Jeffords, Jim, 140, 142, 143

Johns Hopkins University, 137–38

Jones, Georgeanna, 87

Jones, Howard, 87, 88, 95, 308n62

Jones Institute, 87

Journal of the American Medical Association, 44

justice, in Rawlsian theory, 116, 283–85, 333n7

Kass, Leon: background, 182–83, 324n5; charter of President's Council on Bioethics, 325n11; clarification of terminology, 201; concerns about ectogenesis, 72; IVF slippery slope concerns, 46–47, 183; and moral status of human embryo, 323n108; purpose of bioethics, 183; and Stanford University use of "cloned human embryo," 206

Keirstead, Hans, 254

Kennedy, Edward, 48, 140

Keohane, Nannerl, 123

Kim, Sang-Hyun, 335n52

Kinder, Byron, 227–28

King, Patricia, 114, 124, 313n22

Klein, Robert, 217–19, 245–46, 257, 258

knowledge. See facts

Koppel, Ted, 147

Krauthammer, Charles, 186

Kuhn, Thomas, 320n45

Lancet, 58, 86

language. See terminology

Latour, Bruno, 29, 342n40

lay public: ACD concerns about ignorance of, 124–26; defining, 117; disagreements about facts, 172; educating versus convincing, 125, 126–27; experts making judgments for, 9, 55; fears about technoscientific change, 143–44, 146–48; and HERP participation,

lay public (*continued*)
  119–23, 315n48, 315n50, 315nn52–53; and
  HERP recommendations, 124; HERP
  view of, as ignorant, 121, 123, 315nn52–
  53, 316n55; justifications of public
  bioethics bodies for standing in for,
  282–83, 284–88; lack of understanding
  of SCNT, 151; misunderstanding of
  human cloning, 191–92, 226–27, 326n33,
  327n35; misunderstanding of scientific
  shorthand, 200–201, 203, 331n37; need
  to educate about science, 16, 143; need
  to understand language used by public
  bioethics bodies, 188; opposition to
  cloning of humans and legislation
  to prevent, 149–50; and politics of
  hESC as public good, 256; problem of
  defining concerns of, in democracy,
  150; in republic of science, 25; role in
  democracy, 273; and SCNT, 191–93, 198,
  200, 205–6, 326n33, 327n35
Lederberg, Joshua, 291n1, 297n3
Lejeune, Jérôme, 81, 84
life: boundaries of, 3, 4, 5, 165; questions
  raised by human embryo research, 7;
  questions raised by post-World War
  II scientific advances, 3–4. *See also*
  personhood
life-support technologies, and boundaries of
  life, 3, 5
Lo, Bernard, 123–24
"Logical Consequences of the Argument
  from Potential in the Age of Cloning"
  (Charo), 164
Lyons, Michael, 215
Lyons, Moira, 215–16

Mathews, David, 54
McCarthy, Charles: AFS ethics committee,
  94, 309n76; EAB, 57, 65, 68–69, 77
McCormick, Richard: AFS ethics committee,
  87; EAB, 60–61, 62–63, 67–70, 166

McGee, Glenn, 162
McHugh, Paul, 161, 187
McLaren, Anne, 59–60, 91–92, 308n62
Meilaender, Gilbert, 170
Melton, Douglas, 264
Mishkin, Barbara, 57, 65, 77
Missouri court case, 216–17, 223–29, 230–31
Mol, Annemarie, 293n22
Mondale, Walter, 48
monkey cloning, 136–37
moral status concept: AFS definition, 89;
  and biological features of embryo, 166;
  Catholic, 69–70; and consequences
  of use of product, 164–65, 166–67; as
  dissociated from embryo as entity,
  171–72, 275; and EAB, 63–65, 66–72;
  excess embryos, 52–53, 165–66; frame
  of debate, 8–10, 104–5, 293n20; and
  HERP, 112–13; individuality as criterion,
  68; IVF and use of abortifacient
  contraceptive devices as proxies, 119,
  315n47; and NBAC, 169–70; pluralistic
  approach, 115, 198; and public-private
  boundary, 75, 78, 275; and resolution
  of biological status, 95; and SCNT
  products, 162–64; and terminology, 9
Morella, Constance A., 139, 151
Morrison, Bruce, 98–99
Mulkay, Michael, 92
Muller, Hermann, 40, 45, 124–25
Muller, Steven, 112, 120–22, 315n50
Murray, Robert, 62
Murray, Tom, 174

National Academy of Sciences (NAS), 82, 84,
  192, 195
National Advisory Child Health and Human
  Development Council, 97
National Bioethics Advisory Commission
  (NBAC): and ACT human-bovine
  experiments, 169; boundary between
  issues of science and democracy, 169–71;

debate as framed by, 176; dismissiveness of public, 285–86; as enforcing government lag behind science, 143–44; facts/values distinctions, 169–72; formation, 168; and HERP, 168; as moral calculating machine, 175; public versus nonpublic reasons, 171–72; and religious views, 170–71, 173–76, 280–81, 282; report, 175; role, 139, 168

National Commission for the Protection of Human Subjects of Biomedical and Behavioral Research: creation and charge, 41, 48, 294n25; and EAB, 65, 66; effects on human embryo research, 52–53; and elective abortions, 50–51; fetal viability boundary, 52; informed consent, 49, 50; replaced, 77

National Institutes of Health (NIH), 48, 108–9, 124–26. See also Human Embryo Research Panel (HERP)

National Research Act (1974), 41, 48–49, 53, 54, 294n25

National Research Council (NRC), 191–92, 195, 197

National Right to Life Committee (NRLC), 154–55, 311n113

natural law, and moral law, 68

Nature, 91, 96, 133, 200, 287

Nazi human subjects research, 48

Neaves, William, 226–27

neutrality, idea of, as political, 293n24

New England Journal of Medicine, 45, 48

Newman, Stuart, 221–23

New York Times, 46, 162, 177, 263

Nightline, 147

NIH Revitalization Act (S.2507, 1992), 103–4, 108, 128

nonpublic reasons, 22, 116–18, 130, 172–75, 244

normal science, and scientific sovereignty, 146, 320n45

norms: coproduction of knowledge and, 27; crafting of right, 29; of democracy, 235; democratic, 169, 170, 172; and justice, 283–84; operationalization of, 175; practices translated into, 119, 315n47; of public reason in deliberative democracies, 314n35; science as having self-governing, 145–46; study of scientific, as neglected, 28

Norsigian, Judy, 240

nuclear transplantation: confused with human reproductive cloning, 191–93, 198, 200, 326n33, 327n35; and monkey cloning, 136–37. See also somatic cell nuclear transfer (SCNT)

Nuremberg Code, 48

Obama, Barack, 16, 272

Observer, 133

Office for Human Subject Regulation (OHSR), 77

Office of Technology Assessment (OTA), 100–101

Ohanesian, Gail, 220, 223

ontological politics, 8–9, 105, 293n22

Oregon National Primate Research Center at Oregon Health Sciences University (now the Oregon Health & Science University), 136–37

organ transplantation, first heart, 48

Ortiz, Deborah: proposed hESC research legislation, 211, 212; Proposition 71, 242, 247, 254, 259–60, 337n79; stem cell research hearing, 246

Panetta, Leon, 130

Perkins, Tony, 264

Perry, Daniel, 215

personhood: and balancing harm against other goods, 174–75; as beginning at conception, 81–85, 306n22; defining, 81–85, 90, 117, 306n22, 315n41; "human life" amendment to Constitution, 80–81; as not only reason to oppose

personhood (*continued*)
  human embryo research, 166, 323n108;
  and preembryos, 95, 281, 309n78;
  private moral and religious beliefs as
  determining, 85, 86, 306n30; and use
  of IVF and abortifacient contraceptive
  devices, 119, 315n47
Pettrucci, Daniele, 42
Pincus, Gregory, 42, 45
Pizzo, Philip, 206, 245
Planned Parenthood, 239, 241, 242
"Please Don't Call It Cloning" (Vogelstein), 200
pluralism: as approach of HERP, 115–18,
  314n28; and NBAC approach, 168,
  170–71; public bioethics bodies attempt
  to make reasonable, 279–81; reasonable,
  14–15, 21, 116, 117; role in deliberative
  democracy, 22; of values, 21
Polanyi, Michael, 25
"political economy of hype," 266
Political Liberalism (Rawls), 314n32
preembryos: American use of term, 93–96;
  British use of term, 90–93; conditions
  for respect for, 95, 309n78; court ruling
  on term, 310n86; objection to term, 122;
  purpose of term, 105; term coined, 34,
  90, 91, 281, 308n62
pregnancy, as defined by federal
  government, 74
Presidential Commission for the Study of
  Bioethical Issues, 16, 287–88
President's Commission for the Study of
  Ethical Problems in Medicine and
  Biomedical and Behavioral Research, 77
President's Council on Bioethics (PCB):
  formation, 35, 182, 184, 325n11, 325n15;
  product itself and not intended uses as
  issue, 197; proposals, 201; role of and
  robustness of deliberations, 183–84, 281;
  terminology agreed upon, 197, 328n57;
  terminology issues, 35, 185–90, 282,
  325n18

principlism, 65, 66–67, 69, 78, 303n103
pro-life community: and case against change
  in Missouri constitution, 224; and
  reconstitution of EAB, 102–3, 311n113
Proposition 71 (California): background,
  211–12, 213–14; campaign, 213, 214,
  237–38, 252–54, 257–61, 338n84; and
  constitutional position of science, 249;
  court case over pamphlet language,
  216–23, 230–31, 330n22; defeat of, 223;
  democracy as real issue of, 244–46;
  economic impact predictions, 258–60;
  opposition to, 235, 238, 239–41, 244–46,
  261; overview of, 36, 209–10; and politics
  of abortion, 238–43; purpose, 213; and
  religion, 233, 235; and secularization
  thesis, 248; as serving well-being of
  Californians, 251–52; and social contract
  for science, 256–57, 261–62, 337n77;
  terminology use, 214–15; vote, 261
public, The. *See* lay public
public bioethics bodies: disciplining
  function, 117–18, 314n35; as experiments
  in democracy, 15; expertise as
  justification for authority, 14, 15;
  first, 294n25; first to assess IVF, 41; as
  guardians of public reasoning, 175;
  impetus for, 279; Mondale proposal,
  48; reasonableness and presumptions
  of, 11–12, 168, 172; and religion, 236; as
  shapers of public bioethical debate,
  10, 11, 12, 143–44; as stand-ins for
  reasonable public, 14–15, 119–20, 121–22,
  171–72, 282–83, 284–88, 316n57. *See also*
  specific bodies
public bioethics debate
  about cloning as worthless, 200–201
  call for, of IVF and cloning, 44
  citizen participation through practices,
    119–20
  as controlled by public bioethics bodies,
    282–83, 284–88

defining, 292n11

efforts to reform, 205–7

excess embryos to be used in research, 165–67

facts not values as part of, 198–99

as a key pillar of democracy, 16

moral judgments belong to public, 227

and PCB, 184, 187

public bioethics bodies as mediators of, 143–44

science and: constraints on, 191, 326n30; as experts in, 197, 226, 230; as foundational source of authority of, 19–20, 125–29, 142, 143, 145, 149, 227; as manager and determinant of, 145, 167, 199, 202–3, 249–50; role in deliberations in democracy, 84, 85, 100, 200–201, 227, 307n33

terminology: confused use of term human cloning, 191–92, 326n33, 327n35; inability to find common, 190–91; need for precise, value-free, 195, 196, 202; problem of scientific shorthand in, 200–201, 203, 331n37; scientific terms as disciplining, 96, 310n86; use of term preembryo, 94, 105

"thinning" of, 293n20, 325n18

in United Kingdom, 92–93, 193–95

public-private boundaries, 274–79

public reason

    contestability of, 24

    and courts, 216–17

    defining, 18–19

    in deliberative democracies, 314n35

    as delimiter of diversity of reasons, 22–23

    described by Rawls, 116, 314n32

    as disciplined by public bioethics bodies, 282–83, 284–88

    and HERP, 116–18, 130–31

    as model for designing institutionalized power, 26, 296n63

    and NBAC, 171–72, 173

    as normative concept, 19

    rational consistency as necessity of, 174

    religion as opposed to, 244

    as requiring scientific expertise, education, and slow legislative reaction, 143–45

    as requiring understanding of emerging techonoscience, 149

    role in democracy, 21–23, 26, 116, 296n63

    and science: as authoritative in, 23–27, 207–8; as definer of parameters of, 19, 142, 143, 145, 281–82; as model for, 247–48; as not needing to engage with, 24, 26; as prior to and prerequisite for moral judgment, 276–77; using reflective equilibrium to align policy with, 119–20

    shift of parameters, 163–65

purification, 342n40

Rabb, Harriet, 158, 159, 181

Raël, 147

Ramsey, Paul, 43

Rawls, John: deliberative democratic theory, 20–21; political community of reason, 296n58; public reason, 18–19, 21–23, 27, 116–17, 314n32; reasonableness of scientific thinking, 23–24, 27; reasonable pluralism, 14, 116; reflective equilibrium, 118–20; science as legitimate basis of authority, 24–25; territorial sovereignty of science, 25; truth and justice in right social and political order, 116, 283–85, 333n7

Reagan, Ronald, 81, 103

reason: in Catholic theology, 68; political community of, 296n58; values as not subject to, 207

reasonableness: criteria of, 16, 18; and HERP judgments, 114, 115–18, 314n28, 315n41; of methods and conclusions of science, 23–24, 207–8; and public bioethics bodies, 11–12, 168, 172, 279–81; of public

reasonableness (*continued*)
policy, 173; in Rawlsian public reason,
22; science as custodian of, 199–200;
science as key criterion of, 27
reasonable pluralism, 14–15, 21, 116, 117
reciprocity, principle of, 22, 173, 185
recombinant DNA (rDNA), 3–4, 143, 161,
247, 259
Reed, Jack, 143
Reeve, Christopher, 253
reflective equilibrium, 20, 118–20
religion: freedom of, 82–83, 85, 86, 176,
306n30, 307n33; as at odds with
democracy and science, 237, 244, 250–
51; as private and out of realm of debate
in democracy, 235, 236; and Proposition
71, 238–43, 244–46; and public bioethics
bodies, 236; secularization as displacing,
248–49; as used to define science, 244.
See also Catholicism
"Religion as a Conversation Stopper" (Rorty),
236
Report on Research on the Fetus (National
Commission for the Protection of
Human Subjects of Biomedical and
Behavioral Research), 49
reproductive cloning, 192, 193, 194–95, 197,
326n33
republic of science construct, 25
Research Freedom Act of 1990 (proposed), 103
respect for persons, principle of, 65–66,
70–72, 95, 302n102, 309n78
Reynolds, Jesse, 239
rightness, 283–84, 293n24
right public reason: and modernity, 342n40;
and public bioethics bodies, 282–83,
284–85; religion as opposite, 235; science
as definer of, 19, 20, 234. *See also* public
reason; reasonableness
right to privacy, 51, 74–75, 302n91
Rivers, Lynn, 140
Rock, John, 42

Roe v. Wade (1973), 49, 51, 85, 86, 274, 306n30
Rorty, Richard, 236, 237
Rosenberg, Leon, 82, 307n33
Roslin Institute, 136
Rossant, Janet, 269
Royal College of Obstetricians and
Gynaecologists, 92
Rubel, Edwin, 126, 127
Ryan, Kenneth, 110

San Francisco Chronicle, 138
San Jose Mercury News, 206
Schatten, Gerald, 318n14
Schulman, Joseph, 75
Science, 96, 200, 226–27, 271
"Science and Man" (*Washington Post* column
by Lederberg), 291n1
science and technology studies (STS), 28,
296n58, 297n76
science and terminology: authoritativeness,
152–53, 158, 161, 188–89, 202–3; changes
in, 221, 331n37; disagreements among
scientists, 155; issues of defining human
cloning, 150, 151, 152, 154, 185; as political,
222–23; science as supplier of, for public
ethics debate, 19; scientific shorthand in
public debate, 200–201, 203, 226, 331n37;
and SCNT, 151, 187, 191–93, 198, 200,
203–4, 205–6, 326n33, 327n35; use of
"preembryo," 90–93, 308n62; as value-
neutral, 94. *See also* preembryos
science in American democracy, 4, 5, 292n11;
as absent in contemporary theories
of, 288; as allied with, 244, 247–48;
as authoritative in, 14, 15, 23–27, 84,
85, 100, 149, 207–8, 235, 270, 276–79,
307n33; courts as constructors of
boundary, 14–15; as having jurisdiction
over matters of scientific practice
and knowledge, 9, 55; as having self-
governing norms, 145–46; as informing
collective judgment and morality, 8–10;

as key criterion of reasonableness, 27; as measure of progress, 248, 249–50, 335n53; need of law to defer to, 142, 143; need to educate public about, 16, 143; in normative political imagination, 29–30; ontological issues as in realm of, 169–70; oversight, 145–46; as politically neutral, 228; as prior to and prerequisite for moral judgment, 276–77; products of, versus techniques used by, 146, 148–49, 153, 176; as provider of facts, 9, 23–24, 28, 30, 169–70, 278; public fears about, 143–44, 146–48; as reserve power in political culture, 17–18; social contract between science and state, 256–57, 261–62, 337n77; sociotechnical imaginaries in politics, 251–57, 272–73, 336n74; as source of public benefits, 234; "thought communities" and "thought styles" of, 296n58; as value-neutral, 282. See also constitutional position of science

science/scientists
    constraints on authority and ability to weigh in on ethical issues, 191, 326n30; as custodian of reasonableness, 199–200; as custodians of future, 277–78, 289; defining, 28–30, 244; descriptions as analogous to moral reasoning, 115; as distinct sphere from ethics, 9; products of, versus techniques used by, 146, 148–49, 153, 176; public bioethics debate and: constraints on, 191, 326n30; as experts in, 197, 226, 230; as foundational source of authority of, 19–20, 125–29, 142, 143, 145, 149, 227; as manager and determinant of, 145, 167, 199, 202–3, 249–50; role in deliberations in democratic deliberation, 84, 85, 100, 200–201, 227, 307n33; public reason and: as authoritative in, 23–27, 207–8; as definer of parameters

of, 19, 142, 143, 145, 281–82; as model for, 247–48; as not needing to engage with, 24, 26; as prior to and prerequisite for moral judgment, 276–77; using reflective equilibrium to align policy with, 119–20
    religion assumed to be at odds with, 237
    requirements of autonomy and self-governance, 146
    role in deliberations in, 84, 85, 100, 307n33
    and secularization theory, 249, 250, 335n53
    See also science and terminology

Scientific American, 83

Scientific and Medical Aspects of Human Reproductive Cloning (NRC), 191–92, 195

secularization, 248–50, 282, 288, 335n53, 342n40

Seed, Randolph, 75–76, 148

Seed, Richard, 75–76, 147–48, 305n133

Select Committee on Children, Families, and Youth (House of Representatives), 98–100

Sensenbrenner, Jim, 141

Shettles, Landrum, 42

Silver, Lee, 200–201

slippery slope argument, 46–47, 183

Smart, James M., Jr., 229

Smith, Wesley, 221, 332n39

Snyder, Evan, 221, 259

Snyderman, Ralph, 126, 127–28

social contract for science, 256–57, 261–62, 337n77

social imaginary, 249, 335n45

sociology of error, 30

sociotechnical imaginaries, 250–57, 272–73, 335n45, 335n52, 336n74

somatic cell nuclear transfer (SCNT): and animal cloning, 136–37, 292n18; banning of, technique to human biological materials, 152, 153–54, 320n59; boundaries of life dismantled

somatic cell nuclear transfer (*continued*)
by, 162–63, 169; California legislation
to encourage, 211; "cloned human
embryo" as product of, 197–98; embryo
as product of, 154–58; and exploitation
of women, 240, 334n20; human
reproductive cloning confused with,
191–93, 198, 200, 205–6, 326n33, 327n35;
moral status of embryos and products
of, 162–64; overview of questions
raised, 134–35; private funding,
147–48; procedure, 136, 292n18; to
produce specialized tissue versus to
clone humans, 137, 148–49, 153, 318n5;
products as organisms/embryos, 154–
58, 160–63, 169, 176, 322n86, 322nn89–
91; public lack of understanding of, 151;
as research tool in United Kingdom,
194; terminology issues, 187, 203–4. *See
also* cloning; human cloning
Sorkow, Harvey R., 98, 311n92
Soupart, Pierre, 56, 67, 303n107
sovereign science, 25, 146, 320n45
species transformation, 43
Specter, Arlen, 167, 202, 267
Spellman, Mitchell, 71
Stanford Medicine, 215–16, 245
Stanford University, 205–6, 213
Stem Cell Research Act, veto of, 263
"stem cell tourists," 266, 340n16
Stemmler, Edward, 127
"Steps Taken Toward Growing Organs"
(Associated Press), 138
Steptoe, Patrick C., 42; and EAB, 58, 59
Stern, Elizabeth, 98, 311n92
Stern, Melissa, 98, 311n92
Stern, William, 98, 311n92
Stevens, Tina, 242–43
Stillman, Robert J., 99–100
subtraction story of secularization, 248–49
Sullivan, Louis W., 103, 312n113
Supreme Court, 57. *See also* specific cases

surrogacy, 98
symmetry, methodological principle of, 13

Taylor, Charles, 248–49, 335n45
technocracy, deliberative democratic theory
as solution to, 27
terminology: attempt to structure public
moral debate by modifying technical,
94; and ballot initiatives, 214, 216, 223–
24; constitution as provider of shared,
17; definition of human embryo in
Dickey–Wicker amendment, 157–58;
definition of organism, 154–58, 160–61;
litigated in court, 96, 216–31, 310n86,
330n22; and moral status, 9; need
for shared, understood, 94, 188, 194,
200–201, 202, 230, 282; need for
specificity of meaning, 152, 191, 195–96,
327n48; political nature of, 293n24;
and Proposition 71 (California) court
cases, 216–23, 230–31, 330n22; and
public bioethics bodies, 62, 197–98,
302n91; value-free, needed, 195, 196,
202; value-laden, in political speech,
216–17, 225, 231; values versus facts,
219–21. *See also* preembryos; science
and terminology
territorial sovereignty of science, 25
test tube babies, 45, 86, 87. *See also* Brown,
Louise
Theory of Justice, A (Rawls), 283, 333n7
therapeutic cloning, 192, 193, 194–95, 197, 203,
327n33
Thomson, Dennis, 172–73
Thomson, James: and California Proposition
71, 212; human embryonic stem cell
lines cultured by, 137, 138, 162; and
iPSCs, 263, 264
Today (NBC television program), 253
Tribe, Laurence, 82
truth, 283, 342n40
Tuskegee syphilis study, 3

Unborn Child Act (U.K.), 92
United Kingdom, 87, 89, 90–93, 108, 193–95
United Presbyterian Church, 82–83
United States Conference of Catholic
  Bishops, 154, 155, 159–60, 311n113
University of Wisconsin, 137

values: and beginning of human life, 83;
  as belonging to ethics, 9; desire to
  accommodate different, 301n75;
  disagreements over, as legitimate in
  democracy, 169, 170, 172; facts versus,
  21, 24, 26, 175–76, 198–99, 207, 219–21,
  282, 342n40; masquerading as facts,
  199; need for terminology free of, 195,
  196, 202; as not subject to reason, 207;
  as part of public debate, 198–99, 282; in
  PCB terminology, 186–89; privileged
  role of science in deliberations about,
  84, 307n33; role in public policy, 173;
  scientific terminology as free of, 94
Varmus, Harold, 128–29, 130, 143–44, 146, 160
"veil of ignorance," 284, 333n7
"veil of knowledge," 284, 285
verstehen, 297n76
vocabulary. *See* terminology
Vogelstein, Bert, 200–201
voluntary licensing authority (VLA), 90–91

Wade, Nicholas, 162
Wall Street Journal, 201
Walters, LeRoy: AFS ethics committee, 87;
  EAB, 57, 62, 64–65, 73

Warnock, Mary, 87
Warnock Committee (U.K.), 87, 90–93
Washington Post, 45, 291n1
Wasson, Greg, 241
Watson, James, 43–44
Waxman, Henry, 103, 148–49, 156
Weiss, Ted, 102–3
Weissman, Irving: assumptions made
  by, 197; and California Proposition
  71, 212, 220, 252, 254; terminology
  issues, 188–89, 192, 195–96, 198, 201,
  327n48
West, Michael, 153, 157, 161–62
"What Are Clones? They're Not What You
  Think They Are" (Silver), 200
Whitehead, Mary Beth, 98, 311n92
Wick, Doug, 212
Wicker, Roger, 130
Wilmut, Ian, 140, 141, 222
Windom, Robert E., 102, 103
Woollett, Gillian, 152
Wyden, Ron, 101, 102
Wyngaarden, James B., 102

Yamanaka, Shinya, 263, 264, 339n10
Young, Ernie, 244–45

Zavos, Panos, 147
Zeller, Janice, 125
Zinsmeister, Karl, 264
Zon, Leonard, 203, 204
Zucker, Janet, 212
Zucker, Jerry, 212